England's Empty Throne

England's Empty Throne
Usurpation and the Language of Legitimation, 1399–1422

Paul Strohm

Yale University Press
New Haven and London

Set in Palatino by Best-set Typesetter Ltd., Hong Kong
Printed in Great Britain by Bell and Bain Ltd, Glasgow

Library of Congress Cataloging-in-Publication Data

Strohm, Paul, 1938–
    England's empty throne: usurpation and the language of legitimation, 1399–1422/Paul Strohm.
    Includes bibliographical references and index.
    ISBN 0–300–07544–8
    1. Great Britain – History – House of Lancaster, 1399–1461. 2. Richard II, King of England, 1367–1400 – Death and burial. 3. Great Britain – History – Henry IV, 1399–1413. 4. Great Britain – History – Henry V, 1413–1422. 5. Great Britain – Kings and rulers – Succession.
    6. Lollards. I. Title.
    DA245.S77 1998
    942.04'1 – dc21   98–4399
                                                                    CIP

A catalogue record for this book is available from the British Library.

10 9 8 7 6 5 4 3 2 1

07/299—3080X

To Dyan Elliott

Contents

Illustrations

The author would like to thank the British Library for
permission to reproduce the above illustrations.

Abbreviations

Annales Henrici	Johannis de Trokelowe, *Chronica et Annales*, ed. H. T. Riley, Rolls Series, no. 28, pt 3 (London, 1866)
Bourdieu *Outline*	Pierre Bourdieu, *Outline of a Theory of Practice* (Cambridge: Cambridge University Press, 1977)
CCR	*Calendar of Close Rolls*
Chronicon Angliae	*Chronicon Angliae, 1328–1388*, ed. E. M. Thompson, Rolls Series, no. 64 (London, 1874)
CLBI	*Calendar of Letter-Books of the City of London: Letter-Book I*, ed. R. Sharpe (London: Corporation of the City of London, 1907)
Concilia	D. Wilkins, ed., *Concilia Magnae Britanniae et Hiberniae*, vol. 3 (London, 1737)
Continuatio Eulogii	*Eulogium Historiarum*, ed. F. Haydon, Rolls Series, no. 9, vol. 3 (London, 1863)
CPR	*Calendar of Patent Rolls*
Creton	Jean Creton, *Histoire du Roy d'Angleterre Richard*, ed. and trans. J. Webb, *Archaeologia* 20 (1824), 1–402
Dymmok	Roger Dymmok, *Liber contra XII Errores et Hereses Lollardorum*, ed. H. S. Cronin (London: Wyclif Society, 1922)
EHR	*English Historical Review*
Foedera	T. Rymer, *Foedera*, 4 vols (The Hague, 1740)
FZ	*Fasciculi Zizaniorum*, ed. W. W. Shirley, Rolls Series, no. 5 (London, 1858)
Gesta	*Gesta Henrici Quinti*, ed. and trans. Frank Taylor and John S. Roskell, Oxford Medieval Texts (Oxford: Clarendon Press, 1975)
Historia Anglicana	Thomas Walsingham, *Historia Anglicana*, ed. H. T. Riley, Rolls Series, no. 28, pt 1, vols 1–2 (London, 1863)
Kantorowicz	Ernst H. Kantorowicz, *The King's Two Bodies: A Study in Political Theology* (Princeton: Princeton University Press, 1957)
Knighton	*Knighton's Chronicle, 1337–1396*, ed. G. H. Martin (Oxford: Oxford Medieval Texts, 1995)

Lacan, *Seminar*	Jacques Lacan, *The Seminar*: Book 7, *The Ethics of Psychoanalysis*, ed. Jacques-Alain Miller (New York and London: W. W. Norton, 1992)
McNiven	Peter McNiven, *Heresy and Politics in the Reign of Henry IV: The Burning of John Badby* (Woodbridge, Suffolk: Boydell Press, 1987)
Original Letters	*Original Letters Illustrative of English History*, ed. Henry Ellis, 2nd series, vol. 1 (London: Harding, 1825)
PL	*Patrologiae Cursus Completus* [Patrologia Latina], ed. J. P. Migne (Paris, 1857)
Powell, *Kingship*	Edward Powell, *Kingship, Law, and Society: Criminal Justice in the Reign of Henry V* (Oxford: Clarendon Press, 1989)
Privy Council	*Proceedings and Ordinances of the Privy Council*, ed. N. H. Nicolas, vol. 1 (London: Record Commission, 1834)
RP	*Rotuli Parliamentorum*, ed. J. Strachey, 6 vols (London, 1783)
Select Cases	G. O. Sayles, *Select Cases in the Court of King's Bench*, vol. 7, Selden Society, no. 88 (London: Quaritch, 1971)
Usk	*The Chronicle of Adam Usk, 1377–1421*, ed. and trans. C. Given-Wilson (Oxford: Oxford Medieval Texts, 1997)
Westminster Chron.	*The Westminster Chronicle, 1381–1394*, ed. L. C. Hector and B. Harvey (Oxford: Oxford Medieval Texts, 1982)

Preface

This book is configured around an empty place, an event it can only partially know and about which it only occasionally speaks. The event is the deposition and murder of Richard II. The meaning of any event – but especially an event so abrupt in its occurrence and so uncertain in its implications – is always subsequently determined. Its meaning resides in the future, in what it will become or, in the Lacanian rendition, what it 'will have been.' Its significance is thus progressively revealed, a product of its own aftermath. With its meaning not immediately evident and awaiting accomplishment, Richard's death enters the process of symbolization within a broad range of Lancastrian and other early fifteenth-century texts.

What 'Lancastrians?' Dynasties are fragile constructs, and tend to unravel upon closer inspection. John of Gaunt, who laid so many royal foundation stones, seems fitfully to have wished the crown for himself or his sons, but spent most of his last decade as an apparent Ricardian loyalist. Henry IV, said by John Capgrave to have retained the crown only so that he could pass it to his sons, engaged in serious rivalry with his first-born, Henry of Monmouth. Henry V was rivalrous with his brother Clarence, and Gloucester frequently adopted a separate and self-interested line. Early supporters of the dynasty – most obviously, the Percies and Archbishop Scrope – fell by the wayside. Ideologues like Adam of Usk paved the way to kingship but then grew cool. Hardest to assess with regard to their participation in Lancastrian ambitions were the many lords, civil servants, and intellectuals who enjoyed no very close relation at all to what can barely be called a Lancastrian 'court,' but who nevertheless viewed it as an absent object of aspiration and possible identification.

Claiming no stable 'Lancastrian' entity, I treat the Lancastrian cause as a shifting body of ambitions, grudging acceptances, and unrealized dreams; as erratically capable of imposing ideas, rallying support, and affecting historical consequences. Certain Lancastrians enter these pages to the extent that they employed textual processes to imagine the conditions (or to assail the foundations) of dynastic legitimacy. They will be treated, not simply as members of a faceless faction, but in terms of their very particular and 'situated' textual productions.

My approach to Lancastrian texts employs literary hermeneutics in pursuit of historical understanding. I therefore find myself somewhat awkwardly (although I hope productively) stationed at an intersection of literary and historical studies, in ways which may seem at once familiar and unfamiliar to practitioners of each. Literary readers will probably find themselves at ease with my skepticism about the status of the text's face value or 'literal' sense, especially as it bears on the text as an unmediated source of historical information. Less familiar to these same readers will, however, be my constant concern for texts as indispensable (albeit unreliable) sources of knowledge about the status and implications of past events. My habit is to foreground obstacles to full understanding – in fact, to insist upon their problematic status – but from a different point of view from that prevalent in literary studies: less to increase skepticism about the possibility of knowledge than to insist that certain things can nevertheless be known. This knowledge results not from evading textual indeterminacies but from probing them. Expecting no factual kernel or 'nugget' of truth at the text's center, I nevertheless believe its properties (including its fantasies, its omissions, the social 'work' it accomplishes) to be fully historical.

For their part, historians may quail at my habitual redesignation of 'sources' and 'documents' as 'texts,' with the accompanying reminder that meaning is a product of interpretation. Historians will also be asked to accept a more protracted, or at least more public, engagement with interpretative issues than is customary in their own writing. My conviction is that, rather than retarding the historical enterprise, a direct address to issues attending the construction of historical meaning is central to its excitement and vital to its integrity. My objective is thus at once modest and presumptuous: not so much to announce new information, as to offer alternative ways of viewing and entertaining information already considered to be possessed.

All texts are selective, diversionary, and amnesia-prone, forgetting or repressing crucial things about their own origins and those of the events with which they deal. The texts of usurpation and murder are, for obvious reasons, unusually evasive. Nevertheless, their labor of postponement, of holding memorable or crucial events in abeyance, most often turns out to have been spent in vain. For those texts which try hardest to ignore or exclude an event – to 'forget history' – tend to be the very places where the absent event stages its most interesting and complicated return. My own analysis thus continually relies on an enabling paradox: that the places where a text has been most extensively rigged and reworked are the very places where the presence of an event-in-abeyance may be most crucially felt or surmised.

Because I regard a text's ostensible or intended meaning as potentially deceptive, I do not attempt to ground my interpretations upon supposed access to the author's original intent. Professed or apparent intention will be taken into account as one element of a text's staging or enunciation, but rarely or never given the last word. Although I am somewhat more attracted to interpretations based on evidence of reception and afterlife, and gratefully use such information when available, it often remains scarce for the later medieval period. My reliance is finally placed on the act and products of interpretation itself: my quest is not only for what a text intends to say about itself but for those moments of inadvertency or lessened vigilance when it means more than it says.

This book is thus something other than a 'history' of the first Lancastrian decades. It moves among and between different textual concentrations, aiming less at a sequential narration than a series of perspectives on the relations between textuality and political process. Emphasis falls unevenly on different events, but always on symbolic activity as it concerns the making of kingship. This activity is revealing in its successes and also in its failures: its contributions to Lancastrian self-legitimation as well as the frequent occasions when the Lancastrian subject's alternative imagination eludes its control.

Within the circumference of its chosen emphasis on 'Lancastrian textuality,' this study omits several appropriate topics and emphases because they have been published earlier and elsewhere or written by other hands. Within the compass of my own work, I might mention an essay which constitutes a prolegomenon for the present undertaking: 'Saving the Appearances: Chaucer's "Purse" and the Fabrication of the Lancastrian Claim,' previously published in *Hochon's Arrow* (Princeton: Princeton University Press, 1992). Closely related in its concerns is Frank Grady's essay on 'The Lancastrian Gower and the Limits of Exemplarity,' *Speculum* 70 (1995), 552–575. Another subject appropriate for this volume but handled ably elsewhere is Lancastrian employment and encouragement of written English, especially under Henry V, for which see John H. Fisher, 'A Language Policy for Lancastrian England,' *PMLA* 107 (1992), 1168–1180. More, of course, remains to be said on this matter: particularly on Henry V's signet letters and vernacular war dispatches to the citizens of London.

Every book is a collective endeavor, and I have been exceptionally fortunate in my circle of helpers, friendly skeptics, and advice-givers. People who have assisted me at each of this study's several stages are Dyan Elliott, Andrew Prescott, Miri Rubin, and David Wallace. Without wishing to encumber them with its shortcomings, I consider them its co-participants and virtual co-creators. Furthermore, I have benefited more than I can say from the advice of persons who have stepped up at crucial junctures to rescue me from a difficulty or to propel my own consideration of a particular issue to a new and more fruitful level. I am thinking especially of Sarah Beckwith, Linda Charnes, Robert Clark, Carolyn Dinshaw, Louise Fradenburg, Fiona Somerset, and Mohamed Zayani. Other people have, of course, helped me as well, and I have sought to recognize their contributions in my notes. Two readers of the completed manuscript must, nevertheless, be gratefully mentioned: Derek Pearsall (for a grasp of my objectives which seemed at times to exceed my own) and Jill Mann (for a series of valued contributions to the accuracy and felicity of my text).

Unless otherwise indicated, translations are my own. Here as well I have also received advice and assistance, from Dyan Elliott in translations from Latin and from existing translations by C. Given-Wilson (Adam of Usk's *Chronicle*) and Frank Taylor and John S. Roskell (*Gesta Henrici Quinti*).

This study was launched with the assistance of a Guggenheim Fellowship, which permitted a year at Clare Hall, Cambridge. It was concluded during a year as Henry Luce Fellow at the National Humanities Center. My former institution, Indiana University, was supportive throughout. Earlier, shorter versions of two chapters have previously appeared in print: 'The Trouble with Richard: The Reburial of Richard II and Lancastrian Symbolic Strategy,' in *Speculum* 71 (1996), 87–111, and 'Lollards, Counterfeiters, and Lancastrian Unease,' in *New Medieval Literatures* (1998), 31–58. Part of my chapter on advising the Lancastrian prince will appear as 'Hoccleve, Lydgate, and the Lancastrian Court,' in the *Cambridge History of Medieval English Literature*, ed. David Wallace, 1999.

1
Prophecy and Kingship

Concurrently with their military successes, Henry IV and Henry V and their sympathizers explored other, less material, forms of domination. Not content with the forcible dispersal and decimation of their opponents, the Lancastrians entered a field of symbolic action within which adversarial claims might be discredited and even extirpated at their point of origin.

This endeavor may be glimpsed in a contemporary biographer's incidental comment on Henry V's conquest of Harfleur; there, the townspeople having been expelled so that their places might be taken by English immigrants, 'they were proven sojourners where they had thought themselves inhabitants' ('ibi probati sunt hospites ubi se incolas reputabant').[1] Beginning with the practical matter of clearing a town, this observation ends in a fantastical reconstruction. Pragmatically speaking, the introduction of English immigrants secured the city as a staging-ground for English military and commercial initiatives. But Lancastrian genius effects an even more ambitious maneuver, reversing the respective claims of the (native) French and the (colonizing) English. Despite having regarded themselves as inhabitants, the displaced French citizens must now regard their usurpers as rightful heritors and themselves as rootless transients and illegitimate guests. The effects of this reversal are then supplemented and secured by improvised ceremonies of dispossession; fifteenth-century evidence suggests, for example, that Henry had the muniments of the town and the title deeds of inhabitants publicly burned in the market-place.[2]

The Lancastrian interest in domination through displacement and recolonization is not limited to geographical and physical conquest, but is equally applicable to Henry IV's and Henry V's less tangible designs upon their society's crucial places of imaginative production and promulgation. These monarchs regularly engaged in what might

be considered pre-emptive intervention in the practices by which discourse is produced and sustained, in places of daily social encounter
and exchange, and finally even in the 'private' space of the socially
conditioned imagination. This intervention functions pre-emptively
because its purpose is to prevent or otherwise crowd out unwelcome
sorts of imaginative production – first simply by occupying and prolif-
erating within their space, and second in a more complex process of
contesting, revising, or even obliterating any alternative renditions of
historical origin and title which might have been produced and sustained there. The characteristic Lancastrian discovery, as it bears on
questions of ideology and history, is not just that rival accounts are
vulnerable, but that (like the grieving residents of Harfleur, issuing
from the city with their possessions on their backs) they never
deserved the legitimacy they enjoyed in the first place. The Lancastrian
imagination is thus recursive, in the sense that it asserts the claims of a
newly discovered but truer origin which continues through its effects
to govern present arrangements.

The afterword on Harfleur is, of course, that Lancastrian reach (in
the form of the revived dynastic claim to the throne of France) always
exceeded its grasp (in the form of its ability to control French terrain).
The English occupation of Harfleur ended thirty-five years after it had
begun, when 'the English inhabitants, to the number of about 1500,
returned the city of Harfleur to the king of France, departing with
safe conduct for their bodies and their possessions, some to England,
others to Normandy, places held by their party.'[3] Despite the victories
of Henry V, the confused reality of France and French allegiance
remained to confront English occupation with what Castoriadis would
call 'an inexhaustible supply of otherness,' a reality external and excessive to English dominion.[4]

So, by analogy, did much English experience at home as well as
abroad remain 'other' to those officially sponsored symbolizations and
enactments by which the Lancastrian monarchs sought to dominate
their subjects' political imagination. With varying but unceasing intensity over a period of twenty-three years, Henry IV and especially
Henry V sought a symbolic enactment of their legitimacy persuasive
enough to control the field of imaginative possibility. Even as it notices
their many successes, though, my analysis will assert the impossibility
of their task. This impossibility is rooted in their subjects' limitless
ability to imagine alternatives, to preserve alternative images and to
revise newly offered ones.

In this chapter, taking examples whenever possible from early Lancastrian sympathizer Adam of Usk but also ranging more widely, I
want to survey some of the sites of alternative imagination that were

most subject to Lancastrian blandishment and attack. These include chronicle-writing, with its ostensible commitment to progressive narration and its actual investment in retrospection and editorial control; the discourse of prophecy, with divided commitment to recursive and predictive structures; that practice of popular exegesis and its promulgation generally known as 'gossip,' by which consensus about a monarch or a regime is crucially made or unmade; and the imagination itself, understood as the register in which past images can be combined in ways which support or challenge a new status quo. Each case will reveal an early and effective Lancastrian presence, attempting the colonization of what might otherwise be a space or place of dissent. But each case will also reveal an element of alternative and utopian thought which refuses to be bounded, a sense in which, even when partially displaced from its normal foundations, the imagination of alternative possibility manages to exceed (and hence evade) attempts at its own pre-emption.

Gaunt as revisionist historiographer

The fifteenth-century chronicler John Hardyng is an uneven source, but, situated within the household of Henry Percy from 1390 to 1403, he was in a position to hear many things. One such piece of hearsay reveals an ambitious Lancastrian attempt to reconfigure dynastic origins, involving John of Gaunt and Henry Bolingbroke, stretching over a decade and including an assault on chronicle evidence. According to Hardyng, John of Gaunt was disappointed that his son Henry had not been named heir to the throne, and hatched a scheme to enhance the claims of ancester Edmund Crouchback, younger brother of the future Edward I and son of Henry III:

> when the duke of Lancastre wase so putt bie, he and his counsell feyned and forgied the seide Cronycle that Edmonde shuld be the elder brother, to make his sone Henry a title to the croune and wold have hade the seide erle of Northumberlonde, and sir Thomas Percy his brother, of counsaile thereof. . . . Whiche Croncyle, so forged, the duke dide put in divers abbaies and in freres, as I herde the seid erle ofte tymes saie and recorde to divers persouns, forto be kepte for the enheritaunce of his sonne to the croune.[5]

The whole story is, of course, a fabrication, derived apparently from the fact that Edmund was a crusader, and entitled to wear the sign of the cross on his back, and was thus known as 'Edmund Crouchback' or 'cross-back,' not (as Gaunt ingeniously but groundlessly argued) 'Edmund crooked-back.' Even had Gaunt's fabrication been true, it would still have possessed little merit; Edmund, duke of Lancaster was the great-grandfather of Duchess Blanche, Henry IV's mother, and enhancement of his claim would have added little to Henry's own prospects.

If Hardyng were the only authority, his account might be dismissed. Himself a suspected forger,[6] he completed his interested account of Percy gossip about Lancastrian high-handedness under Yorkist – and hence anti-Lancastrian – sponsorship. Nevertheless, other and earlier texts corroborate his account. The *Eulogium* continuator, for example, agrees that Gaunt took the occasion of the 1394 parliament to petition for Henry's designation as heir apparent, and – when confronted by the stronger claims of the earl of March, son of Edward III's second son Lionel – he advanced an ambitious fabrication:

> He said that King Henry III had two sons, Edmund the firstborn and Edward. But Edmund had a crooked back ['dorsum fractum'] and judged himself unworthy for the crown; whence their father arranged it that Edward should reign, and after him the heirs of Edmund, and made Edmund duke of Lancaster; and from him was descended Henry, rightful son of his mother, who was daughter of said Edmund.[7]

Henry IV seems in turn to have revived this story as one element of his claim to the crown. Chronicler Adam of Usk was among the committee of doctors, bishops, and others chosen to discuss the subject of deposing King Richard and substituting Henry, duke of Lancaster, and to provide reasons for these actions.[8] If Adam is representative, the members of this committee must have passed an exacting political screening, and some of them turn out to be even more actively complicit than Adam himself. Some, for example, seem already acquainted with, or briefed about, the Edmund story, and ready to put it to use:

> One day, in a meeting of said *doctores*, it was mentioned ['fuit tactum': it was touched upon] by some, that by right of succession from Edmund, duke of Lancaster – declaring Edmund to be the firstborn of king Henry III, but excluded from the succession on account of his infirmity and his younger brother Edward being set in his place – the direct line ought to be denied to Richard.

At this interesting juncture, the evidence of pedigrees and chronicles is sought, and Edward's primacy is upheld with reference to the most authoritative existing chronicles and compilations: the Polychronicon, Nicholas Trivet, and the Chronicle of Robert of Gloucester. And so this particular argumentative attempt is buried under a mountain of learned citation.[9] The learned *doctores*, whose own authority is grounded on the written record and constraints upon its use, have marked a limit to how far they are ready to go. This is not to say that this bunch of cynical connivers believed the chronicles to be inevitably true or to be proof against tampering and other forms of interested manipulation.[10] But they apparently did regard the chronicles as a collective argumentative resource held in common by all members of the clerical-legal establishment, rather than as the property of any one of its sectional interests.[11] The chronicles, in other words, were open to interested interpretation and to case-by-case revision, but their rhetorical force was limited to piecemeal application, rather than whole-sale dynastic purposes.

Still, deciding to make only local rather than global use of the chronicles, the *doctores* hardly found themselves hampered in the production of pro-Lancastrian argument. They rapidly and ingeniously produced a plethora of formal and informal *causae* for Richard's deposition.[12] Adam informs us that they reached unanimous agreement about Richard's perjuries, sacrileges, sodomies, insanity, the impoverishment of his subjects and their reduction to servitude, and the feebleness of his rule. The committee took the argumentative high ground by consulting justifications for deposition in the Decretals, noting Richard's own preparedness to resign voluntarily, and studying forms and ceremonies of deposition. But it obviously made room in its considerations for the more varied terrain of polemic, scurrilous hearsay, and other forms of interested critique. Adam himself embraced innuendo about Richard's illegitimacy (amounting to a 'shortcut' attack on Yorkist dynastic claims), and his subsequent text abounds in anti-Ricardian prophecy, gossip, calumny, and other pro-Lancastrian invention designed to further the contention that, not only is Richard now displaced as king, but he *was never entitled to be king in the first place.*

Something other than high historiography, these stratagems might be considered as entries into the quarrel over succession by alternative, often less formal, and argumentatively more economical means. Of course, the introduction of a new discursive route (or the revival of an established one) is like the construction of a new highway, whose builders will have limited authority over which vehicles will drive upon it or with what cargo. Official recourse to such varied routes as political prophecy, sensational anecdote, partisan legislation, and legal ingenuity can result in temporary argumentative advantage, but at the cost of opening these same routes to alternative action and imagination, rejoinder or other reply. Complicated by this possibility of counter-deployment, each alternative or supplementary strategy must be considered not only in terms of its Lancastrian use, but also as a new place for the proliferation of alternative or oppositional tactics.[13]

The uses of prophecy

During the fateful autumn of 1399, as a member of Richard's entourage, the chronicler Creton spoke with an 'ancien chevalier' attached to Duke Henry. As they rode side by side during the forcible relocation of Richard from Conway to Chester, the old knight told him

> that Merlin and Bede had prophesied the taking and destruction of the king during their lifetimes ['que la prise du roy et la destruccion avoient Merlin et Bede prophecise des leur vivant'] and that if I were in his castle he would show it to me in the form and manner in which I had seen it come to pass, saying thus: 'There shall be a king in Albion, who shall reign for the space of twenty or two and twenty years in great honor and great power, and shall be united with those of Gaul, which king shall be undone in the parts of the north in a triangular place [by implication, Conway Castle].' . . . Thus the said knight held this prophecy to be true, and accorded it great faith and belief, for they are so disposed in this country, that they believe completely in prophecies, phantoms, and sorceries, and employ them readily.[14]

The superstition-ridden country to which Creton refers is presumably not Wales (albeit known for such things) but England (*also* regarded, at least in France, as a wellspring of superstition!). The English fondness for prophecies, and especially those of Merlin, has elsewhere been remarked by French commentators. The seventeenth-century historian De Mezeray, describing Edward III's deployment of a prophecy of a merged crown to introduce his claim to France, summed up a traditional French view when he observed that 'Les Anglais commençaient toujours leurs harangues par une prophétie de Merlin.'[15] But the old knight employs prophecy in a way characteristic of the parties of Henry IV and Henry V and highly congenial to their aims. For the old knight's invocation of prophecy is less vatic or predictive than it is retrospective or backward-looking. Prophecy as prediction is best suited to those out of power and wishing for an amelioration of circumstance. For those *in* power, or even with a finger-hold on power and seeking its consolidation, a retrospective emphasis on prophecy's fulfillment is far more serviceable. Lancastrian prophecy is therefore almost invariably retrospective, designed both to secure the throne and to pre-empt more visionary, and hence more dangerous, forms.

The old knight's Lancastrian analysis finds Henry IV and his son summoned to rule by a previous prophetic destiny. His prophecy's retrospection is revealed by its timing, in that it 'predicts' events which have already happened or are already inevitably in process. The old knight has every reason to suppose (and Creton, writing his account from France in the months following Henry's coronation, can be certain) that Richard's term is about to end in the course of its twenty-third year. Events having once assured Henry's access to rule, prophecy is then produced to show that his accession was inevitable; was, in the fullest sense of the currently prevalent phrase, 'always already' foretold.

The old knight was not the only one whose thoughts turned to prophecy at this moment. Henry IV's accession was accompanied by a blizzard of prophecy, most newly generated, but all presented as matter already known, the pertinence of which is suddenly recollected under incentive of emergent events. The authenticity of the old knight's prophecy, *as* prophecy, is guaranteed by its prior inscription in a book, purportedly available for inspection in the old knight's castle. But it might have lain there forever, imminent or latent but unrealized, had not the event of Henry's accession refreshed its significance. Its meaning thus in every sense comes 'back from the future.'

Could the old knight actually have possessed a book of Merlin or Bede which embraced such particulars as twenty-two years of Ricardian rule, or his undoing in a northerly and triangular place, or which predicted the predominance of Lancaster as early as 1361? A few of these elements might be generally adumbrated in the widespread 'Prophecy of the Last Six Kings of England' or 'Six Kings after John,' in which Richard was understood to be the 'lamb' or 'crowned ass' fifth in succession, and Henry the mole or 'moldwarp' who should follow him.[16] But nothing else in the Merlin or pseudo-Merlin tradition would permit such confident attribution of detail. The closest thing in a *pre-Lancastrian* manuscript to the old knight's particularities appears in the widespread 'Prophecy of the Eagle,' an apparent thirteenth-century spinoff of the Merlin texts which enjoyed wide popularity in the fifteenth century. In that prophecy, a white king ('rex albus' – subsequently understood to be Richard) will, and will not, be king, and will then be unseated by the eaglet ('pullus aquilae' – subsequently understood to be Henry), who will cross the sea to Britain on horses of wood in a mode of conquest:

> Then the white and noble king will go to the west surrounded by his multitude to the ancient place near the flowing water. Then his enemies will attack him and each in their own place will be arranged against him and the army of his enemies will be arrayed in the manner of a shield ['deinde ibit albus rex et nobilis, versus occidentem suo circumdatus examine ad antiquum locum juxta currentem aquam, tunc occurrent ei inimici sui et suis quisque locis ordinabitur contra eum et exercitus inimicorum ejus ad modum clipei formabitur'].[17]

The old knight has it as a place in the north, in the shape of a triangle; the prophecy of the eagle has it in the west, faced by an army in the shape of a shield. The similarity to Henry's array about Conway Castle is arguable, but dim. But such similarities, however much imaginative augmentation they require, have their corroborative role to play.

The role was a popular one, as we see from Froissart. Reflecting on Richard's death, Froissart recalls his first trip to England, when, in the service of Queen Philippa and with the Black Prince still living (but Richard not yet born) he heard a prophecy that the house of Lancaster should rule England:

> For the first year that I was in England in the service of the noble queen Philippa, king Edward and queen Philippa and all their children were at Berkhamstead, to take leave of the prince and princess of Wales who were departing for Aquitaine, and there I heard a very old knight ['ung bien anchien chevallier'] named Bartholomew Burghersh, who was chatting with some damoiselles of the queen (who were from Hainault) and said thus: 'We have a book in this country, which is called the Brut ['qui s'appelle le Brust'], which says that neither the prince of Wales, nor the duke of Clarence, nor the duke of Lancaster, nor the duke of York, nor the duke of Gloucester shall be king of England, but the kingdom shall return to the house of Lancaster.' Now I, named Jean Froissart, author of this history, say that, all things considered, [Bartholomew Burghersh] was right, for I and everyone saw Richard of Bordeaux rule as king of England for twenty-two years, and, still living, come and return the crown of England to the house of Lancaster.[18]

Somewhat less than fully content with the prophetic explanation, Froissart then adds a causal one: 'Henry was crowned king under the conditions I have explained, and would not have thought of the crown, or even considered it, had Richard conducted himself more familiarly and amiably toward him.' But the prophecy, anchored by careful atten-

tion to setting, speaker, audience, and – of course – the authority of the
Brut, is what energizes Froissart's recollection. The fact that it was
uttered prior to the birth either of Richard or of Henry, and remained,
as it were, innocently available for retrospective confirmation, is why
Froissart finds it remarkable. This is how prophecy functions best for
the Lancastrians: as a pre-existing repository or, actually, junkyard of
utterances abounding in curiosities and irrelevancies, many of which
will remain unclaimed, but including the occasional usable obscurity.
Far from imposing themselves, such utterances await discovery, as
discrete prophetic elements are selectively validated by the progression of events.

This retrospective use of prophecy may be illustrated by
Walsingham's citation of a Bridlington prophecy, upon the seizure of
Archbishop Scrope of York in 1405. The prophecy actually cited is an
ambitiously reworked combination of two different Bridlington passages, originally treating the falsity of the Flemish after Crécy and the
death of the master of the hospitallers, and now applied to the seizure
of Scrope by the earl of Westmorland.[19] Scrope having been seized, and
the prophecy of fraudulent machination and the inevitable death of
a hierarch being applied, Walsingham comments, 'This being done,
that fevered prophecy of Bridlington might be found true, an obscure
prediction a present fact' ('Quo facto, potuit illud febricitanis
Brudelyntone vaticinium fore verum, praedicentis satis obscure
praesens factum' – p. 270). Emphasis is laid, in other words, on the
*un*intelligibility of the Bridlington utterance – fevered and obscure –
until it is rendered legible by a subsequent event. Such a use of
prophecy – and its concomitant, which is its severance from its own
stabilizing context – will be seen as a characteristic Lancastrian operation, visible in Adam of Usk's regular employment of Bridlington
prophecy, in a radically decontextualized and hence usable form.

The very notion that the Bridlington prophecies, in their obscurity
and presentational chicanery, should resist subsequent appropriation might itself invite surprise and skepticism. But, trumped-up
and fictitious as they were, they did in fact possess a very specific
and time-bound set of original purposes. In an act of apparent self-
authentication positively Borgesian in its ingenuity, the original
Bridlington prophecies are introduced by a humble commentator, one
'John Ergome,' who (under this or another name) was probably their
original author. Ergome declares himself to have collected these prophetic verses and to have composed his accompanying writings and
annotations for Humphrey de Bohun, earl from 1361 to 1372 ('haec
scripta et annotationes super versus prophetiales in honore vestri a me
collectas'[20]) and his composition dates from around the mid-1360s. His

disposition is to be extremely diffident about his findings ('nec dico me in omnibus invenisse veritatem' – p. 214), but he nevertheless mounts a series of claims for prophecy's value, including its capacity to fore-warn about impending dangers ('ille qui cognoscit istam prophetiam a periculis imminentibus potest se custodire' – p. 125). Since prophecy is presented in terms of the control it promises over contemporary and near-future events, its value depends upon (rather than deliberately evades) historical specificity. Ergome accordingly uses his position as finder and glossator literally to enclose the Bridlington prophecies in closely confining and localizing commentary. Although the prophecies are offered in the form of a fevered and disconnected vision-poem, their *ordinatio* involves tables of contents, frequent subdivision, ten-dentious headings, and – especially – Ergome's own detailed, phrase-by-phrase, commentary, all designed to lock the prophecies into a highly specific relationship to certain events, mostly preceding and some barely following the verses' authorship.

Although obscured by various devices which the author explains to us, the first two books remain completely historical in their impetus, accumulating interpretative authority by reporting under the guise of prophecy various things that have already happened in the reigns of Edward II and Edward III, with special emphasis on the battle of Crécy and its aftermath. The first two books conclude in the early 1360s. Building on the credibility gained by the backdated or pseudo-prophetic relation of known events, the third ventures into prophecy. But even here the prophecy is near-term and explicitly programmatic and reformist. Ergome's commentary relates it to a lapse into unfortu-nate practices by Edward III, and then bends his prophecy to reformist purposes by predicting his regeneration. The work concludes by fore-seeing victories for the Black Prince in France and the union of the two crowns under his sway.

Each of the first two books is held within a strictly and frequently reiterated chronological frame. The second book is introduced with the rubric, 'The author resumes his prophecy, containing the English occurrences from the first disposition toward the battle of Crécy, namely the year of Christ 1345. . . .' Treatment of the battle of Crécy itself is introduced in the second chapter, which 'shows the occur-rences and events of war at Crécy,' commencing with,

Jam crescunt bella, crescunt ter trina duella,
Alma maris stella, fer nunc vexilla, puella.
Bis dux vix feriet cum trecentis sociatis
Phi. falsus fugiet, non succurret nece stratis.
['Now battles increase, thrice three duels increase,

Bear now the standard, kind star of the sea, maiden.
Twice the leader will scarcely strike with 300 companions.
The false Philip will flee, nor will he succor those overthrown by
   slaughter.']

The specificity of these lines is extended – beyond the reference to King
Philip's cowardice – within the accompanying commentary. *Bis . . . vix*
are shown, in ways too complex to repeat here, to work out numerically to '1346,' the date of the battle. Moreover (abbreviating slightly)
the commentary goes on to assert that

> This chapter contains the occurrences at Crécy and Durham, the
> former dating to October 1346 and the latter to November of that
> year. The author begins by showing many future battles, imploring
> the aid of the blessed virgin Mary for king Edward. . . . As it hap-
> pens, conflicts will occur between men of two kingdoms, but all will
> be singular in nature, between knights of England and France.
> . . . *Phi. falsus fugiet*: Phillip king of France, [will flee] from that battle,
> *non succurret nece stratis*: nor will he succor those overthrown in this
> battle . . . but will abandon them; and thus it happened ['ita factus
> est']!

As may be imagined, the close constraints that Ergome places on his
own meaning constituted at least a momentary or provisional barrier
for the many subsequent commentators who sought to apply
Bridlington to their own situations and designs.

The original intentions of the Bridlington text having been invali-
dated by the Black Prince's decline and death in 1376, its prophecies
could be delivered to later ages and wider use – but only upon condition of bypassing their original contextualization and use. The essential
first stage of this endeavor was, of course, the separation of the prophecies from their author's carefully created and highly constraining
frame, and this was easily enough accomplished by the simple
expedient of recopying the prophetic verses independent of 'Ergome's'
headings and exposition; that this was done is evident from a review of
fifteenth-century manuscripts, most of which present the bare verses.[21]
With that step accomplished, the intriguingly suggestive and gnomic
verses are thrown open to new application within an enlarged
appropriative field.

Adam of Usk is among those fully ready to forage among the
Bridlington remains in order to harness their authority to his narrative
task. Describing the return of Bolingbroke from exile, Adam returns to
the verses we have just considered, but reworks them in a very deliberate and unapologetic way:

Returning from exile, the said duke of Hereford, and by the death of his father now duke of Lancaster, thus having been made duke twice over, according to this Bridlington prophecy, whence the verses:

> Bis dux vix veniet cum trecentis sociatis.
> Phi. falsus fugiet, non succurret nece stratis.

Displaced is, of course, all the number symbolism of *Bis . . . vix*. Now the leader ('dux'), no longer Edward III, assumes its alternative meaning of 'duke,' and Henry reasonably enough becomes 'twice duke.' The 300 companions become, by implication, the small band with which Henry returned to England; as Adam goes on to say, Henry landed with scarcely 300, as previously said ('vix cum ccc., ut premittitur'). Finally, (although not many have been slain yet) Richard, awkwardly absent in Ireland, stands in easily enough for the false Philip. Thus, Richard himself through cowardice and misadvice, is shortly depicted as having senselessly, with few followers, fled to Carmarthen: 'ad Carmerthyn circa mediam noctem cum paucissimis vecorditer *affugit*' – p. 27.

The reworked Bridlington prophecy having 'previously said' that Henry would land with scarcely 300 followers and that Richard would flee in disarray, Henry's and Richard's actions in the autumn of 1399 can now be viewed as surrounded by an aura of inevitability. The demonstration that Henry's unfolding narrative has been 'said before' bestows enormous Lancastrian premiums in its suggestion that, far from being an adventurous usurper, Henry is actually engaged in fulfilling a venerable prophetic mandate.[22] The advantage of stripping and using a prophecy of Bridlington in this way is that Henry thus arrogates to his own narrative all the prestige of a crucial native figure, John of Bridlington, additionally regarded as a miracle worker, a sanctified object of veneration, and one operating – according to Ergome's commentary – under the direct inspiration of the holy spirit.[23]

Notoriously multivalent in any case, prophecy becomes even harder to control when loosed from its contextual moorings. Adam, for example, follows his account of Henry's arrival with 300 followers by a brief flirtation with the possibility of identifying him as the eaglet, but then opts for the surprising and rather unique alternative of the dog:

> According to the prophecy of Merlin, this duke Henry is the eaglet, for he was the son of John; following Bridlington, however, he should rather be the dog, because of his livery of linked collars of greyhounds, and because he came in the dog-days, and because he

drove from the kingdom countless numbers of harts – the hart being
the livery of King Richard. (Usk, p. 53)

Adam does a series of deft associative pivots: from Henry as the
vaunted *pullus aquilae* via the Prophecy of the Eagle (which often
accompanied Merlin in the manuscripts) and because of a link between
his father John of Gaunt and the evangelist John whose emblem is the
eagle,[24] to Henry as dog because he arrived in the 'dog-days' of Cancer
in the month of July and because his livery of the greyhound-collar
banished Richard's livery of the white hart from the land.[25] Part of
Adam's activity here amounts to a kind of conscious overdetermina-
tion, in which different causalities (historical, biblical, familial, astro-
logical) are seen to point to the same eventuality. But part would seem
to result from a certain skittishness about identifying Henry and his
reign with any single prophetic determinant. Because prophecy is
fickle, the short-term gain of one prophetic identification is likely to be
negated by a subsequent turn of prophetic events.

The eagle, for example, does well in the Prophecy of the Eagle, but is
assigned a highly equivocal role in an even more influential prophecy,
that of the pseudo-Merlin prophecy of the 'Six Kings' to follow John.
Dating from the late thirteenth or early fourteenth century,[26] this
proliferated during the Lancastrian era. One of its several contentions
was that the lamb (or ass) usually taken to signify Richard will assign
his lands to the eagle, who will govern well but will be slain by his
brother's sword, with rule returning to the lamb:

> This lambe shal . . . gif an Lordeship to an Egle of his landes; and this
> Egle shal wel gouerne hit, til the tyme that pride shal him ouergone,
> – allas the sorwe! – for he shal dye through his brotheres suorde.
> And after shall the lande falle to the forsaide lambe, that shal
> gouerne in pees al his lifes tyme.[27]

Henry would have had every reason to avoid identification with *this*
eagle; the more so since rumors of Richard II alive in Scotland and
eligible to resume rule persisted throughout Henry IV's kingship and
endured even to 1420–21 when Adam was probably finishing off his
work.[28] The task for the deft Lancastrian apologist was to harness all
the positive imagery of the arrival of a *pullus aquilae* from across the
sea, without being inextricably bound within any of the possible negative repercussions of the association. Adam managed this task with
aplomb.

Such corroborative operations were valuable to the Lancastrians, as to any successful user, for their production and delivery of legitimacy within a closed symbolic economy. If a dynastic event can be shown to fulfill a prediction, then the event will acquire the prestige of Merlin, John of Bridlington, or its other predictor. The consolidation of its effects will be abetted by a sense of inevitability, that it could not have been otherwise, and it will also arrogate to itself all the displaced and deferred content of the prophecy. This last, and most important, respect repeats the pattern of biblical typology, as established in the relation of the New Testament to the Old and as repeated in many systems of later medieval figuration. An earlier utterance or event which is assigned a prefigurative role is effectively drained of its own meaning, with an accompanying transfer of meaning to the subsequent event which 'completes' it, into the reality of which the meaning of the earlier event is subsumed. This arrogation of meaning explains the relative heedlessness about the narrative context or intention of the predictive event, especially as practiced in the biblical typology of the later Middle Ages. The intention or self-understanding of the original actor is negated, since the relation of the initial action or utterance to its context is adventitious in any case.[29] Only in the revelation of its relation to a subsequent act is the meaning of the prophetic utterance revealed, and its meaning is 'spoiled' or transported elsewhere at the very moment of its revelation. But its value survives the act of spoilage as, reworked, it is put to the service of the subsequent event it edifies – in this case, within the varied narrative of Lancastrian ascendancy.

*

The vindicatory or triumphalist use of prophecy, in which past prophecy is stripped of its capacity to cause or make things happen and is recruited to bear fitful witness to a current inevitability, is naturally enough favored by those interests already enjoying possession of power and seeking its consolidation or extension. For parties in power, prophecy is expected to be tributary and supine; not to insist on its own applications or interpretations, or to surround itself by surplus and potentially disturbing commentary. This proposition may be illustrated by the fates of prophets who had the audacity to come before Richard II (when he was king) and Henry IV (now that he is king) in their own person, not just to prophesy but to urge their own, very particular, prophetic interpretations. A prophet whom the *Annales Ricardi* identify as one William Norham came in the spring of 1399 to the archbishop of Canterbury, and subsequently to Richard himself, demanding that Richard reinstate those lords whom he had dispossessed and had disinherited in the last parliament, or else both archbishop and king would be overtaken in a short time, by such dire news that it would make the ears of anyone who heard it tingle ('tam dira nova . . . ut quicunque audiret, tinnirent ambae aures ejus').[30] Richard, doubtful about the self-styled prophet's ragged condition, but still intrigued, proposed that the prophet walk on water to confirm his status as a messenger of God. The prophet, explaining that he was not a saint who performed such miracles but reasserting the force of his prophecy, was ordered to the Tower. There, the *Annales* say, he remained until he saw his prophecy fulfilled ('qui mansit ibi donec videret impleri suum vaticinium'). This prophet may, in turn, be the same who, having foretold the future for Richard, now sought to do the same for Henry[31] – and, once again, to rail at him besides ('Regi moderno prophetare nititur, et minus prudenter invehitur contra ipsum' – p. 372). Henry's solution was more direct than Richard's: convicted of lies, the prophet was beheaded at York ('convictus dixisse mendacium, decollatus est' – p. 373), dying a traitor's death.[32] The outrage, in each case, would seem to involve the attempt to turn prophecy to unauthorized account, to inveigh against a seated monarch on its presumed authority.

The Lancastrians quickly understood the importance of suppressing any prophecy promulgated beyond their immediate purview, as in Henry's early proscription of any divinations originating in Wales. In parliament, in 1402, it was agreed that

> no wastrels, rhymers, minstrels, or vagabonds should be sustained in Wales, to make tumultuous gatherings among the common people, which by their divinations, lies, and excitations are the cause of the insurrection and rebellion occurring there now ['par lour divinationes, messonges, & exitations, sount concause de la Insurrection & Rebellion q'or est en Gales'].[33]

The disturbing element of these Welsh divinations was, of course, that they were somebody *else's* prophecy, prophecy directed within a non-Lancastrian teleology to a decidedly anti-Lancastrian end. But, for reasons to be considered, Henry's attempt to proscribe alternative prophecy must be compared in its possible effectiveness to Darius's decision to scourge the unruly sea.

However effective the Lancastrians may have been in silencing alternative prophecies and prophetic voices, they could never have succeeded in restricting the vast and unruly field of prophetic utterance to their own use. Retrospective and pro-Lancastrian uses of prophecy might succeed in their own terms, but could not prevent potential rivals and out-of-power rivals from seizing upon the same or related prophecies, yoking them to the narrative of their own hoped-for emergence. Of particular utility to Henry IV's early opponents was an association available within the 'Six Kings,' in which Henry was viewed as the sixth (and last) in the succession. Within this prophecy, Richard was commonly understood to be the fifth king, the lamb (or cursed or crowned ass), and Henry was considered to be his successor, the ignominious moldwarp or mole: 'a Moldwerpe acursede of Godes mouth, a caitif, a cowarde as an here'.[34] This moldwarp will have rough skin like a goat, and in his first year will enjoy plenty but his pridefulness will incite God's anger and the moldwarp's subsequent overthrow. Or, in the highly jaundiced version of MS Cotton Galba E. ix,

> A swith grete wretche the moldwarp sal be;
> In euerilka nede fast sal he fle. . . .
> And on him sall light, who so right redes,
> The vengance of God for ald euill dedes.
> He shal be ful wrangwis in euerilka wane [dwelling],
> And grace in his time gettes he nane.[35]

The critical point about the moldwarp was not, however, his disagreeable features, but the finitude of his term of rule. The prophecy imagined the moldwarp's demise through the joint action of a dragon, a wolf of the west, and a lion of Ireland:

> Than sall cum a dragon ful fell & full scharp,
> And he sall raise were oganis the moldwarp;
> And als with that dragon than sall be prest
> A wolf that sall cum out of the west. . . .
> Out of Yreland sall cum a liown,
> And hald with the wolf and with the dragown:
> Than sall all Ingland quakeand [sic] be,
> Als leues that hinges on the espe tre.

The prophecies end with minor but telling local variations, though always with the conclusion that England will be divided into three parts, ruled by the three beasts.

This must be the prophecy to which Glyndwr hopefully alluded in the 1401 letters he wrote to his *consanguinei* in Ireland and Scotland, seeking to rally them against the common Saxon enemy. Far from the fulminating seer of Shakespeare's *Henry IV, Part 1*, the Glyndwr of these letters maintains a slightly provisional stance in relation to prophecy, but a determination not to forgo the practical and argumentative advantages that prophecy might confer. Expressing to the lords of Ireland his own determination to rebel, he observes that prophecy requires something of them too; his request for arms and men is grounded on a need to follow prophecy's stipulations:

> It is commonly said in the prophecy ['quia uulgariter dicitur per propheciam'] . . . that, before we can gain the upper hand in this contest, you and your noble kinsmen in Ireland shall come to our aid in this matter.[36]

Expressed here would seem to be a version of Žižek's 'cynical belief,' in which the political actor 'knows better' but still behaves *as if* he or she believed; behaves, that is, no differently from a believer, and hence effectively does believe. This is the same provisionality, issuing from a desire to believe or at least an absence of anything else to put in belief's place, that animated Richard's followers in the years after his death (see Chapter 4, pp. 108–111). At its ultimate extension, this stance toward belief models a relation to ideology (that is, to the process of social belief) itself: a process in which ideology is at once 'seen through,' yet continues to influence social decisions and things social actors do. These actors are, again, in the position of Žižek's cynical subject, who 'is quite aware of the distance between the ideological mask and the social reality, but . . . none the less still insists upon the mask.'[37] Glyndwr, that is, stands rather urbanely aside from prophecy, describing it as a popular phenomenon ('uulgariter dicitur'), but then seems at once to bend it to cynical use (as an excuse to demand Irish aid) and conditional belief (expressed as an unwillingness to ignore any term of prophecy's fulfillment).[38]

This condition of hesitant wishfulness – in which one does not believe yet effectively believes, in which one seeks to use prophecy and is in turn used by it – is attributed to the principal anti-Lancastrian conspirators, when they sought to rally after the devastating defeat of Percy and the Scots at Shrewsbury. Here is the fullest chronicle account of the terms in which Glyndwr, Mortimer, and the earl of Northumberland swore allegiance in 1405:

> if, with God disposing, it should appear to the foresaid lords in the course of time, that they are the same persons of whom the prophet speaks, among whom the realm of Great Britain ought to be divided and partitioned, then they will labor, and, both of them will labor to the best of their abilities so that this matter would be brought effectually to completion [. . . si disponente Deo, appareat praefatis dominis ex processu temporis, quod ipsi sint eaedem personae, de quibus propheta loquitur, inter quos regimen Britanniae majoris

dividi debeat et partiri, tunc ipsi laborabunt, et quilibet ipsorum laborabit juxta posse, quod id ad effectum efficaciter perducatur].[39]

The conditionality of this passage depends not just on a reverent uncertainty about God's will, but on a question in the three rebels' minds as to whether they *are* the dragon, the wolf, and the lion to whom the prophecy of the 'Six Kings' assigns tripartite rule. Their subjunctively posed question weighs their ability to step into prophecy's pre-established frame; whether, to continue the analogy between the operations of prophecy and ideology, they can successfully heed, and shape their behavior according to, prophecy's interpellation.

However seriously prophecy was or was not taken, the co-conspirators are shown using prophecy in a potentially productive way: as a source of alternative social representations within which a utopian or resistant stance toward an unwanted state of affairs might find a place of attachment and propagation. Again, like ideology itself, prophecy was impossible to avoid, both for those intent on justifying a social order and those intent on changing it. Actions are produced within prophecy in order to assure their intelligibility, and completed actions are judged and categorized as prophetic effects. Here, rather than facilitating a desired outcome, prophecy turns out to have promoted a temporary delusion. But prophecy is understood by all concerned to have altered the course of unfolding events.

As normally displayed to us, Henry Percy might seem to provide a counter-example. Shakespeare was true to his chronicle sources in portraying Henry Percy as one determined to live in the real world, to avoid self-deluding interpretations. The *Eulogium* continuator gives us a Percy who delivered a lecture on *realpolitik* to the followers of the late King Richard who showed up on the eve of Shrewsbury still wearing his livery: 'He caused it to be proclaimed that he was one of those who had striven greatly for the expulsion of Richard and the introduction of Henry, believing himself to have done well. And because now he knew that Henry was a worse ruler than Richard, he therefore intended to correct his error.'[40] Yet even Percy is elsewhere returned to prophecy's shifty dominion. The *Annales Henrici* draw upon a well-established anecdotal frame when they have him, learning before the battle of Shrewsbury that a nearby village was called Berwick, blanching and heaving a great sigh, and saying to a servant,

I know indeed that my plow has reached its last furrow; for I have heard through prophecy ['per fatidicum'] . . . that I should undoubtedly die in Berwick. But I was deceived, alas, by confusion about the name ['sed decepit me, proh dolor! nominis hujus aequivocum'].[41]

The implication is that Percy had resolved to avoid Berwick upon Tweed! Here, though, another Berwick manifests itself, to his undoing and the greater prestige of prophecy. This story's status as an obvious invention matters less than the habit of mind it reveals; a habit in which actions are, willy-nilly, subjected to prophecy's dominion.[42]

Even those who seek not to live in prophecy are imagined to have died in it. By the same token, the Lancastrians, who sought to control prophecy, could not fully elude its control. In his report of King Henry's death in 1413 even the generally pro-Lancastrian Adam of Usk cannot resist the assertion that Henry IV's ending was already knowable, and legible, in his beginning. He notes that Henry died of a putridity of the flesh ('carnis putredine' – p. 242), and that 'this festering was foreshadowed ("portentebat") at his coronation, for as a result of his anointing then, his head was so infected with lice that his hair fell out, and for several months he had to keep his head covered' – p. 243.[43] At this point, however, we have begun to shift registers – from prophecy to portent – with a corresponding adjustment of audience, expectation, and discursive situation.

Gossip, portentous talk, and public opinion

Access to, and exegesis of, written prophecy is normally a learned operation, and frequently a clerical one. As with the more academic forms of biblical citation, reference to particular passages of a heavily glossed and often monastically copied Latin text like that of Bridlington belongs to a process of verification congenial to a learned elite. Adam of Usk's recourse to Bridlington is, in a sense, scholarly as well as political, asserting and maintaining the internal consistency of a body of written texts. At stake is an explanatory economy, in which a providential pattern is found to regulate apparently disparate events. Ingenuity and interpretative *force majeure* are enlisted in support of this economy and the social arrangements to which its authority is loaned. But, if the linguistic competences and interpretative tools normally prerequisite to such exegesis are those of an intellectual elite, the same exegetical impulses and procedures were also more widely distributed. One thus encounters a very broad sharing out of these procedures – the confidence in intelligibility of seemingly fortuitous or incidental details, the reclamation of such details in a new pattern based on precedent and previously unnoticed congruence, the citation of pattern for persuasive purposes – all deployed in the stream of everyday conversation, as it occurs in the alehouse, between neighbors, on journeys, or in workshop or field.

Adam himself engages frequently in forms of speculation and argumentation which, rather than simply belonging to a learned elite, were broadly available across the strata of society.[44] He shares with every subject the need for a king's death not to be a death alone, but to *mean* something. The connection between Henry IV's problems of rulership and the lice caused by his coronation oil would, for example, have been available to persons other than Latin exegetes. Here Adam manifests a certain interpretative restraint. The lice predict Henry's death, rather than something even more ambitious, such as failed unction or the corruption of his reign. In this treatment may be read both Adam's faith in prophetic structure and his position as Lancastrian ideologue (a potentially embarrassing message is better withheld than uttered). His restraint may also suggest a certain faith in his readers' interpretative capacities: the implication of this anecdote, his manner suggests, can be trusted to their own well-practiced competence.

A closely related, and more congenial, subject on which Adam had no difficulty finding his voice is that of Richard II's death. Once again he relies upon a premonitory structure, but inhabits it with evident verve:

> At this lord's coronation, three symbols of royalty foretold ['portentebant'] three misfortunes which would befall him: firstly, during the procession he lost one of the coronation shoes, so that to begin with the common people rose up against him, and for the rest of his life hated him; secondly, one of his golden spurs fell off, so that next the knights rose up and rebelled against him; thirdly, during the banquet a sudden gust of wind blew the crown from his head, so that thirdly and finally he was deposed from his kingdom and replaced by King Henry. (p. 91)

The coronation of Richard II was described in minute detail in several texts,[45] but none mentions any of these three irregularities – nor, for that matter, does Adam himself, in his initial report of the coronation. This, added to the commonsense fact that crowns seem unlikely to be blown by gusts of wind from royal heads, suggests that much of the substance of Adam's passage must be considered invention (whether by Adam himself or by another author). Other evidence suggests, however, that one of the three – the loss of the slipper – may have been extra-textually suggested. An inventory of the regalia taken in 1356 includes 'deux chaunceons de samyt rouge' (two slippers of red silk) as well as 'deux pairs desporons',[46] and in 1390 Richard sent a new pair of red velvet shoes to the monks of Westminster, designed, according to the Westminster chronicler, as a replacement for those that were lost in circumstances which he describes:

> when the coronation was over a certain knight named Simon Burley picked up the king, still dressed in his regalia, into his arms, entering the palace by the royal gate, with crowds rushing to meet them and pressing against them, and in transit lost one of the blessed royal shoes ['unum de sotularibus regalibus benedictis'] through negligence. (pp. 414–416)[47]

The chronicler's primary interest is in preservation of the coronation regalia, a responsibility of the Abbey, and not in Burley's or Richard's misfeasance or the contours of Richard's reign.[48] Precisely because this mention of the slipper's loss is incidental to another, supradynastic, concern, it would seem to be politically innocent with respect to Richard's reign, and thus believable. Still, whatever aid to Adam's invention real events might have supplied, his exegesis must be considered mainly purpose-built rather than 'historical.' 'A fact,' as the narrator of Don DeLillo's novel *Libra* observes, 'is innocent until someone wants it,' and the 'fact' of the lost slipper remained latent and unemployed until Adam wanted it, for what must be regarded primarily as an imaginative construct, weaving actual and invented details into an explanatory pattern.

With Adam's enterprise may be compared a more ambitious, but less persuasive, attempt by a fellow chronicler who, learning of Richard's death by starvation, sought to draw a larger cluster of disparate details together under the dominion of a single portent. He says that Richard was starved at Pontefract,

> in order that the prophecy might be fulfilled ['ut adimpleretur prophecia'] of a certain knight of France who was present at his coronation, where he saw the king's slipper falling to the ground and saw the king at the banquet vomiting his food ['ubi vidit regis sotularem ad terram cadentem et regem ad prandium cibum suum evomentem']. He explained it thus: 'This king will be glorious and extremely abundant in food, but he will lose the *dignitas* of the realm and in the end will die on account of hunger.'[49]

Adam's remix of fact and fiction, and the presumed invention of a prophetic 'knight of France,' function within what I am calling the 'Lancastrian' mode; the mode, that is, of seated power. The effect is once again recursive, showing that the present moment is the consequence of an inevitable and unalterable pattern, the necessary fulfillment of tendencies long in motion which could not have turned out other than they did. The difference, when compared with Adam's mobilization of Bridlington, is simply that one need not know so much; that the point of prophetic origin is no longer in difficult Latin hexameter, but is observable in mundane events: a dropped coin, a lost slipper, childish nausea in the middle of a turbulent and exciting day.

Merlin and pseudo-Merlin and John of Bridlington were manipulated in such a way as to offer maximum scope to the interpretative imagination. But possibilities multiply exponentially when the entire body of written and spoken exemplum and anecdote is opened for investigation and application. A well-worn anecdote could be summoned and repeated (with minor recasting or no recasting) for *ad hoc* prophetic purposes. Consider Adam of Usk's recital of the story of Richard's fickle greyhound. Like any good storyteller, he recounts it as something he witnessed at first hand, applying it to a transitional moment that makes the dog into something of a popular prophet (if not a popular exegete!). He explains that the dog was Richard's constant companion until, when Richard's prospects began to wane (and Richard himself behaved ignobly),

> deserting him, it made its way . . . alone and unaided, from Carmarthen directly to Shrewsbury, where the duke of Lancaster, now the king, was staying at that time with his army, in the monastery there, and, as I stood watching, it went up and crouched obediently before him, whom it had never seen before, with a look of purest pleasure on its face. (p. 87)

Lest the point be missed, Adam subjects the dog to another test. Richard having been deposed, the dog is brought to him, but the dog 'did not recognize him or treat him in any way differently from any ordinary person.'

The anecdote is by no means Adam's own.[50] This kind of migratory anecdote functions as does a remembered image in the medieval thought process, to be adduced, de- or re-contextualized, and applied, in order (as in this case) to serve as an indicator of an important shift in loyalty. It functions like prophecy, to predict the imminent conversion of a duke to a king, and then to go on confirming that this event could not have been otherwise, that its import is legible even (in Froissart's version) to the 'congnoissance naturelle' of Richard's (and now Henry's) dog.

This highly mobile hound traverses narrative and linguistic barriers to corroborate a variety of claims, both military and royal. It participates, that is, in fictions identical in structure to some of the most learned applications of Latinate prophecy. This corroborative view of the world, unconfined to formalized systems and disciplines of explication, is equally at home in casual conversation, or even in outright gossip. For, as the Lancastrian judiciary was quick enough to recognize, informal exchanges of 'nouvelles' contribute significantly to creating the kind of climate of general consensus that can confirm a new regime's power – or encourage its overthrow. As it touches on the deposition of Richard II and the accession of Henry IV, for example, the written record (especially chronicles, augmented by treason trials in King's Bench) affords repeated glimpses of a climate of lively talk, in which ordinary subjects probed issues of rule and sought consensus on such questions as the logic and inevitability of Richard's deposition.

Disgruntled talk occurred all the time, as when William Mildenhale of London confessed in 1391 that his father had regarded the king as incompetent, and had wished that 'he were in his gong ['latrina'], where he might stay for ever without further governing any.'[51] But the utterances which interest me here are those structured according to recursiveness, suggesting that the king (for example) has been unfit for rule from the very beginning – that he has, in effect, 'always already' been unfit – and seeking a consensus for this view.

Particularly apt for such purposes were rumors concerning Richard's birth, since, were Richard thought to be a bastard, his disqualification from rule would be evident and acceptable to all. Adam outlines such a view in his discussion of Richard's deposition, mulling over his tendency to debase the noble and to exalt the low, and adding in an explanatory way that, considering his birth,

> many unsavoury things were commonly said, namely that he was not born of a father of a royal line, but of a mother given to slippery ways ['lubrice uite dedita'] – to say nothing of many other things I have heard. (pp. 62–63)

Extramarital antics on the part of the queen mother are, Adam suggests, legible in Richard's flaws. Such antics would, moreover, have disqualified Richard from the start, creating a context in which he *should never have been* king at all. So promising was this claim from the anti-Ricardian and pro-Lancastrian point of view that it was widely encouraged. A variant version of Creton's account of Richard's humiliation at the hands of Henry IV in London has him exhibited in degrading circumstances to citizens who disparage his legitimacy: 'Next day the king was carried through the city from Westminster on a sorry horse, with an open space around him, that all might see him, and lodged in the Tower. Some had pity of him, but others expressed great joy, abusing him, and saying, "Now are we avenged of this little bastard, who has governed us so ill."[52] The French *Chronicque de la Traïson et Mort* repeats the anecdote, saying that Richard is first hailed by a boy and then shouted down by the crowd, which (according to the manuscript in question) variously denounced him as 'petit bastard' and 'mauuais bastart.'[53] Froissart imagines Henry accusing Richard of bastard birth during their pre-deposition interview in the Tower:

'It is commonly held ["commune renommée"] in England and else-where that you are not the son of the prince at all, but of a clerk or a canon. . . . [For I have heard that your mother], having succeeded in marrying the prince by subtlety and guile, fearing that he would divorce her, made herself pregnant ["fist tant qu'elle fut grosse"] and had you and another before you. Of the first one I cannot judge, but of you, whose manners and conditions are visibly so different from the valiance and prowess of the prince, it is said in this country and elsewhere that you are son of a clerk or a canon – since at the time that you were engendered and born in Bordeaux there were many very beautiful and young ones in the household of the prince. All this is commonly believed by people in this realm, and properly so, because your works have confirmed it ["et bien en avés par expérience monstré les euvres"], for you have always chosen their company and have wanted to make peace with them, to the confu-sion and great dishonor of our realm.'[54]

This biology-is-destiny argument is, of course, sharpened in the case of a king, whose clear title is based on his birth.

Such claims were never simply promulgated 'from above'; although reliant on the same retrospective recasting of origins that marks learned use of prophecy, this structure was fully available to those without access to learning. Consider a piece of reported (or imagined) domestic talk, from the 1387–88 treason accusation against Thomas Austin, who let his wife carry on against the king and (almost as bad from the point of view of the accusation) failed to correct her: 'diuerse tymes his wiffe hath seyd that serteynly that the kynge was neuere the prynses sone and also sche hathe seyd that his moder was neuere but a strong hore and that same Thomas was neuere that man that onys wolde beddyn here holdyn here wordys but cherschid here in here malyse.'[55] Mrs Austin was precocious, in that her household harangues were supposed to have taken place *c.* 1383–84; but if true, or even if simply common enough to be plausible, her sentiments offer a glimpse into a moment of micro-causality, a single moment that contributes to a generally held view. Unsurprisingly, Henry IV would himself be subject to accusations of bastardy by partisans of Richard, as in 1402 when a Welshman named John Sperhauke had a conversation with a tailor's wife who told him that 'the present king was not rightful king . . . and that he was not son of the noble prince John, duke of Lancaster, whom God bless, and that he was born also to a butcher of Ghent'.[56] She, according to John, had heard this claim from a friar or hermit who had recently been imprisoned at Westminster, and he, in turn, had the misfortune to repeat it to several citizens of Morden – one John Taylor, as well as a beggar and his wife and more.

Such networks and chains of informal talk weave a consensus, a view so 'commonly held' as to constitute proof and a basis for political action. No wonder that kings and regimes against which they were directed took action against the tellers; the whole Austin family ended up in court, and Sperhauke lost his head for his tale-telling. By compromising a regime's legitimacy at its source, such talk can solidify to make itself, like prophecy, 'come true.'

Imagining the king's death

Adam of Usk turns directly from one disciplinary parable (concerning the execution of William Sautre) to another, describing the fate of one William Clerk. Concurrently with the same parliament in which Sautre was burnt, William was judicially condemned and subjected to an emblematic punishment:

> While this parliament was going on, a certain William Clerk, a scribe from Canterbury who had originally come from the county of Chester, was condemned by judgement of the court of chivalry ['militaris curie iudicio dampnatus'] firstly to have his tongue cut out, because he had spoken disrespectfully of the king . . . , secondly, to have his right hand cut off, because it had written these things down, and thirdly, by penalty of talion, to be beheaded at the Tower, because he had not been able to prove his false allegations. (p. 123)

Because William's case was not heard in King's Bench, its records have not been preserved and Usk's veracity in this instance cannot be assessed. Even if an invention, however, its manifest and multiple determinations place it in a vivid and fully historical context of contemporary contention over what might be spoken and written about the new dynasty. The instability of William's vocation (is he scribe or clerk? is he simply named 'Clerk' or did he gain that title through vocation and function?) broadens the cautionary impact of his fate to embrace an entire lettered class. His present location in Canterbury, the seat of the archbishopric, coupled with his origin in Chester, the hot-bed of pro-Ricardian agitation, inscribe him as a man of shady origins, now dangerously placed. The venue of his trial in the court of chivalry flags his offense as treasonous in nature.[57] His punishment (along with the amorphous nature of his crime) serves as a warning to those who speak and those who write of matters disagreeable to the king. Notable in its extreme theatricality, the punishment is rooted in the homely *contrappasso* of the pillory and the stocks but considerably more ambi-tious than hanging a spoiled cod around a fishmonger's neck. Its site – the Tower – is a place of royal authority within the city walls, with access to mass spectatorship. In all these ways, this brief narration has much to offer a regime interested in silencing opposition and wielding punishment theatrically to secure its claims.

As the fate of William Clerk might suggest, the Lancastrians were no friends to spoken or written critique. Celebrated occasions of permis-sible dissent – like Repingdon's admonitory letter – turn out upon closer inspection simply to be more artfully arranged instances of complicity.[58] This distaste for criticism was hardly unusual among medieval monarchs. But the innovative element in the reigns of Henry IV and Henry V is the extent to which, rather than waiting for instances of public criticism to arise and responding accordingly, these mon-archs regularly attempted pre-emptive intervention at the imaginative, geographical, and discursive places of insurrectionary possibility.

Of what was William Clerk actually guilty? The charge against him would seem to embrace what he said and wrote, and hence to consti-tute a precocious example of what has been called 'treason by words.' Spoken and written words are equally involved here, but the whole notion of treason by words during this period remains potentially misleading. This notion originated in a misconceived scholarly sugges-tion that the 1352 treason statute required an 'overt act' for conviction, and that words alone (which had always been liable to prosecution in common law) were reasserted as a basis for conviction during the reign of Henry IV.[59] In point of fact, the 1352 statute requires no overt act for conviction, and it is applicable to a wide range of situations 'quant homme fait compasser ou ymaginer le mort notre Seigneur le Roi.' 'To compass or imagine' the death of the king is to commit treason, whether or not a concrete action ensues, and the evidence of words spoken or written is subordinate to (although clearly contributory to) a determination.[60]

In cases like that of William Clerk, spoken and written dissent is obviously a contributory factor, but only within the more general claim that the death of the king has been compassed or imagined. 'Compasser ou ymaginer' is itself, however, a phrase that needs to be disassembled in order better to be understood. Seeming at first glance to be one of those legal catchalls or omnibus phrases in which the same thing is repeated in all its variants in the interest of comprehensiveness, it is in fact a union of two slightly different terms. To 'compass' the death of the king is to lay a plan for it, to undertake a series of steps leading to its fulfillment; to 'imagine' the death of the king is to form an image or phantasm of the king's death in the mind.

This apparent difference is partially mitigated by the physiological basis of the medieval imagination, and by the belief in its material and sensual staging. In its most minimal and literal sense, later Middle English *imagination*, together with its counterparts in Latin and French, refers to the faculty of forming mental images from sense data and of retaining them. Even when abstracted as objects of thought these images retain a sensory character. As Mary Carruthers conveniently summarizes the medieval understanding, taking Thomas Aquinas as her case in point, 'even in describing so purely "mental" an activity as abstraction seems to us to be, a physical analogy persists. Thomas, as we have seen, regards the production of phantasms as a process of physical changes.'[61] The sensory basis of images or phantasms might be differently described or illustrated from system to system, but remains fundamental to every medieval conception. The fact that thought relies upon sense-derived images or phantasms constitutes a partial explanation for the criminal nature of treasonous imaginings; thought is, in a very important sense, more tangible and real to the medieval understanding than to our own.

Nevertheless, the less tangible and more creative element of unregulated imagination increases when it is understood to embrace, not just things seen or observed, but (here borrowing from Kurath and Kuhn's *Middle English Dictionary*) 'the power of forming mental images of things not experienced.'[62] So seen, the imagination is not just a storehouse of inert forms, but renders images or phantasms which can be configured or reconfigured to represent the possible. Carruthers discusses Thomas's distinction between a retentive imagination ('phantasia') and a composing imagination ('imaginativa'), observing that the two might be combined and called simply 'phastasia seu imaginatio' (p. 51). This case, in which images can be recalled or combined without external stimulus, is similar to what Morton Bloomfield, in a useful preliminary survey of the subject, designated 'an internal sense, . . . generally known as the *vis imaginativa*, or *vis phantastica* (the imaginative power).'[63] Although I would stop short of Bloomfield's subsequent identification of imagination with divine inspiration and the operations of prophecy,[64] I would point out that imagination in its 'internal sense' is potentially creative, in its capacity to realize at the imagistic level things that have not occurred.[65] This is the hypothetical sense which Augustine (in non-Aristotelian terminology) called spiritual, as opposed to corporeal, vision: 'the spiritual vision by which we think of absent bodies in imagination – whether recalling in memory objects that we know, or somehow forming unknown objects which are in the power of thought possessed by the spirit, or arbitrarily and fancifully fashioning objects which have no real existence.'[66] Augustine is skeptical about the prophetic power of such vision, but, if something less than prophecy, creative forethought can replicate the capacity of prophecy to capture the future – or to be discovered retrospectively as the origin of a future event – under the aegis of desire.

The medieval imagination may, in this respect, be seen as a creative force, based in the senses but not limited to them, possessed of the capacity to open the space of the hypothetical or the possible, the space which I have elsewhere (Chapter 4, pp. 108–111) described as that of *tanquam . . .* or *si*. It is a provisional mode, a mode that participates in the provisionality which invariably accompanies imaginative entry into the register of the symbolic and the symbolization of desire. Precisely because it is disconnected from any existing state of affairs, representing a kind of openness with regard to possible outcomes, it is a potentially transformative mode. And, to the extent that it is transformative, the Lancastrians would have had cause to regard it as repugnant and dangerous.

One may entertain imaginative alternatives without formally participating in a plot or machination; yet, on the other hand, the entertainment of a notion may precede its implementation. This is what Chaucer reveals when he describes the 'heigh ymaginacioun' of the iniquitous fox in the *Nun's Priest's Tale* – an imagination which, unbound to the present and free to sift images of Chauntecleer's undoing, enables him to settle upon his treasonous plan.[67] This is also the 'fals ymaginacioun' by which Gower's future Pope Boniface undid his predecessor Celestin through 'supplantacioun.' Only when he enlisted a young clerk to do his 'wille' by duping Celestin into believing that God sought his resignation might we say that Boniface entered into a plot or conspiracy, but his foresight of an alternative possibility, imaginatively embodied, was the essential precondition of his false action.[68]

To imagine is to engage in an implicitly utopian activity, to deploy images according to the plasticity of desire. To loose one's imagination on the king is temporarily to suppose him other than he is, even to suppose him supplanted or transformed (from Richard II to Richard, knight of Bordeaux, from Henry IV to Henry, duke of Lancaster), or deposed, supplanted, or dead. No wonder the Lancastrians (together with other reigning dynasties) sought to curb imagining – or to substitute for unruly imagining a more officially approved and structured imagination, stabilized and externally available in sponsored descriptions and official enactments.

Many strands – the dangers of false prophecy, of uncontrolled rumor and false report, the dangers of subjective and unregulated imagination – are woven together in a statute of 1406, framed against Lollards and others who would dispossess spiritual, and ultimately temporal, lords of their estates.[69] Several features of this statute remain unexplained, including its presentation as a parliamentary petition under the primary sponsorship of the Prince of Wales, its temporary duration (until the next meeting of parliament), and the odd incommensurability of its stated attempt to control Lollard threats to the realm at a time when the Lollards had been relatively silent for several years.[70] Most likely, its actual purposes are only to be glimpsed, as it were, awry, in utterances incidental to its stated objects.[71] My interest here is not, however, so much in the tactical purposes of the petition, as in its disclosure of other assumptions. Which is to say that a 'dishonest' petition can still reveal much about what its framers take for granted about the framework of shared assumptions in which their text is drafted and within which it will be received; its sham targets and bogus accusations are nevertheless advanced in the expectation that they will command assent, that they speak to matters of common concern.

The petition's preamble, for example, invokes 'Lollardes, & autres parlours & controvours des Novelx & des Mensonges' – suggesting wholesale dissemination of lying gossip and destabilizing novelty, presumably not unlike the sort that the Lancastrians had earlier been happy to sponsor in the case of Richard II. Now that he is 'late king' rather than reigning monarch, Richard is no longer a suitable subject for prophecy:

> Evil men and women . . . by false assurances and signs, so far as they are able, publicize and evilly cause to be publicized, falsely among the people of your [that is, Henry's] realm, that Richard lately king of England, is supposed to be alive ['duist estre en plein vie']. And others write, license, and publicize to the people diverse false and pretended prophecies ['diverses fauxes pretenses Prophecies'] and have shown schedules and books to the same people.

Reappearing, too, is the Lancastrian frustration with those who cynically pander to the wish that Richard were alive, in the case of 'celuy fool q'est in Escoce' and those enemies in Scotland who sponsor him in order to create 'division' in the realm.[72]

Lying reports, false assurances and signs, substitutive and imitative practices – all are inimical to a settled social order as this petition evokes it. The keystone of this order is, of course, the holy Church, supported by its articles of faith and (in an invariable point of Lancastrian emphasis) as embodied in its sacraments. Henry IV's progenitors, the petition observes, have always been 'obedient to holy Church and firm in the Catholic Faith, have maintained and defended that Faith and the Sacraments of the holy Church.' The Church has been endowed with temporal possessions in defense of its prerogatives, and those now engaging in novel incitement against such possessions not only endanger an order and its guarantees, but would go so far down this slippery slope as to threaten temporal lordship itself. Against this disruption of ecclesiastical and lay responsibility is posed an edifice of laws and customs, assertive of the rightness of ecclesiastical possessions; possessions of which the Church's ministers

are surely, loyally, and rightly endowed and possessed as it has been best considered and imagined by the Laws and Customes of your Realm ['come il ad peu este mieux avisee ou ymaginee par les Loys & Custumes de vostre Roiaume'].

How are we to understand this legally and customarily 'imagined' state of affairs? Not, apparently, as something material or fully realized, but as a construct or an aspiration, imaged forth in laws and customs.

Recast in late twentieth-century terminology, the mobilization and presentation of images in written laws and customary practices rest more properly within the symbolic than the imaginary, are more a matter of agreed-upon and officially sponsored symbolism than imagination *per se*. But herein lies exactly the explicitly Lancastrian political wish of the 1406 petition: that in place of the unregimented and potentially transformative imaging or imagining of the social order by individual subjects, should stand an officially sanctioned symbolic order. In other words, the categories and limits of the subject's imagination should be contained by and within state-sanctioned symbolism. The decidedly Lancastrian result would be the elimination of the alternative or utopian imagination. The suppression of such an imagination would mean loss of those powers conferred by the medieval theory of the imagination: powers to form mental images of things not experienced, to constitute hypothetical alternatives to the present disposition of things, to engage (in James Simpson's words) in moral reflection across time.

Whatever the immediate purposes of the 1406 petition, it harbors a political wish which exceeds any finite objective: the annihilation of the utopian imagination by superimposition of its own sanctioned symbolism on the individual capacity to image alternatives. Even modest success in so ambitious an enterprise requires the complicity of other military and political events and realities. These include the failure of possible opponents like the Percies and Scrope and Glyndwr to consolidate their military activities; Henry IV's simple duration on the throne and his prevalent deference to aristocratic property rights; his success in establishing his eldest son as heir, together with the incremental legitimation derived from a second generation on the throne.[73] But such favorable developments might be consolidated by aggressive symbolic initiative, including proscription of competing analyses and symbolic programs. Consider, in this regard, the immense success of Arundel's *Constitutions* of 1407–9 in quelling the dissemination of Lollard opinion and in chilling other comparably imaginative projects.[74]

Despite the advantages of incumbency and despite the supplementary assistance of an ingenious symbolic program, oppositional imagination remained vitally alive throughout the Lancastrian decades. This imagination may be glimpsed in such surviving anti-Lancastrian rumors as gossip about Henry's high taxes and his regime as 'bad weather,' wishes that Richard might still be alive, and diverse imaginings of Henry's supplantation. Functioning as a political unconscious, the oppositional imagination produces an unending stream of representations alternative to every established or agreed-upon signification.[75] Operating under the permissive dominion of the pleasure principle, the imagination is inherently erratic in its functioning and cannot be relied upon as a docile or workaday provider of positive or hopeful alternatives. Yet, in any given social situation, the inevitability of imaginary excursions and fanciful extrapolations must comfort those who hope for change. The inability of the Lancastrian endeavor to pre-empt unruly and evasive imaginative processes stands as a reminder of the inherent futility of attempted social-symbolic domination.

2

Heretic Burning: The Lollard as Menace and Victim

Lancastrian accounts of the Lollard movement are marked by a recurring two-sidedness. The Lollards are insistently portrayed as aggressors: as unruly insurgents bound by conviction, perversity, or sheer wantonness to force the authorities' hands. Yet these same accounts cannot seem to resist a counter-tendency, in which the Lollards are exposed as dupes and fumblers, as persons beaten from the start and unable to understand the magnitude of resources already arrayed against them. Although ostensibly premised on the Lollard threat to religious and civil order, ecclesiastically and civilly sponsored documents turn out again and again to include or even to rely upon the discovery that a present threat of Lollard assertion or misrule actually exists because it is *suffered* to exist, because it is tolerated or encouraged by structures already in place but concealed from view. The joke, in such moments, is always at the expense of the Lollard. The structure of the revelation is typically joke-like, with a denouement or punchline unexpectedly but devastatingly revealing the Lollard as a witless and powerless buffoon.

Such a moment occurs in the course of priest William Sautre's 1401 heresy trial, as presented in the *Annales Henrici Quarti*. Archbishop Arundel having pronounced Sautre's degradation, we read,

> ... to whom the debauchee ['ganeo'] responded with pride, 'Your malice is already consummated. What more evil will you be able to visit upon me?' 'I,' replied the archbishop, 'commit you to secular judgment,' saying to the marshal, 'Take him, so that he may be punished according to your law.' He was led to Smithfield and there, with many people watching, was burned. (pp. 335–336)

Embraced within this anecdote are both ways of representing the Lollard threat. As a *ganeo*, a sort of ribaud or clown,[1] Sautre embodies the arrogant challenge of the Lollard gone out of control, the derisive swaggerer who threatens social norms and decorum. This is the same Sautre who is depicted in the trial records as responding to requests for information with mirth or outright derision – 'ridendo sive deridendo.'[2] Yet the chronicle account (and the trial record) cannot forgo the concurrent opportunity of presenting him as a figure of complete impotence, a pitiable dupe oblivious of his actual peril. Not comprehending his situation, he evidently cherishes the obsolete assumption that (as would have been the case in the Ricardian era) his degradation will conclude the process; that, the Church having done its worst, he may expect to resume his life as an untonsured layperson.[3] In the denouement or punchline which exposes Sautre's folly, the marshal turns out already to have been summoned, and a new horizon of judgment and punishment is revealed. Finally, erasing any uncertainty about the import of the marshal's presence, the account ends with a notice of Sautre's burning at Smithfield.

Here revealed for the pleasure of the orthodox is the extent of this Lollard's self-deception; thinking he controls his own circumstances, he is completely – ultimately fatally – unaware of the groundwork already laid for cooperation between the religious and secular arms, the ecclesiastical court and the secular marshal. He is, in the terms of Aristotle's *Poetics*, subject to a surprise, but a surprise placed at the moment of its revelation in a cause-and-effect relation to previous actions: the surprise is his prompt delivery to the secular arm for punishment, and its latterly revealed causation involves prior collusion between the secular arm and the institutions of the Church.

As here presented, the Lollard is most fully under control precisely at those self-fancied moments of greatest autonomy and freedom. I have referred to this effect as a counter-tendency, a secondary or seemingly incidental contention, whose genius is comfortably to coexist with its more prepossessing opposite: the depiction of the Lollard as initiative-taker, as genuine threat to theological and social stability. Of course, a representation need not be consistent in order to do its work. In this case, anti-Lollard writings accomplish most by advancing multiple (albeit contradictory) contentions at the same time: the Lollard is both menace and victim, bully and dupe. Only the historian – as opposed to the rhetorician or political strategist – is obliged to press the subsequent question: was the Lollard a genuine threat or a political pawn, agent of destabilizing challenge or a hapless creation of self-legitimizing Lancastrian discourse?

This question is worth posing again because twentieth-century historians have usually reproduced the dominant contention of the official texts on which they have been obliged to depend. This analytical complicity often takes the form of a direct and uncritical reiteration of medieval claims about a Lollard menace, which is then seen as having provoked a measured and reluctant sanction. I find this tendency in K. B. McFarlane's argument that 'the real drive against the heretics did not begin until the heretics under Oldcastle's irresponsible leadership had also become traitors' – suggesting that the labeling of Lollards as 'heretics' somehow preceded and remained dissociated from other aspects of repression until the Lollards themselves provoked it.[4] Similar reasoning underpins Peter McNiven's suggestion that 'Arundel's progress to the highest position in the English ecclesiastical hierarchy was almost exactly paralleled by the development of Lollardy. . . . His responsibility for combating heresy was therefore bound to increase as his career advanced' – overlooking precisely those respects in which Arundel's rather explicit interest in defining and persecuting heresy was an element in his career advancement.[5] R. N. Swanson has more recently observed in the same vein that 'The absence of large-scale heresy from England before the appearance of Lollardy meant that there was no need to create a machinery to deal with it'[6] – implying that heresy somehow precedes heresy's repression; is recognizable prior to any of the sanctions mobilized against it.

In all these formulations, this need for sanction against heresy is considered to exist without agency, to arise only in reaction to a provocation. 'There is' or 'there is not' a need for repression, to the extent that heresy rears its head, but the repressive agency (presumably civil order, due subordination, the unimpeded narration of the English 'story') remains unspecified. Rather than seen as active co-creators of heresy, socially vested institutions (the orthodox Church, the legitimate state) are absolved of any responsibility for heresy's suppression: they only did what they had to do, what the 'threat' of heresy exacted from them.

My analysis will treat recurrent references to the Lollards' comic insufficiency more seriously, taking them as potentially valuable indicators of an alternate possibility. This is the possibility that the Lollard position was *always* one of weakness rather than strength, that the Lollard was from the beginning less a real threat to orthodox control than orthodoxy's rhetorical plaything. Here I must pause, however, to consider a possible shortcoming to my argument. For, crudely considered, my discovery of an 'actual' position of Lollard weakness might be considered less a matter of conscientious historical investigation than a simple hermeneutic maneuver. Indeed, it does rest on a deconstructive commonplace, that language affords 'the possibility of substituting binary polarities such as before for after, early for late, outside for inside, cause for effect, without regard for the truth-value of these structures.'[7] The textual critic operating according to this perception is well positioned to identify 'causal fictions' – as, in this case, the instatement of an effect or outcome (Lollard persecution as enemies of the state) as a cause (as enemies of the state, Lollards must be persecuted). The identification of such a causal fiction permits an after-the-fact act of rectification and redress, in which Lollards are found to be the victims of aggression, and the Lancastrians its perpetrators, rather than the other way around. But has so much really been accomplished by employing a form of 'substitutive reversal' to replace a fiction (Lollard aggressiveness) by its opposite (Lollards as victims)?[8]

Caution is appropriate; one would not, in seeking to right a discursive wrong, want simply to instate its equally exaggerated opposite. Yet we are playing something other than an entirely textual game here. Much, but not everything, can be accomplished by interrogating the texts at our disposal, turning them around and upside down. Much else finally depends on the materiality of texts and, especially, textual consequences. Textual analysis can reveal the persistence of certain discouraged possibilities – of traces and absent causes, the remnants of erasure or the felt pressure of an incompletely symbolized pressure from an unreclaimable Real. But these traces must then be evaluated by whatever other categories of extra-textual evidence, common sense, and knowledge of parallel situations the investigator can bring to bear.

One consideration adding evidential weight to the suppressed account (Lollard as victim) over the dominant one (Lollard as menace) is that the original discursive process, in which the relations of cause and effect are initially determined, does not operate in a textual exemption zone. In the fifteenth century, as today, differential access to material wealth and organized agencies of dissemination resulted in differential access to textual processes. Most texts bearing on Lollard persecution are, after all, orthodox productions. An analytical technique that emphasizes orthodoxy's obscured opposite is invaluable precisely because it promises to redress a skewed textual situation, in which a particular assignment of cause and effect enjoyed privileged expression in the first place.

Textual claims of Lollard menace and puissance were thus called into question by external evidence of the actual ease with which Lollardy was suppressed, its followers silenced and its leaders taken to the stake. In this process, both the ominous and threatening Lollard and the pitiable and derided one are delivered to the material sphere of corporeal coercion, involving a real place with a stake, a barrel, faggots, burning coals. So do submerged textual implications of 'othering' and incrimination intersect with the material at every turn. Spies and informers collect money from the Exchequer, ropes bite flesh, barrels sear and fires burn. Beginning in textual process, the chastisement of heresy issues in an occasion of unavoidable, ostentatious, display. Originating in the imaginary and manifesting itself in the symbolic, the Lollard figure of fun meets a terrible and very material end. A world of material consequences reminds us that the processes of victimization occur outside, as well as inside, textual bounds; that some elements of this process stand outside, and evaluate, textual claims.

Considering its material consequences, the barely suppressed mirth which percolates up through anti-Lollard texts may come closest to depicting the actual degree of Lollard impotence. For, external to Lollardy, the activities of the Ricardian Courtenay, the Ricardian/ Lancastrian Arundel, and finally the Lancastrians themselves may be viewed as those of well-situated adversaries who have successfully achieved dominion over broad areas of Lollard endeavor, including even the terms of their enemies' self-assertion. Positioning themselves at both ends of a process leading from discovery to rebuke, the Lancastrians participated in shaping and focusing the very threat which they then obliged themselves to chastise, in times and places and via procedures of their own selection.[9]

Discursive fuel for a real fire

A step so drastic as burning a dissenting neighbor is taken only within various authorizing and acquiescing structures. With respect to authorization, several scholars have painstakingly explored the legislative and statutory stages by which canon and civil law, sacerdotal authority and lay power joined forces to identify and discipline heresy in the first years of Lancastrian rule.[10] But another precondition for this drastic act is, in a word, imaginative. Aided by learned rhetoric, pulpit invective, and everyday talk, a society that had not customarily burnt heretics somehow found itself imaginatively able to contemplate so extreme a practice. The initiative of Arundel and Henry IV, come suddenly to power and disposed to its use, cannot be ignored; but Sautre could probably not have been burnt, were it not for a period of some twenty years in which anti-Lollard sentiments were consolidated and burning emerged as a natural and even inevitable penalty for lapsed heretics among the clergy and, ultimately, for all categories of Lollard believers among the laity of the land.

The Lollards were placed at a discursive disadvantage from the outset, when first branded as 'Lollardi.' This term appeared, in Latin rather than English, early in the definition of the Lollard movement, and (as in the case of Quakers, Ranters, Shakers, and other stigmatized sects) played an undoubted and complicated role in its formation. In mid-1382, during that very brief heyday in which certain Wycliffite tenets were accepted as near-orthodoxy in and around Oxford, one Henry Crump, master of theology, was disciplined by the university chancellor for calling Wyclif's followers 'Lollardi.'[11] Whatever the details of its etymology, this term would appear to gain at least some of its anti-heretical force from its near-homology with the Latin term *lolium/lollium*, already well established in late-twelfth-century and subsequent orthodox discourse. A *lolium* is a cockle or tare, and the metaphorical corruption of good grain by tares provided an obvious, and highly suggestive, metaphorical vehicle for orthodox distress over invasive and unwelcome doctrines. Around 1179, Peter of Blois, hearing of a heresy in the see of York, wrote to the archbishop to remind him that he was a steward of the 'vines of the Lord,' responsible for watching over them and for doing whatever was necessary, so that 'ne degenerent propagines vineae in labruscam, *frumenta in lolium*, aurum in scoriam, oleum in amurcam' ('the shoots of the vines would not degenerate into wild vines, *grain to cockle*, gold to slag, oil into its dregs').[12] This same metaphor flourished into the fifteenth century, where, for example, we find Adam of Usk lamenting the pernicious consequences of Lollardy for orthodox faith: 'Among other evils . . . there arose errors and heresies in the catholic faith on account of the seeds sown by a certain Master John Wyclif, whose noxious doctrine contaminated the faith as if by tares' ('pestifere doctrine uelud lollio eandem fidem corrumpentis') (Usk, pp. 6–7).

The notion of faith as a field of grain, subject to invasive corruption by 'bad seed' and yielding in turn to adulterant cockle or tare, posits a status quo ante as the site of originary purity, with any invasion or alteration immediately knowable as decline. But it also possesses an added layer of implication, owing to the doctrinal, and often specifically eucharistic, instances to which it was usually applied. A network of associations widely represented in art and sermon literature in and after the twelfth century portrayed Christ as good grain, as spiritual food, ground and milled in the crucifixion, and offered for the salvation of humankind in the figurative bread of the eucharistic host. This is the motif of Christ as the 'mill of the host,' often paired with the 'mystical winepress' in the treatment of Christ's body as the true, and pure, substance of the bread and wine.[13] The corruption of good grain by heresy thus has an added consequence, disastrous in the thirteenth and fourteenth centuries, during which the Corpus Christi service was composed and the sacrament of the eucharist celebrated with increasing fervor. In defiling the host itself with material dross or bran or worse, and in resisting its sacramental conversion into the body of

Christ, the heretic was placed in a relation of estrangement and danger to the larger community of the orthodox. The vexed destiny of the Lollards was thus anticipated early on by their incriminating association with *lolia* or cockles threatening debasement of Christ's pure sacrifice. Inscribed at the very beginning were the anger directed against Lollardy, an aggressive determination that these heretics be 'extirpated' or 'uprooted,' and even the extent to which Lollard error was epitomized in and around a matter of belief about material persistence (and hence spiritual adulteration) of the host.

Wyclif and his immediate followers were subjected to verbal admonition and doctrinal prescription in the Oxford condemnation of 1381 and the Blackfriars condemnation of 1382. Yet, in retrospect, the language of official disapproval seems quite restrained in relation to what would follow in the next decade. Archbishop Courtenay's post-Blackfriars letter forbidding the teaching of Wyclif's heresies and errors in Oxford labeled his utterances as serpentine, venomous, and pestilential, but suggested only that anyone espousing them should 'flee' or 'shun' them forthwith.[14] The tone had noticeably shifted a decade later when the chronicler Knighton retrospectively composed his account of 1382; Lollards were identified by name as a *secta nefanda*, observing tenets and educational practices that estrange them from the populace at large. Complaining that their conspiracy is all the more cursed for its intransigence, he invoked God in their destruction:

> Accursed be their pertinacious assembly! May God destroy them, and tear them out, and drive them from their tabernacles and uproot them from the land of the kingdom! . . . confound them, and let them perish with their doctrine into eternity ['Confundantur et pereant cum doctrina eorum in eternum'].[15]

Although figurative and subjunctive, this talk of uprooting and destruction quickly came to typify the anti-Lollard discourse of the later 1380s and 1390s. In 1392 the royal council inveighed against the possibility that the contagion of heresy might 'infect' the populace (with the accompanying assumption that it should be 'cured'),[16] and a conciliar resolution of 1395 called for a military 'assault' ('expugnatio') on the heretics.[17]

Such ominous language is the stock in trade of ecclesiastical controversy. More to the point, and a good deal more omninous in the light of future events, is that language which contemplates destruction of heretical adversaries by fire. An example in which discourse outruns concrete action (even while paving its way) occurs in Knighton's discussion of the heretic Swinderby who, he says, having been publicly convicted of heresies and errors, deserved to be food for the flames ('pabulum ignis digne effici meruit').[18] Sympathizers, and especially John of Gaunt, are said to have interceded with the bishop to seek a lighter sentence ('ut penam eius transferret in aliam penitenciam' – p. 312). The account is, of course, fanciful, since no heretics had been officially burnt in England, and because such a penalty would in any event have been a matter for secular rather than ecclesiastical determination. The notion that certain offenses *deserve* burning was, nevertheless, beginning to enjoy some currency. Describing the anti-Lollard surge of the late 1380s, Walsingham notes that *one* ecclesiastical diocese had no problems; that Bishop Despenser of Norwich quelled heresy by threatening to burn or behead any member of that 'perverse sect' who presumed to preach there ('Quod si quisquam de secta perversa praedicare praesumeret in Dioecesi sua, vel ignibus traderetur vel capite privaretur').[19]

Similar ideas and images waxed in the later years of the century. Boniface IX, declaiming against the Lollards in 1395, wished them destroyed, so that not even a hidden spark should remain among the ashes ('sic quod nec favilla cineribus operta remaneat').[20] Responding, like Boniface, to the Lollard provocations of 1395, Roger Dymmok pondered the precedent of Joshua, who did away with malefactors and who destroyed idol worship in his kingdom, burning the idolatrous priests upon their áltars ('et sacerdotes ydolorum super aras combussit').[21] Underlying all this rhetoric is the influential example of the Continent, where, as English churchmen were enviously aware, the practice of burning heretics was already well established. The link between continental precedent and English reasoning is made in a somewhat mysterious document, composed by the archbishops of Canterbury and York or else hypothetically assigned to them, around the year 1397. In this communication, the archbishops point out that in other Christian realms those condemned by the Church for heresy are promptly handed over to the secular arm to be put to death ('en autres roiaumes subgitz a la religion cristiene quant aucuns sont condempnez par leglise de crime de heresie ils sont tantost liuerez a seculer iuggement pour estre mys a mort').[22]

All this talk about eradication and extirpation, burning and sparks and ashes, need not have eventuated in actual deeds. Yet, a tacit connection would seem to exist between a vivid imagination of such punishments, and their actualization.[23] In this case, the increasingly animated (but still mainly clerically sponsored) discourse of treason and burning under Richard II may be considered a kind of imaginative groundwork for what was to come, when the introduction of a new secular authority with its own reasons for embracing an anti-Lollard

program would permit a translation of words to deeds. This translation would occur early in the second year of Henry IV's reign, with the
public burning of lapsed priest and chronic troublemaker William
Sautre at Smithfield.

Manufacturing consent

The various terse chronicle entries on the death of Sautre are notable
not only for what they declare but for their intuitions and guesses. The
Eulogium continuator, for example, implies a link between Sautre's
death and the parliament of 1401:

> During this parliament ['In hoc parliamento'] the archbishop of
> Canterbury degraded a certain heretic, who said that accident is
> not without a subject in the sacrament of the altar and that bread
> remains; who was burned at Smithfield ['qui Smythfeld combustus
> est'].[24]

Sautre was indeed burnt during parliament, but the burning's problematic relation to parliamentary process is more difficult to ascertain.
The Hilary parliament of that year met more or less concurrently with
(and down the road from) a provincial council or clerical convocation
presided over by Thomas Arundel, archbishop of Canterbury, held at
the chapter-house of St Paul's. Parliament convened on 10 January and
concluded on 10 March, and the convocation convened on 29 January,
sentenced and degraded Sautre on 25–26 February, and then went on
to other business prior to its nearly simultaneous conclusion on 11
March. This spatial proximity and temporal overlap permitted an
elaborately choreographed series of communications and visitations, a
sharing of personnel, and – ultimately – a cluster of artfully interwoven
documents that rely upon borrowings, echo-effects, and other textually
enacted gestures of complicity.

The convocation opened with a statement by Arundel to the effect
that its major business would involve an inquiry into clerical and lay
heresies and errors ('super erroribus et haeresibus nonnullorum
presbyterorum, clericorum, et laicorum'), and especially those concerning the eucharist.[25] This statement having been briskly dispatched,
the convocation was joined by a lay delegation, especially sent from
parliament, consisting of Constable Henry Percy, Chamberlain
Erpingham, and Treasurer Northbury – a group which, according to
McNiven, 'represented, almost too obviously, virtually every aspect of

royal policy of which the Church could be expected to make acknowledgment' (p. 80) – together with other lords and noblemen of the
realm. The expressed wish of this delegation was, uncoincidentally,
that something be done about heresies and errors indeed widespread
in said realm ('de haeresibus et erroribus sic modo generali, in dicto
regno Angliae'), a view held by many – both clerics and laypersons –
as they said ('per nonnullos tam clericos, ut dixerunt, quam laicos').
Having thus deftly interwoven their words and demands with
Arundel's own, the delegation promised the aid of the secular arm in
doing whatever might prove necessary to defend the realm. The delegation then exceeded the archbishop in at least one respect, suggesting that clerical offenders should be canonically and publicly punished
– that is, liable to punishment not only by canon law but by secular
proceeding (presumably including the death penalty itself).[26]

Arundel responded to the delegation's words by endorsing close
cooperation on this and other matters, and put his own words into
effect by abruptly postponing the convocation for seventeen days so
that he and his fellows could attend to necessary business connected
with the parliament then meeting. One item of parliamentary business
involved a petition presented to King Henry from an unspecified
group of prelates and clergy of the realm; a petition that does not seem
to have issued from the convocation itself (since it has no place in the
record of the convocation's official business), but which must have
been prepared by a drafting committee of persons looking ahead precisely to the convergence of parliament and convocation, and wishing
to make major headway on the Lollard question at that propitious
time. This petition turns out to embody in a remarkably mature form
virtually all the leading contentions of a composite anti-Lollard
intertextuality that had been in process of active formation since 1381–
82. Present in its preamble is the definitive version of an anti-Lollard
brief, touching upon such points as the novelty of the sect, its operations under the cover of simulated sanctity, its promulgation of its
views in both public and covert situations (including its manipulation
of vernacular publication and new practices of lay education), its propensity for seditious and insurrectionary machinations, and its creation of divisions among the people. This brief would be reiterated
again and again, in one form or another, throughout the first half of the
fifteenth century, providing a kind of template for anti-Lollard legal
documents and justification for varied prosecutions. The crucial inno-
vation of the petition, however, related to the additional matter of legal
sanctions, particularly as they touched upon the interface of ecclesiastical and lay responsibilities. For the petition concluded with the recommendation that

county officials shall be personally present at sentencing to receive the defendant, and should do whatever is further incumbent upon them . . . ['ulterius agant quod eis incumbit . . .'], lest such wicked doctrines and heretical and erroneous opinions, or their authors and maintainers, should be sustained or in any way tolerated.[27]

The suggestion that secular officials might, in effect, proceed by any means necessary can be read in several ways, with imprisonment and other forms of duress as possibilities. But the petition may offer a thinly veiled invitation to institute the death penalty.

Whatever the petition's intentions in this matter, they were respecified and solidified in Henry's *responsio*. His response parallels the petition in a number of procedural respects, including provision for arrest and detention of suspected heretics until they have purged themselves – although adding certain specifications pertaining to the augumented role of the secular court and to fines payable to the king. Continuing with the case of heretics who refuse to abjure their beliefs, he then offers this noteworthy amplification:

after the sentence is handed down [the secular officers] shall receive them, and cause them to be burnt publicly in a prominent place ['coram populo in eminenti loco comburi faciant'], so that such punishment might inspire fear in the minds of others. (*RP*, vol. 3, p. 467)

Henry's response is, at the very least, a fulfillment of clerical wishes, and may reasonably be read as signaling a measure of resolve which exceeds that of the clerical petition.

These two documents reveal an impressive and highly orchestrated degree of complicity, as does the resultant statute, generally known for its embrace of Henry's proposed punishment as *De haeretico comburendo*. With a minimum of verbal improvisation and elaboration, this statute interweaves the original clerical petition and Henry's own response to create a single document from their varying voices. One of the document's few newly fabricated passages reveals its consistency of purpose. It is drafted

for the avoidance of dissensions, divisions, injuries, scandals, and perils in posterity, and so that this wicked sect, preachings, doctrine, and opinions should cease from now on, and should completely be destroyed ['penitus destruantur'].[28]

Extirpation, destruction: an ambitious program, but definitely a mutual enterprise of state and Church, and one which set the stage for an easy articulation of aims and means between the civil and ecclesiastical arms.

This spirit of cooperation is epitomized within the trial itself when Sautre, having been ceremonially stripped of each church order (priest, deacon, subdeacon, acolyte, exorcist, reader, and doorkeeper), stands at the very brink of degradation to the status of layman, in which he is stripped of his tonsure and a cap emblematic of lay status is – presumably mockingly – placed upon his head. The account now reveals that, as contemplated in the clerical petition and the royal response, representatives of the secular arm have indeed been invited to witness the final deposition: that 'constables and marshals of the secular courts of the realm being personally present,'[29] the final deposition may proceed. Perhaps the secular officers have been present all along, or perhaps a one-day delay between sentencing and the formal ceremony of degradation was introduced in part to allow them to attend. In either case, no scrambling after appropriate officers is indicated in the record; as in the anecdote of the *Annales Ricardi*, they are *already there*, their presence suggesting that advance planning underpins a seemingly unpremeditated series of events. Sautre is then handed over to these same civil officers with a pro forma request for mercy, with Arundel 'asking that the same court might wish favorably to receive said William, committed to them.'[30]

The general public, and even astute observers, came quickly and understandably to the conclusion that Sautre had been burnt under the statute (*De haeretico comburendo*) which issued from joint ecclesiastical, royal, and parliamentary action. Walsingham, for instance, observes of Sautre's burning that the statute had now been put into practice ('practizataque fuit haec lex').[31] Yet, parliament did not conclude its work until 10 March, whereas the king's writ of 26 February, issued on 2 March, provided the authority to burn Sautre while parliament and the convocation were still in session. Issuance of the writ suggests that, far from wanting to conceal his activities behind the processes of parliament and the convocation, Henry was prepared to be recognized as its author, as a driving force in the process. A royal writ is, after all, the pre-eminent vehicle for revelation of a king's will, and this one – issued on behalf of the king and additionally his council (and by implication parliament as well) – seems deliberately designed to assert Henry's unambiguous intent.[32]

Affirming that his action is taken in concert with the convocation and its conclusions, and discharging the Church of any responsibility for further actions, Henry goes on to direct that before the people he be publicly committed to the fire, and in the same fire caused actually ['realiter'] to be burned up, in detestation of this kind of crime, and as a manifest example to other Christians.[33]

The wording of the writ is ambiguous, at once acknowledging its origin in a special situation and denying that the situation possesses any unusual features at all. This ambiguousness is apparent in Henry's self-representation within the document; in choosing to represent his motives, Henry is confessing to a departure from the ordinary, though the tendency of his remarks is to deny any exceptionality to the case:

> We therefore, enthusiast of justice and laborer for the Catholic faith, meaning to maintain and defend the Holy Church and its rights and liberties, and to extirpate such heresies and errors from the realm of England as much as we are able, and to punish heretics with appropriate sanctions, and awaiting the time when such heretics have been convicted, according to divine law, human law, established canons, and the custom of this region, they should be burned with the heat of fire ['juxta Legem divinam, humanam, Canonica instituta & in hac parte consuetudinar' Ignis incendio comburi debere']. (*RP*, vol. 3, p. 459)

Henry's writ seeks to naturalize his action by appeal to divine law, human law, canon law, and national custom. Some precedent may be found in each of the first three categories, although variably so; but little or no precedent for burning heretics existed in English custom. Divine law was easily enough illustrated within the Bible and biblical commentary, centering on such key verses as John 15: 6 ('If a man abide not in me, he is cast forth as a branch, and is withered; and men gather them, and cast them into the fire; and they are burned'). Human law was erratic, since burning for heresy came only slowly and latterly to be regarded as a responsibility of the secular arm, but influential legislation was embraced by Peter of Aragon in 1197, by Frederick II in 1224, and elsewhere. Henry de Bracton does include the penalty of burning for heresy and sorcery in thirteenth-century England,[34] but without any apparent consequences in actual practice. Canon law was, of course, particularly rich in this area, embracing such key moments as Lucius III's decree that heretics should be turned over to the secular arm for punishment (1184); Innocent III's Lateran demand that the secular powers agree to exterminate ('exterminare') heretics marked by the Church (1215); Gregory IX's unambiguous embrace of the death penalty in a papal decree (1231); Innocent IV's bull *Ad extirpanda* (1252).[35]

Yet Henry's assertion about English 'custom' lacks substantiation, and purported evidence tends to vanish when closely scrutinized. The closest of quasi-official precedents, Henry II's sentence of outlawry upon a hapless band of Flemish 'Cathars' found in London in 1166, is remote in time and circumstances from Sautre's case, and amounts to something other than a *de jure* death penalty in any event.[36] Witchcraft *was* a civil crime in medieval England, but no documented burnings are to be found. The celebrated early fourteenth-century case of Dame Alice Kyteler occurred in Ireland, and Dame Alice was freed on condition of pilgrimage and fines.[37] Burnings were rife on the Continent, including mass exterminations during the Albigensian 'crusades' in the early thirteenth century and the condemnation and mass public burning of Templars in the earlier fourteenth century. It is to such burnings that the clerical establishment of England admiringly alluded in the previously mentioned petition to the crown seeking the death penalty for heretics, noting that confiscation and death were common penalties abroad and wishing for their introduction to England.[38] But this petition itself constitutes evidence that officially sanctioned burnings had not yet occurred. Henry's claim that custom would be served by burning Sautre was, in short, a screen, an invention, a bluff. In burning Sautre by royal writ, he moved ahead of his own carefully forged consensus, laying deliberate claim to the burning as a distinctive component of his personal political program.

The (trial as) mousetrap

The fact that something is asked *as if* the content of the answer matters does not mean that it matters.[39]

The point of dogma upon which suspected heretics were most closely examined was the doctrine of transubstantiation and Christ's presence within the consecrated host. If only because of the vastly expanded importance of Christ's embodiment as a basis for sacramental community in the thirteenth and fourteenth centuries, special attention to the eucharist was inevitable. Yet eucharistic doctrine also enters the present interrogation scene as a matter of prosecutorial convenience. The diversity of opinion on the subject, and its potential to draw even the theologically sophisticated out of their depth, rendered it ideal for purposes of interrogative entrapment. Thus, as urgently as eucharistic subjects mattered at the end of the fourteenth century, another sense exists in which eucharistic questions may be found hardly to matter at all, except as a means to another, previously established, objective.

Sautre held controversial views on a wide range of issues, of which his eucharistic doctrine was only one, and never at the head of any personal list. During a prior imprisonment – probably in Norwich in 1399 – he launched an appeal to be heard by king and parliament on the seven following points: 1. his intent to worship the cross only 'vicariously,' as a sign of the passion; 2. his inclination to worship the saints rather than the true cross; 3. his preference for preaching over services of the hours; 4. his privileging of other clerical vocations over the services of the hours; 5. his preference for charity over pilgrimages; 6. his belief that the sacramental bread is both bread and the body of Christ; and 7. that a predestinate man is more worthy of adoration than the angels.[40] Subsequently, when called before the convocation, he was accused of a slightly revised list, in which worship of a temporal king is now preferred over the cross, other minor adjustments are introduced, and the persistence of the material substance of bread is now eighth among eight. Finally, another, and slightly altered, list of ten points, on which he was accused in Norwich in 1399, carries forward his eucharistic views as the eighth item. Challenged at the convocation to defend himself, he launched into an energetic defense on all the eight points on which he was accused. Yet, we learn from that record that it was primarily – or, really, exclusively – the matter of the eucharist on which he was examined:

> Immediately omitting all other articles, conclusions, and responses recorded above, the archbishop interrogated said William Sautre especially ['specialiter'] upon the sacrament of the altar: first, viz. whether in the sacrament, after the pronunciation of the sacramental words, material bread remains, or not? (*Concilia*, p. 256)

When responding across a broad range of issues, Sautre had tackled the eucharist with confidence and clarity, arguing that the consecrated wafer was 'panis cum corpore Christi' – at once bread and the body of Christ. Now, brought to a more special focus on the eucharist alone, he faltered: 'to which question [he] responded as though hesitating ("quasi vacillando"), saying, he did not know about that.' The point is, of course, that the question of the eucharist involves some extremely recondite theology. And so well may William *not* know, especially when pressed by a mixture of condescending simplification and theological mystification:

> And then the lord [Arundel] asked, whether that bread – material, white, and round – fit and disposed upon the altar for the sacrament of the body of Christ, suited in all respects to its function, by virtue

of sacramental words rightly spoken by the priest, is transubstantiated ['transubstantiatur'] into the true body of Christ? (*Concilia*, p.
256)

Taxed during a two-day oral examination with exasperating
simplicities about whiteness and roundness on the one hand and with
the vexed and (even for the orthodox) incompletely resolved high-
theological issue of transubstantiation on the other, Sautre can be for-
given a certain cognitive confusion. The trial record – which naturally
functions not as an objective document but as a persuasive assignment
of guilt – informs us that he now replied derisively ('quasi deridendo')
that he did not know, and announcement of his conviction and sentencing soon follows.

As thoughtful a commentator as McNiven suggests (p. 83) that this
is an argument which a superior theologian like Wyclif might have had
a chance of winning. I am more inclined to think that this debate could
never have been won, situated as it was on a ground so argumentatively vexed that no position could confidently be sustained against the
full weight of orthodox institutions. Over a period of some twenty
years, beginning in 1381–82, the question of the eucharist had been
deliberately installed as the litmus test of orthodoxy, precisely because
its internal paradoxes and contradictions were so pronounced, and its
own understanding among different camps of the orthodox so
fissured, as to constitute a ground so uneven that no one meant to
stumble could fail to stumble.

The Lollards' heresy was effectively founded – ironically, through
no particular choice of their own – in the quarrel over the eucharist,
and specifically over the orthodox claim that the *accidentia* or visible
material attributes of the consecrated host persisted without a subject,
sine subjecto. Whatever artificial or imagined unity might be brought to
the theory of the eucharist, the inner diversity of the debate guaranteed
that it was never – and in fact could never be – concluded or closed.[41]
The installation of a single, orthodox doctrine on transubstantiation
(sometimes retrospectively supposed to have occurred in 1215, or in
the Thomistic synthesis) turns out on inspection never really to have
occurred; to the extent that attempts were made to close, or significantly to narrow, a very broad discursive field, they must be deemed
unsuccessful. Innocent III's promulgation of transubstantiation in his
Lateran decree of 1215 was accompanied by no definition of the term,
or of the specific theory of Christ's embodiment being advanced.[42]
Thomas Aquinas's use of the Aristotelian vocabulary of subject and
accident to argue for the status of the consecrated wine and bread as
'accidentia sine subjecto' was influential, but did not quell debate.[43]

Subject – or substance – and accident had been mainstays of eucharistic discussion since the eleventh century, when (ironically, given his eventual disrepute as arch-heresiarch) Berengar of Tours introduced a grammatically derived concept of subject to argue the proscribed and eventually heretical position that an accident or external appearance and its subject were inseparable, and that the bread of the eucharist must therefore remain bread (enjoying a figurative, rather than actual, relation to the body of Christ).[44] Although Aquinas's particular solution, in which accidents existed only as quantity and otherwise without a subject (their subject having been miraculously transubstantiated) was influential, it by no means ruled the field.[45] Duns Scotus and Ockham were, for example, subsequently to argue that bread and wine were annihilated in consecration, and theirs is the view against which Wyclif was principally to reply.[46] As Gary Macy persuasively argues, an active contention of different views of the eucharist continued not only past 1215 but well into the fourteenth and fifteenth centuries; theories which one might espouse within the boundaries of orthodoxy ranged from those in which Christ's body was *substituted* for the bread and wine (Duns Scotus, Ockham) to those in which bread and wine were *transmuted* into Christ's body (Albert the Great, Thomas Aquinas), with only ideas in which the substance of bread and wine *coexisted* with Christ's body liable to suppression – such suppression occurring only rarely and only when the theologian's work contained other troubling opinions.[47]

No wonder, given this climate of potential diversity, that Wyclif and the Lollards themselves reveal a certain bemusement over the sudden emphasis given to this rather recondite subject. One of the discussants of Wyclif's *Trialogus*, a work completed shortly after the 1382 Blackfriars Council, comments that attention is owing to the eucharist because 'there's a real brawl going on about the eucharist right now' ('quia hodie circa eucharistiam est dissensio plus brigosa').[48] Partly as refuge, but also partly in apparent puzzlement, Lollards comment again and again that this is a terribly specialized matter to receive the kind of attention it does. A generation later, according to his account of the matter, Lollard William Thorpe, questioned by Archbishop Arundel about whether material bread remains after the consecration of the host, would explode that the question of whether the host is 'accident withouten soget' is a 'schole-mater' about which he has never concerned himself, adding that 'I committe this terme *accidentem sine subiecto* to tho clerkis which deliten hem in so curious and so sotil sofestrie.'[49]

An explanation for this apparent anomaly is that the eucharist was not so much chosen by the Lollards as thrust upon them. Certainly, the subject of the eucharist resonated with a view of society and social order which guaranteed its attraction for any person or party with an urgently held view of community and its foundations. But, in a more practical and immediate sense, the uneven terrain of eucharistic discussion, riddled with theological pitfalls and places of potential doctrinal entrapment, rendered it a perfect ground for the analysis and discovery of error. It offered, in other words, a discursive minefield into which Wyclif (and, soon after, the Lollards) could be drawn; a field which, once delineated as the ground of contestation, could then be subdivided in ways which would isolate Wyclif and his successors and expose them to reprisal.[50]

The chronicler Walsingham alludes to the creation of such a field when he describes 1381 as a year in which the Church was placing special emphasis upon the doctrine of transubstantiation ('eo praecipue tempore quo specialem de transubstantiatione Corporis Christi facit sacrosancta ecclesia mentionem').[51] The compiler of the *Fasciculi Zizaniorum* likewise sees Wyclif *entering* this discursive field in the summer of 1381, when he first began to pronounce ('dictare')[52] and determine ('determinare') upon the matter.[53] Wyclif's Oxford condemnation of spring 1381 was actually set in motion by the then chancellor William de Berton who appointed an investigating committee in spring 1380.[54] Provided to the committee was a fabricated and rather miscellaneous list of twelve 'Conclusiones Wycclyff de Sacramento Altaris.'[55] The mixed and improvised quality of the list seems to spring from two causes: (1) a determination that his views of the eucharist should be at the forefront of consideration, and (2) the fact that none of his major writings on the eucharist, including *De Eucharistia* and *Trialogus*, had yet appeared. (Wyclif's undated *De Eucharistia*, usually held to have provoked his 1381 Oxford condemnation, alludes to what he has 'often said in public,'[56] and projects a clear sense that the current climate of controversy is what now obliges him to formalize his hitherto informally articulated views.) The condemnation itself was produced very promptly, early in 1381, and lays as much emphasis on his and other people's intra- and extra-mural utterances as on two of his particularly annoying writings ('tam in ista universitate, quam extra, publice dogmatizant; due inter alia sua documenta pestifera asserentes').[57] Wyclif's rejoinder, the *Confessio*, was evidently produced at white heat and is dated 10 May 1381,[58] with other, more formal statements of his position to follow.

We here encounter a tangled, and very condensed, field of speculation and argumentation about the theology of the eucharist. Oral arguments – and, subsequently, written documents – were issued at such a clip that careful commentators have increasingly emphasized the uncertainty of the field's inner chronology.[59] Given previously defined contours of ecclesiastical dogma (as summarized in early fourteenth-century Decretals), and given the fact that Wyclif had been telegraphing his own views on the persistence of the substance of bread since his earliest works of the 1360s,[60] this field *might* have been constituted at any point in the last third of the century. Wyclif's *Confessio* begins almost wearily, with a sense that the present accusations deal with matters he has repeatedly publicly avowed ('Saepe confessus sum . . .'). What *is* new, in 1380–81, is the mobilization of institutional authority against specific points of eucharistic dogma, points long familiar, but suddenly no longer to be excused.

Condemned in 1381 were two positions: that the substance of material bread and wine remains after consecration, and that the presence of Christ in the sacrament is neither essential nor substantial nor corporeal, but figurative or 'tropical.'[61] Following in May 1382, the aggressive William Courtenay having replaced the more hesitant Sudbury as archbishop of Canterbury, was the Blackfriars Council, at which the list of heretical conclusions was headed by tightened versions of these same tenets: that the substance of material bread and wine remains after consecration ('quod substantia panis materialis et vini maneat post consecrationem in sacramento altaris') and that accidents do not remain without a subject after consecration ('quod accidentia non maneant sine subjecto post consecrationem in eodem sacramento').[62] The Blackfriars condemnation was promulgated with all the elements of a conscious campaign. Concurrently, Archbishop Courtenay petitioned parliament against the heretics; the latter document is now lost, but the parliamentary rolls for 7 May cite unlicensed preachers for sowing discord and dissension, and grant added powers of arrest and detention.[63] In May and June Courtenay effectively suppressed Wyclif's followers at Oxford, wielding the conclusions of the Blackfriars Council as his authority.[64] The condemnation was read from every pulpit in the province of Canterbury, and a religious procession was held in every diocese at the end of May.[65] Knighton describes a general procession by citizens of London designed to consolidate support for Courtenay's initiatives, in which varied estates, clerical and lay, walked 'nudis pedibus' to hear an anti-heretical sermon by a Carmelite doctor, followed by a miracle in which supposedly Wycliffite knight Cornelius Clone saw flesh and blood when the host was broken at the ceremony of the altar.[66]

Of course, an orthodox field of belief cannot be consolidated all at once, especially around so slippery a concept as transubstantiation. As attested by Wyclif's own controversial writings in 1382–84, he and his followers were not slow to speak up for themselves. The Michaelmas parliament of 1382 saw a counter-move against the previous session's statute against wandering preachers, suggesting at least some resistance in the Commons to such bids for orthodox control.[67] Under accusation in that same year, the Wycliffite preacher Swinderby thought it worth his while to seek redress from Lancaster and the king.[68] In the next decade Lollards frequently took the offensive, as in 1395 when they publicized twelve highly assertive conclusions (including one on transubstantiation as a 'feynid miracle,' mocking Thomas and the pope for finding a miracle in the emergence of a chicken from an egg).[69] Nonetheless, a certain discursive purification was proceeding apace, in which an ever-narrower range of reply on eucharistic questions was permitted to those whose orthodoxy had come under suspicion.

Those suspected of heresy made a wide range of supple and ingenious attempts to reconcile their views with the orthodox position, including Wyclif's suggestion that Christ is more present in the eucharist than in other sacraments,[70] Henry Crump's theory that the eucharist 'mirrors' Christ in heaven,[71] Sautre's ideas of vicarious adoration and the simultaneous material and divine existence of the 'bread of life,' Purvey's suggestion that the host is visibly bread and invisibly the body of Christ,[72] and so on. But the point is that none of these compromises was invited or encouraged. Complete and unequivocal submission, and certainly nothing remotely approaching an exchange of views, was the only goal of the interrogation. Thus, after Sautre had been driven to confused retreat and last-ditch profession of ignorance, Arundel asked the only question that really and truly mattered: whether Sautre would stand by the determination of the Church ('utrum vellet stare determinationi ecclesiae')?

If resignation to the authority of the Church is all that is actually sought, and if interrogation about eucharistic belief is only a pretext for demanding such a resignation, then can the question be said really to matter? So considered, the question does not matter, is arbitrary and empty, except as the means to an altogether different end. The real question is always, as with Sautre, whether the subject will submit in the end, whether he or she will stand by the determination of the Church. As Thorpe tells it, his attempt to plead lack of interest in the arguments of clerks – that is, not to 'play' – cannot succeed, precisely because the point is that he has never had a choice, he has no alternative other than to play:

And the Archebischop seide to me, 'I purpose not to oblische the to the sotil argumentis of clerkis . . . but I purpose to make thee to obeie the to the determynacioun of holi chirche.'[73]

The question is in no way designed to elicit information, but rather to bring the accused to a point of realization: that he or she is captive to the political authority of the orthodox system; that the only available choice with regard to dissenting beliefs is to renounce them or to die for them.[74]

The staging of the trial as a belated affirmation of a guilt already known is reinforced by another familiar trial element, in which a written document is produced, as though incidentally, but with the effect of rendering the outcome of the trial foregone.[75] This stratagem was employed, for example, at a critical juncture in the 1392 hearing of Henry Crump. Throughout most of his trial, that Cistercian master successfully denied the views attributed to him, producing a *schedula* containing nine different (and less sensational) conclusions that he stood ready to defend. The proceedings were drawing to a reluctant close, with his accusers grumbling that a fuller account of his views must exist somewhere, when a remarkable discovery was announced:

> in the house of the brothers preachers of Oxford, by chance and unexpectedly ['casualiter et inopinate'] in a kind of old chest a certain public instrument was found, drawn up in the manner of an indenture, with the seal of the bishop of Meath (and with a notorial seal) upon it.[76]

The seals being opened and the document examined, it was discovered that, as a relapsed heretic, Henry Crump was thus eligible for more severe punishment. This opportune discovery permitted the council to establish the inveteracy of Crump's heretical opinions: he had long been guilty of precisely those points of which he was now accused.

So, too, does Sautre's trial pivot on a supposedly adventitious discovery. Sautre having been found guilty of heresy (which, if it were a first offense, would not necessarily have exposed him to burning) was then found to be a relapsed heretic, because of a document from Norwich, the existence of which was rumored (*Concilia*, p. 255), but which had not been produced. The trial was then recessed for four days, during which the document came to light, via the rather mysterious agency of a friend of Henry Despenser, bishop of Norwich, who happened to be present at the convocation:

> Henry, bishop of Norwich, following the order of the archbishop of Canterbury, presented William Sautre with a certain process, sealed and closed, with the assistance of a friend of his who was present at the council ['per quendam familiarem suum in concilio hujusmodi praesentem'], the veracity of the process secured by seal, faithfully

placed there by worthy witnesses ['fidem hujusmodi sigillo per testes fide dignos imposuit']. (*Concilia*, p. 257)

Ostentatiously tricked out with emblems of legitimacy, and read out in its entirety and entered in the record of the convocation, this document foreclosed the possibility that Sautre might save himself through recantation. The archbishop and 'many others' now charged him, and the record notes his retreat into ironical denials and ultimate silence.

The theater of orthodoxy[77]

Strategically viewed, an inquiry into heresy cannot fail. If the heretic repents in time to escape destruction, the mercy, clemency, or persuasive power of the civic officials is fruitfully demonstrated; if the execution proceeds, the secular arm is provided with an unmatched opportunity to demonstrate its commitment to defend orthodox belief.[78] But, by the common consent of everyone involved and most particularly the king, Sautre's destination appears always and irreversibly to have been the burning-place at Smithfield. Certain points were evidently to be made about the orthodoxy of this regime and the impotent malice of its dissenting subjects; in any event, commentary on the burning suggests that such points were conveyed.

Henry's own order for burning repeatedly insists upon the public and exemplary nature of the proposed spectacle:

[Sautre is to be] committed to the flames in a *public and open place, publicly, before the populace*, in detestation of this kind of crime, and as a *manifest example* ['exemplum manifestum.]'[79]

Far from unique to such situations, the idea of *exemplum manifestum* is pervasive in a culture where words and deeds, characters in written narrative and real people, were found constantly to engage in meaningful performance for the edification of all beholders.[80]

King Henry was not alone in assigning exemplary value to Sautre's burning. A Commons petition framed in obvious reference to Sautre's case and submitted to the parliament then sitting urged that 'anyone' taken in Lollardy and held in prison should receive the judgment he has reserved, 'as an example to others of that evil sect' ('en ensample d'autres de tiel male secte').[81] So, too, does the resultant statute *De haeretico comburendo* argue that burning occurs in order that the deed might inspire fear in the minds of others ('ut hujusmodi punicio metum incuciat mentibus aliorum').[82] Chronicle accounts, likewise, underscore the spectacle's exemplary value, stressing the impetus it provided toward recantation among Sautre's fellows. Thus the *Eulogium* continuation argues that 'After this terrible example other of his accomplices personally recanted their heresies at the cross of Saint Paul.'[83] That some highly public and ceremonial rendition of recantation was arranged at St Paul's can hardly be doubted.

An attempt was rather obviously made to generate momentum toward recantation during the period of the 1401 parliament and concurrent convocation at St Paul's. Most conspicuously, past and future Lollard John Purvey – no doubt impressed with Sautre's fate[84] – folded up like an accordion before the same tribunal just three days after the Smithfield burning, and the very next day permitted himself to be hustled into a public, English-language ceremony of abjuration.[85] The archbishops' registers abound in proximate accounts of Lollard conversions.[86]

But some were not swayed. A case indicative of the complexities of such persuasive attempts is that of John Seynonus, known to have claimed that his views about the eucharist were unaffected by Sautre's fate:

> He said and avowed that our decretal and that of our prelates, and the clergy of our province of Canterbury in our last convocation, together with the consensus of the lords of our realm, and the nobility and magnates of the last parliament, against the heretic recently burned in the city of London ['contra haereticum in civitate Londoniensi nuper combustum'], was insuffICENT to change his belief, that the substance of material bread persists in the sacrament of the altar, just as before. . . .[87]

The irony is that this insight into Seynonus's hold out is conveyed within the form of an abjuration and public performance of his acceptance of the authority of the Church. What failed, evidently, to persuade as pure performance became sufficiently persuasive when linked with threatened sanctions – and the threat of sanctions is always somewhere in the wings of this theater of hegemonic power.

As the only public burning during the ten-year period between 1401 and 1410, Sautre's punishment would always have a more emblematic than practical significance. That it was repeatedly invoked seems clear, not just from the fact, but the wording of Arundel's reported threat to William Thorpe:

> 'But I seie to thee, lewid losel, eithir now anoon consente to myn ordynaunce and submytte thee to stonde to myn decree, or bi seint

Tomas thou schalt be schauen and sue [follow] thi felow into Smethefelde!'[88]

Noteworthy here is Arundel's casual, part-for-whole allusion: 'shaven' for 'degraded' and 'follow to Smithfield' for 'be burnt there.' The mundanity of 'giving a shave' or 'sending to Smithfield' both conceals and sharpens the sense of underlying menace, in much the same way that the calculated everydayness of the carpenters of the York crucifixion or the homely slang of Elaine Scarry's Philippine torturers conveys the same effect.[89] Thorpe seems to get it right when he concludes that Arundel is feeling no sorrow for having burnt Sautre at Smithfield, and he may also be right when he suggests that 'the Archebishop thirstide yit aftir the schedynge out of more innocent blood'.[90] But Arundel's threat evidently remained linguistic and symbolic, and was never enacted in Thorpe's case. For the Lollards of the first Lancastrian decade, an interlude was afforded, in which to draw their own conclusions from the charged *exemplum* of Sautre's trial, degradation, and very public burning at Smithfield.

Sautre had, of course, always been an 'example' of *something*, from the time that his doings first entered the textual realm. But the semiotic weight of his case deepened measurably with his trial at St Paul's during a session of parliament at which opinions were expressed about the ideal disposition of the case; *lingua materna Anglicana* was employed during crucial episodes in his trial; the public rite of his degradation was accomplished in the usual, highly emblematic, way, with Sautre led out in priestly habit and then stripped by seven stages of the dress and emblems of rank, finally being shaved and his head covered by a layman's cap. But the most heightened theatrical moment was that of the burning itself, a moment for which several days' thoughtful preparation were evidently required. Dated 26 February (the day of Sautre's degradation),[91] Henry's writ for the execution was not implemented until 2 March. Among other motives for the postponement must be reckoned the fact that this was the first public and officially sanctioned burning for heresy conducted within the realm.[92] As such, and in consequence of its exemplary importance, some decisions had to be made about the procedures to be employed, and about their particular symbolic resonances.[93]

Adam of Usk's spare account – possibly that of an eyewitness, but recollected from later years – is the most detailed. Usk says that he was taken to Smithfield and,

posti derecte stando catenatus ac dolio, ignitis focalibus circumdatus, in cineres redactus existit [fettered upright to a post standing in a barrel surrounded by blazing wood, he was reduced to ashes]. (Usk, pp. 122–123)

Several elements present themselves for analysis, most notably the location at Smithfield, the deployment of chains and tun or barrel, and Sautre's reduction *in cineres*, to ashes.

Smithfield may be understood as a practical choice because of its convenience: it was an open space several hundred yards northwest of the city walls, close enough to attract a crowd and large enough to accommodate it. Yet executions might occur elsewhere – in Cheap or Tyburn, for example – and such places could accommodate large crowds as well. The choice of Smithfield would seem to bear some relation to its past history and symbolic resonance. Most obviously Smithfield was associated with the assertion of royal prerogative, indelibly established in 1381 when the young Richard led the rebels there and when (in an exhibition of cooperation between king and urban patriciate) Mayor Walworth slew Wat Tyler and the rebels were dispersed.[94] Richard may well have sought to revive such associations when he made his 1390 Smithfield tournament the ceremonial centerpiece of his revived kingship and the place where he instituted his newly founded Order of the White Hart.[95] Compatible with the history of Smithfield as a place of royal and civil importance is its complicated legal title, as explored by Sheila Lindenbaum, who finds that 'It had an ambiguous legal status that made it seem to belong to the king and the city at the same time: medieval documents refer to it both as the "king's field" and the city's "common ground." '[96] Apparently the city's ownership was confirmed in 1400, and Henry's own writ is addressed to the mayor and sheriffs of London, in acknowledgment of the city's jurisdiction. But its earlier identity as a place of jurisdictional encounter lingered, in complement to its reputation as a place of spectacle and public display. As the fifteenth century progressed, heretics and traitors were often haled to the place where their crime was thought to have occurred, as when Oldcastle was burnt in St Giles's Fields, the site of his supposed rebellion. Smithfield, with its own rich history as a site hospitable to royal and civic prerogative, was an ideal place of punishment for Sautre, found guilty of crimes against the secular state.

Burning, although less common than Henry's writ would imply, had taken hold in the public imagination as the accepted form of punishment for heresy, and Sautre's standing position, chained against a post, was conventional.[97] More remarkable is the decision to stand Sautre in a *dolium*, a cask, tun or barrel. Once employed in Sautre's case, it would be used again. Walsingham, for example, has Badby, nine years later, in similar straits: 'enclosed in a barrel ["dolio includitur"], afflicted by devouring flames,'[98] and 'Gregory's Chronicle' has 'the tonne putt ovyr hym ande fyre put unto hym.'[99] But the device itself seems not to be well understood, even by those employing it. Badby was described as having met his fate bound to a stake with iron chains, 'enclosed with a certain concave vessel' ('quodam vase concavo circumplectus').[100] But, as to the rationale for such a vessel, nothing is said. Perhaps, as in the choice of Smithfield, the *dolium* may have been a simple matter of expediency, a way of assuring completion of the job without scattering of ashes, in the form of an inconvenient (or even subversively tantalizing) remainder.[101] Yet an emblematic impulse might be involved here as well. Dante's Farinata, isolated in his tomb, has been taken to exemplify the heretic's separation from the common body of the orthodox. Sautre, in his barrel, might be seen as similarly cut off.[102]

A desired step in assuring exemplary status for a heretic is, of course, confession or compelled speech, in which the heretic recants and endorses the orthodox view. This is what the prince sought with Badby and Arundel at least briefly achieved with Purvey.[103] But, if the heretic cannot be persuaded or hectored into orthodox utterance, then his or her silence is greatly to be preferred to unorthodox speech. This whole process may be illustrated in the trial of Sautre, in which he is first enjoined to speak, and then converted to a static icon. In its early stages, the trial permitted Sautre a good deal of latitude, both for written and oral response. Then, the grounds of the discussion narrowed to the issue of the eucharist, and very technical questions being posed and re-posed, his replies are repeated only in indirect discourse and short summary ('dixit, se hanc materiam nescire . . . dixit, se hoc non intelligere . . . quasi deridendo, respondit dicens, se hoc nescire . . . adeo quod interim praefatus Will. aliter noluit respondere' – *Concilia*, p. 256). Pleas of ignorance, and other sorts of mocking evasion, are to be treated by examiners as equivalent to admissions of guilt.[104] Subsequently permitted only words of self-incrimination, he is reduced to silence during the ceremony of degradation, and evidently during the burning as well. Allowed in Adam of Usk's version to speak, he is treated as later chroniclers were to treat Oldcastle, as a spouter of grandiose prophecies; Usk has him, after his condemnation, threatening Arundel with the claim that he and his clergy and the king would die an evil death ('mala morte morituri') and that a foreign tongue ('extranea . . . lingua') will arrive to assume rule. The replacement of Sautre's usual pithy, and more genuinely challenging, utterances with what I take to be pseudo-Bridlington rant, is a final attempt at his neutralization.

The non-*arbitrariness of Henry's choice*

Thus far I have argued for a certain arbitrariness – both in the selection of William Sautre as a subject of Lancastrian rebuke and in the employment of certain highly specialized and relatively belated points about transubstantiation as the litmus test for orthodoxy. But from a slightly different perspective Sautre may be seen as a completely plausible (and perhaps even inevitable) victim, even as the eucharist may be seen as the crucial (and truly inevitable) test for orthodox belief.[105]

One vital consideration is that Sautre was both a priest and a relapsed heretic, the former status exposing him to ecclesiastical trial and the latter to what amounted to a death penalty (since, in 1401, even the most zealous proponents of orthodoxy had not yet imagined the possibility of burning anyone who had not entered the doubly degraded state of relapse). Another, and closely related, element of prosecutorial advantage is possession of Sautre's earlier trial records in a form that could be brought judicially to bear. But he turns out to have left in his wake a still more extensive parchment trail.

For one thing, rather than concealing his previous conviction, Sautre seems to have raised it to maximum visibility. The *Fasciculi Zizaniorum* discovers and reprints a petition evidently sent by Sautre to king and parliament, seeking an opportunity to address them on precisely the points of his April 1399 Norfolk conviction:

> I, William Sautre, declare myself unwilling to defend myself with respect to any and all conclusions, considering myself to have been persecuted and violently imprisoned as a result of connivance and without sufficient deliberation, supplicating my lord king and all parliament, that I might be able to come to an open hearing by my lord king and all parliament, to whom and to which hearing I appeal, on account of the health and peace of the whole realm.[106]

An 'appeal,' in the medieval system, has more the effect of an accusation than a request for a second hearing, and Sautre's petition conveys more indignation than abjection. He considers himself deprived of essential protections, and to have suffered unwarranted brutality in his imprisonment. The points on which he wishes to be heard are central to Lollard belief, and are, in fact, the very points cited as the basis for his Norfolk conviction in the conciliar proceedings.[107] Presumably, his request for a hearing came prior to his submission, though (in the light of his subsequent preparedness to reassert his positions) not necessarily so. In any event, it amounted to a request for a national discussion of Lollardy, in the highest tribunals of the land.

Additional evidence touching on Sautre's activities during the year before his January 1401 trial suggests that he was fully prepared to create problems on a national scale. For his name appears, rather astonishingly, on a list of suspect persons arrested and tried in Oxfordshire in connection with the Epiphany rising against Henry in January 1400. The persons listed in this exceptional and anomalous document have been rounded up the week following the unsuccessful rebellion of the earls, and it records their hearing as conducted in the presence of the king himself ('in presencia ipsius Regis'), as a hearing of the Court of the Verge, conducted within an area of twelve miles around wherever the king was resident.[108] The principal perpetrators having already been summarily executed by local initiative, this hearing involves a number of smaller fish, including most notably Sir Thomas Blount and a handful of other knights and esquires, together with several score associates and servants. Various sentences are recorded, with the leaders hanged, decapitated, and quartered for treason; a mixed group of servants and followers pardoned outright because of their limited responsibility; and an additional group found at fault ('culpabiles . . . de prodicionibus et feloniis') but pardoned by the king for various reasons; and a final group found to deserve death but who on account of their positions in the households of major figures were thought not to have acted voluntarily so should therefore be pardoned of their capital offense. Among this group of convicted but pardoned felons is 'Williamus Sautre, clerk.' Sautre/Sawtry/Chatrys is a reasonably common name, but the occupational and status designation of 'clerk' in this document (and *capellanus* in the Patent Rolls) seems to indicate that this is our man.[109]

How Sautre managed to involve himself in this ill-fated venture, in which Lollard participation was not large, must remain a matter of conjecture – especially since his participation would put him in the surprising company of conservative Ricardian diehards like Bishop Despenser, the very cleric who had recently hounded him from the Norwich diocese.[110] All that can be said on the matter, for now, is that some of the plotting for the rebellion of the earls would seem to have gone on in London and Westminster in the autumn of 1399 – involving alleged meetings in St Paul's and in Baynards Castle and Dowgate wards with the participation of Thomas Merks, bishop of Carlisle, and other clerics – and that Sautre was also resident in London during the months between his recantation in May 1399 and his arrest in January 1400.[111]

Alongside this bare *opportunity* for the malcontent Sautre's recruitment may be considered certain affinities or points of possible commensurability between Lollardy and anti-Lancastrian activity, as potential ground for Sautre's involvement. Although the linkages between Lollardy and pro-Ricardian sedition were never as numerous as the Lancastrians imagined or claimed them to be, such linkages may have occurred from time to time. The Lollards did not rally to Richard early, or in great numbers, but a number of incidental details between 1400 and Oldcastle's final affirmation of belief in Richard alive in Scotland in 1417 point to the grounds on which such a consolidation of Lollard belief could at least be imagined.[112] Owing in part to its Wycliffite origins, Lollard dogma was always strong on loyalty to the crowned king. One of the central points in the 1401 accusation against Sautre was that 'he chose to venerate a temporal king rather than the wooden cross on which Christ was crucified' (with respect, he explained in his behalf, to the material cross).[113] For the crowned king, like a saint or a predestinate man, presented an analogy to the human and divine Christ, as an exemplification of humanity raised sacramentally to a more perfect state. Believing, though, in the special status of a legitimate king, the Lollard could hardly be sanguine about his displacement, or about any sacramental process that promised to dissolve or obliterate the claims of a regnant king and to transfer them to a new incumbent. This, in turn, becomes a question of sacramental efficacy – and a question, especially, of the sacrament of the eucharist.

Even more foregone than the selection of Sautre as victim was the principal charge under which he was tried: 'specialiter super sacramento altaris,' or 'especially upon the sacrament of the altar'; that is, the eucharist. This is the charge which moved so rapidly to the top among the various heresies and errors with which Wyclif was initially charged, and it remained at the top of the list of forty-five proscribed views officially adopted by the Council of Constance in 1415.[114] The irony here is that, even though attention given to the eucharist remained anomalous and disproportionate within the primarily moral and social program of the later Lollards,[115] they found themselves unable to extricate themselves from its conditions. Not of their own choosing, the subject of the eucharist was nevertheless one which they could not fail to acknowledge as central to theological and societal understanding. Thus, they found themselves obliged to assume a discursively dictated role in an argument they could not win.

The unavoidability of the eucharist revolves around its emergence as a subject, not just of doctrinal, but also of social contention. For the orthodox, the eucharist became a sacramental guarantee not only of God's compact with humankind but also of a social order at once closely bounded and infinitely renewable. The visible social order, in this view, is a sacramental derivative or by-product, infinitely subject to sacerdotal transformation and interpretation. The Lollard view, if so sweeping a generalization may be attempted, is sacramental too, but considers the sacraments to be symbolic in nature, less the determinants of social meaning than a symbolic addition or complement to visible meaning.

Rather than differing in all respects, the views I am calling orthodox and Lollard are actually very close; but in the theory of the eucharist their difference becomes apparent. The quintessential articulation of the orthodox position as it bears on the events of 1401 is Roger Dymmok's rejoinder to the Lollard contentions of 1395. To the Lollard insistence that absence of material change means that Christ's body cannot have entered the host, he replies that sacramental action constantly affirms and reveals the possibility of inward change without outward change:

> For if this [Lollard] argument should thrive, it would destroy all the sacraments of the Church, all the oaths of kings, and the political association of all men with one blow. . . . I ask, what sensible change do you see in a boy newly baptised, in a man who has confessed, in a boy or man who has been confirmed, in consecrated bread, in a man ordained into the priesthood, in marriageable persons betrothed or joined? All receive a new virtue, except the bread, which simply ceases to exist without any kind of sensible change, and is transubstantiated into the body of Christ. In what way also is the body of a king changed, when he is newly crowned, or anyone similarly advanced? (p. 130)

Dymmok offers us, in effect, a chain of sacramental signification, in which inward change is accomplished without alteration of outward appearance. This chain, as such, would present no problems of belief for the Lollard, who also believes that *every* sacrament confers a new virtue, symbolically and relationally ('habitudiner').[116] But the orthodox differ in locating the chain's symbolic efficacy in a single, irrational point: in the eucharistic bread, which is not only symbolically transformed but obliterated, to assume a completely new substance. This eucharist is discontinuous, does not make sense, and thus protects the entire symbolic sequence, serving in Lacanian terms as a completely sealed and veiled mystery, a place always sought but completely inaccessible, an enigma which functions at once as pure signification (in effect, as 'accidens sine subjecto') and also as pure presence (the whole and entire body of Christ).[117]

What the Lollard view threatens is not the sacral *per se*, but the exceptionality of the host within the sacral, and hence its function as that point of irrationality that secures (in Lacanian terminology 'quilts') the entire ideological system. In one sense, the Lollard view thus threatens very little and, in another, everything under the sun. Revealed in this contention is a certain Lollard intransigence, a stubbornness about the nature and extent of sacramental transformation. Prepared to believe in sacramental symbolism by which a new layer of signification is added to an existing entity, the Lollards stopped resolutely short of the belief that a sacrament can refashion or utterly replace substance with new substance. Dymmok's own statement seems to hesitate over this point. The king, by virtue of coronation, receives a 'new virtue,' which is a matter on which the Lollard (who thinks the consecrated host consists of bread *and* the body of Christ) might be expected to agree. But Dymmok then presses his argument to an extreme with which the Lollard would presumably not agree, suggesting that a sacrament (or even a quasi-sacramental rite like coronation) might effect a total inner transformation, even while external accidents remain unchanged ('In what way also is the body of a king changed, when he is newly crowned?'). With this view a Lollard, stubborn about the persistence of substance and all that persistence implies, might be expected to demur.

Here the disagreement between orthodoxy and Lollardy bears powerfully upon Lancastrian dynastic hopes. Here rests the point of possible connection between Sautre's two offenses, the one doctrinal and the other political. For a Lollard, skeptical about orthodox claims of sacramental power to infuse new meaning in defiance of outward appearance, might well cling to a literal view about whether a king can be unmade, or whether a new king can be created from un-regal matter. The orthodox interpretation of transubstantiation implies an infinite capacity for the world to be destroyed and miraculously remade. By no means refusing an access of symbolic meaning, the Lollard view of the sacrament nevertheless starts with the observed world and grants that world a certain irreducibility. Dymmok believes that the accidents of humble bread are severed from any taint of bread-ness by the incarnation of Christ and that a human body can be made by coronation into a king; Sautre doubts that a sacrament, let alone a quasi-sacrament, can do so much. And, if coronation in the absence of other entitlement cannot make a king, a usurping dynasty cannot expect to rest easy on the ground.

3
Plots

No strangers to mortal plots, the Lancastrians dealt with them on a regular basis. During Henry IV's first decade as king, he and his sons were constantly in arms against one plot or another: starting in the first months of his reign with the rather feeble scheme of Thomas Blount and the earls; continuing more dangerously in 1401–4 with the varied machinations of Owain Glyndwr, Henry Percy, and the earl of Northumberland; threatening always to involve and engage France and Scotland; and finally ebbing out at the end of the decade with the death of Archbishop Scrope and the collapse of armed opposition in Wales. Henry's fortunes narrowly survived the battle of Shrewsbury. Had any combination of these adversaries been able to oppose him in concert, his reign would have been short indeed.

And these were just the real plots. As if real dangers were not sufficient, Henry IV and V were constantly surrounded by fancied schemes and intrigues of every description. Such fanciful initiatives might originate with enemies, but their textual promulgation was often sponsored by friends and well-wishers or even by the Lancastrians themselves. In the atmosphere of betrayal, animosity, and aggressive intrigue engendered by the Lancastrian usurpation, the traitorous plot itself became a key structuration and tool of thought through which different issues, not just of loyalty and disloyalty but also of kingship and dynastic survival, might be affirmatively symbolized and constructively engaged.

Consider this story of malicious intrigue and narrow escape told by Thomas Walsingham of Henry IV in the second year of his reign:

> When, on a certain night, the King was getting into bed, he escaped a deadly danger with God's protection. By the cunning of a certain traitor, an instrument made of iron was placed in his bedstraw,

fashioned with three teeth, having three long hooks subtly rounded, pointed with the sharpest barbs at the ends. The intent of this ingenuity was that, when the King should have pressed the bed-straw with the weight of his body, he would have been wounded, or even killed, by these same barbed points. But, by the will of God, the King unexpectedly ['inopinate'] perceived the death-dealing instrument, and avoided this peril.[1]

This anecdote was probably written down early in the reign of Henry V, by which time Walsingham may be considered a fully complicit writer.[2] Whether or not it was actually created and promulgated by the Lancastrians, they must certainly have tolerated its dissemination, and understandably so.[3] For here a blatantly imagined variant of the dangers that Henry IV constantly faced is bent to the task of reassurance through the agency of narrative control.

Obscured in the narrative is the motivation of the cunning assailant. We are told what we most need to know, that he is a *proditor*, a traitor, an enemy of Lancastrian promise. Rather than dwelling upon his rationale (over-detailed attention to which could only, after all, prove a distraction at best and a Lancastrian embarrassment at worst), attention is displaced to his fiendish contrivance. But the reader is returned to the question of motive, or at least of modality, by the machine's deployment, in the most private space of Henry's chamber and the most domestic precinct of his bed. Implied here is a key Lancastrian fear, that of domestic treason, of treason from within the household, at a point and place and time of special trust.

'O perilous fyr, that in the bedstraw bredeth!' exclaims Chaucer's Merchant, over Damian's betrayal of January his lord from within his own household, and then goes on to point the sense in which the domesticity of his crime increases its fault: 'O servant traytour, false hoomly hewe/Lyk to the naddre in bosom sly untrewe . . .' (IV, ll. 1783, 1785–1786). Here, then, is treason in its most pernicious form: domestic, false-fronted, involving violation of trust, exploiting that constant element of Lancastrian anxiety, the possible difference between seeming and being, appearance and intent. Of course, the Lancastrian king – considering himself rightly ordained and entitled to his subjects' obedience – considers domestic treason the very essence and type of treason, since *all* treason in one way or another involves the violation of a privileged bond. Hence, control over this seemingly special case of treason offers the gratification of temporary control over every kind of treason.

This narrative controls anxiety, not just in its denouement, in which the device is discovered, but also in the partially visible rationale of the discovery itself. Henry's preservation is God's intent; his escape occurs as a result of God's protection ['Deo protegente'] and the discovery of the device is a consequence of God's will ['Deo volente']. Henry finds the device *inopinate* or unexpectedly. Although he was not systematically searching for any such device, it was nevertheless revealed to him. The lesson here is directed against potential plotters, assuring them that, even should Henry's attention stray, he will enjoy God's providential protection. The climax of the anecdote has Henry avoiding the peril in which he was placed ('. . . et periculum devitavit'), and *devitare* possesses the special sense not just of 'to avoid' but 'to leave unfulfilled.' The danger falls short of fulfillment because – in the narrative's reassuring implication – an alternative fulfillment is already guaranteed by God's special protection, a fulfillment bound up in the providential narrative of Lancastrian kingship.

However cheaply such narrative reassurances (and admonitions) might seem to come, the Lancastrians found them invaluable. Lancastrian records abound in threatened empoisonings and ambushes, often violative of domestic and private space or (in their more ambitious renditions) relations of special trust. The Henries could hardly plan a Christmas season without some threat of its violation, either invasion of the household at Epiphany in January 1400,[4] by poisoned food at Christmas 1400,[5] by Lollard mummers in 1413–14,[6] or in a host of other ways.[7] Of interest here is not so much the invention of such plots, of which chronicles and treason trial records and other sources afford almost endless evidence, but a related contention: that the invention and control of such plots by narrative means was found so serviceable to the institution of Lancastrian kingship that both Henries participated with energy and creativity in the wholesale creation of their own violent and traitorous opposition. A pioneering effort in this regard may be found in Henry IV's relations with the Lollard conspiracy, and in his leading role in forging a link between Lollardy and sedition (see Chapter 2). But his son hardly lagged behind, and at two crucial junctures in the early years of his rule discovered ambitious plots requiring prompt action and resolute succession. Unsurprisingly, each of these plots is treated as a threat to the king's life, as an unspeakable violation of special bonds of trust, as an occasion on which the plotters (though not Henry and his supporters) are taken by surprise, and as an opportunity for revelation of God's providential plans for the king and his dynasty.

Reconsidering the 'Oldcastle Rebellion'

Something happened at St Giles's Fields (or Fickett's Field) on 10 January 1414 (or the night and early morning of 9–10 January). But, as tends to be the case with those occasions of special intensity or importance which come to be perceived as historical events, certainty about what did happen becomes less distinct as particular contours are sought. Obviously, an event cannot mean the same thing to everyone, whether in prospect, as it is happening, or in retrospect. But one thing is certain: if a faction or party with sufficient access to civil or cultural power decides that an event is to occur (or that it has occurred), then it *will* occur (or will have occurred). Other parties or participants may revise, demur, or otherwise register opposition to the prevailing view, but they have little choice in their acquiescence to the postulation of *évenémentielle* status.

The 'event,' once so registered, becomes an object of commentary, an occasion for speculation and especially writing, whereby interested parties seek (but never completely successfully) to exhaust or control its meaning. This is the sense in which an event is, in Lyotard's phrase, a 'bidon vide,' an empty barrel, in which written commentary is endlessly poured, but which never achieves plenitude.[8] Commentary generally seeks to provide an illusion of plenitude, in the form of complete or at least sufficient explanation, and the very first accounts of the 10 January 1414 event possessed such completeness in extremely satisfying degree. Its main features were specified in writing on the very morning it happened, and – incorporated into statutes and parliamentary records, and abetted by chroniclers and pro-Lancastrian biographers – these features commanded rapid and general assent. The main elements of an agreed-upon narrative were consolidated in the indictment sworn by the jurors assembled on the morning of the revolt: that the rebels conspired to assemble in St Giles's Fields; that on the early morning of 10 January 20,000 of them from all parts of England gathered there under the leadership of chaplain Walter Blake and knight Roger Acton; that they were treasonously arrayed for war and would have slain the king had he not scattered them, slaying some and arresting others.

Variously embellished, this account held the field throughout the fifteenth century. Its prestige untouched by that century's magnate controversies, it flourished equally among Lancastrians, Yorkists, and early Tudors. Various parties of Lollards and their sympathizers must surely have had their differences with this account, but such were the persecutions and suppressions visited upon the Lollards (including, of course, textual suppressions, especially after the promulgation of Arundel's 1407–9 Constitutions)[9] that no alternative written tradition seems to have survived the century. Less inherited than reinvented, an alternative written account would emerge in the mid-sixteenth century under the sponsorship of Tyndale, Bale, and Foxe, not coincidentally but with the institutional and political support of an emergent state Protestantism. This account, which reversed the poles of analysis and portrayed Oldcastle as victim and Henry V as aggressor, was in turn to prevail for 300 years.[10] It remained essentially unquestioned until overthrown by a group of late nineteenth and early twentieth-century historians, including James Tait,[11] J. H. Wylie,[12] and, especially, W. T. Waugh.[13] Acting in the name of a return to the fifteenth-century records, and hence to a more scientific historiography, these historians did indeed re-read Walsingham, Elmham, and the other fifteenth-century writers. Theirs was, however, a credulous science, accepting and reinstating the main outlines of these Lancastrian accounts, while modifying them with respect to certain matters of detail. (For example, the frequently repeated assertion that 20,000 Lollards gathered in St Giles's Fields was altered by Waugh to a 'hundred' [p. 647], though without any change in the general contours of the account.)[14] Exhibited here, in the name of historiography, is actually an extreme complacency and passivity towards documents that have made a previous investment in the work of their own narration.

Twentieth-century accounts of the Oldcastle rebellion consistently yield to the demands of narrative over the obligations of analysis.[15] That such a preference should characterize the work of several late-Victorian historians is not in itself surprising; what is surprising is that their work, and most centrally Waugh's 1905 essay, has not been seriously scrutinized in the intervening years. Although additionally emended with respect to matters of detail, their account of the 'Oldcastle Rebellion,' effectively rehashing claims shaped and sponsored by the Lancastrians in the period 1414–20, prevails today.[16] Here proposed is less a review of additional details and factual claims bearing on the events of 10 January (an activity which more archivally experienced scholars are in any case better prepared than I to perform) than a reconsideration of the very narrative contours of the event, as initially and so promptly provided under the auspices of Lancastrian textual production.

Constituting the event

The occurrence of 10 January issued in an initially savage repression (including the hanging and hanging/burning of some forty dissidents on gallows specially constructed at St Giles) and a longer-term process of intimidation (including the formation of special commissions that encouraged local juries and investigators to 'name names' of Lollards and traitors). Repressions and intimidations are characteristically justified by discovery of the cause and necessity of repression in the bad character and evil intentions of the repressed. This formula is implemented by the Lancastrian strategy of *hysteron-proteron*, or reversal, in which results and consequences are substituted for causes and origins, and the reverse.[17] Thus, the outcome of the rising, in a swift and highly punitive judgment against the plotters, is carried back to become an account of origins, via the assertion of a prior Lollard plot.

As everyone agrees, the Lancastrian response to whatever haltingly oppositional gestures were made on 10 January was breathtakingly swift and sure. Everyone also agrees that the effectiveness of the Lancastrian response is the result of extensive planning. The issue rests elsewhere: in the question of whether such planning was undertaken in response to a growing Lollard threat, or whether it included the fabrication of the Lollard threat. Some evidence bearing on this question – and weighing heavily on the side of 'fabrication' – is available within the Issue Rolls of the Lancastrian Exchequer. With the understanding that the dates of the items refer to their inscription, rather than to the originating dates of the writs and warrants recorded there, and that the dates thus provide a *terminus ad quem* rather than a *terminus a quo*, here are three crucial items bearing on the question of Lancastrian planning for the occurrences of 10 January 1414:

(1) 11 December 1413: payment of five marks to Robert Warner, sheriff of Middlesex, for his expenses and costs in constituting and summoning a panel for Lollards already insurgent against the king ['pro lollardis iam raro insurgentibus contra dominum Regem'] and seven pounds to Richard Mayhew and his fellow jurors summoned and in attendance at Westminster for certain necessary reasons touching upon the convenience of the king.[18]
(2) 5 January 1414: grants to John de Burgh (carpenter) and Thomas Kentford for detecting and revealing 'coniectamenta proditoria' – treasonous conjectures recently proposed and imagined against the king's majesty by certain persons called Lollards.[19]
(3) 7 January 1414, to sheriffs: since captured Lollards have confessed intent to make illicit congregations and conventicles in various parts of the realm, in destruction of the king's person and also that of lords and the Church, proclamation is to be made against participating in these gatherings under forfeit of life and limb.[20]

These items, each referring to an action prior to 10 January, speak far less to the question of Lollard treason than to Lancastrian planning, aimed at controlling the parameters of an event toward which they stand in a relation of partial sponsorship. Reviewing them, item by item: (1) Particularly notable here is the constitution of jury panels as early as December 1413 – ostensibly for events that had already occurred, though no such events are recorded and no records of jury proceedings are to be found. Such evidence of early foresight may be, and usually has been, taken in confirmation of Lancastrian alertness and the new king's leadership capacities. My own, contrary, suggestion is that it indicates advance determination that an event will occur, under conditions at least partially of Lancastrian choosing. The actual thrust of these expenses appears to be toward summoning a jury and maintaining it in a state of readiness. (The sum in question – seven pounds – is not a fortune, but is sufficient to finance a significant amount of groundwork in identifying and preparing jurors, in order to have a panel at hand on the crucial morning.) This supposition is, in turn, verified by a February entry pertaining to events of January, recording final payment to John Mayhew and his fellow jurors empanelled to inquire into matter of certain traitors recently captured ('super certis proditoribus iam raro captis')[21]. (2) Similar payments to observers and *exploratores* are recorded elsewhere in the Exchequer Rolls. Of interest here is the non-clandestine nature of the entry (enrolled just a few days before the 10 January event to which it might refer). Also relevant is the occasion taken to specify the treasonous nature of the designs in question; the Lollards' indulgence in treasonous imaginings against the king's majesty opens them to severe reprisal; this wording, along with that of many similar texts, may be considered a contribution to a pre-woven Lollard indictment. (3) More important for this repressive purpose is the proclamation against congregations and conventicles. Earlier proclamations and statutes had sought to regulate Lollard sermonizing and teaching.[22] This one renders all Lollard gatherings inherently seditious, and opens them to reprisal, claiming their attempt manifestly to destroy the king and the spiritual and temporal magnates of the realm. Subsequent to 10 January, and on the momentum generated by that repressive event, these provisions against Lollard assembly would be written into law.[23] For now, the proclamation was sufficient to allow the king to do what he intended to do. Armed with the kinds of preliminaries indicated here, Henry was able to discover and dramatize in the events of 10 January the preferred Lancastrian pattern: potent and malicious schemers against the realm are shown to have been anticipated, *gylours* are always already beguiled, traitors always already betrayed.

The traditional date of the planned rising is 10 January, and historians – unable to explain how a rising could both occur and be judged by legal process on the very same day – have assisted the record by suggesting that the engagement in question actually occurred between the hours of midnight and dawn very early in the morning of that day.

Given this modest explanatory boost, the following, rather remarkably paced, set of texts may be assembled:

10 January 1414: a broadly worded commission to the mayor of London, Henry Lord Scrope, and others, to the effect that the Lollards have treasonously conspired ('proditorie imaginauerunt') the king's death and that of others, and that he wishes them punished according to their crimes ('iuxta eorum demerita . . . castigari & puniri').[24]
10 January 1414: the presentment of an unnamed jury before those same commissioners, indicting Walter Blake, Roger Acton, and others for planning to rise treasonously in St Giles's Fields on that very date.[25]
10 January 1414: an arrest warrant issued for Blake, Acton, and others.
[10 January 1414]:[26] £2.16s.8d. expenses for breakfast ('gentaculum')[27] for the mayor, Scrope, and other commissioners 'appointed . . . to try certain traitors who recently rebelled against the person of the Lord the King.'

Quite a day – especially if, in addition to these judicial procedures and the accompanying breakfast in the Tower, a rebellion were to have been put down as well! Nor was there much rest the next day, on which an inquiry on Lollard activity was launched in twenty counties,[28] and a nationwide offer of generous rewards was made for the apprehension of Oldcastle,[29] the latter text stating that some Lollards had already been taken and condemned to die ('capti, ac . . . morti adjudicati existunt').

On the unlikelihood that such convergences might be innocent in nature, or even possible without advance preparation, I defer to Foxe: 'Seeing this equitation or riding toward Saint Giles field was vpon the Wednesday next after the feast of Epiphany (as in this Indictement and processe of outlawry is aboue certified) which was the tenth daye of January, and commission also the same day was charged, the Jewry moreover impanelled the same daye, & yet no Jewrer named, [&] the verdict the same day presented, how all these can concurre together, and all in one day, let the reader after he haue well consideered the matter, use his iudgement therin, not only whether it be like, but also whether it be possible' (*Acts*, p. 576). Labeled 'absurd' by Waugh (p. 646), Foxe's argument seems to me so persuasive as to be very nearly definitive. Consider that the commissioners were not only in the wings but sufficiently so to enjoy a ceremonial breakfast; that the jury was either pre-constituted or never existed; that ambitious drafting projects and processes of accusation were completed with near-magical speed;

that convictions were evidently handed down the same day. Here are all the hallmarks of an event which was either invented, or, if not invented, at least so extensively managed as to constitute a virtual invention. We will later see Walsingham's and other accounts in which dazed Lollards fall like stunned birds into the arms of the king's men; unlike real-life scenarios, which involve messy and unpredictable resistances, cross-currents, and delays, we here encounter an unencumbered event, with contours that stand forth so vividly as to suggest its planned and scripted nature.

Against such evidence of Lancastrian planning must be weighed the contrary claim, that the origins of the conflict lay in Lollard aggression. Certainly, Lollard sympathizers must have been on some kind of 'alert' following Oldcastle's condemnation on 25 September 1413 and his escape from the Tower with probable Lollard connivance on 19 October.[30] Subsequent indictments and chronicles suggest the existence of some kind of communications network, involving preachers like William Ederyk of Derbyshire and Walter Gilbert of Leicestershire.[31] But evidence of the extent and refinement of such a network is nevertheless compromised by the means of its gathering. Most of what is known about this network's existence, and the content of its communications, derives from the surviving returns of the county commissions issued by king and council on 11 January, through which information was sought about local Lollard activities.[32] These commissions were sent to twenty counties and localities, especially in the north and west midlands, seeking information about Lollard activities. But the commissions are not only framed in a way which presumes guilt, but also in a language and scope immensely encouraging to 'naming names' and seeking convictions.

According to one of these nearly identical commissions, in this case directed to the earl of Oxford, Henry V has been fully informed of the treasonous activities of those popularly called Lollards ('lollardi vulgariter nuncupati'), some of whom are already captured ('quorum aliquam capti existunt').[33] Bound by his duty as a Christian prince, he wishes to resist them, believing them worthy to be held and punished according to their wrongdoing. Notable here is the exceptional breadth of this aspect of the commission. As in the commissions of inquiry following the rising of 1381, and again in the 10 January commission, the suggestion that 'iuxta eorum demerita . . . castigari et puniri' opens the way to proceedings of exceptional scope and flexibility. Following upon this enlargement, the jury charge is itself sweeping in its intent, including a gathering of names of all Lollards and others who have sought his death or contemplated ('imaginaverunt et proposuerunt') other evils and wrongdoing, who have not yet been captured. He wishes to know of all matters and guilty parties they have been able to find, and wishes the perpetrators to be arrested and imprisoned, and information to be forwarded to him under commissioners' and jurors' seals.[34] Only after this sweeping mandate do we encounter the more usual, and circumspect, suggestion that these steps are to be taken according to the law and custom of the land: 'secundum legem & consuetudinem dicti regni.' Given the receipt of these commissions by trusted officials, and their implicit invitation to create loyalist and activist juries, one can only be surprised that so few, rather than so many, names were gathered in response.

Surviving returns taken before the commissions suggest that sixty or so lesser clergy, artisans, and peasants did set out for London in the first week of January; if all the indictments were in hand, numbers might run to two or three times as many. But, despite certain more concrete claims made within the indictments, the purpose of their travels and the question of whether they considered themselves to be involved in a rebellion remains entirely unresolved. The usual form of these indictments is to note that persons have, in effect, 'left town' ['devillaverunt'] under suspicious circumstances, their presumed destinations being St Giles's Fields and their presumed objective being to aid Oldcastle. Some are vivid in their ascription of motive; the most vividly realized of all has a group setting out from Derbyshire and planning to assemble at a Smithfield inn called the Wrestler on the Hoop ('in quodam hospicio vocato les Wrastelere on the hope' – KB9, 204, 58). Yet many of the returns state with becoming reserve that the intentions of people setting out for London were completely unknown to the jurors (for example, no. 4, in which a group of seven set out from the village of Thaxtede toward London, 'quo proposito aut intencione penitus ignorant'). The indeterminacy of such accusations, especially when the final destination and activity are unknown, may be illustrated by the case of one Philip Turner, whose own claim was that he left town on the vigil of Epiphany planning to buy wine in London ('in vigilia Ephiphanie . . . fuit devillans, causa emptionis vini versus Londonium'). He was arrested upon his return, and taken back for imprisonment in London, where he broke from captivity and fled to parts unknown. He is, the account concludes, a Lollard: 'et est lollardus.'

Because these inquests are framed to serve as possible indictments in cases of sedition, the most frequent suggestion is that the activity in question was aggressive in nature; that those leaving town were *armata et arraiata*, or *modo guerrino arraiati*, or otherwise arrayed for insurrection against the king. The latter cases, however, may be understood in part as satisfying the requirements of possible prosecution, the more so because the phrases in question are well established in legal custom, and have even more proximate sources in the indictment drawn against those arrested in St Giles's Fields on 10 January and its closely related variants.[35] The language of these returns is, in fact, so formulaic that Edward Powell has surmised that a protocol or other source document was read to the jurors to assist them in the framing of their conclusion.[36] This is a tempting conjecture, although, in accordance with the forms of textual economy by which anti-Lollard language is frequently shared,[37] the language of the many returns may also be found in numerous pre-existing texts. Most commonly, the language of the 11 January commission – itself a direct borrowing from the abbreviated 10 January commission for the investigation of the events at St Giles as it appears in the Patent Rolls (C66/393, mem. 30d) – is forthrightly cannibalized in the wording of the county commission indictments. The indictments produced at Ware and Baldock, Hertfordshire, on 29–31 January, for example, typically begin with a recitation of the general charge, and then follow it with a particularization in which the same language is applied to a local case.[38]

Considering these indictments in the aggregate, I remain unconvinced that much more is illustrated by them than the power of a royal proclamation, directed to loyalists and known adherents in the several counties, to elicit a predictable result: in this case, a quantity of hearsay and supposition about presumed or rumored activities of seditious troublemakers and Lollard believers loose in the land. In his careful study of these indictments, Edward Powell has 47 people accused of Lollardy and rebellion, 115 of rebellion alone, and 52 of Lollardy alone.[39] In addition to being (in Powell's words) 'pitifully small,' this purported turnout is fractured in other ways. If not motivated by Lollardy, then what did these 115 seditious people think they were doing: what was their grievance and what did they hope to gain? And, although the 52 Lollard stay-at-homes (together with seven persons named only as owning English books) swell the total numbers, they add nothing to an account of the events at St Giles's Fields.[40] The suggestion that owning a Lollard book, or preaching a sermon against the power of pilgrimage, or simply being a 'strong Lollard' goes far toward proving seditious intent seems far-fetched indeed. One cannot help but entertain special respect for those juries, like many in Hertfordshire, 'who say under oath that there are no Lollards [in their county] to their notice, nor any others who falsely and traitorously imagined the death of the lord King against their allegiance, or any others who imagined or proposed the destruction, either of the catholic faith or the estate of lords and magnates of the realm of England' (no. 118).

Narrative control

Whatever actually happened that morning at St Giles's Fields, the renarration of this one-sided and brief scuffle exhibits already familiar devices of narrative control. The pre-written (or else *very* hastily produced) indictment of 10 January is founded on the rhetorical divide between orthodox and heretic, and tacitly advances a series of prophetic and providential claims. As a spectacular success at what it sets out to accomplish, this text commands respectful attention; its devices, subjected to such attention, turn out to be surprisingly frail.

After a formulaic review of the seditious nature of Lollard activities (including their intent to slay the king and his brothers, to destroy religious orders and raze churches, and to name Oldcastle as regent), this text lays down the definitive account of the events at St Giles's Fields:

[the defendants] did falsely and treasonably propound and decree that they, together with 20,000 men from various parts of the realm of England . . . should raise a secret rebellion and should assemble, one and all, and come together on Wednesday after the Feast of the Epiphany . . . at the town and parish of St Giles outside Temple Bar in London in a certain great field there in order to fulfill their evil purposes. . . . And on that Wednesday the aforesaid Walter, Roger, and the others . . . falsely and treasonably proposed and plotted ['falso et proditorie proposuerunt et imaginauerunt'] to slay our aforesaid lord the king . . . and they rode there towards the aforesaid field, arrayed like traitors in warlike fashion ['modo guerrino arraiati'] in form of rebellion against their allegiances, and would have made war upon our said lord the king, had they not providently been forcibly restrained by him ['nisi per ipsum manuforti graciose impediti fuissent'].[41]

Exaggerations like the convergence of 20,000 upon St Giles notwithstanding, numerous surface features argue for this narrative's reception with a good deal more caution than has been the case. For one thing, the Lollards in this indictment lack a leader. As I will argue below, this early 'core' or first-stage indictment names only Blake and Acton in that capacity, and Oldcastle is nowhere to be found. Furthermore, these conspirators are said to be heading toward an indeterminate place – here, St Giles's Fields, elsewhere, Fickett's field – about which little agreement is to be found in fifteenth-century texts.[42] Finally, the language of the indictment itself is woven from established legal formulas (cf. 'modo guerrino arraiati') which would appear to be included more to ensure conviction than to mirror external reality.

Of course, a good causal narrative can soar over such factual contradictions, and the present text possesses a causal core: treasonous Lollards in warlike array, forestalled by the king. This causal core in turn embraces and overrides all sorts of contradictions; in fact some of its strength seems to derive from the divergent emphases it can simultaneously contain. This capacity for contradiction may be illustrated in relation to a single clause: 'nisi per ipsum manuforti graciose impediti fuissent.' On the one hand, the king's success is *graciose*: by grace of God, based not on merit or personal fortitude but on provident fortune. On the other hand, it is achieved *manuforti*: by military might, good planning, and overwhelming strength. This simple contradiction is, in turn, elaborated in subsequent narrations.[43] The Lollards are immeasurably strong and can be overcome only by providence or immense force; yet they are weak, liable to yield and melt away upon the merest turn of luck or most modest martial display. The king is terribly vulnerable; yet he possesses immense reserves of divine grace and military acumen. And so we encounter a cacophony of analyses and claims. Representations of the Lollards, strong as they are reputed to be, are penetrated by evidence of weakness and inevitable defeat; representations of the king, weak as he is reputed to be, cannot refrain from asserting his total foresight, his pre-emptive possession of the entire conflictual field. Yet, for all their persuasive verve, such cacophonous representations also risk a certain dispersal of effect, a long-term loss of their power to persuade.

The captivating energy of this narrative core *and* the precariousness of its persuasive power are on display in the first really ambitious extra-judicial rendering of the rising, by chronicler Thomas Walsingham. After certain preliminaries about plans to destroy the king while he observed Christmas at Eltham,[44] and about the ineradicable malice of the Lollards, Walsingham launches into his central account:

> They came in the first part of the night to a field called St Giles near London, where their leader ['campi-ductor'], 'Oldcastille,' lord of Cobham, brought his followers to be concealed. You might see by paths, by lanes, by crossroads, crowds thronging together, from almost all the counties of the realm, solicited with grand promises, to meet at that very day and hour. Asked why they were rushing so, panting to get there, they responded that they were hastening to the lord of Cobham, who had summoned them to be gathered there with his rewards.

But the king, not unaware of all this ['non ignarus omnium praemissorum'], at a well-chosen moment of the same night ordered his followers to be prepared in arms, before all else announcing to his followers what he had decided to do. . . . [After reassuring nervous followers, and insisting on his line of action because of his awareness of the dire results of Lollard success] the king, with so many evil ones opposing him, offered himself to danger, against the wishes of his followers ['Rex, tantis malis se objiciens, ingessit periculo, contra vota suorum'], entering the field a little after the middle of the night, where he established his position, that he might be prepared ['praestolaturus'] whatever should happen the next day. Whence it happened that many from remote places who would at first have entered the hostile camp entered, by error, the royal camp, where, when asked whom they sought, responded: the lord of Cobham. On account of which, contrary to their hopes, they were seized and committed to prisons.

This report reached the leaders of the enemy party; namely, that the king, with strong force, had occupied the neighboring field, and had captured many of their followers. The greater part were terrified, because they saw no one venture from London, whence they were expecting thousands to rush to their aid. . . . [The king had ordered the city gates closed and guarded.] And it is true that, had not the king conducted himself with this shrewdness ['hac calliditate'], on this very night, as has been said, 50,000 servants and apprentices, together with some of their masters from among the citizenry, would have sallied forth against the king.

The common impulse among the Lollards, the king having indeed already established his forces in the same field, depleted in spirit, was to seek the protection of flight; the royal forces followed them, capturing some and killing others.

In order that their leader might be forestalled, or at least something might be learned, the lord king had promised with the public voice of a herald 1,000 marks from his purse to whomever betrayed him, and maximum liberties to the cities or districts which should detect him. Whence it could be inferred that almost all the country had embraced his dementia, since nobody might be found who, with respect to such reward, wished to reveal him.[45]

One of this text's structuring oppositions is between the vulnerable king (dissuaded by his anxious supporters from engaging the Lollards by night and offering himself to danger only because of the gravity of the situation) and the puissant and authentically menacing Lollards (converging in great numbers from all corners of the kingdom with mayhem on their minds). In his assertion about Lollard strength, Walsingham repeats a standard element of Lancastrian representational strategy, as when the officially drafted core narrative of the rising argued that 20,000 Lollards had taken the field. But Walsingham is so intent on establishing the Lollard threat that he stumbles into even more absurd claims – claims that, were they to be believed, would effectively disqualify the king from any entitlement to rule – such as that 50,000 London servants and apprentices, together with citizens too (in other words, a number nearly equal to the total population of the city) were predisposed to rise against the king.

But such representations of a towering Lollard menace are also, and invariably, accompanied by a second motive, in which a present threat of Lollard assertion or misrule is found actually to exist under the sufferance and full dominion of structures already in place but concealed from view. Such an alternative structure is certainly present in Walsingham's passage, and in an unusually heightened form. Even prior to the passage in question, we have been told that certain among the conspirators had been stirred by fear to warn the king of danger and how it might be avoided (*Historia Anglicana*, v. 2, p. 447), and a strong secondary theme of this passage concerns the extent to which he has taken advance account of every stratagem directed against him. We are told that the king is aware of the Lollard plan from the outset, and that he chooses exactly the right moment in the night to make his move; that the king is prepared when the right moment comes; that his plans exhibit consummate shrewdness ('calliditas'); that he is already in possession of the field before his enemies can make a move. The Lollards, faced with such foresight, seem strangely paralyzed; indeed, they fall, trancelike and unaware, into the hands of the royal forces. Having asserted Lollard strength and menace, the author thus counters with a contradictory analysis: the Lollards actually never had a chance, were beaten before they started, were wholly undermined by superior insight – were, in fact, no worthy adversaries at all.

This same tissue of contradictions is repeated within the characterization of the Lollards and their motivation. Against all common sense – given Oldcastle's fugitive status and scant resources – Walsingham writes off the loyalty of his followers as craven desire for reward. The Lollards, Walsingham says, streamed toward St Giles's Fields because Oldcastle had promised them rewards. Later he will exemplify this claim in the person of one William Murlee of Dunstable – mockingly (and snobbishly) described as a rich brewer, who had come hoping for a knighthood, and had brought his own gilt spurs and other equipage for the ceremony (ibid., v. 2, pp. 448–449) – an illustrative tale that serves his purpose well, and has, surprisingly, impressed twentieth-century historians as well. All this being said, however, he veers to a directly contradictory assertion – that Henry, having offered a handsome reward for Oldcastle's capture,[46] found no takers, thus concluding 'almost all the country to have been seized of his dementia.' The reward was, in fact, to stand for three more years, and Oldcastle to remain at large throughout the period, before he would be captured and the reward, eventually, claimed. In the meantime, the unclaimed reward remains in unresolved opposition to Walsingham's claims about Lollard greed.

A leaderless revolt?

Coherent as the narratives of the 10 January indictment and the Walsingham elaboration might seem at first exposure, they thus not only harbor, but are founded upon, a series of irreconcilable contradictions: Lollards as limitlessly threatening/as pathetically feeble; the king as imperiled/never in trouble; Lollards as precocious planners/as belated dupes; rebels as overpowering in their numbers/as stragglers and no-shows; Lollards driven by ambition or greed/as beyond ambition or greed. Each of these contradictions effectively surrounds an unrepresented place: the place of unscreened information, the 'undoctored' account, the balanced assessment of 'what happened.' Pre-eminent among these unrepresented places is one as yet undiscussed: the place of leadership, the enigmatic location of Oldcastle himself. For Oldcastle, the presumed (or at least legendary) mover and field leader of this event, is himself lost somewhere between inexplicable absence and absurd over-presence in these accounts.

Evidently lingering in London after his escape, in the autumn and winter months leading up to and embracing the events at St Giles,[47] Oldcastle seems never to have shown up on the morning of 10 January. His presence is not even hinted in the original 10 January indictment, where Acton and Blake are treated as leaders of the rising and Oldcastle himself is mentioned only as a possible regent of the realm in the rebels' long-term plans. He is, on the contrary, everywhere in Walsingham's account, but always as an object of aspiration and desire ('when asked whom they sought they responded: the lord of Cobham') and never as tangibly present at the scene. Furthermore, the first official notice taken of Oldcastle, on 11 January, a proclamation directed to the sheriffs of the counties and offering reward for his seizure, concerns not his *presence*, but his *absence* from the events at St Giles's Fields and their aftermath.[48] Rather than asserting Oldcastle's presence or participation, this proclamation contents itself merely by asserting his general support for the Lollard cause, his condemnation for heresy and his unorthodox preaching, the general conspiracy of Lollards seeking the king's death, the capture and sentence of death on Lollards and others already taken at the previously mentioned event ('occasione praemissa'), and then offering a reward for Oldcastle's arrest. In short, this proclamation is marked by two telling blind spots: the first its failure to specify the nature of the 'occasione praemissa,' and the second its failure even to claim Oldcastle's presence there.

Oldcastle's absence constitutes an undoubted affront to the satisfactory completion of a conspiracy theory, a representational breach that demanded swift repair. The repair in question was to be textual in nature, and, gaining wide and rapid acceptance, it would ultimately be codified and officialized in a single text, the compilation of judicial documents relating to the events of 10 January, as preserved in what amounts to its Lancastrian 'record and process': the *Coram Rege* Roll or records of the court of King's Bench, Public Record Office MS. KB 27/ 611/ (rex) mem. 7. This compilation includes the original indictment, but no longer in what can be considered its original form. It is a 'working' text, a text bent and reshaped for the accomplishment of shifting social objectives.

In its subsequent appearances (as recopied, for example, in the Rolls of Parliament,[49] and most recently in the superb modern edition of G. O. Sayles), this judicial compilation looks like a finished document. But the actual King's Bench manuscript constantly betrays its own synthetic nature: by internal, linguistic markers, and also by varying hands, inks, dates, and one extended erasure and overwriting. Certain of its duplicities have been noted (though not to my knowledge since the nineteenth century), but never extensively pursued.[50] The unrivaled duplicity of this text can be understood only with and through identification of its several compositional strata, the diversity of its sources, and the distortions introduced at each stage of its composition. Because this text embraces other documents, now lost, I will follow the order in which the source-documents were originally composed.

The *first state* of the text, probably entered in mid-February, consists of the following strata:

(1) A reiteration of language appointing the 10 January commission, in verification of its charge.[51]
(2) The commission's 10 January issuance, upon presentment of twelve unnamed jurors, of a *indictamentum* or indictment of Blake and Acton for masterminding the treasonous gathering at St Giles's Fields.

(3) Notation that these documents have been called before the king. Blake and Acton are presumably in custody, but the sheriff is instructed not to fail in arresting them.

(4) Following, still copied in the same ink and the same hand, are the judgments against Blake and Acton, the former rendered on 24 January and the latter on 9 February.

The *second state* of the text includes alterations and emendations introduced no earlier than 1 July 1414 (the date of Oldcastle's outlawry), all in lighter ink and apparently in a single hand. These include:

(5) Two and one-quarter lines of erasure,[52] into which, in a new ink and hand, the following is written: 'per litteras ipsius domini Regis patentes assignatis apud Westmonasterium die Mercurii proxima post festum Epiphanie Domini anno regni Regis Henrici quinti post conquestum primo per sacramentum xii juratorum extitit presentatum *quod Johannes Oldecastell de Coulyng in Comitatu Kancie Chivaler dominus*,' now followed by the names Walter Blake, chaplain, and Roger Acton, knight as additional defendants.[53]

(6) Addition of the word 'dictum' ['dcm'] before the original mention of Oldcastle, as Blake and Acton's choice for regent of the land.

(7) Appended is a description of the steps leading to a 1 July 1414 declaration of Oldcastle's outlawry.

A *third state* of the text involves an addendum, in another ink and a third hand:

(8) A notation that the foresaid 'record and process,' as it touches upon said John Oldcastle, has been brought before the parliament for Oldcastle's final trial, on 14 December 1417.

Much representational ground is traversed in the development of this highly synthetic text. It begins by mingling excerpts from the original commission of inquiry, in which no names of suspects appear, and the original indictment, in which Blake and Acton are named as co-leaders of the conspiracy, with Oldcastle mentioned only subsequently as the intended regent of the realm. Also included, without reference to Oldcastle, are the judgments against Blake and Acton. The crucial stage in Oldcastle's insertion occurs with an erasure and the somewhat awkward insertion of 'Oldecastell' ahead of Blake and Acton as principal defendant in the case.[54] This insertion requires, in turn, the addition of 'dictum' before the passage which was formerly his first mention, in relation to his intended regency. This section might have been added at any time between the declaraton of Oldcastle's outlawry on 1 July 1414 and the preparation of a *separate* copy of the record and process for the use of parliament on the occasion of Oldcastle's final trial on 14 December 1417, although probably closer to the former than the latter date. Finally, a concluding (and misleading) notation to the effect that the foregoing material was brought before parliament. The version taken by Chief Justice Hankford to parliament was, however, an *edited* version, consisting of the record and process with respect to John Oldcastle ('recordum et processum . . . quo ad dictum Iohannem Oldescatell').[55] The reasons for this parliamentary text's condensations are clear enough: Blake and Acton being out of the way, and thus finished items, Oldcastle is now parliament's sole concern.[56] Nonetheless, the parliamentary document has the effect of completing an established trajectory, instating Oldcastle as the sole leader of the conspiracy. 'Johannes Oldecastell . . . et alii, Lollardi vulgariter nuncupati' now become the objects of the indictment, with Blake and Acton thrown into the general Lollard pool, appearing only as 'alii,' and with proceedings against them completely omitted.

This same progression, in which Oldcastle is brought forward and Blake and Acton are set aside, occurs within the textual record as a whole. None of the 10–11 January texts asserts Oldcastle's presence at St Giles's Fields; he appears in the texts of the second day as a missing person, one who, *not* present at St Giles, is now sought. Only with the forgery now before us, and narratives composed in 1416–22, does Oldcastle assume his designated historical role as leader of the 'rebellion' which bears his name: as (still absent) rallying point in Walsingham, and finally in the *Gesta Henrici* as a doubly dastardly personage, as arch-plotter who is excessively present but who, upon learning of the king's arrival, *then* cravenly disappears ('adversarius vero inde premonitus disparuit').

The question remains why Henry V and advisers like Arundel (who suddenly appears along with the commissioners at the 10 January breakfast at the Tower) and a host of Lancastrian ideologues collaborated so energetically in the creation and personalization of their own opposition. Perhaps the case against Oldcastle, including evidence of sedition and a claim of his earlier outlawry, was being strengthened in preparation for his parliamentary trial.[57] But Oldcastle's own status as a condemned heretic, previously delivered to the secular arm for punishment, and his escape from the Tower would surely have sufficed for his 1417 conviction. The motive here instead seems characteristically Lancastrian: the objectification of opposition in a sufficiently vivid form to permit a reciprocal stabilization of the Lancastrian king as the guarantor of civil order and ecclesiastical orthodoxy. This objectification permitted a shaping of the supposed conspiracy in terms of agency and malign purpose, into a form suitable for narration. This form was far more amenable to the highly dichotomized or polarized narrative which Walsingham and other Lancastrian writers were shortly to produce.

Subsequent to his 1413 breakout from the Tower, Oldcastle must have found himself the object of a very powerful – almost society-wide – act of interpellation, shared by foes and probably some friends as well, in which he was portrayed as a revolutionary leader and imaginer of carnage on the grandest of scales. Yet this was finally a refused interpellation, in the sense that the historical Oldcastle, holding tenaciously to his reformist religious views, left no unequivocal evidence of having accepted the revolutionary social mandate the Lancastrians sought so persistently to thrust upon him. He lived to see the beginnings of his own fictionalization, a process continued soon after his death in texts like the Carsewell confession (see Chapter 5), eventually travestied in Shakespeare's Falstaff/Oldcastle,[58] and celebrated in seventeenth- and eighteenth-century romantic biography.

Between Oldcastle's 1413 prison escape and his 1417 condemnation and execution, he became a kind of will-o'-the-wisp, sighted everywhere and firmly located nowhere. His presence can be glimpsed, but fleetingly and in the act of disappearance, in the prison break itself, residual signs of occupancy in previously vacated houses, odd manifestations to wayfarers and non-allied conspirators,[59] together with a hundred other schemes and plots and dead ends and false clues. His final identity is phantasmagorical, in the sense that his last years were lived – as Antigone lives in Lacan's formulation[60] – between two deaths. As a convicted heretic, and escapee from the Tower and an indicted traitor, he had already (like Antigone) undergone the first death, or death to the symbolic order; awaiting him, like Antigone in her tomb, was the second, or corporeal death-of-the-body.[61] Oldcastle, in other words, becomes effectively spectral, which is to say that his extraneous presence 'haunts' these texts, challenges them with reminders of what they have excluded.[62] Rather than a documentable presence which seals and guarantees Lancastrian conspiracy claims, Oldcastle is an absence who, endlessly written about, still eludes his representations, in ways which persistently challenge the Lancastrian account.

Providential history

Oldcastle's strange mix of absence and presence, vulnerability and menace, renders him an apt leader for a movement already contradictory in its attributes and burdened with so many unlikely objectives. His own role, and that of the flawed movement he supposedly led, become coherent only when they are taken as illustrations of the peculiar logic and surprising manifestation of providential history. At the providential level God tolerates – in fact sponsors – apparent discrepancies in order to institute exemplary lessons of his own choosing, as when Walsingham suggests divine management of the whole affair, with God intervening to be certain that Henry will prevail:

> God Omnipotent did not want the innocent to perish at the hands of the guilty; but he sent his fear into the hearts of certain conspirators, who warned the king to avoid danger. (p. 447)

As is frequently the case, Henry is briefly found *inopinate*, unaware of the plot against him. But, rather than exposing a weakness, his lack of foresight prepares the way for a demonstration of God's providential concern for Lancastrian well-being. Henry is promptly – even gloriously – restored to a position of superior knowledge. These divinely inspired double agents enable him to overcome the asserted Lollard advantage in personnel and tactics. Made temporarily to seem weak, he is promptly revealed as divinely aided and hence invincibly strong.

Even as prince, Henry seems to have grasped the possibilities of this trope. Reporting to his father on one of his victories in Wales, the younger Henry portrayed his own forces as numerically inferior, but nevertheless able to conquer by God's favor: 'but it is well seen that victory does not lie with the multitude of people, and this was well demonstrated there, but "en la puissance de Dieu."'[63] Subject to endless elaboration in relation to Henry's career as king, this same observation served equally well on occasions when it was objectively true (as in analyses of the victory at Agincourt) and when it was not. It permeates the pro-Lancastrian *Gesta Henrici Quinti*, at a particularly deep level. Here, the consistent purpose is to reveal Henry, at home and abroad, as the true elect of God: 'ut verus electus dei.'[64] This author frames his account of St Giles's Fields so that Henry not only prevails, but prevails in an instructive way, as part of a probationary process. For all his apparent might, Oldcastle is in turn reduced to an agent of divine destiny:

> God . . . in order that at once vexation might promote understanding and that his elect might have been proven ['probaretur'] in the furnace of tribulation, allowed an adversary to rise against him, a certain John Oldcastle. . . . (*Gesta*, p. 2.)

As with all such cases of proving or probation, care is taken to specify that God's chosen party remains unsubjected to frivolous temptation or testing, or at least that elements of temptation are introduced only purposefully and within limits. Referring to pre-trial interviews between the king and Oldcastle, the author reassures his reader that limits are in place: 'holy and merciful God . . . permits nobody to be tempted beyond their capacities' (ibid., p. 4).

God's role as benign stage-manager is palpably asserted, in this text, by a detail found nowhere else: once Henry has taken his position at St Giles's Fields, a brilliant sign appears in the sky: 'suddenly, seen to our west, the sky seemed to open and a splendid star to issue forth which, descending, soared between the poles between us and the north, and with a great flash of light grew in length until it was extended two bow-shots.' (ibid., p. 10). The author leaves the matter of interpretation to God, but notes that many considered it as a beacon of faith ('ad illuminacionem fidei'). Although modern historians have been inclined to take this assertion at face value,[65] it bears all the hallmarks of an invention, staged in relation to its designs within the signifying order.

From the standpoint of providence, Oldcastle appeared independently strong but was always a minor component of God's plan, raised up in order to fail; Henry appeared vulnerable but was always numbered among God's elect. Both Oldcastle and Henry experienced God's scourge, but in order that one might be consumed (like a false coin in the fire of probation) and the other consummated (or made complete in his Christian destiny): 'Istum ut consumeret, alterum ut consummaret.' In this respect, apparent contradictions can be resolved and converted to meaningful commentary, within God's providential order. As in the previous anecdote of the infernal machine in the bedstraw, even seemingly discrepant details are functional and contributory to this new order of meaning. Oldcastle is, for example, assigned a position of trust within the king's very household: 'unum de precarissimis et magis domesticis suis' (ibid., p. 2). But the point here (as with the domestic origin of the earlier plot) is less to describe a position actually occupied by Oldcastle, than to point a particular perfidy unsettling to the order of things, which is to be set right as a consequence of God's intervention (there, *deo volente*; here, because Henry is *electus dei*).

The sense of the Lollard-scourging Henry V as *electus dei* is preliminary to that even grander assertion of his providential mission, and vindication of his claims, through his subsequent victories over the French and arrangements to regain the French crown. The author of the *Gesta* already knows of his success at Agincourt, and expects even grander consequences from the coming campaigns about which he enthuses at the end of his work. But, even at the moment of most prepossessing success in France, the utility of the Lollards as a necessary antagonism and a continuing spur to Lancastrian accomplishment and consolidation is not forgotten. Euphorically celebrating the triumph at Agincourt, the *Gesta* thanks God's special relation to the English people as the source of all success, and then reminds readers of the need to please God continually. As it happens, the avenue to God's pleasure is already familiar to us: England is to do its part by extirpating heresies and errors.[66]

*

This discussion of providential framing does not result from facile skepticism about the eligibility of texts to provide historical information. Tools of late twentieth-century textual analysis encourage the discovery of structuring oppositions in all kinds of texts, yet the existence of inner contradiction need not disqualify the text as a source of information. The point is, rather, to decide *what sort of information* a text can reasonably be expected to provide. Some texts, constituted by processes of opposition and exclusion, may nevertheless be aligned with or provide information about actual occurrences. Other texts, effectively invented within large and commonly held interpretative structures, are likewise historical, but only in the sense of providing information about time-bound patterns of perception and belief. The extremity of Walsingham's and the *Gesta*'s divisions, and the extreme undecidability of their rival claims, urge their inclusion in the latter category. Certainly, they are fully 'historical,' in the information they provide about what fifteenth-century society was prepared to believe about Lollards. And beliefs are themselves 'historical,' issuing in very material and poignant consequences of anti-Lollard persecution. But I would not turn to them for information about what happened on 10 January, or John Oldcastle's whereabouts on that disputed day.

The obscure and apparently disparate occurrences at St Giles on 10 January achieved coherence as an apparent event primarily as a result of Lancastrian will. Interestingly, the record of Lancastrian actions subsequent to 10 January suggests a rapid dispersal even of Lancastrian insistence on this event's solidity, a withdrawal of the very conviction that underwrote its *événémentielle* status in the first place. Not only the narratives of the event but also the records of prosecution show a continuing confusion over the issues of Lollardy vs. sedition, with the two offenses coinciding in a minority of cases.[67] The rarity of the coincidence is undoubtedly traceable largely to issues of separate ecclesiastical and civil jurisdiction, and to other variables such as recantation. Nevertheless, uncertainty on this issue even on the part of commissioners, investigators, and juries suggests a high degree of continuing confusion over the precise nature of the offense in question. Focus was also blurred by a surge of unanticipated accusations and denunciations, issuing from beyond immediate Lancastrian control and from motives beyond the scope of Lancastrian interest; slippage in Lancastrian control over the contours of the event is indicated as early as 11 January, when a royal proclamation forbade accusations of Lollardy for private gain.[68] Issuance of wholesale pardons commenced soon after the first mass execution of rebels on 13 January. Henry Dene, fuller, received a pardon on 23 January.[69] Others followed on 28 March[70] and 9 December (Thomson), with a specific offer of pardon to Oldcastle himself on 16 December 1415.[71] The earliest pardons are themselves broadly concessive on matters of evidence and its reliability; although reiterating the broad outlines of the Lancastrian account of the conspiracy, the 28 March pardon also notes that many basically loyal subjects may have been victims of malice or untrue information.[72]

The Lancastrians were in a good position to relinquish their proprietorship of this event and its narration – not only in order to seize an opportunity to present the king as merciful as well as severe,[73] but also because a host of objectives had already been attained. Vividly demonstrated were the king's providential foreknowledge of events, his capacity for prompt action against civil and ecclesiastical schismatics, and his unifying gift of mercy to dubiously worthy subjects. Henceforth, his position as agent of God's providence and defender of orthodoxy would be transferred to other arenas.[74] Now, having thoroughly exploited 'the Oldcastle rising' as an occasion for consolidating his position, he could well afford to relax the resolute attention which permitted this diffuse and occluded moment to be grasped and handled as a 'rebellion' at all. Considering its consequences, he had reason to consider 10 January a day well worth the labor of its own invention.

The Southampton conspirators

On the morning of 10 January 1414, Henry, Lord Scrope, one of the commissioners charged to hear and determine the extent of sedition in the St Giles rising, joined a handful of other royal insiders for the celebratory breakfast served that morning in the Tower. The following year, Scrope was himself arrested, tried, and executed as one of three principal conspirators against the king's life in that feeble, puzzling, and almost inexplicable conspiracy known as the 'Southampton Plot.'

Henry V and his intimates appear to have been somewhat less active in shaping and promulgating this event than they were in the case of the Oldcastle rising. Then, Henry played a leading role in consolidating an event from which he clearly expected to reap tangible propaganda advantages. The Southampton conspirators seem initially to have been slated for a quieter prosecution, with a minimum of publicity and a bias toward representational economy. In the solicited confessions of the conspirators and the documents of the trial itself, potentially embarrassing disclosures and novel interpretations are consistently minimized, in favor of well-worn and even platitudinous accusations and observations. Nevertheless, the operations of what might be called 'Lancastrian propaganda' never depended on the will of the king alone, or even that of his immediate advisers and council, but resulted from the initiative and actions of a considerably more dispersed group of Lancastrian-aligned commentators. Enjoying varying degrees of relation to the throne, members of this extended group ranged from Thomas of Elmham and the author of the early *Gesta Henrici Quinti* (whose services were presumably remunerated) through the still-Lancastrian but more detached observations of chroniclers like Walsingham (once bitterly opposed to Lancastrian fortunes) and those of mixed affiliation like Waurin (who fought on the side of the French at Agincourt before aligning himself with the English) through others whose complicity was entirely a matter of subjective wishes and desires and whose participation conferred no practical advantage at all. Members of this diffuse alignment collaborated in reworking the events and records of this potential embarrassment to turn them to Lancastrian account. Many of their representational strategies – including near-obsession with being and seeming, claims of royal foreknowledge, emphasis on divine probation and providential legitimation – are familiar. But activation of these strategies within a potentially inhospitable body of materials necessitated refinement of the tools of Lancastrian apologue.

The dynamics of self-accusation

The 'Southampton Plot' appears not to have reached the stage of a finished conspiracy (or, in the words of participant Scrope, a 'grounded purpose')[75] when the earl of March revealed it to Henry V shortly before the departure of his first expedition to France. It seems to have been at a conversational and exploratory stage, during which several far-fetched scenarios were being bandied about among a small group of malcontents, when the earl lost his nerve and reported his associates to the king. Henry immediately ordered the arrest of the three principals: Richard, earl of Cambridge, Henry, Lord Scrope of Masham, and Thomas Gray, knight, of Heton. All promptly confessed to varied wrongdoings. Gray, as a simple knight, was tried, convicted, and executed by jury, before the king's commissioners, on 2 August 1415; Cambridge and Scrope, as peers, were convicted by a distinguished group (including accuser March) gathered and awaiting the expedition to France, and were executed that same day, 5 August 1415.

The earl of March's conversation with his king remaining off the record, the confessions of the three principals constitute the only evidence in the case. Written in the conspirators' own hands in the hope of eliciting a merciful response from the king,[76] these confessions convey an oddly selective view of events. They are, indeed, discursively ample – Gray insists with some persuasive force that 'I have wretyn to yowe al that I knaw' – but they remain curiously unrevealing with regard to the conspirators' motives and long-term objectives. Attaining frequent and rather manic heights of self-indictment, they strike the reader with an odd sense of second-handedness, belatedness, and comic-opera intrigue. These oddities are, I believe, traceable to the complicit and purpose-written nature of the confessions, including an anxious accommodation to things the Lancastrians might and might not have wanted said. So eager are the conspirators to seek exoneration through self- and mutual incrimination that they give an impression of almost apologetically hastening themselves off-stage in order to clear the way for more important Lancastrian business to follow.

The plan, as briefly outlined in Cambridge's confession to Henry V, was to enlist the earl of March, as true heir, and

> to have a hadde the forseyd Erle in to the lond of Walys wyth outyn yowre lycence takyng up on hym the sovereynte of thys lond yif yondyr manis persone, wych they callyn Kynge Richard hadde nauth bene alyve, as y wot wel that he nys not alyve . . . ; and as for the forme of a proclamacyoun wych schulde hadde bene cryde in the Erle name as the heyre to the corowne of Ynglond, a geyns yow, my lege Lord calde by auntreu [untrue] name Harry of Lancastre usurpur of Ynglond . . . , havyng wyth the Erle a baner of the armes of Ynglond, havyng also the coroune of Speyne on a palet, wych my lege lord is one of yowre weddys [pledges].[77]

Additional elements of the supposed plan include bringing the Richard imitator as well as Harry Percy from Scotland and encouraging risings and castle seizures in Wales. Every one of these stratagems – with the pathetic exception of displaying a former crown of Spain – had been attempted without success during the reign of

Henry IV, and none of them had even as much chance of succeeding now. Attempts to rally around the earl of March in Wales had failed even when Glyndwr was at full strength and the Percies and Northampton had yet to take the field. So much less chance would such an endeavor enjoy in 1415, with Glyndwr having not mounted a foray since his desperate defeat in 1410, and now only weeks from his dismal and solitary death; with Henry Percy's heir and namesake a successful petitioner of the king and about to return to England on harmonious terms with the Lancastrians;[78] with the earl of March wholly in Henry V's power, as a result of his indebtedness to the king for his marriage;[79] and with even the Richard *imitator*, Thomas Ward of Trumpington, dead since 1414.

In fact, the impracticality of this plan does not await discovery by the modern historian; the confessions produce their own, internal critique – not only implicitly but also explicitly in the despairing analysis that Scrope claims to have offered March, in an attempt to dissuade him from the venture:

> y schewid hym quat perils wolde faule yif he drue to Loulardis thai wolde subuert this londe & the chirge . . . if they made hym take a felde ye schulde com on hym . . . & distrue hym & yif he wente in to Wals he schulde be enfamind & lost & yif he went by se with weselz of awauntage he schulde be takin & undon. . . .

Scrope undoubtedly somewhat overestimates the Lollards as a revolutionary force, but he is certainly right in his suggestion that they would be incompatible allies. He is also right about Lancastrian military superiority; the provident Henry had, in fact, arranged to post garrisons to assure civil order in his absence,[80] and the previous misadventures of Archbishop Scrope, Northumberland, and other would-be rebels suggest that these conspirators would have fared no better in the field. So, too, do the effective collapse of Glyndwr's rebellion and that leader's own fugitive status suggest that Wales would have been an ineffective place of resort. Finally, Henry having marshalled the largest naval force of the century for his invasion, Scrope is right to assign him effective control of the sea.[81] In other words, Scrope's analysis is everywhere on the mark, and wholly devastating to the conspirators' prospects.[82]

Might this pathethic plot simply be a 'mock-up,' invented so that its supposed principals would have *something* to which they might confess? This conclusion gains some support from the worn and tawdry nature of the materials from which it is assembled. It is, in the final analysis, a conceptually threadbare fabrication, a plagiarization from scraps of actual 1400–5 conspiracies that happened to be lying around.

Both accusation and confession seem to have been imagined into being according to the general model of the Epiphany rising of 1400, in which a handful of disgruntled and under-preferred earls sought to extinguish the Lancastrian line by taking and killing Henry IV and his sons in ambuscade. The one charge indignantly rejected by Scrope – that of imagining the death of the king and his brothers – seems a deliberate prosecutorial reprise of that earlier fiasco. Additionally, as Cambridge tells it, in the passage which was also to be adopted as the core of the indictment at his and Scrope's trial, other elements of the plan appear to have been borrowed from the Mortimer–Percy intrigues of 1402–4. The whole notion of a Welsh-based rising on behalf of Richard, should he live, echoes the strategy and even the language of that earlier time.[83] An additional, and even closer, counterpart is to be found in Lady Despenser's failed attempt to abduct the young earl of March and his brother to Wales in 1405.[84]

What process (other than torture, which is said not to have occurred),[85] could have persuaded the conspirators to plead guilty to so unpromising a plan? Some derivative of 'approvership,' in which a criminal seeks a pardon by cooperating in the conviction of his former associates, may have been at work here. But a deeper and less pragmatically based form of complicity seems to be involved as well. A starting-point for the analysis of this complicity might be the breadth and fervor of the conspirators' self-accusations. Well beyond the imaginings and deeds of which they are accused, they repeatedly acknowledge deeper and even more perverse betrayals, as in Gray's confession of 'vngracius and mesheffus gouernauns.'[86] This same notion of malicious malignity would, of course, be a frequent resort for subsequent commentators. (In the account of Tudor chronicler Hall, for example, Henry can only imagine the conspiracy to have originated in 'madd imaginacion,' in 'some priuate Scorpion in your hartes, or some wild worme in your heads.'[87]) Such an explanation in turn suggests an analogy between the abject Christian before his judgmental/merciful God and the guilty subject before his judgmental/merciful king. Gray addresses Henry 'withe hert knelyng and body knelyng [before] yowr powr,' finding 'no men be twene God and me but yowe.' Like Marlowe's Faustus facing judgment from his God, Gray shrinks from this terrible and final conclusion, imagining himself obliterated, buried alive, his name unknown: 'qweke dolfyn . . . my name never to be rehersit.' Obliteration not being possible, Gray (again like Faustus) turns eucharistic, expressing his fervent 'lofe of yowr gracius hert and body,' above any earthly thing of this world. In a mangled but tantalizing passage, Gray seems even to suggest that frustration of his fervent admiration for the king has brought him to something analogous to a state of religious despair, that 'powert cofetice and princepaly yowr hegh . . . hafe broghte me to this . . . shame' (ibid.).

Similar ambivalences lurk in the confessions of Scrope (who could confess to the charge of planning a rebellion in Wales but indignantly reject any suggestion that he might have imagined the death of the king) and Cambridge (who seemed never, despite his rebellious plans, to cease describing himself as Henry's 'liege man,' or considering himself eligible to be taken 'into the hands of your merciful and piteous grace'). Naturally enough, they rely on the king's mercy now that they have no other hope; but also evident in these passages would seem to be a certain desire for ingratiation, their desire to erase shame by associating themselves with Henry's intentions and destinies – if necessary, by proving themselves to be the very plotters he has accused them of being.

Acknowledging themselves guilty of something very close to original sin (albeit with the spiritual realm transposed to the allied realm of sacramentally invested power), these suspects are offered a species of redemption, which accords them a place in the larger Lancastrian design. For even the snake (like other low plotters) has a part in the drama of redemption. The condition of their entry into the drama of Lancastrian triumph is their acceptance and willing elaboration of their assigned role as treasonous plotters. The mechanisms of such an acceptance have been observed in other connections. In *Darkness at Noon*, for example, Koestler suggests that confessed plotters cease to distinguish between actions committed in fact and those which they merely should have committed as a consequence of their opinions. Acknowledging themselves guilty of certain doubts about Lancastrian legitimacy, our plotters seem ready to accuse themselves of anything under the sun, almost (though not quite) to the point – as in Shakespeare's elaboration of the same scene – of rejoicing in their capture. Like Koestler's Rubashov, they discover a measure of purpose in turning themselves into object-lessons (in Rubashov's case, making way for the Stalinist project of socialism in one country; in this case, for the destinies of Lancastrian kingship).

Discovering God's will

With parliamentary ratification of the executions in November 1415, the Lancastrians scored at least a short-term victory in their quick and apparently costless dispatch of several aristocratic malcontents. In fact, during the years immediately following, the circle of complicit Lancastrian commentators set out to convert the plot into a positive opportunity for propagandist advantage.

The central theme of Henry V's first years might be said to involve justice, as exercised by the king and as the basis for divine support of his endeavors. Henry Beaufort, bishop of Winchester, summed up the Lancastrian credo in his opening address to the parliament of November 1415 – that parliament in which the condemnation of the Southampton conspirators was ratified, and, more importantly, the parliament at which the recent Agincourt victory was celebrated. Among the formal *theames* of the parliament was Henry's watchword against the French, which, according to Beaufort, was 'Certa pro justicia, & Dominus pugnabit pro te' – strive for justice and God will fight on your side.[88] Henry's domestic hallmark emphasized justice too: 'Sine justicia non regitur respublica' – without justice the republic is not ruled. This formula, in which Henry shows himself to be a just ruler, and thus to be worthy of God's support, seemed to many commentators immanent in his handling of the Southampton plot.

Once again, an apparent problem for Lancastrian rulership is converted into a valuable resource for its vindication. The avidly pro-Henrician *Gesta Henrici Quinti*, for example, frames the entire episode as a trial, in which God, wishing to test the constancy of his elected ruler, permits him to be assailed ('deus, volens experiri constanciam electi sui, permisit eum iterato temptari').[89] The trial is quickly passed, through God's deliverance and the less likely vehicle of March's confession:

> But He who sits above the cherubim and beholds the depths, and knows how vain are the deliberations of men, soon delivered the just from the ungodly ['cito liberavit iustum ab impiis'] and revealed the Judas-like iniquity and treason of these evil men through the lord Mortimer. (*Gesta*, pp. 18–19)

God's favor is revealed simply through the exposure of the plot, but it is the *just* king who is delivered, and Henry vindicates his delivery by revealing his justice in several ways. One is by his relative lenience, with none of the three being disemboweled or hanged. Only Scrope, as a Garter knight and (in the words of the *Gesta*) 'the more culpable an enemy because the more intimate a friend,' is publicly drawn to his place of beheading. Chronicler Walsingham comments on this lenience, observing that 'the king pardoned them the other penalties which might have been imposed by law,' and suggesting that 'he is said to have wept at their reversals' ('deflevisse vices eorum fertur').[90]

Henry's restraint is accompanied and recognized by his selection as the vehicle of God's plan. The detection of his adversaries once again proceeds, according to Walsingham, 'Deo volente,' by God's will.[91] The chronicler of Cotton Claudius A. viii. 8 observes that 'almighty god of his grete grace held his holy hand ouer hem and saued hem from this perillous meyne.' And the Digby poet, writing around the time of Henry's coronation and not necessarily in relation to this particular event, emphasizes the divine aspect of Henry's success:

> Men do in derk, god seeth in lyght
> Synne, morthere, derne tresoun,
> Not may be hyd fro goddis syght.
> To ryghtwys Iuge, god geueth the crowne.[92]

Penetrating treasonous schemes, God awards the crown to the just king. The king's justice is revealed relationally, and sin, murder, and treason have their place as foils to his righteousness, restraint, and legitimacy. In pursuance of this logic, the treasonous content of the conspiracy received early and extensive elaboration.

The principal expression of Henry's concern for justice was his demand for the crown of France, and the principal evidence of God's support for Henry was his success in the French campaign. Accusations of treason against the conspirators were therefore magnified by the suggestion that they had practiced not only against the king and his brothers, but against his plan to invade France. This suggestion is essentially avoided in the indictment, and then merely shadowed in the peers' final judgment that Scrope had rebelled against his allegiance and against his native land as well – 'contra Dominum suum Ligeum & linguam in qua natus est.'[93] This avoidance, in an indictment otherwise shaped almost entirely toward conviction by any available means, becomes all the more remarkable since the conspirators' confessions open the door to this very accusation. According to Gray, at any rate, Scrope had opined to Cambridge that it was 'best to breke this viage if hit meghte be done,' and the two men had talked together about destroying the ships gathered for the invasion, with Cambridge concluding that 'hym thoghte best to bren the sheppes. (ibid.).' Presumably, in the days prior to Agincourt, such suggestions, even if available within the written record, were too hot to handle. Once Henry had scored his signal success at Agincourt, restraints were removed, and important capital was to be had for his subsequent French endeavors by documenting the futility of opposition to his earlier invasion plans.

Such documentation proceeded apace in the post-Agincourt era, with increasing elaboration of the plotters' Francophile motivations. First off the mark was the *Gesta Henrici Quinti*, an entire work authored, in the view of its modern editors, to generate support for

Henry's designs on the throne of France. There we read that the conspirators were 'corrupted by a desire for domination, but more by the
odor of French promises or rewards' ('potius odore promissorum vel
munerum Gallicorum') '. . . to the hindering of the proposed expedition.' Walsingham likewise suggests that Scrope intrigued with the
enemy ('tractabat cum hostibus,' p. 506), and Adam of Usk adds
an occasion and a motive: that the French ambassadors, supposedly
treating for peace in the weeks before the invasion, bought Scrope's
cooperation in killing the king or hindering his voyage with a great
sum of gold ('in magno redemerunt auro': pp. 254–255). The notion of
lucre, having been introduced, became progressively central. A mid-
century poem has it that 'Lordys of this lond oure Kyng gan there sell,/
For a million of gold as y herd say.'[94] The Davies chronicle, of *c.* 1460–
70, says that the three lords 'had receyued an huge summe of money,
that is to say, a milion of gold, forto betraie the king and his bretheryn
to the Frenshemen,'[95] and the late-century chronicle of Cotton MS.
Claudius A. viii embraces the same accusation (f. 2), linking it with the
claim that only God's 'holy hand' could have saved the king in this
desperate case. Such matters of motivation and proof were hardly at
issue in the original trial of these openly confessed traitors. Now they
are amply supplied, but with emphasis moving to where it always
implicitly lay: on Henry's own probation and vindication as a vehicle
of God's will.

Constantly at the edge of the Southampton discussions, and soon
moved to the center, is the deceptiveness of external evidence and the
necessity for rigorous probation in the distinction between the false
and the true. The author of the *Gesta* supposed that God had framed
the Southampton plot in order for Henry to be tested or tried
('experiri', 'tentatari') and shown worthy, and probation of the conspirators now reveals them as flawed or corrupt. This emphasis on
probation addresses a point of Lancastrian anxiety, that corruption
cannot always be detected from external appearance. Henry, a promising king, had to be proven in practice, and duplicity from within
his circle of peers and (in the case of Scrope) Garter knights could
not have been predicted from their external appearance of loyal submission. A possible disjunction having been opened between outer
appearance or display and inner disposition, 'proof' is needed to
repair or close the gap. Probation of visual phenomena and the critical
disparity of inner and outer are, of course, general medieval themes
and by no means specific to the Lancastrian era. Nevertheless, as
thematized in the poetry of Hoccleve and Lydgate, and as realized in
Lollard trials and recurrent attacks on counterfeiting and other dis-
simulative practices, the possible disparity between seeming and being

reached crisis proportions in Lancastrian England (see Chapters 2 and 5). Opportunities to pursue the issue in terms favorable to Lancastrian claims, as here, were seldom spurned.

In addition to exposing dissimulation, the Southampton accounts emphasize the ties of loyalty which should have bound the conspirators and their king. Scrope is singled out for particular attention in both regards. Walsingham, for example, finds him a master of hypocrisy with respect to outward deeds. Rising to classical citation, he borrows from Claudian against Rufinus in order to judge him guilty of simulating faith, concealing the menace in his countenance with a smile, even while full of savagery and desire for cupidinous reward ('lucrique cupidine fervens') (*Historia Anglicana*, vol. 2, p. 305). This trope solidifies in numerous subsequent accounts; Capgrave's mid-century chronicle is representative, in its sole emphasis on Scrope and its observation that 'Sobir was the man in word and chere; and under that ypocrisie had he a ful venemous hert.'[96] Walsingham also, however, finds in Scrope's behavior a failure of office and patriotic responsibility. In negotiations with the French (in which the historical Scrope did indeed play a part), he pretends publicly to favor his own people but inwardly supports the enemy ('fronte favens suis, mente vero Gallis') (ibid.).

As in the case of Oldcastle (but with slightly more foundation), Scrope's perfidy is amplified by a substantially invented recital of the offices of trust and friendship he enjoyed with the king. Walsingham insists that his pretended gravity in counsel was so persuasive that Henry invariably followed his advice, as if it were an oracle fallen from heaven ('velut oraculum e coelo lapsum') (ibid.). This notion of Scrope as a false counselor is, in turn, augmented or replaced in other accounts by an even more pervasive portrayal of Scrope as a false friend. The author of the *Gesta* struck the same note when describing him as a worse enemy because a more intimate friend. This line of possibility comes to fruition in Waurin and subsequent accounts. As Waurin has it, Scrope was so intimate with the king he often slept with him, and even in his own chamber: 'lequel par pluiseurs fois avoit couchie avec le roy et en sa chambre.'[97] Confronted with such a defection, Henry can either be angered (as in Waurin, who finds him 'moult courouchie') or driven to tears (as in Walsingham). In the sixteenth century, Henry's susceptibility to such intimate betrayal undergoes bathetic expansion, when he offers himself, like Christ in late medieval lyric, to an insufficiently grateful populace: 'I embrace you all,' he says in the *Vita Henrici Quinti*, 'with an extraordinary love, and from that source my sorrows overflow' ('amore singulari vos omnes complector, et ex illo fonte omnes mei dolores redundant').[98]

Henrician fabulation

The most ambitious fifteenth-century reworking of the Southampton plot, and especially its discovery, belongs to a French chronicle tradition – present in le Févre,[99] and drawn here from Waurin. This tradition attaches to Henry an anecdote which, although pre-Lancastrian (and certainly pre-Henrician) in origin, touches upon a number of crucial Lancastrian themes. This anecdote presents Henry both as protagonist and as storyteller or fabulist in his own right. The fable, of which Henry is both subject and object, narrator and protagonist, is ultimately Aesopian.[100] The fable is, of course, an enormously flexible and mobile idiom; here it is enlisted on behalf of power, and the capacity of power not only to control discourse but to infiltrate and overbear the sites of alternative imagination.

The situation is this: the conspirators, thinking themselves the more cunning fabulists, approach the earl of March and suggest that he employ a 'fiction' to absent himself from the French expedition, after which they will conspire in Henry's absence to instate March as king. Henry, having learned of the plot, assembles his council and princes and captains (including the conspirators) and spins out an invented, or at any rate hypothetical, fiction of his own, 'en termes per maniere de fiction.' It seems, he says, that some of his subjects had been working ('aulcuns de ses subgects avoient pratiquie') against him and his crown, and he asks how the assembled group would counsel him. He begins with his greatest lords (who counsel severity) and then turns to the three conspirators, who respond,

> 'Sire, he or those who would devise or practise such treason against you, are worthy to suffer a death so cruel that it may be an example to all others. . . .' This counsel having been held, and all the opinions heard, . . . the king caused [the three conspirators] to be confronted and made them to speak in each other's presence . . . and there, without much fine language and without gainsaying, the above-mentioned lords confessed the said deed. . . . Then the king, very angry at the thing which had come to pass through the said lords, whom he greatly loved . . . , had them all three beheaded, then cut into four quarters and sent to the four principal towns of England.[101]

The conspirators here occupy the role of the villains in what the *Motif-Index of Folk-Literature* identifies as type Q581, 'Villain nemesis,' in which a person is condemned to the punishment he has suggested to others.[102] Caxton's Aesop contains at least two variants – one of which might be taken to find the villain in the stronger, the other in the weaker, position. In the fable of 'The Fox, the Wolf, and the Lion,' the wolf, wronged by the fox, suggests to the lion that his adversary be skinned and the skin used for medicinal purposes. Owing to the superior deceits of the fox, it is the wolf who suffers the recommended fate. To whom the fox: 'Who so euer maketh the pytte redy for his broder ofte it happeth that he hym self falleth in the same and is beten with the same rodde that he maketh for other.'[103] In another, a bee, rewarded by Jupiter, overreaches in his request: 'graunte that who so euer shal come for to take awey my hony yf I pryke hym he may sodenly deye.' But Jupiter replies that 'whoso euer shalle goo to take they hony yf thow pryke or stynge hym Incontynent thow shalt deye.'[104] Either way, it is the person lacking mercy or restraint whose words recoil upon him; just as, in this case, those who counsel a cruel death for conspirators have one straightway visited upon them. Whereas this Aesopian structure might be bent against an unjust judge or figure of authority, it is here bent against the weakest persons in the room, the last in order of precedence, with the 'sage et ymaginatif' ruler elevated to an ethically untouchable position as architect of exposure and as final arbiter of justice.

This superior position with respect to the narrative is closely related to another familiar Lancastrian emphasis, upon the sovereign's pervasive powers of discovery and foreknowledge. This power, we learn in Henry's case, is not only prophetic and divinely conferred, but practical as well. Scrope claims to have warned his colleagues prior to their apprehension that 'playnly ye hadde men on euery syde to aspy swilche maner of gouernauns,' and the intelligence that enables the wise and imaginative Henry to bait and spring his trap would seem to bear out Scrope's forebodings.[105] Recognizing the importance of foreknowledge, the Lancastrians not only encouraged stories about it but sought actually to procure it. From the evidence of the Exchequer Rolls, Henry V was unusually involved in surveillance practices during the first years of his reign, particularly with regard to the activities of John Oldcastle. Payments to John de Burgh, John Barton, and Thomas Burton and others who kept watch on Oldcastle and observed houses he was supposed to have occupied have already been noted; the Issue Rolls for 22 February also record payment to a certain valet for reporting on the governance of 'Ewain Glendourdy' (E403/614). Other spies were hired in 1417, including William Scalby and Thomas Horneby in relation to Henry Talbot's conviction for the abduction of the earl of Fife (E403/630) and William Wykeham, servant of the sheriff of Southampton, to locate Lollards Richard Wyche and William Broune (E403/633).[106]

The king's foreknowledge leaves the Southampton conspirators no

option save immediate and confused confession, with less to say and
know about themselves than he can say or know about them. They are,
in a way, emptied out – voided – left with no choice but to substitute
the king's will for their own. This anecdote, in effect, starts them down
the path where they will end in Shakespeare's *Henry V*: glad of capture,
delighted that their pathetic schemes will occasion no interruption
of their monarch's destiny and grand design. And, for now, it offers
additional insight as to why – in these Lancastrian-sponsored confessions and trial records – the conspirators have so little to say for
themselves. Even when eager to confess their guilt, they must fall back
on outworn schemes and exhausted conspiracies of the former decade.
Full comprehension, in this case, is withdrawn from the failed actors
and reassigned to the king who knows their purpose, not only in
advance, but more fully than they can know it themselves.

The return of the Yorkist repressed

The readiness of the conspirators' self-accusations, and the brevity of
the three-day period between the arrests and the first execution, permitted an exceptionally clean trial record from the Lancastrian point of
view. That is, convictions were obtained and the power to eliminate
vestigial dissent was demonstrated without suffering much in the way
of alternative or anti-Lancastrian representation to enter the written
record. The few details in any way disparaging to Lancastrian dynastic
prospects are so hedged by denial and other devices of minimization
that they would hardly seem to constitute a long-term problem, or
even to mark the trace of one. March is mentioned in Cambridge's
letter and in the trial records as 'heyre' to the crown, but only within
the disparaging context of the 'proclamacyoun wych schulde hadde
bene cryde in the Erle name'; only, that is, within that farcical production involving the used crown of Spain and other pitiable
paraphernalia. (This is the same March whose claims are additionally
reduced elsewhere in the record, as when Gray and Lucy agree that he
is a coward and a *hogge* for failing to pursue his title claim.) Presented
by the conspirators without genealogical reasoning or other argumentative support, and without defiance, this description of March as
'heyre' is plainly intended to debunk the very idea, in a manner wholly
satisfying to Henry and the other recipients of Cambridge's written
confession of shame. So, too, with the suggestion that the same proclamation might include reference to 'my lege Lord calde by auntreu
name Harry of Lancastre usurpur of Ynglond'. The notion of Henry V,
via his father's deed, as 'usurpur' of the crown is broached (and even,
one might say, creatively broached, since this is the first known usage

of this form of the word in written English) but is hedged by multiple denials: that Henry is acknowledged in the very sentence as Cambridge's 'lege Lord,' that the title 'usurpur' is branded as 'auntreu' even by its coiner, and, again, by the tawdry nature of the whole charade in which the assertion is embedded. Given the difficulties of convicting anybody of anything without granting some degree of recognition to their claims, the Lancastrians would seem to have attained a maximum prosecutorial leverage with a minimum admission of unwelcome material to the written record.

Mentioned only as part of a self-evidently crazy scheme, and in connection with the greediest self-interest, the argument for March's title might seem to have been successfully neutralized or contained.[107] Any such temporary containment was nevertheless eligible for violation – and in fact was to be violated, as soon as subsequent alterations of dynastic fortune rendered the Mortimer/March claim visible once again. The Yorkist resurgence in and after 1460 not only permitted a revival of the notion that the Lancastrians were usurpers of the throne, but quickly advanced 'usurper,' in all its variants, as a central term of later fifteenth-century political discourse. Repressed for a half-century, it surges to the forefront of parliamentary discussion with formal acknowledgment of Richard, duke of York's claim in 1460, and with the accompanying conclusion that Henry IV's claim to the throne as 'right enheriter' was 'oonly to shadowe and colour fraudulently his said unrightwise and violent usurpation, and by that moyen to abuse disceyvably the people stondyng aboute him.'[108] Edward IV, claiming the throne in 1461, sponsored language to the effect that Henry 'usurped and intruded upon the Roiall Power ... taking upon hym usurpously the Croune and name of Kyng.'[109] Then ensues a blizzard of like accusation: 'the seid *Usurpour* late called Kyng Henry the sixt, to th'entent that in his opinyon he myght the more surely stand and contynue in his *usurpacion* ... and for the execution of his malicious and dampnable purpose therin, in a pretence Parlement, by him and his *usurped* auctorite holden at Coventree, the xxxviii yere of his *usurped* Reigne ... juged the same noble Prynce Richard. . . .'[110]

The revised political situation not only ushered in a new rhetoric, but supplied a new foundation of analysis, in which the Mortimer/March claim was bolstered by detailed genealogical argumentation. Acknowledgment of Richard, duke of York's claim in 1460 was accompanied by detailed reiteration of the entitlement of the Mortimer heirs, through Lionel, third son of Edward III, suggesting that Henry IV unrightly seized the throne, 'to the which [title] Richard Duc of York, as son to Anne, [wife of Richard earl of Cambridge and] doughter to Rogier Mortymer Erle of Marche, son and heire to the said Phelippe,

doughter and heire to the said Leonell, the third gotten son of the seid
Kyng Edward the third, the right, title, dignite roiall . . . apperteyneth
and belongeth, afore eny issue of the seid John of Gant, the fourth
goten son of the same Kyng Edward.'[111] This genealogical reasoning
was extensively canvassed in the fifteenth and sixteenth centuries, and
would permit an augmented and revisionary re-reading of the Southampton plotters' motives. The Tudor chronicler Halle, for example,
gives full attention to the basis for March's title, and asserts Cambridge's additional interest in advancing his family's claims should
March remain childless: 'And therfore beyng destitute of comfort and
in dispayre of lyfe, to saue his children he fayned that tale, desiryng
rather to saue his succession then him selfe, whiche he did in dede.'[112]
The point is that even the most discredited plots remain eligible for
revival, if and when new circumstances open them to reconsideration
within new distributions of interests and powers.

4

Reburying Richard: Ceremony and Symbolic Relegitimation

Throughout the turbulent early years of the fifteenth century, magnates were having more than usual difficulty gaining access to, or
remaining in, their own graves. One of Henry IV's first acts upon
acceding to the throne was to move Thomas, duke of Gloucester to a
better location in Westminster Abbey.[1] After defeating Henry Hotspur
at Shrewsbury, Henry IV first permitted his burial but then disinterred
him and displayed his body suspended between two millstones to
prove he was really dead.[2] Consumed with a sense of his own sinful-
ness, Henry IV eschewed the Westminster burial dictated for him by
tradition, and chose to lie in Canterbury instead.[3] And of course the
remains of Henry IV's victim, Richard II, lay out of place for thirteen
years at Langley Abbey before the new king Henry V arranged his
reburial in his previously commissioned sepulcher in the Abbey of
St Peter, Westminster.[4]

These restless migrations invite attention to a deeper stratum of
aspiration and anxiety, having to do not only with the desire to attain
(or deny) a final resting place, but also with the meaning of interment
for the great of a realm and especially for a king. In his testament of
April 1399, Richard II pauses in the midst of a detailed specification of
funeral observances to entertain a disturbing possibility. God forbid
('quod Deus ex sua misericordia avertat'), his body might be lost at sea
or in tempest or snatched from the sight of men ('per maris turbines aut
tempestates seu quovis alio modo corpus nostrum ab hominum
aspectibus rapiatur'); nonetheless, he consoles himself by insisting that
obsequies go forward with or without his corpse.[5] Hostile rumor
among Henry IV's French detractors had it that the bargemen delivering Henry's own corpse to Gravesend dumped it overboard to quiet a
tempest and that his obsequies were in fact so conducted, at an empty
tomb.[6] Richard's French adherent Creton went a step farther, rewriting

history via a remarkable imaginative flight, in which he supposed
Henry shipwrecked on his cross-Channel voyage to England in 1399
and his body lost forever: his flesh food for birds and fish, his spirit
raving through different regions of the air and his bones tossed on the
shore in the sands by the movement of the waves ('qu'à celle heure les
jours de sa mauvaise et honteuse vie fussent finis et que sa chair fust
demourée viande à oyseaux ou aux poissons et son esprit foliable par
diverses regions de l'air, et ses os sustraits en la rive de la mer dedans
le sablon par le deboutement des eaux.')[7]

The problem with these unburied bodies – or, seen from another
point of view, their grisly potential – is that their troubled spirits
continue to walk the earth. Denied a final resting place, the spirit
receives in return an uncanny and disturbing power.[8] Neither fully
alive nor satisfactorily dead, it inhabits the troubled zone described by
Lacan as the space 'between two deaths.'[9] A person enters this zone
by dying symbolically (like Antigone who, in Lacan's example, dies by
tyrannical decree) prior to dying a natural or biological death. Or, as
alternatively set forth by Slavoj Žižek in a form more pertinent to the
murdered monarch, the corpse of a person who has suffered biological
death may be refused its full settlement of symbolic accounts through
funerary and other rituals.[10] Either way, a figure suspended in the
space between two deaths is inherently spectral, less and more than
real, charged with what Lacan (still dwelling on Antigone) regards as
a terrible beauty and his follower Žižek (having switched his attention
to *The Night of the Living Dead* and *Pet Semetary*) regards as a kind of
shambling and awkward persistence.

Every symbolically unincorporated death gives us a ghost who
walks the earth in beauty, buffoonery, or terror. The phantasmic figure
possesses an even more disturbing potential for persistence when it is
that of a late medieval king. From the end of the thirteenth century, the
entombment of the king's corpse, joined with its idealized effigy, was
a crucial expression and summation of the relation between what
Kantorowicz has described as the king's 'two bodies.'[11] Previously
joined in the king's life, as Kantorowicz has explained, were his 'body
natural,' subject to death and decay, and his 'body politic,' his imperishable *dignitas* or majestic aura, a property of his office. Now the two
are at once joined and separated – the perishable body below in its
tomb and the sacral body displayed above as idealized effigy, crowned
and accompanied by symbolic regalia. This juncture, at which the
natural and ideal aspects of kingship are arrested for display, is complexly sought and refused, desired and denied. It secures the symbolic
legitimacy of the king's reign, but also marks its end; it images the
dignitas of which he was possessor, but announces its eligibility for

transfer. With a denial of proper burial, the royal *dignitas* is rendered ineligible for orderly transfer, is unsecured and effectively at large.

Richard's burial at Langley Abbey was a Lancastrian improvisation, but it was not grossly rude or ignoble. He was, after all, buried in hallowed ground, within the precincts of a flourishing foundation.[12] The denial of his Westminster sepulcher may reasonably be dismissed as a relatively unimportant instance of the displacements inevitably accompanying an unauthorized dynastic supplantation. Yet we are not here dealing with an entirely reasonable phenomenon. A king's exclusion from proper burial in his own tomb must reverberate deeply within the symbolic, in ways which rebound upon the order of things.[13] Loosed, the king's body politic is (like the ghost of Hamlet's father) a recurrent reminder, not just of its own discontent, but of all the problems generated by an improper succession and the extent to which they lie beyond the powers of the new incumbent to resolve.

Richard's displaced burial thus presented his foes and friends with a special crisis and opportunity. For, ominously or auspiciously, depending on one's loyalties and wishes, failure to secure his aura within an ordered succession prolonged its availability as a source of unease or a locus for desire. As an object of conjuration, this aura could not fail to produce a specter, and this specter comes bearing a demand for practical and restorative action.[14] The specter appears as an interruption, in this case interrupting the Lancastrian attempt to 'get on with it' by enacting a progressive history of untroubled dynastic succession.[15] Well might a Lancastrian, besieged by apparitions and rumors, hope to close the troubled space of their origin by returning Richard to his proper grave. Henry V's decision to effect this return is here treated not as an isolated act of piety but as a positive political stratagem – a form of symbolic struggle which addressed (though it could not settle) continuing problems of Lancastrian legitimation.

Richard's 'first death'

Within the limits imposed by his responsibility for Richard's death and his own clouded claim to the throne,[16] Henry IV made a strong bid for the early settlement of Richard's symbolic accounts – at least to the extent of proving him dead and burying him *somewhere*.

In February 1400, Richard having been imprisoned out of sight for several months, Henry's own council deliberated the matter and reached a practical conclusion. In its list of actions, the council reaffirmed its determination that a living Richard must be closely guarded, but that a dead Richard should be displayed to the people. The council's minutes reveal its inclination to the latter option, verging on a recommendation of its implementation. With exquisite dubiousness and a general note of reluctance, the official record of council actions suggests that *if* Richard, former king, still be living, as some suppose that he might be ('si Ricardus nadgairs Roy soit uncore vivant a ce que len suppose quil est'),[17] that he be carefully kept. But, the minutes suggest, with a perceptible brightening of tone, should he be dead he might be shown openly to the people so they would know it ('il soit monstrez overtiement au poeple quils en puissent avoir conissance'). Henry quickly availed himself of this thinly veiled advice, in all its aspects. It was put about that Richard had starved himself, and had died on Saint Valentine's Day.[18] His body was brought from Pontefract to London, where it was publicly shown after the office of the dead, and the next day after mass, and again at his exequies at St Paul's with Henry and the citizens of London attending.[19] Adam of Usk, probably present at the funeral, adds that his face was not covered but was shown openly to all ('non velata facie sed publice cuique ostensa' – pp. 44–45).[20] Froissart reports with less authority that more than 20,000 men, women, and children viewed Richard as he lay in state 'descouvert,' and an accompanying fifteenth-century illustration now in the British Library depicts Richard's first cortège, issuing with face and body in plain view from the Tower en route to St Paul's, accompanied by torchbearers (their torches marked by quartered arms of England and France) and mourning friars.

Establishing Richard's 'first death' was, of course, the easy part. The usurping Henry IV was considerably less well situated to provide for his 'second death,' through proper interment and an acknowledgment and respectful resettling of his symbolic aura. The problem was starkly framed for Henry by the fact that Richard's Westminster tomb was previously commissioned and built and conspicuously ready for occupancy. Upon the death of his beloved Queen Anne in 1394 Richard had provided for their matched sepulchers, the most sumptuous ever built in England, and Anne was already interred there.[21] A feature of the tomb was its splendid marble effigies of the king and queen – Richard's effigy existing, along the lines described by Kantorowicz, not as a likeness of his body natural but as a visible display of sacred transcendence. Prepared to grant Richard the office of the dead, to sponsor and attend his exequies at St Paul's, Henry was in no way prepared to grant his predecessor the honor of a Westminster burial, in which his physical body would be perpetually joined to the representation of the very *dignitas* from which the Lancastrian articles of deposition had sought so conclusively to sever him.[22]

1. The funeral of
Richard II.

Richard was thus buried respectably, but out of the way, among
the brothers of Langley Abbey. Even the resolutely Lancastrian
Walsingham draws a distinction between the public nature of
Richard's funeral and the privacy and hugger-mugger of his Langley
interment, without the presence of magnates or the populace, and
omitting even the concluding ceremony of a post-interment meal for
the ecclesiastical guests ('sine magnatum praesentia, sine populari
turba; nec erat qui eos invitaret ad prandium post laborem').[23]
With Richard's remains away at Langley, a remarkable state of
affairs was then instituted, in which anniversaries and other

observances – including attention to such matters as chimes, candles, and distribution of alms to the poor – were conducted by the brothers of St Peter's, Westminster at Richard's empty tomb, financed by Richard and perhaps by Henry as well![24] The monks of Westminster were performing an obligatory duty they probably thought routine, and not macabre. Nevertheless, these ceremonies for the absent dead were inherently empty at the center so long as Richard's remains rested at Langley, and this emptiness assured a failure of ritual purpose. The linking of the king's mortal remains with the emblems of his dignity at once celebrated his possession of the kingly aura and rendered that aura eligible for transmission to its next earthly embodiment. Unsecured, attached to no mortal simulacrum, and hence symbolically ineligible to pass to the king's rightful successor, his aura or transcendent body was loosed in the land.[25]

Rumor

Even while Richard yet lived, in Henry's custody, a look-alike named Maudelyn, a priest from his own retinue, imitated him in various parts of the land in a vain effort to rally his followers.[26] But it was in 1401–2, the year after his funeral, that the rumor that Richard 'still lived' began to make serious headway.[27] In May 1402 the king and council had issued a proclamation against seditious preaching in taverns and other places where people gather ('in Tabernis, & aliis Populi nostri Congregationibus').[28] And in June 1402 the council followed on with a complaint about the people's desire to hear rumors and to immerse themselves in lies ('qui Rumores audire desiderant & Mendaciis assuescunt'), thus opening themselves to seditious suasions. Central among these lies is the belief of some foolish persons that late King Richard is alive in Scotland, whereas 'in truth said Richard is dead and buried' ('in rei veritate praefatus Ricardus sit Mortuus et Sepultus').[29] The very breadth of the rumor's promulgation may be measured by the fact that the council that same spring sent messages to every county, seeking the punishment of persons who had proclaimed the late king to be alive.[30] Its breadth was social as well as geographical; the *Annales Henrici* would report in 1404 that rumors had gained ground not only among the people, but even in the household of the king ('non solum in vulgari populo, sed etiam in ipsa Domini Regis domo.')[31]

Successful rumors require sponsorship, and the rumor of the living Richard did not lack support among the former king's followers and the present king's rivals. The Scottish court provided an early haven for rumor-mongers, and would ultimately offer long-term credence and financial support to a Richard imitator, one Thomas Ward of Trumpington.[32] The official promulgators of the rumor in England between 1402 and 1404 included such arch-Ricardians as former chancellor William Serle and Maud de Vere, the countess of Oxford. When finances failed, the conspirators made do, appropriately, with devices of dissimulation – or, as we would say today, 'simulation' itself. As chancellor, Serle had fled with the king's private seal, and affixed it to a flood of counterfeit letters to Richard's former intimates; the countess engaged in artful deceits and forgeries of her own, including the large-scale fabrication and distribution of Ricardian badges of the white hart ('Fecitque fabricari cervos argenteos et auratos plurimos, signa videlicet quae Rex Ricardus conferre solebat suis militibus, scutiferis, et amicis').[33]

But, if sponsorship can explain the initial dissemination of a rumor, it cannot finally tell us why the rumor was *embraced* – especially so widely in the kingdom and so deeply within social strata where no evident interest was served. To be sure, the populace as a whole was disappointed to find no improvement – and perhaps even some deterioration – in its material circumstances during the early years of Henry's rule. Despite the fact that Henry made a conscious effort to withhold taxes on the commons during his first years of rule,[34] we are told in the *Eulogium* continuation that the people began to complain against Henry and to long for Richard, saying that the former was taking their goods without giving them anything in return ('quia dicebant quod ipse cepit bona eorum et non solvebat' – p. 389). But the material conditions of the populace had not necessarily grown more harsh in the first years of the new century, and a satisfactory explanation cannot be found in that quarter alone.

Despite the absence of a material explanation, the Richard rumor continued to flourish, supported not just by former Ricardian magnates with axes to grind, but by middling citizens of the realm. Treason trial records, which appear in profusion during and after royal suppressions in 1402, repeatedly document the rumor's propagation through face-to-face contacts between private persons who rallied to Richard less from presumptive advantage than strong personal conviction.[35] Brought in June 1402 to testify before the King's Bench, John Bernard of Offey, Hertford said that around the feast of the Ascension he was plowing near his village ('il fuist al charu en mesme la ville') when along came a certain William Balsshalf of Lancaster. When he asked Balsshalf what was new ('demanda de dit William queux nouels'), William told him that Richard the late king was alive and well ('en plein vie') in Scotland and that he would return to England around the next feast of St John the Baptist. Balsshalf additionally claimed that

William Serle was making the arrangements, and that Henry was planning to abscond with his wealth to Brittany where he would court the duchess, and that John should gather men and await Richard's coming at Atherstone near Merevale Abbey.[36] The remarkable thing is that John Bernard appears to have recruited two of his fellow villagers – John White and William Thresshere – who promptly agreed to join his venture ('Ils tantost a ceo assenterent').

Bernard seems to have been prepared, by a certain recognition of affinity if not by personal acquaintance, to trust Balsshalf, and White and Thresshere were inclined by personal trust to follow Bernard.[37] But an incentive, a certain impetus or motive, still seems missing from this explanation. How could so far-fetched an escapade possibly have gained the assent of such presumably practical-minded men of toil? What put Balsshalf on the road and what motivated Bernard to follow him, even to the extent of leaving his plow, gathering followers and procuring arms and leaving home to wait in the precincts of Merevale Abbey for so conjectural a coming?

The (inevitably) complicated answer to this question revolves around the simultaneous demand which the phantasm makes upon the beholder and the beholder simultaneously makes upon the phantasm. As Derrida suggests in his discussion of Hamlet's father, the ghost and its beholder are conspirators in a complex feat of conjuration, the ghost posing its demand and the beholder embracing the ghost in reciprocal desire.[38] ('Is not,' he pertinently inquires, 'to possess a specter to be possessed by it?' – p. 132.) At its ultimate reach, this reciprocity of demand and desire is messianic, and supposes the ultimate unsettlement of things. Balsshalf and Bernard, waiting there at the abbey for Richard's return, may in this large sense be associated with recurrent messianic prophecies and yearnings, as manifested throughout the later Middle Ages; to this extent, their decision to take up arms for Richard's vainly awaited coming may be informed by broader patterns of popular expectation, sometimes (as in the Arthurian materials) collected around the second coming of a neither wholly dead nor wholly living king. For now, however, I would like to pursue one side of this demand/desire dyad, that of the desire or wish that brings the form of an absent object before a mourning subject's eyes.

Fausse *joy*

In the years after 1402, the certainty that Richard was alive and well in Scotland seemed less tenacious than the desire that it be so. Perhaps the last people actually to believe Richard alive were the duped Welsh volunteers who showed up for muster prior to the battle of Shrews-bury wearing the livery of Ricardian white harts; according to the *Eulogium* continuator, Henry Percy was so exasperated with their credulousness that he paused to give them a short lecture on political reality, saying that he was one of those who had thrown out Richard and who now, finding Henry worse, wanted to throw him out too.[39] Once the Welsh volunteers removed their emblems, people seem to have found a way, while not exactly believing, to exist in a hypothetical state of partial or conditional belief, sustained in the face of over-whelming counter-evidence by the force of their own desire.

Of course, kings are always the objects of such desires. They create themselves as kings by stirring and promising to fulfill them, and – as Louise Fradenburg has observed – the king's *absence* may actually abet rather than hinder this imaginative process: 'Distance, absence . . . is not necessarily . . . a liability for a king. The sovereign is created as distant, and the distance allows him to be desired in a particular way, as ideal, as disembodied. . . . Thus sovereignty promises a fantastic, a perfect but imaginary, closure to the very yearning it brings into being.'[40] This very circuit of imaginary closure is suggested in a 1402 letter addressed to Richard by his steadfast admirer Creton. Creton, first-hand observer of the events of 1399 and now valet de chambre of Charles VI of France,[41] writes tentatively but hopefully to the absent sovereign in Scotland, saying he has heard that Richard still lives and that he prays it is so ('por ce qu'on dit par deça que tu es sains et allegies, desquelles choses Je prye Nostre Seigneur qu'ainsi soit'). He adds that of those who speak of the matter or hear it spoken, the great majority cannot believe him dead. He describes his own obsessive return to an image of Richard: 'I do not know how [it is that] the representation of your image comes to me so often before the eyes of my heart, for by day and by night all my mental imaginings have no other object than you.' ('Je ne scais comme la réprésentation de ton image me vient si souvent devant les yeux de mon cueur, car de jour et de nuit toutes mes pensées imaginations ne sont aultres sinon pensées à toy.') Creton is fully aware of his own creative role in the production of Richard's image. Provoked by Richard's absence and his own desire, he engages in 'thoughtful imaginings' – a phrase that Robert Clark, who has assisted me with this passage, considers to embrace both 'the thought process and its product.' The result is not just an image but a double removal – the representation of an image – and Creton knows that he solaces himself with 'fausses' rather than 'vraies' joys: 'ainsy medelictent les fausses joies puisque les vraies je ne puis avoir.' His joys are false because of the role of imagination in their production;

Richard's *figure* – whether taken to mean his countenance or his entire being – is brought before the eyes of his thought by the force of his desire.

As it happens, Creton spent time with Richard in the last year of his reign, and can bolster his imagination with his own recollections. But, even if he had never seen Richard, he would still have access to the separable and immortal symbolic body of his absent king. Richard's image might be said to assume its plasticity at a point of conjuncture, between the imaginary and the symbolic – between Creton's desire-driven thought-work on the one hand, and an enlarged repertoire of past and potential royal symbolizations on the other. Richard's physical absence facilitates this process, by enabling a direct circuit between the subject (as source) and the king (as object) of desire.[42]

Apparent in Creton and in most of the Richard imaginings and sightings is a kind of hypothetical register, a tendency to act 'as if' he were alive. Serle's forged letters seemed to Richard's friends *'as if* sent by himself' ('tanquam ab eodem missae').[43] The hypothetical vein in which these letters were received would seem akin to the vein in which the Richard accounts were themselves received. This would seem to have been the state of mind of the doomed friar who, asked by Henry whether he believed that Richard yet lived, replied that 'I do not say that he lives, but I say that *if* he lives he is the true king of England' ('"Non dico quod vivit, sed dico si vivit ipse est verus Rex Angliae."').[44]

An ability to enter a hypothetical register, the register of *tanquam* . . . or *si* . . . , is the precondition of all these instances of belief. They share, in other words, all the provisionality with which one imaginatively enters the register of the symbolic. A similar provisionality invariably accompanies professions of belief in the living Richard. The elder Edmund of Mortimer, writing to his tenants to explain his alliance with Glyndwr in 1402, says that *if* King Richard is alive he intends to restore his crown, and that *otherwise* his nephew who is rightful heir to the crown should be king of England ('si le Roy Richard soit en vie de luy restorer a sa coronne, et sinoun qe mon honore Neuewe q'est droit heir al dit coronne serroit Roy d'Engleterre').[45]

A still more attenuated quality of belief is precariously maintained in the 1415 confession of Richard, earl of Cambridge, whose 'Southampton plot' involved the advancement either of the pseudo-Richard or of the earl of March. The plan outlined in his compelled confession is 'to have hadde the forseyd erle [March] into the lond of Walys wyth outyn yowre lycence, takyng upon hym the sovereynte of thys lond; zyf yondyr manis persone wych they callyn kynge Richard hadde naught bene alyve, as y wot wel that he nys not alyve. . . .'[46] At issue here is not whether Richard is still alive but whether his dubious substitute Trumpington remained alive (he actually died in 1414), and in fact Cambridge is at pains to deny that 'he' (whether Richard or Trumpington) yet lives. Yet a symbolic space is carefully maintained, within which the phantasmal Richard might have his hour. Apparent in Edmund's and in Cambridge's equivocations is a refusal wholly to abandon the wish for Richard, despite persuasive evidence to the contrary. The stubborn persistence of the wish, even in the face of overwhelming proof, surfaces in the forger Serle's 1404 confession. He admits that he journeyed to Scotland to see whether Richard still lived, and that, discovering only a person resembling Richard, he nevertheless continued to maintain the fiction ('Nihilominus tamen, ut illuderet Scotis et Anglis, affirmavit hunc esse Ricardum Regem proculdubio, praeservatum ab aemulis divino miraculo.')[47]

In none of these instances is belief founded on the conviction of Richard's physical survival. Rather, it is founded on something less material and less susceptible to physical proof: the continued availability of Richard's symbolic or sacral body to utopian desire. These otherwise enlightened believers inhabit the zone of what Žižek calls 'ideological fantasy,' in which the subject no longer believes, but behaves 'as if' he or she believes. This is a 'cynical' subject – in the sense of knowing better but behaving *as if* he or she believes; no significant difference divides the cynical and credulous subjects, since they finally behave identically. 'Knowing' at some level that Richard does not live, yet behaving as if they did 'not know,' they allow the plasticity of their desire to confect an imaginary Richard from available symbolic materials.[48]

Preferring the phantasm

I am saying, in effect, that undead Richard commanded such attention not *in spite of* his absence from the scene, but at least in part *because of* it – an absence that need be no liability for a king. The functionality of Richard's absence is most forcibly conveyed in a fact we have already glimpsed: that an undead Richard was actively preferred to the concretely available and thoroughly visible alternative claims of Edmund, earl of March.

Edmund's father Earl Roger was held in many quarters to be the logical successor to a childless Richard II, as a result of his descent through Lionel, second son of Edward III (as opposed to the Lancastrian claim through the third son, John of Gaunt). The always judicious

Westminster Chronicler, for example, pronounced his the line upon which the crown, in the event of Richard's failure to produce an heir, would pass by hereditary right ('jure hereditario' – p. 194), and a less reliable embroidering of this claim – to the effect that Richard himself endorsed Roger as his heir in 1385 – found its way into the *Eulogium* continuation,[49] and thence to other chronicles as well. With Roger's death in 1398, the young Edmund arguably became the heir to the throne, and he remained available as a rallying point for anti-Lancastrian activities throughout the reigns of Henry IV and Henry V, and into the childhood of Henry VI.

Despite the strength of his claim, and the anti-Lancastrian ground-work laid by his uncle and namesake in Wales, and his close family ties to the rebellious Percies, Edmund remained oddly inconspicuous in the broils of the first quarter-century. To be sure, his name does surface from time to time. A treason case of 1402 involved Welshman John Sperhauke, who had the misfortune to repeat a rumor he had heard from a certain tailor's wife of Baldock, to the effect that the present king was not the true son of Duke John but was born to a butcher of Ghent and that the earl of March was in fact king by right.[50] In the same year, Mortimer's uncle and namesake joined in coalition with Owen Glyndwr, explaining to his tenants his support of Richard if he were alive and otherwise of his nephew as 'droit heir.'[51] In 1405, Edmund and his brother figured in a bizarre kidnapping attempt in which they were to be abducted from Windsor Castle, apparently to become rallying points for anti-Lancastrian activity, probably with their Uncle Edmund in Wales.[52] As late as 1415, one of the options supposedly entertained by the Southampton conspirators against Henry V was (according to Richard, earl of Cambridge's undoubtedly coerced confession) to have had the earl of March 'into the lond of Walys . . . , takyng upon hym the sovereynte of thys lond.'[53] Nevertheless, Edmund's uncle and Richard, earl of Cambridge and most of the other high-echelon conspirators who mentioned his name tended to treat Edmund not as a first conspiratorial resort, but at best as a fallback should Richard really turn out to be dead and no good impersonator present himself.

This effective neutralization of Edmund's claim was accomplished in part by the brilliant machinations of the Lancastrians. In a move that conveyed multifold practical and psychological advantages, the newly crowned Henry IV promptly took the young Edmund and his brother Roger into his personal custody. Practically speaking, Henry controlled their extensive lands and rents, and the Patent Rolls for 1399–1413 abound in his awards of sergeancies, stewardships, custodies, and wardships to Henry's loyal followers. At the same time, Henry gained psychological advantage by treating Edmund less as a prisoner than as a child-dependant; Henry was generous in his annuities (ranging from £300 to £500) and, in the years prior to the attempted abduction of 1405, even boarded the two brothers with his own younger children.[54]

Yet, however beneficent its face, the Henries' control was absolute. Henry IV, for example, granted the right to arrange Edmund's marriage (and to collect a brokerage fee) to his queen in 1408,[55] and while still Prince of Wales the future Henry V (who had become Edmund's keeper in 1409)[56] prudently and privately bargained to gain personal control of these same marriage rights.[57] When Edmund came of age in 1413, Henry V was pleased to accept his homage and grant him full livery of his estates,[58] but then in a stunning volte-face of 1415 assessed a financially debilitating fine of 10,000 marks for Edmund's forthcoming marriage to his second cousin Anne.[59] This fine was not only to be a source of bitterness to Edmund, but would involve him in 'hugh chefesaunz' or indebtedness to Lord Scrope, and would become a partial incitement to his embarrassing involvement in the blundering and truncated Southampton conspiracy of 1415. Shortly after the deaths of his co-conspirators, apprehended as a result of his own confession and plea for clemency, Edmund won from Henry a blanket pardon for his crimes.[60] But, as T. B. Pugh concludes after his careful analysis of the documents of the conspiracy, 'after 1415 the earl of March was bound to remain a discredited figure in English politics for the rest of his short life.'[61]

A conversation reported in the documents of the Southampton conspiracy has Sir Thomas Gray speaking dismissively of Edmund, offhandedly saying to Walter Lucy that 'the Erle of the March was but a hogge.' Lucy, for his part, agreed, and (implying that he found March something less than a man) said that 'he shulde be fonde mon and chalange his reghte.'[62] Despite the fact that March was found fully capable of military service and other jobs the Lancastrians would send his way, their policy seems to have been overwhelmingly successful in portraying him as their ape, as something of a feckless fool, and hardly an apt focal point for opposition to the shrewd and beforehand Henry V.

The success with which dead Richard eclipsed living Edmund did not, however, depend upon Lancastrian disparagement of Edmund alone. Richard's pre-eminence as an anti-Lancastrian rallying point was ultimately secured by the potent and less than rational considerations which comprise the heart of my analysis in this chapter: by the fact of his anointment and the creation of his second and imperishable 'body politic,' and by the relocation of that body to a place in the symbolic order where it remained, physically absent but available to his former subjects' desire. In this sense, Edmund's greatest apparent advantage – his very 'presentness' – was his greatest disadvantage. For, as even Henry V was to acknowledge by encouraging or permitting representations of Richard as his benignly remote well-wisher, the father as absent guarantor of law and rule is always to be preferred to his more human and more oppressively present avatars. The king, as an object of desire, occupies less a physical than a symbolic space. However many subjects may view a king (alive or dead), the king functions still more critically as a beholder of his subjects, ideally observing their actions from that absent but all-seeing place in the symbolic order from which the subjects wish to be observed. This role, already that of the living king, is of course ideally suited to the absent one, the one unseen but still able to see.

Henry V's two fathers

Ricardian rumors thus resurfaced periodically,[63] and with particular vehemence in 1413–14, the critical years embracing the final illness and death of Henry IV and the accession of Henry V. According to a July 1413 indictment of King's Bench, a remarkable character named John Wyghtlok, onetime groom and yeoman of King Richard, had allied himself to the supporters of Scottish Richard imitator Thomas Ward of Trumpington, and had hatched private schemes over a period of seven years.[64] Together he and his allies had crisscrossed the whole of England and Wales, or most of it, announcing that Richard was alive in Scotland and would soon return. Then, in a height of contempt, they revealed themselves in sanctuary in Westminster, where they defiantly remained from March to June of that year, using it as a base of operations. During this period Wyghtlok audaciously launched two different campaigns, in each of which causing a broadside to be placed on the doors of the church of Westminster and throughout the city and its environs, swearing in English that King Richard was the 'same persone . . . in warde and kepyng of the duk of Albanie in Scotland.'

Wyghtlok's first campaign coincided with the last parliament of the ailing Henry IV; his second coincided even more embarrassingly with the coronation and first parliament of Henry V. Wyghtlok seems to participate in the mixed and unstable nature of the apparitional king in whose name he performed his deeds – sometimes as a less than fully serious prankster, and sometimes as an unappeased spirit seeking revenge. And he seems also to have participated in Richard's inherently evanescent nature: in a stunning preview of Oldcastle's escape later that year, Wyghtlok escaped from the Tower before coming to trial and then disappeared from the written record. Surely his evasion of punishment was a further provocation to Henry V, his new and serious-minded king.

Whether provoked by Wyghtlok or acting on a longer-standing resolve, the newly crowned Henry V quickly and conspicuously moved to rebury Richard, with appropriate obsequies, in Westminster Abbey. Walsingham observes that, 'In this year (1413) the body of Richard, former king of England, that had been buried ("humatum") in Langley, was raised and transported to London, and regally entombed ("tumulatum") in Westminster; and not without great expense ("non sine maximis expensis") to the present king.'[65] As Walsingham suggests, a considerable ceremonial and fiscal gap separates a simple burial (stripped even of the amenity of a funeral luncheon) and a regal entombment. One post-contemporary account has it that Richard's body was brought to Westminster 'in a riall chare couered wyth blake veluetis baners of diurse armes aboute and all the horse drawyng the chaire were napped in blak and brun with duierse armes and many a torche byrnnyng.'[66] Moreover, this assertion is confirmed by the 1 Henry V Issue Rolls, which reveal the detailed attention given to the reburial, with respect to the transport of the body and its interment, as well as (despite the fact that the tomb itself was bought and paid for) the considerable sums involved. The entombment itself appears to have occurred in mid-December,[67] with expenditures spread from 1 December through to 22 February.[68] Some of the more suggestive include: payment to John Wyddemer, joiner of London, to make a bier ('libitina') for carriage of Richard's body ('pro cariagio corporis Ricardi') from Langley to Westminster Abbey for reburial ('de novo sepeliendo') (1 December); to Giles Thornton, household servant, for providing 120 torches to burn about Richard's body along the way (1 December); to Thomas Barbour and John Broun, valets of the earl of Arundel, to provide candlewax for the hearse recently ordained for Richard's anniversary (and for thriftily saving the wax for the king's reuse!) (4 December); to Wyddemer for a *horsbere* and a coffin ('cista') for carriage of the body (20 February); alms for the brothers of Langley, and for distribution while conveying the corpse (22 February). The grand scale observed throughout may be measured in the 1,000 marks distributed for Richard's soul along the route of the cortège bearing his bones (11 December) – in contrast with the meager 20 shillings distributed by Henry IV during Richard's original funeral at St Paul's.[69] Although falling short of the ambitious funeral plans outlined in Richard's own will,[70] Henry exceeded Richard's hopes in his expenditure on torches and distribution of alms.

The Issue Rolls for 1 Henry V suggest that his expenditures on

Richard were comparable to those for the recently completed burial of his own father. And, in certain cases, the new king did not shrink from audaciously intermingling their funeral trappings. An item for 1 December 1413 orders that banners provided for the anniversary of Henry IV be placed upon the hearse ordered at Westminster for the anniversary of the Lord Richard, late king of England, there recently entombed ('pro vexillis que ordinata fuerunt pro domino Henrico patre domini Regis nunc pro anniversariis suis apud Cantuarium de dicto archiepiscopo & priore ecclesie christi Cantuarii mutuandis ad supponendum super herceam ordinatam apud Westmonistarium pro anniversario domini Ricardi nuper regis Anglicorum ibidem de novo tumulati').[71]

Lancastrian chroniclers located Henry V's motive in his respectful piety toward Richard, his childhood king. 'And anon,' says one representative summary, 'the firste yeer of his regne, for the grete and tendre loue that he hadde to King Richard, he translatid his body from Langley vnto Westmystre, and buried him beside Quene Anne his firste wiff, as his desire was.'[72] Fifteenth-century chronicles emphasized the extent of Henry's exertions on Richard's behalf, and their efficacy as well. One end-of-century chronicle in the British Library argues that Henry V set about deliberately to reverse his father's offense, and notes the differential result of his endeavor (compared with his father's less materially and spiritually generous response):

> And for as moche as his fader had deposid by his labour the good kyng Richard and petyously made hym to die . . . he had sent to Rome to be assoilled therof for which offence the pope our holy fader enioyned hym to make hym be praide for perpetually and . . . he shuld do founde iiii tapers to bren perpetuelly a boute his body that for the extinction of his bodyly lyffe his soule may euer be remembred and lyve in hevyn in spirituall lyfe. And also that he shuld euery weke on the day as it comyth aboute of his deth haue a solempne masse of requiem on the eyvn to fore a dirige with ix lessons and a dole to pore peple alwey on that day. . . . And to euery monke to haue xx shillynges which all these thynges performed this noble kyng, for his fader for Kyng Henry the iiii his fader performed not it duryng his lyfe whome as it is said god touched and was a lepre er he dyed.[73]

For all the 'goodnesse' this chronicle attributes to Henry V, its account introduces his father's shriveled body as a cautionary reminder of the necessity for restitution in order for subsequent Lancastrians to enjoy unblighted reigns. Emphasis on benignity and love is, in other words, an oversimplification, both of mourning in its more general aspects, and of particular objectives served by the reburial itself. Mourning has, after all, its aggressive and triumphal elements, and even in its most benign forms it seeks, as one recent commentator observes, 'to exorcise [the past] albeit under the guise of respectful commemoration.'[74] Once a king's spirit is set down, its *dignitas* resecured, the business, not of memory, but of forgetfulness can begin. Forgotten is the deposed king as the source of strident and unaccommodated demands. The memory which is tolerated is memory in its most narrow and functional sense, with the king treated as a figure in a line of willing transmission and restored succession. Kantorowicz anticipates this aspect of the reburial, in his suggestion that the king's *dignitas* must be assigned before it can be *re*assigned; that, as a quality that cannot be held or enjoyed by two persons at once, it must be firmly linked to the term of one finite life before it can then be assumed by a rightful successor. Henry IV sought unsuccessfully to elide a step in the transfer, effectively loosing Richard's *dignitas* in the process of prematurely stripping it away,[75] and then proving unable to recapture it in his own behalf. In contrast, Henry V may be said to have managed the reburial in ways conducive to the orderly transfer of Richard's sanctified aura to his own kingship.

Supplementing the pomp of the translation, and the piety expressed through accommodation of Richard's own wishes, and the propriety of Westminster as the burial site for a relegitimized king, was another aspect of proper interment which Henry IV had been unable (or in any event unwilling) to provide: the new king's presence at the interment of the old. Elizabeth A. R. Brown has revealed the importance of the successor's presence, in her discussion of the second funeral that the eventual successor Philip of Poitiers staged for his brother Louis X of France, after having been unable to attend the obsequies accompanying his burial a month before.[76] As sponsor of Richard's reburial, Henry V was able to display himself in a role of rightful successor that was unavailable to his own usurping father. Henry V's capture of the symbolism of rightful succession required, however, an active suppression. Absent from the ceremony, and in fact doubly absent in his Canterbury grave, was Henry V's natural (but dynastically illegitimate) father, Henry IV; in his place was Henry V's chosen (and dynastically legitimate) father Richard, to whose paternity he was about to lay brilliant symbolic claim. The paradox is as intriguing as it is obvious: the symbolic strategy which Henry V was so brilliantly to adopt had the effect of disavowing the actual basis of his claim on the throne, through his natural but usurping father, and asserting a fictitious claim, through the implication that Richard II was his 'true' spiritual mentor.

Having ended Richard's corpse's awkward odyssey and rejoined it to the symbolic representation of his royal dignity, Henry V now reaped the fruits of Richard's benign sponsorship of his own career. Central in this enterprise was fabrication and circulation of the rumor that Richard was himself the future Henry V's foremost patron, having foretold and blessed the young Henry's ascent. The ardently Lancastrian Thomas of Elmham, for example, says that (evidently upon first encountering the young Henry) Richard – aided either by prophecy or by the grace of his prerogative – recognized something in Henry's countenance that caused him to burst forth to him and to all present that 'We have heard that our England should foster a certain prince Henry, who, with respect to the nobility of his manners, the exceeding greatness of his deeds, his immense soldierly industry, the high renown of his deserved fame, will shine forth abundantly through the whole world, and that according to what an occult book ["liber secretus"] that he has frequently consulted has said, he is certain that this is that very Henry.'[77] Not only was Richard portrayed as benignly interested in the young Henry's career, but Henry was portrayed as regarding Richard with the affection one owes to a true father; Walsingham concludes his account of the reburial by noting that Henry considered himself to owe (to Richard) as much veneration as to his own fleshly father ('qui fatebatur se sibi tantum venerationis debere, quantum patri suo carnali').[78] Drawing upon this cluster of associations – although in this case for ironic intent – is an illustration of Creton, British Library MS. Harley 1319, in which Richard bestows knighthood on a kneeling Henry during his Irish expedition in the ominous spring of 1399.

Richard's reburial may thus be seen as Henry's exceptionally imaginative and adroit attempt to encourage and effect a form of transference – in this case, a transference of emotional affiliation from Richard's residual aura to his own.[79] Remembering that misrecognition of the object of one's desire is an essential element in the process of transference, Henry may more precisely be seen as attempting a form of 'managed misrecognition' – offering devious but persuasive grounds for his subjects to shift their mistaken allegiance from the residual aura of their long-dead king to his own royal person. Having successfully put his guilty, overly-knowing and excessively present biological father out of the way in Canterbury, and having instated Richard as the benignly absent guarantor of succession, Henry V was well positioned to inherit the mantle of complete – two-personed – kingship and to exercise mature rule.[80]

2. Richard II knighting Henry of Monmouth (later Henry V) in Ireland in 1399.

Two specters meet

Records of Richard recurrences suggest that the reburial was successful in securing (and hence removing) Richard's free-floating spirit
as a rallying point for alternative desires – but not immediately or all at
once. Claims and sightings of the years 1414–20 suggest an initial
refusal by many subjects of Henry's proposed transfer of allegiance –
a refusal, that is, wholly to cede their desire to recognize Richard as
their legitimate king. Richard rumors may, in fact, even be seen to
proliferate in this period.[81] But Henry's success resides in the fact that
they proliferate in a new key: hit-or-miss, spontaneous, idiosyncratic,
mainly divorced from any sort of programmatic opposition to Lancastrian rule.

In 1416, Richard Woolman, hosteler of London, and John Bekeryng,
'Gentilman' of Lincoln, were indicted for asserting the claims of the
Scottish Richard-imitator Trumpington, and for writing a letter of

complaint to the Emperor Sigismond, from whom they seem rather fancifully to have expected redress. Bekeryng died in Newgate and Woolman was drawn, hanged, beheaded at Tyburn, and his head set upon London Bridge.[82] In 1420, well after the death of Trumpington, one Thomas Cobold, a fishmonger who had recently returned from Scotland, came to London where he stayed at the home of William Norton, barber, and spread seditious rumors about Richard. He was imprisoned as a person 'male fame.'[83] Cobold was probably just trying to tell a good story, as his fortunate exemption from most of the penalties for treason would suggest. In another episode of 1420, we encounter that ultimate stage of proliferation in which invention, accepted as fact, begets second-order invention. Roger Oliver, draper, was accused by sometime accomplice John Russell, of forging an indictment, backdated to 1408, naming a list of sixty-one Londoners who believed that Richard was still alive. The bogus indictment said that these Londoners had maintained their claim in battle with a hundred bailiffs of the king, slaying five of them. Oliver is said to have forged this indictment in order to obtain forfeiture of the goods of the sixty-one, and also to obtain release for friends imprisoned by any of the sixty-one for debt. This unlikely invention showed, in turn, a remarkable power to attract adherents and converts; Roger Oliver, going to search his conscience with cleric Roger Lawsele, ended up taking money from Lawsele to include additional names of the latter's suggestion to the list! Unwieldy as Oliver's superimposition of a forged Richard fabrication upon a pre-existing tissue of Richard fabrications might seem, it was well on its way to judicial success when it was blocked by action of the king's council.[84]

The later Richard rumors do touch ground in one definable milieu and possible site of opposition to Lancastrian claims, however, in their association with some of the more seditious aspects of Lollardy.[85] The subjects of religious heresy (especially as enacted by the Lollards) and sedition (especially as conducted in Richard's name) had always coexisted in the same Lancastrian discursive register, and in some respects the broader Lancastrian strategy of linking, 'othering,' and demonizing real and imagined enemies had always encouraged the imaginative association of heretics and traitors to the realm.[86] In a parliamentary petition of 1406, for example, anti-clerical and pro-Ricardian sentiments are condemned within a single text, though they are never quite permitted to intermingle. Directed against 'Lollardes, & autres parlours & controvours des Novelx & des Mensonges,' this petition accuses 'some' of arguing against the establishment of the Catholic faith, and 'others' of stirring discord between lords temporal and spiritual, and 'others' of reporting false prophecies, and yet 'others' of preaching that Richard, recently king, who is dead, is alive ('qe Richard nadgairs Roy, qi mort est, serroit en pleine vie') or giving credence to that 'fool' who is in Scotland, falsely pretending to be King Richard who is dead ('celuy fool q'est in Escoce . . . fauxement pretendent d'estre le Roy Richard qi mort est').[87]

A series of conjunctions suggesting that a link between Lollardy and sedition might actually have occurred, or at least that it was ever more deeply rooted in the prosecutorial imagination, emerges in trial records of the second decade of the fifteenth century. Recall the case of John Wyghtlok, the anti-Lancastrian who used the protection of sanctuary to disrupt Henry IV's last parliament and Henry V's first parliament with rumors of Richard alive. On both occasions he sallied forth to post broadsides on the doors of churches and public buildings in Westminster and London and the environs, including one, in English, which offered in support of his claims an oath so grisly and terrible that it could not but command respect – first on the host ('I will swere it on Goddis body sacrid and vse it yat it is kyng Richard persone') and then on his own soul ('I betake the devil evir to lie in helle body and soule with outyn departyng and nevir to haue mercy of God ne parte of no priere in holichirche from this day in to the day of doome, but that persone that was sumtyme kyng Richard be alive in Scotlond'). These rather astounding oaths might support a claim that Wyghtlok was the most fervent of believers *or* disbelievers, that – for example – he was either more or less than usually committed to the idea of the sanctity of the host, and thus intimately linked to the most crucial subject of Lollard contention and anti-Lollard agitation.

Another partially stifled suggestion of religiosity appears in the indictment of Henry Talbot, the 1415 kidnapper of Murdoch of Fife. Talbot claimed in his 1417 appearance before the King's Bench in Westminster that all he had done was consistent with Henry V's own campaign to destroy sin in the realm of England ('ad destruendum peccatum in regno Anglie') and that he had acted on the advice of some of his confessors, including bishops and other ecclesiastics ('per consilium quorumdam confessorum suorum, tam episcoporum quam aliorum vivorum ecclesiasticorum'), and that God knew his intention and purpose to be good.[88] This confidence in his own divine authorization was to form the basis for his stubbornly iterated defense: 'Deus vult et Deus scit.'[89] In other roughly contemporary cases the linkage of Lollardy and sedition is more explicitly made. In 1417, Thomas Lucas, 'magister in artibus' and 'Gentilman,' claimed Richard was still living and Lucas was said to have conducted a handbill campaign in Canterbury and London. According to the indictment, he had consorted with Lollards and dallied in the views of Oldcastle, both with respect to

Lollardy and to treason ('idem Thomas fuit et est consenciens . . . et socien omnibus operibus Johannis Oldcastell' tam in oppinionibus lollardyie quam in omnibus aliis suis malitiosis proditionibus').[90]

The crucial link between assertions of a living Richard and Oldcastle's heresy was attributed to Oldcastle himself, in his reported response to the chief justice that Henry's courts did not have jurisdiction over him, since his liege lord was living in the realm of Scotland (as reported by Walsingham, 'respondit se non habere judicem inter eos, vivente ligeo domino suo in regno Scotiae.')[91] Either he actually said it, or – much the same thing – it is now the kind of thing Oldcastle was generally expected to say. This invocation of Richard sealed a convergence which appeared at the outset as a creation of Lancastrian policy, and which now seems to have gained a belated head of steam. Walsingham was following chronology, and was also relying on his own sense of significance, when he placed his entry on Henry V's reburial of Richard II within the following narrative sequence of his *Historia Anglicana*:

1. Oldcastle, found guilty of heresy, escapes the Tower.
2. Many English die of pestilence.
3. The body of Richard II is reburied in Westminster.
4. The Lollards mount a conspiracy to seize the king at Eltham.
5. The Lollards gather in force in St Giles's Fields. (vol. 2, pp. 296–297)

Leaving aside the tempting conjecture that pestilence was itself a figure for the spread of Lollard opinions (see Chapter 2, pp. 36–40), Henry V's decision to move Richard's body is taken, and executed, in the midst of a season of Lollard unrest – an unrest that was, according to Walsingham, seen as likely to spread widely among the servants and apprentices of London and many of their masters, and also as enjoying broad support in the countryside (ibid., pp. 298–299).

Yet, uttered in 1417, Oldcastle's defiant declaration of allegiance stands very near the end of one cycle of attention to the claims of that absent king. The close conjunction of the Richard rumor's apparent greatest success and its precipitate decline suggests that Henry's reburial ceremony might have been more effective than was immediately apparent, in foreclosing a troubled emotional space where oppositional ideas and wishes might be sustained. Several revealing linkages among and between the reburial, the Lollard heresy, and the suppression of anti-Lancastrian alternatives are made in a poem in which Thomas Hoccleve imputes an oddly expanded aura of implication to the removal of Richard's bones from Langley to Westminster.[92]

Hoccleve begins his poem not with Henry, or Richard, but with the spread of heresy in the land:

> Allas! an heep of vs, the feith werreye;
> We waden so deepe in presumpcioun,
> That vs nat deyneth vn-to god obeye.

Henry is, in turn, introduced to the poem as 'Champioun/For holy chirche' and 'Crystes knyght,' battling against 'this Rebellioun.' Hoccleve pauses to entertain a disturbing thought: that England might have found itself with a king prepared to sponsor heresy and subvert the faith, but rejoices that this is not so. Then he considers the form of Henry's battle, which turns out to *be* the reburial:

> Our kyng Richard that was yee may wel see,
> Is nat fled from his remembrance aweye.
> My wit souffysith nat to peyse and weye
> With what honour he broght is to this toun,
> And with his queene at Westmynstre in thabbeye
> Solempnely in Toumbe leid adoun.

Several implied or disguised terms or filters are needed to make sense of Hoccleve's implication that Henry somehow defeats heresy by reburying Richard. One is that heresy disrespects continuity and tradition as lodged in 'sad byleeue & constant vnion,' and that disrespect for continuity is, as he characterizes it at one moment in the poem, a form of 'Rebellioun.' The reburial of Richard is, in contrast, a display of constancy and respect for tradition, and hence a riposte to heresy's insurrectionary force. Repairing the rupture opened by his own father's initial act of insurrection and re-establishing dynastic solidarity, Henry thus repossesses – and paves over – heresy's breeding ground.

This poem's muted suggestion that heresy is a form of rebellion is complemented and completed beyond its immediate textual bounds, in its implied link between rebellious heretics (in the poem) and traitors against Lancastrian rule (outside the poem). The poem addresses this fear by reknitting the fabric of continuous tradition, by eliding Henry IV's act – and, for that matter, omitting Henry IV altogether[93] – in favor of a reverent and loving transfer from Richard II as predecessor and Henry V as successor. In other words, the poem seeks, like Henry's own ceremony of reburial, to close the emotionally unsettled space in which unseated and unburied kings live a vexed half-life, available as a rallying point for plotters against those who unseated them.

Oldcastle's own profession of Ricardian allegiance seems to argue for the failure of Henry's attempts at symbolic closure, but may actually argue for their success. Here we have Oldcastle, finally captured, wounded, humiliated by circulation of the story that he was captured by an old woman who broke his leg with a footstool,[94] and stood up for trial before full parliament. That he was permitted to invoke Richard at all, and that such an invocation was permitted to enter a much-doctored written record, argues less for the potency of the Richard rumor than for its now-denatured quality.[95] The absurd invocation of Richard, alive in Scotland, as late as 1417 possesses less menace than poignancy, in the sense that here two specters meet. Oldcastle, taken at last and speaking in the context of a show trial just preliminary to his death, is spectral in the Lacanian sense of one who is now condemned to die within the symbolic, and only awaits his second or biological death. (The author of the *Gesta*, writing *c.* 1416 and acknowledging Oldcastle still living, nevertheless regards him as experiencing a form of living death, of surviving 'in mortis simulacrum.'[96]) Richard, biologically long dead, has now ebbed as a potent force within the symbolic, to the extent that his mention need no longer unsettle Lancastrian complacencies or claims.

Even (or perhaps especially) when linked in a kind of redoubled subversion to the activities of the now scattered and demoralized Lollards, the Richard rumor after 1413 progressively lost its points of contact with persons and programs able to affect the order of things. Its last status, conjoined with declining Lollard fortunes, is that of a sponsored rumor, a rhetorical convenience permitting a Lancastrian-dominated judicial system to frame vivid charges and obtain easy convictions of persons whose activities are suspect or who have otherwise offended king or council.[97] The period 1417–20 thus marks the end of a cycle of urgent and consequential symbolization.

Richard's return

Henry V having reasserted oversight and even sponsorship of the most central sites of Ricardian symbolization, the urgency of Richard representations dwindled. As former monarch, Richard could not be wholly expelled from the symbolic, and was maintained in royal chronology and genealogy as negative example, and even (after his reburial) ironically as benign sponsor. But in all these respects he might be said to have survived as a place-holder, a minimized though unavoidable link in a chain, a trace or even a trace of a trace. Richard may be encountered in this aspect in a host of genealogically inspired works of the

3. Richard II and Henry IV share a roundel in this genealogy of French and English kings.

mid-fifteenth century, in which his image is blandly reinserted in one or another argumentative chain or regal succession, the fact of traumatic rupture minimized or suppressed.

An intriguing and rather ingenious example of such a minimization occurs in the genealogical table designed to vindicate Henry VI's claim to the throne of France, prefatory to the sumptuous compilation of romances presented by John Talbot to Margaret of Anjou.[98] This genealogical table is arranged in the form of a fleur-de-lys, the middle of whose three branches depicts the direct line of French kings from St Louis to Charles IV, the left the collateral Valois line to Charles VI, and the right the English kings from Edward I – all three uniting in Henry VI. The genealogy is staged generationally, according to degrees of descent from St Louis, with the roundel of the fifth generation shared (non-regally) by the Black Prince and John of Gaunt, and the roundel of the sixth generation by 'le roy Richart' and 'le roy Henry.' A mild contentiousness might be implicit in the representation, in which

Henry IV faces Richard, in profile, gesticulating with hands apart. And, in a contradiction of ritual possibility, each sovereign bears his own scepter. Nevertheless, the temporal fold or stutter allows the designer/ artist of the roundel to repackage a disputed succession as a simultaneity, and thus to minimize its impact. This is a dishonest and messy jointure, one which seeks to elide the fact of rupture, but reluctantly acknowledges it. Others are more successfully 'forgetful.' Consider, in this regard, the bland impassivity of the carved choir screen at York Minster, in which the image of Richard unproblematically holds his place in a regnal succession originally culminating in Henry VI.

The reinsertion of Richard in an ordered chain of succession signals a suppression of his special woes that amounts to a form of forgetting. But, ironically, such forgetting prepares the way for another kind of return; a trace is, in this sense, not only a remainder, but an anticipation of things to come. Precisely in the short-term success of the reburial as a form of respectful commemoration and hence as ritualized forgetting lay the conditions for the long-term failure of Henry's stratagem.[99] With the reburial of Richard, his specter quieted as object of unruly desire and source of unfulfilled demand, he is paradoxically freed for another kind of return. His place as an active contestant ceded to others, he is liable to return, not as king in his own right, but (rehabilitated in ways the Lancastrians could neither imagine nor approve) as martyred sponsor of a new royal line.

In this case, as always, the repressed/excluded returns not from the past but from the future, from the emergence of a new set of circumstances which allow a revision of past events from an altered vantage point. I am, of course, referring to the events of the mid-century and the new possibilities they opened for a Yorkist reconsideration. Richard, having ceased by degrees to function as insurrectionary will-o'-the-wisp and phantasm, the attractions of living claimants might gain a previously unachieved status. The marriage of the formerly laughable Richard, earl of Cambridge and disparaged Mortimer heiress Anne, daughter of the earl of March, had produced a son (Richard) who would become duke of York and would gain title to the crown in 1460. A year later his son became the first Yorkist king of England, and the Rolls of Parliament for 1 Edward IV (1461) endorse a new and argumentatively augmented genealogy of English kingship. Henry IV, now branded usurper, is said to have dealt in this way with his predecessor Richard:

> . . . the more grevous thyng attemptyng, wykidly of unnaturall, unmanly and cruell tryanny, the same Kyng Richard, Kyng enoynted, corouned and consecrate, and his Liege and moost high

Lord in the erth, ayenst Godds Lawe, Mannes Liegaunce, and oth of fidelite, with uttermost punicion attormentyng, murdred and destroied, with moost vyle, heynous and lamentable deth.[100]

Richard as king 'anointed, crowned, and consecrate' is here restored to a semblance of his pre-usurpation situation, now as Lancastrian victim rather than as benign sponsor.

The virtual forgetting of Richard – his exclusion (except as ancestor, sponsor, and place-holder) from the realm of the symbolic, turns out to have been a precondition for his return from the 'real,' in both its lay and its Lacanian senses. He returns, that is, under the very practical and material sponsorship of a new dynasty, and also from the extra-symbolic, in a new and more comprehensive symbolization. This mid-century Yorkist symbolization may be considered more comprehensive in the sense that it restores repressed/excluded features of Richard's sorry case. These features (including Richard's title and his victimhood) had no place in the Lancastrian symbolic program, but remained latent, awaiting more propitious circumstances for rediscovery.

Genealogies and commentaries produced under mid-century Yorkist sponsorship are obviously no less political and cynical in their motivation than those of the Lancastrians. Yet the Yorkist re-representation argues that extreme forms of enforced historical forgetfulness do invite their own retribution. This retribution occurs in the form of a return from the future which reinstates repressed materials precisely at their moment of apparent elimination from symbolic consequence.

5
Counterfeiters, Lollards, and Lancastrian Unease

William Carsewell's bad Pentecost

Arrested in 1419 on suspicion of counterfeiting and other treasonous offenses, William Carsewell confected a remarkable confession that drew upon some of the most sensational materials of his day.[1] The purpose of his confession was to secure for himself the role of king's approver or 'probator domini regis,' and to seek his own exoneration by giving evidence leading to the conviction of his confederates. A successful approver's confession had to establish grounds for conviction, meeting several standards along the way: it had to incriminate the approver along with several confederates; to reveal their guilt of felony or other substantial crime; and to weave a supportive narrative rich in persuasive detail.[2] Carsewell delivers handsomely, offering a narrative which invites shocked attention to its cast of conniving counterfeiters, insurrectionary traitors, and blasphemous Lollards. Imaginatively reprocessing these seemingly disparate activities, it reveals their communality as threats to Lancastrian repose.

As he told it to the king's coroner, Carsewell became involved with the prior and cellarer of Wenlock Abbey in 1417, when they approached him with a bar composed of silver clipped from the king's good money and asked him to cast it into the likeness of the king of England's money, artificially fabricated with letters and signs belonging to (the coin called) the groat ('ad similitudinem monete domini regis Anglie de grotes . . . , artificialiter cum litteris et signis ad grossum pertinentibus fabricato'). This session being successfully completed, the prior promised Carsewell ten pounds to teach him the art of multiplying gold and silver, and Carsewell became a regular guest at the priory.

On Tuesday after the close of Easter, he was brought into a special dining chamber of the priory called 'le misericorde.'[3] There he was introduced to the indicted and outlawed traitor John Oldcastle, who was in turn accompanied by an Irish chaplain and a Welsh yeoman. The prior and Oldcastle then sat and dined at high table ('ad discum'), where they discussed counterfeiting schemes, and Carsewell and the chaplain were seated at the end of the same table, where they were served food and drink by the yeoman and the cellarer. The result of these discussions was a bastardized oath of fealty, in which Carsewell swore in or within the hands of the said Oldcastle ('in manu') to keep faith with him in all things:

> He was retained ['retentus fuit'] with Oldcastle to multiply, die, strike, and forge gold and silver in likeness to the coin of the king ['in similitudinem cunee domini regis']. . . . Moreover, he was sworn to come to the said Oldcastle at his manor at the next feast of Pentecost ['ad festum Pentecostes extunc proximo sequentem'], and that in the meantime he would wait in the countryside near the previously mentioned manor until summoned by Patrick the chaplain, at which time he would assuredly come to the said Oldcastle ['quando in certo idem probator veniret ad ipsum Iohannem Oldecastell'].

Carsewell's narrative seems not to have had its intended effect. The prior was declared innocent by the jury and, although detained for other possible offenses, was bailed by gentlemen of his county. Carsewell, vanishing from the record, remained in prison, presumably like most approvers to perish there.[4]

An approver's narrative that did its job in other respects was not necessarily expected to be true. Indeed, I take Carsewell's story for a wild invention, not just because of its inherent unlikeliness but also because so many of its elements would, in effect, have come to him imaginatively pre-structured, already conveniently available in popular discourses of his day. But, even while supposing his story an invention, I want to claim for it another kind of historical truth. This historical truth consists, not in the verifiability of Carsewell's claims about his and Oldcastle's activities, but in the historical specificity of the structures within which he devises his claim. What is historical, in other words, is not so much what he did or did not *do*, as the time-bound, meaning-making structures he employs.

At the notional center of these structures lies a cluster of anxieties more broadly late medieval than specifically Lancastrian, but imaginatively central to Lancastrian kingship. These rather fraught notions become historical, not by being verifiable or true or lending themselves to description of how people necessarily behaved, but by their contribution to contemporary (and hence historically specific) self-understanding, as crucial components of the structures within which people produced and understood their own actions. Among these notions I will touch upon: (1) continuing – although, after 1408–9, largely unreasoned – Lancastrian fears of sedition and insurrection; (2) nationalistic mistrust of monastic internationalism; (3) the ever-widening ambit of treasonous activity; and (4) fear of contamination and blasphemy, especially blasphemous emphasis on the materiality of the eucharistic host.

Insurrection

Oldcastle and his purported retinue show up trailing such a semiotic overload of insurrectionary implications as to become ludic in their final effect. April 1417 – the occasion of the incident in Carsewell's story – was the absolute peak of Oldcastle's celebrity as arch-heretic and arch-fugitive. Four years earlier convicted of Lollard heresy and sedition, breaking prison and supposedly sponsoring the St Giles rising of 1414, declared outlaw and now still at large, he was the most celebrated symbol of opposition to the established Church and the new Lancastrian king. In January 1417, Henry recirculated a remarkable promise that had gone unclaimed for three years: an immediate pardon and a reward of 1,000 marks and 20 pounds annually to anyone bringing Oldcastle before the king, and a remission of taxes forever to the city, borough, or town responsible for his capture.[5] That was also the year in which Oldcastle's goods were finally declared forfeit and seized; among evidence relating to their enumeration and reassignment is the remarkable Exchequer entry to the effect that the king's escheator in the county of Kent required an escort of twenty and sometimes thirty horsemen, 'for fear of the soldiers and other malefactors adhering to and obstinately favouring John Oldecastell.'[6]

Oldcastle's companions in crime include: Patrick Trim of Ireland ('de Hibernia') as Oldcastle's personal chaplain or *capellanus*; John Harlech of Harlech in Wales ('in Wallia') as yeoman; and Hugh Sheldon, a lapsed or degraded priest ('nuper clericum'), evidently of the Lollard persuasion. Represented by this band are the principal hostilities over which England perceived itself to have little control. France and Scotland were, after all, rival kingdoms, and armed warfare with those countries was at least partially subject to modulation through embassy, treaty, and England's own decision to assert or withhold its aggressive designs and claims. But the process of domination affecting Ireland and Wales was, by definition, incomplete; having staked infinite claim to these regions by right of ancient conquest, England was in a sense put in the reactive and colonialist situation of having to brook endless agitation and outrage from these subject but unsubjugated peoples.[7]

The continuing sense of Ireland and Wales as zones of disturbance is suggested in the summons to Henry IV's parliament of 1405–6, in which the cause of the meeting was alleged as the depredations committed by the rebels in Wales and also the activities of enemies in 'Guyen, Caleys, & Ireland, come en les Marches d'Escoce.'[8] Unlike the kingdom's other enemies, the rebels of Wales and the 'wilde Erish'[9] who resisted English domination were treated less as honorable adversaries than as brutes, primitive and superstitious. The rebels of Wales, in particular, were thought to live not in houses but among rocks and caves. Their savagery in and after battle was memorialized by Walsingham, who reported that atrocities committed after the capture of Edmund Mortimer in 1402 included castration of the slain by Welsh women, who desecrated the dead by placing their penises in their mouths and hanging their testicles from their foreheads.[10] Welsh triumphs in battle resulted not from military might but diabolical arts, practiced by Glyndwr and by allied Minorite friars, including the raising of windstorms, hail, and snow.[11]

No wonder that anti-Irish and anti-Welsh sentiment led to periodic attempts at expulsion. In 1393, and again in 1413, attempts were made to banish Irish from the realm, and additional 'wylde Irishmen' were expelled in 1422.[12] Welsh scholars and retainers were expelled from universities and the court in the first decade of the fifteenth century. Not that such attempts were wholly successful, but Patrick of Trim and John of Harlech were, in a real sense, matter out of place in the English homeland. Moreover, each enters the narrative with a name, or location, suggestive of additional perturbation. Trim retained its association as the castle of Edmund Mortimer, earl of March, killed in Ireland in 1398, and grandfather of the true and living heir to the English throne. It was attached to the Mortimer earldom, and hence to the fortunes of the strongest rival claim to the Lancastrian throne, throughout the fifteenth century, finally passing to Richard, duke of York and then to the first Yorkist king, Edward IV, as he ascended the throne.[13] Harlech was one of Edward I's castles and a symbol of troubled English dominion in north Wales; more relevantly, it was one of the English castles successfully seized by the Welsh rebels during the Glyndwr rebellion, and the last to be relinquished, in 1409.[14] The subjects of Mortimer claims and unrest in Wales had recently converged in the loyalist imagination when in 1415 Richard, earl of Cambridge and others were accused of conspiring to draw Edmund, earl of March to Wales where they would proclaim him true heir to the throne and would seize Welsh castles and hold them until aid came from Scotland and the north.[15]

In 1417, the date of Carsewell's arrest and narrative confession, the Welsh threat had subsided but not disappeared and Ireland remained incompletely subdued.[16] The total effect of Oldcastle's disturbing accompaniment is thus greatly to enhance his seditious credentials, and the former priest Sheldon likewise seems to have been a strenuous Lollard of seditious persuasion, on the run with Oldcastle since his 1413 breakout and full participant in his treasonous schemes of armed rebellion. Oldcastle is in incontestably 'bad company.'

Incipient nationalism

But what prompted Carsewell to grant the prior of Wenlock Abbey a place in this treasonous scheme? No ordinary house of English monks, Wenlock was what we now loosely call an 'alien priory': a Cluniac house, allied to a mother-house in France. As Knowles has pointed out, suspicion of these houses' foreign domination and consequent pressure upon them grew steadily throughout the wars between England and France.[17] Two crucial occurrences, each related to these suspicions and pressures, flank the events of 1417. The first is the passage in 1414 of a parliamentary Act of Denization, which gave statutory sanction to the expulsion of foreign religious and the confiscation of their possessions.[18] This Act seems to have put the matter to rest, except that the end of the papal schism in 1417, with its effect of reuniting England and France under the same papal dominion, encouraged the abbots of Cluny to attempt to regain control of their English houses.[19] Only at the end of the century, in the reign of Henry VII, were the English Cluniac houses placed formally under the visitation of the archbishop of Canterbury, and only four years after that did Wenlock petition for formal exemption from the administration of Cluny.[20] Thus, 1417 was a year of heightened concern over the status of houses like Wenlock and the possibility of their involvement with foreign enemies of the realm. The inherently and deeply treasonous nature of the prior's counterfeiting scheme would have seemed only too logical to persons already worried about the affiliations and loyalties of this alien outpost on native soil.

Treason

The inner logic of Oldcastle's presence may be further exposed via a popular presumption of the day: that, as traitors and as inherent falsifiers, Lollards and counterfeiters had a great deal in common.

The traitorous nature of counterfeiting is attested by a long series of treason statutes – from Justinian through Bracton and Glanvill in the thirteenth century to the definitive English statute of 1352 – which agree that counterfeiting is a form of lèse majesté. Enumerating treasonous acts in terms of their gravity, the 1352 statute specifies: plotting the death of the king or those close to him in succession; warring against the king or adhering to his enemies; and then 'si homme contreface les grant ou prive sealx le Roi ou sa monoie.'[21] Linking these false seals and coins as counterfeit is their bogus claim to the authority of the king, impermissibly arrogating his aura or *dignitas* to sanction their otherwise inert matter, and also the more particular sense in which they misuse and abuse his royal image. Carsewell's narrative depicts him and his colleagues engaging in counterfeiting of an undoubtedly treasonous variety; the false groats they were striking imitated silver coins of about four pence in value, the *signa* or emblems of which were a full-face portrait of the ruler on one side and a Christian cross on the other.[22]

The association of heresy with treason was slower to develop and less explicitly codified, although the Lancastrians placed themselves in the forefront of its development and implementation. In the two years after his coronation, assisted by Archbishop Arundel, Henry IV was in some haste to articulate and dramatize his own doctrine of the 'two swords' (of interdependent ecclesiastical and lay authority) and the 'double death' (or multiply signifying punishment visited upon the convicted heretic).[23] According to the former doctrine, the heretic was normally convicted by the ecclesiastical arm and then delivered to the lay arm for corporal punishment. According to the latter doctrine, the condemned heretic was both burnt and hanged – or sometimes both at once – in order to suggest offense against both religious doctrine and the civil state. As the most prominent heretic of his century, Oldcastle was thus regarded as having transgressed with respect both to his Church and to his king. Ecclesiastically condemned in October 1413, he escaped the Tower in the middle of that same month. Hasty proclamations were made seeking his capture (E403/614, 10 October 1413), and the more detailed proclamation issued in January 1414 specified both the religious aspect of his offense ('in Haeresin Dampnatus') and the treasonous threat that he and his fellow Lollards posed to king and country ('Mortem nostram . . . falso & proditorie imaginaverunt').[24] The definitive linkage of heresy and treason was effected by an official proclamation (and hence statute) of Henry V's first parliament, in April 1414.[25]

Yet heretics and counterfeiters have more in common than a penchant for treason. Oldcastle's heretical identity embraces an enlarged repertoire of half-concealed metaphorical connections underpinning the repeated association of Lollard heretics and adulteration or falsification of coin. The notion of proof by assay, and the equation of truth with good coin and falsehood with bad coin, was commonplace in the ancient world; Page duBois has shown that the classical association of torture and truth relies on an underlying metaphor, through which true gold is separated by assay from its counterfeit.[26] The association is no less true for the medieval period, where ideas of 'assay' and 'proof,' drawing their communicative vitality from the continuing practices of alchemy and metallurgy, control discussion of the affirmative separation of God's saints from their debased or less worthy contemporaries as well as the negative or stigmatic separation of the false heretic from the body of the faithful and true. Early in the fifteenth century, Jean Gerson would wield this metaphor ambitiously in his 'De Distinctione Verarum Revelationum a Falsis,' where he explains that those who would assess the validity of revelations should function as spiritual money-changers ('nummularii seu campsores spirituales'), shrewdly and accurately examining the precious and otherworldly coin of divine revelation, lest demons who seek to corrupt and falsify ('corrumpere falsareque') any divine and good money, should substitute false and worthless for true and genuine money.[27] Gerson's metaphor is deployed for theological purposes and within theological discussion, but the conception of such probation or trial was widespread in later medieval secular literature as well. 'Greet skile,' Chaucer's Clerk suggests, 'is [God] preeve that he wroghte' (IV, l. 1152), joining his predecessor-authors in invoking a metaphor of founding or casting and metallurgic assay to hail Griselda's survival of her test, and Chaucer's narrator in the *Book of the Duchess* urges the sorrowing Knight to 'preve' his good offices 'by assay' (l. 551). The same metaphor is very much at work in the judicial process; we need only recall that Carsewell's official role in the recorded proceedings is that of *probator*, assisting the king by furnishing evidence by which falsehood may be assayed and known.

In this charged metaphorical climate, the Lancastrians and their supporters proclaimed themselves eager for probation, whether divine or human, and considered themselves certain to pass the test. Heretics like John Oldcastle are raised up, according to the author of *Gesta Henrici Quinti*, that the faithful might be proved in the furnace of tribulation ('in conflatorium tribulacionis probaretur electus eius').[28] So, on the other side of the coin, must heretics be proven or assayed so that their falseness may be revealed. According to the author of the *Gesta*, Oldcastle is not what he seems, his corruption hidden under the cloak of sanctity ('sub velamine sanctitatis' – *Gesta*, p. 10) and, according to *De haeretico comburendo*, 'sub simulate sanctitatis colore.' More relevantly, he is portrayed as false or corrupted matter, who once, according to Hoccleve, 'shoon ful cleer,' but now has undergone a 'permutacion' from truth to falsity which may only be cured by purgation.[29] Walsingham portrays him as dear to the king on account of his probity, but nevertheless suspect as a result of his twisted or distorted hereticality ('propter haereticam pravitatem' – *Historia*, p. 291).

From time to time, these tacit connections are brought together in more manifest and explicit associations. A fifteenth-century treatise on excommunication, for example, associates under one rubric 'alle eretekkes that done wyttyngly ayeynis the lawe of Crist' and those who 'falsen the kyngis money, or clyppith it.'[30] Trying not to cluster these metaphorical associations too tightly, I would nevertheless say that Oldcastle is brought into association with false permutation and with corruption of the pure and true; he has, that is, his own inherent affinity with falsification and false coin, in terms that are implicit rather than explicit in Careswell's narrative, but that nevertheless offer a contextual explanation for the seemingly unmotivated alacrity with which he accepts the prior's wicked design to corrupt and alloy the good money of the king.

Blasphemy

Carsewell's and Oldcastle's proposed consummation of their scheme on Pentecost, the feast celebrating the descent and dissemination of the holy spirit, suggests a knack for malicious blasphemy. Important aspects of the link between counterfeiting, Lollardy, and treason are revealed by inquiry into the precise nature of the blasphemy as it is imagined. Based on the descent of the holy spirit on the apostles and the bestowal of the gift of tongues as recounted in the Acts, the feast itself was honored in England as a time of purification and baptism.[31] Its essence seems to involve the free gift of the holy spirit to the community of the devout, and the impetus to the apostolic life, to the spreading of the gospel by the original apostles and their successors. The gift of the holy spirit is liturgically emphasized by the singing of the hymn 'Veni, sancte Spiritus' during the sequence of the Pentecostal mass, with its emphasis upon the spontaneous gift of enlightenment to those in a state of deprivation or lack:

> Veni, pater pauperum;
> Veni, dator munerum;
> Veni, lumen cordium.

. . .

Da virtutis meritum
Da salutis exitum,
Da perenne gaudium.

[Come, father of the poor; come, giver of gifts, come, light of
hearts. . . . Give the merit of virtue, give salvation in the end, give
everlasting joy.][32]

The related idea of Pentecost as a time of dispersal and dissemination is perhaps best conveyed in its literary uses; in particular, in its
traditional invocation in the *Queste del Saint Graal* and in Malory as the
season at which the grail quest was initiated, at which time Arthur's
knights went abroad in the world in pursuit of the ineffable goal of
spiritual perfection.[33]

The goal of the knights' Pentecostal quest is, with the possible exception of the host itself,[34] that most overdetermined of medieval symbols,
the holy grail. But one of the grail's implications, and presumably the
central one, is of importance to an understanding of the particular
blasphemy of Carsewell's and Oldcastle's counterfeiting scheme: for
the grail was characteristically regarded as the pre-eminent source of
pure, authentic (or non-counterfeit) production. The uncanny nature of
the grail's productivity lies, as Marc Shell points out in his discussion
of the grail romances, in its capacity to transmute materiality into
spirituality, physical properties into spiritual gifts.[35] The grail may, in
turn, be aligned in this symbolic function with the two other pre-
eminent late medieval places of production: the altar upon which the
ceremony of the eucharist transforms material bread with its capacity
for corporeal nourishment into the purely symbolic 'food' represented
by the host, and the Royal Mint, in which ingots or inert matter are
granted symbolic sanction by the addition of the image of the king.[36]

The idea of boundless productivity as an antidote to spiritual or even
material lack might seem to embrace these counterfeiters, with their
determination to flood the country with bogus coin at the time of
Pentecost. Aptly enough for Carsewell's invention, 1417 (the year in
which he is said to have minted more than thirteen marks' worth of
coins) came at the heart of the great 'bullion famine' of the second
decade of the fifteenth century, and was the very year in which the
English money stock declined to a record post-plague low.[37] In certain
respects, then, the minting and distribution of good coin might be said
to offer a symbolically robust equivalent to the pure productivity of
the grail and the host, instituting a kind of effortless productivity to
remedy a serious lack. But the coin in question is, of course, bogus

rather than good, and therein lies the blasphemy. The distribution of inert (and therefore false) coin on the very day of Pentecost constitutes a tacitly sacred, as well as criminal, offense.

The blasphemous implications of this Pentecostal counterfeiting scheme are anticipated and redoubled in the broadly shared medieval understanding of the non- or in fact anti-material nature of God's gift to the apostles. Although given to the poor, it is a gift not of earthly treasure but of the spirit: of light, of virtue rewarded, of salvation through grace, of everlasting joy. This same point is made more explicitly in the *Cursor Mundi*, the pre-eminent spiritual manual of orthodox laypersons in the fourteenth and fifteenth centuries, where the story of Pentecost is framed by narratives of mistaken persons who have committed precisely the error of confusing spiritual and material reward. The *Cursor* tells, for example, of the fates of Ananias and his wife Sapphira who, having vowed to give their goods to the apostle Peter, greedily retained half and were struck dead for their reward, and of the error of Simon Magus, who thought that the gift of the holy ghost could be bought.[38]

But more remains to be said of John Oldcastle's contribution to this blasphemous scene. As a manifest traitor whose public identity was already at least partially identified with motivationless mischief-making, Oldcastle seems more or less at home in this conspiracy scene. But, as arch-Lollard, Oldcastle was associated even more particularly with a notorious doctrinal insult to the Pentecostal promise of spiritual transformation.

A theologically simplified, but widely held, contemporary stigmatization of Lollard spirituality emphasized its insistence on the separateness of spirit and matter and on the immutability of matter. In the view of the orthodox, this Lollard opinion was nowhere expressed more scandalously than in and around that site of pure spiritual productivity, the consecrated host. More shocking than any other Lollard transgression was their denial of the doctrine of transubstantiation, in which material bread was transformed into the spiritual body of Christ. Oldcastle's contention on this point during his 1413 trial was, according to Walsingham, that 'in the sacrament of the altar is the true body [of Christ] and true bread; the bread that we see and the body of Christ veiled in it which we do not see' (*Historia Anglicana*, vol. 2, p. 294). The heretical content of this apparently unexceptionable utterance resides in Oldcastle's insistence that the consecrated bread remains bread, even as it acquires an additional symbolic property as the body of Christ. Here he references a whole tradition of Lollard reasoning, including the contention of William Sautre, first heretic burnt by the Lancastrians in 1401, that 'after the pronunciation of the sacramental words of the body of Christ, the bread remains . . . *and* the bread with the body of Christ; that it does not cease to be ordinary bread, but that it remains bread [and also the] holy, true bread of life.'[39] To this contention that the bread in any sense remained bread, the orthodox rejoinder relied upon the Thomistic assertion that the bread continued in appearance only, as 'accident' of bread remaining in its nature 'without a subject' – which is to say that, the material bread having been wholly transformed into the body of Christ, its subject has been sacramentally removed.[40]

The point of passionate difference in this seemingly rather abstract discussion rests on the issue of transubstantiation. And transubstantiation, in turn, suggests an elaborate commerce between the material and the spiritual, in which, even without apparent alteration, the substance of the material can be utterly transformed by the action of the spirit. Although by no means disbelieving in the spirit, the Lollard places a heightened valuation upon it by maintaining its separation from the world of matter. Denied, in the process of Lollard reasoning, is the possibility of easy transition between the realms of matter and spirit. Baldly put, this is why Lollards distrusted material images, like representations of Christ's cross, as objects of spiritual veneration in their own right. Oldcastle declared at his 1413 trial that the body of Christ alone, and not the cross on which he was crucified, was and is to be adored, and he was thought scandalously to have effaced sacred images in devout books that had fallen into his possession.[41]

To the orthodox understanding, the Lollard inhabited a world desperately stripped of symbolic meaning, a physical world without reference to the spiritual realities beyond. In denying transubstantiation, and thus driving a wedge between the material and the spiritual, Lollards like Oldcastle were thought by the orthodox to overestimate the material, without concern for its substance or ultimate symbolization in a sacramental world of migratory meanings. The threat of heretical materiality is connected with the host and with issues of counterfeit in a sermon of the period, in which the preacher describes the wafer as if it were a coin, 'graven' on one side with truths and plain on the other as a reminder of the plainness and self-evident qualities of authoritative revelation. The sermonist warns that, if you look at the host with overmuch certainty in your own senses, 'than thou may sone counterfett the sight of thin eyn. For it semeth to thin eye but as a litill brede, but yitt it is no brede but Goddes owne flessh and his blode.'[42] Oldcastle is a counterfeiter because he sees only the material host, and misses its spiritual transformation. Just such an attachment to materiality underpins Oldcastle's imagined involvement in a scheme to flood the country with bogus, dead symbols on the day reserved for celebration of the living spirit.

Lancastrian legitimacy and the motility of the sign

Pervasive royal, and royalist, concern about counterfeiting may be explained in part as a deliberate discursive strategy. In the act of defining an illegitimate and non-orthodox opposition, the Lancastrians tacitly asserted and effectively staged their own legitimacy and ortho-doxy. But Lancastrian concern with the counterfeit also expresses a deeper and less tractable unease. For the *ultimate* counterfeiter, who cannot be prosecuted or even named, is the usurper-king. At once completely illegitimate and the very guarantor of legitimacy, he is, in Derrida's phrase, 'an outlaw and the very figure of the law.'[43] As usurpers, the Lancastrians entertained the concern of every counter-feiter: to stamp their kingship with the available images of legitimacy and to gain its willing acceptance. In fact, buoyed by their possession of the ceremonies and symbols of kingship, they conceived a higher ambition still, moving beyond the counterfeiter's strategies of re-signification to the alchemist's reconstitution of matter.

Even before Henry IV's usurpation, the Lancastrians were dis-playing an interest in self-transformative practices. John of Gaunt con-nived to alter chronicle records by inclusion of the bogus story of ancestor Edmund Crouchback's disparaged claim.[44] Henry IV devised novel coronation ceremonies designed to portray him as God's elect, and encouraged the understanding that he was the first king eligible to be anointed with a newly rediscovered coronation oil of unction deliv-ered directly from the hand of the Virgin to St Thomas of Canterbury.[45] Henry V reworked existing prophecies on his own behalf, and designed a reburial service for Richard II that portrayed his deposed predecessor as a benign sponsor of his reign (see Chapter 4, above). The presumption of all this machination was that appropriate ceremo-nies of election, coronation, and consolation can *transform* a claimant into a king.

The Lancastrians' point was made for them by royalist theologian Roger Dymmok who, writing at the end of Richard's reign, was in turn to become a Lancastrian stalwart. Dymmok's argument in this case is against Lollards who believe sacraments such as consecration of the host to be invalid because they do not effect visible transformation.[46] 'Should,' he rejoins, this argument hold sway, all the sacraments of the Church, all the oaths of kings, and all political intercourse would be completely destroyed. He goes on to offer a series of examples of transformation without outward change, including the case of a child newly baptized, a man confessed, a boy or man confirmed, a wafer consecrated, a man ordained into the priesthood, or marriageable persons newly betrothed or joined in their infirmities. All, he says, receive a new spiritual virtue ('uirtutem nouam spiritualem recipiunt')

– except of course for the bread, which is completely transubstantiated. He then turns to his clinching example: 'In what way is the body of a king changed, when he is recently crowned ["cum nouiter coronatur"] . . . , when such new authority is conferred upon him? He acquires no bodily change as a result.'

This reasoning, promising an influx of spiritual virtue with the power to transform a claimant into a king, holds clear appeal for the newly self-instated Lancastrian dynasty. Against the notion that through anointment the king might acquire a second or sacral body was pitted the Lancastrian discovery of a Lollard conspiracy within the land, wedded to a literal and material notion of what might (for simplicity) be called 'the king's one body.' William Sautre sought to defend his refusal to worship abstract symbols like the cross of Christ with an argument that might have been supposed pleasing to an incumbent ruler, saying that 'I prefer to adore a temporal king, than the aforesaid wooden cross, with respect to its material nature' ('volo magis adorare regem temporalem, quam crucem ligneam praedictam, quantum ad materiam in se').[47] Sautre here equates the temporal king and the material cross, and says in effect that each is what it is . . . and that a king is a king, no more and no less. By the same reasoning, he goes on to say that he would rather adore the bodies of saints than the true cross, and would rather adore a confessed and contrite man than the cross, or a predestinate and contrite man than an angel of God. The cross appears as brute matter; the predestinate man and the saint (along with the king) as matter distinguished by function or personal attainment; the angel is superior but intangible and remote and thus inaccessible to direct veneration.

Sautre's reasoning must trouble a usurping dynasty, for what is denied is precisely the symbolic process that might transform a non-king into a king. Latent in his argument is the contention most feared by the Lancastrians: that Richard – or, if not Richard, his legitimate heir – should still be king. This argument was in fact made; not, in the first instance, by a Lollard, but by one of the obstinate friars condemned to death by Henry IV in 1402. Suspected of complicity in the rumor that Richard yet lived, this friar of Aylesbury was said to have been interviewed personally by the new king.[48] Asked by the king if he would do battle for Richard's right, the friar responded in the affirmative. Asked if he wished Henry and his associates dead, the friar responded in the negative. Asked what he would do with Henry if he should gain victory over him, the friar responded, 'I would make you duke of Lancaster' ('Facerem vos ducem Lancastriae').[49] No reply could have been more galling to the new and insecurely seated king. This is, in fact, the very point on which his outrage came to rest when he wrote to his council from Burton upon Trent on 17 July 1403, rallying them against Henry Percy and complaining that he has risen against the king and his regal prerogative ('contre nous et notre regalie') and that, as recently established, he is calling Henry by nothing except his ducal title ('nous avons napelle fors Henry de Lancastre') – not to mention the usual, that 'le Roy Richard est encore en vie.'[50] Henry's vexation revolves around the danger that, his coronation notwithstanding, he might be regarded as what he always was: the duke of Lancaster, still. Supposing Henry to be only a duke, and the Prince of Wales to be only the son of a duke, then Richard (should he yet live) would still be king. And this is why Oldcastle, at his final hearing in 1417, was reputed to have defied the justices, saying that 'his liege lord Richard still living in Scotland, they had no right of judgment over him.'[51]

The Lancastrian commitment to ideas of transformation, so intense that it may be considered obsessional, is justified and defended by a strategy of doubling or division. Good transformation – that is, sacral transformation, elevation of inward properties without outward or apparent change – is reserved to the king. Bad transformation or counterfeiting – which begins and ends with brute matter and cynically sidesteps or even actively travesties the transformative power of the royal sign – is decisively split off from the royal purview and assigned to a host of obstinate materialists. The Lancastrian program was reliant upon signs and more signs: more efficacious, more numerous, more motile and transferable. Lollards (whose heightened respect for the spiritual encourages respect for matter's stubborn resistance) and counterfeiters (who cynically impose life-giving signs upon inert or dead matter) pose a closely allied, if not identical, threat to the Lancastrian symbolic. The idea of counterfeit, sublimated within the orthodox and Lancastrian system, is thus projected outward and upon them, as enemies of the transformative sign. No wonder that, from the Lancastrian-loyalist point of view, their identities sometimes became less than distinct.

Legitimacy and the Lancastrian poet

Fully implicated in the Lancastrian task of legitimating self-transformation was the Lancastrian poet. Long recognized as practitioners and exemplars of poetry as 'symbolic legitimation,'[52] Lancastrian poets like Lydgate and Hoccleve moved well beyond the frontiers of simple ingratiation and into a zone of complex complicity, the hallmark of which was their easy occupancy of a symbolic place analogous to that of the king. The place of the Lancastrian king was one of profound doubt and unease, marked by guilty concealment and by fitful hope of definitive self-legitimation. And do not these terms also describe the place of the Lancastrian poet? No serene guarantor of the symbolic, the earlier fifteenth-century poet was beset by doubts about legitimacy and mandate, and bedeviled by the need for secure insertion in a legitimate and legitimizing literary succession.[53]

Issues of being and seeming surface repeatedly in Lancastrian poems, including Hoccleve's 'Series,' the one I will pause to consider here. The form of this conflict in the 'Series' involves the narrator's recent emotional affliction that affected his relations with his friends and caused him to stop writing poetry, and his proposal to use this new work as a means of documenting his recovery and re-entry to the public sphere. The problem of recovery turns out, however, to hinge on familiar Lancastrian issues of genuineness and counterfeit, being and seeming, the possible incongruity of outward appearance and inner reality. Even though the narrator's wit is fully recovered, many deem him still unwell, and he realizes that he cannot make his case on external appearance alone:

> Vpon a looke is harde, men them to grownde
> what a man is; therby the sothe is bid.[54]

His vindication will require an exposure of his inner life, and his poem will in fact play a vital role in 'proving' his recovery ('Dialogue,' l. 444).

In the process of stabilizing and asserting his own claim, Hoccleve works his way through varied observations on surface and depth and the problems they pose for determining legitimacy and illegitimacy. Within this process of self-analysis and self-legitimization stands a passage that we might now consider almost predictable, if not mandatory, but which has seemed to Hoccleve's twentieth-century readers an occasion of aesthetic disproportion and blemish upon his work.[55] This passage is a lengthy tirade against counterfeiting, and, although it invariably strikes modern readers as labored and inexplicably over-strenuous, its problems paradoxically derive not so much from what it says as from what it does not say. Borne within it, but left tacit and latently available for the early fifteenth-century reader, is a cluster of partially developed and implied connections to urgent public issues of the day.

Counterfeiting enters the poem rather casually, via Hoccleve's observation that he could understand stigmatization if he had done something really serious, such as commit homicide, or extortion, or robbery, or clip coins, or war against the faith, or participate in bogus legal actions. But he then pauses, to say that 'amonge the vises that right now/rehersed I, *one* of them' is particularly hurtful – that of debasement of currency or 'feble moneye' (ll. 99–102). In a 100-line passage, he urges the penalty of hanging for 'falsynge of coyne,' whether by clipping or shaving or sweating, for their offenses against truth and harm to the poor. 'God grant,' he urges, 'that ther be no slowthe,/of this treason punishement to do' (ll. 152–153), especially since this practice is 'to owr Kynges preiudice,/and harme to all his lige people trewe' (ll. 162–163). The rather understated link between Hoccleve's immediate problem and his outcry against counterfeiters is that the latter employ various metals 'to make all seme gold' (l. 144). Counterfeiters are, that is, over-focused and over-reliant on the *appearance* or the surface of matter, in a way that undervalues or deliberately distorts its *substance* or its inner reality; just as, he has complained, people are overly concerned with his own unchanged appearance, erroneously assuming that if he looks the same his substance or inner state must remain in disarray.

Accepting the modernist (if not post-modernist) notion of stable selfhood as the *terminus a quo* of literary composition, we might mistakenly conclude that Hoccleve has appropriated the notion of the counterfeit, and its over-reliance on outward appearance in relation to inner legitimacy, in order to facilitate his self-disclosure. But the medieval (and pre-modern) writer is more likely to deploy the self, not as the ultimate center of interest, but as an imaginative exemplification of broader issues.[56] Rather than wielding the counterfeit for purposes of self-representation, Hoccleve offers up a highly stylized self as an instance of the loyal subject's essential project of eschewing the counterfeit and adhering to the legitimate within the potentially deceptive terrain of Lancastrian politics. With implications far beyond the presenting issue of a single poet's effort to gain the public estimation he deserves, this passage constantly invites rearticulation with the largest public issues of appearance and substance, matter and meaning.

In keeping with the breadth of his emphasis, Hoccleve continually affirms the urgency of counterfeiting as a matter of public concern. For example, Hoccleve seems to have rewritten his own tirade, inserting a rather breathless up-to-the-minute report that parliament has now passed a law pertaining to the weighing of gold:

no statute made was then as that now is . . .
now tyme it is unto weightes vs drawe
sythen that the parlyament hathe made it a lawe. (ll. 136, 139–140)

The session of parliament in question is presumably that of 9 Henry V (1421), in which the Commons brought forward a whole series of interrelated petitions, having to do with the restoration of 'loial Moneie' through the establishment of its 'joust pois' (including the

establishment of money exchanges throughout the realm) and punishment of 'fauxsours & controvours de faux Pois.'[57]

We have already seen that parliament's insistence on 'loial' terminology is not accidental, with falsification of the king's image and
currency regarded as one of the most gravely treasonous of offenses.
The gravity of the counterfeiter's offense is underscored, in Hoccleve's
suggestion not only that counterfeiters' work and sweat will purchase
them a seat in hell (ll. 141–147), but that their crime is one of 'treson'
itself (l. 153). This claim is itself supplemented by the suggestion that
counterfeiters should be hanged, the traditional punishment for traitors ('he that in falsynge of coyne gilty is/hathe great wronge that he
nere on a gebet' – ll. 129–130) and is substantiated by the assertion that
counterfeiters' activities cause direct injury to the king ('Alas that to
owr Kynges preiudice . . . Continue shall this fowle and cursed vice/
of falsynge of coyne' – ll. 162–165).

The link with treason suggests the symbolic reverberation of counterfeiting, and Hoccleve's passage is replete with implied suggestions
that the offense does not end with the activities of a handful of
wretched coin-clippers. The activities of Hoccleve's counterfeiters are
amplified through two different metaphorical clusters, one of which
would see practitioners as a 'cursed meynye' (l. 178) or band of followers united to a common end, and the other as a 'falce secte' (l. 191)
or sectarian deviation within the larger community of the faithful. Seen
as 'meynee,' and linked with the sponsorship of great and unruly lords
of the countryside, counterfeiters are at least glancingly associated
with the quarrels over illicit distribution of livery and disruptive sponsorship of unfounded legal actions that divided English society in the
later fourteenth and fifteenth centuries.[58] Seen as 'secte,' counterfeiters
and their activities gained an even more ominous resonance.

The language in which Hoccleve describes his 'falce secte' draws
heavily upon the association we have already seen in Carsewell's
narrative, between counterfeiting and Lollardy. Consider the peroration with which Hoccleve concludes his tirade:

> Nowe in good faythe I drede there shall be
> suche multitude of that falce secte
> with-in this two yere or ellis thre,
> but yf this stynkynge errowr be correcte,
> that so myche of this land shall be infecte
> there-with, that trewthe shall a-downe be throwe,
> and that cursed falshed it overgrowe. (ll. 190–196)

The crucial terms here would seem to be: (1) counterfeiters as, or
modeled upon, a 'secte' or deviant group; (2) the danger of their

proliferation; (3) their preference for falsity over faith, for error over truth; (4) the images of foulness and, especially, contagion with which they are associated. These terms are, in turn, contemporaneously associated within one – and only one – textual matrix: in that contemporary discourse of orthodoxy and heresy by which the Lollards were defined and separated from the community of the faithful.

These supposed Lollard attributes are all fully in play within the statute *De haeretico comburendo*, promulgated to justify burning Sautre in 1401, the second year of Lancastrian rule:

> perfidious and perverse members of a certain new sect ['diversi perfidi & perversi cujusdam nove Secte'] . . . openly and secretly preaching in these days perversely and maliciously within different parts of our kingdom diverse new doctrines and opinions [which are] iniquitous, heretical, and erroneous ['doctrinas & opiniones iniquas hereticas & erroneas'], and from such sect and its evil opinions they generate conspiracies and illicit alliances . . . and stir up as much sedition or insurrection as they can ['ad sedicionem seu insurreccionem excitant quantum possunt'] . . . and perpetrate and commit other varied enormities horrible to be heard.[59]

This sect spreads its opinions through preaching and other means, is dedicated to error and heretical iniquity, and is bent on seditious insurrection. Only missing (albeit implied) in the cluster of terms just enumerated is the imagery of pestilential contagion, but it is richly supplied elsewhere. In the proclamation against Lollards issued by Henry V during the first year of *his* reign, this same 'Nova Secta Lollardorum' is accused of operating under the color of preaching to sow discord among the people ('ad seminandum discordiam in populo nostro') and to raise up the pestiferous seed of Lollardy and evil doctrine ('Semen pestiferum Lollardriae & Male Doctrine').[60] Dymmok's rejoinder to the Lollards, written at the end of the fourteenth century and continuously popular in the Lancastrian era, describes them as the modern heretics who have infected or corrupted our island ('moderni heretici sic nostram insulam inficerent') and as this pestilential people ('hec pestifera proles' – p. 6). Hoccleve himself, hailing the burning of heretic Badby in the presence of Henry, Prince of Wales, detests the stench of his error ('the stynkyng errour that he was inne').[61]

Hoccleve's reprobation of Lollardy, and assertion of his own orthodoxy, recurs constantly in his poetic corpus, as in his poem of animadversion against John Oldcastle, or, again, in his *Regement of Princes* where he wishes all heretics 'i-served' like John Badby, burnt for heresy in 1410.[62] Inveighing against heresy, Hoccleve thus bends the energies of his text to an assertion of the representational divide that the Lancastrians themselves were intent on driving between seeming and being, outer and inner, counterfeit and real, material and ineffable, heretical and orthodox, illegitimate and legitimate; his text, moreover, everywhere announces its preference for the orthodox and the legitimate in their struggle against adulteration. Simultaneously, Hoccleve puts his narrator in the position of his Lancastrian monarch, as one who has effected genuine self-transformation: on the one hand, from duke or duke's son to king; on the other hand, from a victim of irrational self-beguilement to an adviser fit to please and instruct a prince or a king. Hoccleve's prince and his narrator would, put to the test, be 'proven' transformed and true.

The motile sign is a crucial element in the Lancastrian prince's and poet's self-transformative project. But in order to perform its legitimizing function the sign must be stabilized in the end. The stabilization of the monarch's claim rests on true title, as conveyed by unclouded inheritance and just descent. That is the very dream of Lancastrian kings and their followers – unaccountably, as they tell it, thrown away by Lollards, counterfeiters, and their ilk. Would you not, cries Hoccleve in what I take to be the most deeply felt lines in his declamation against Oldcastle, defend land

> Which that thy fadir heeld in reste & pees,
> With title iust & trewe in al his age,
> And his fadir before him brygelees,
> And his and his . . . ? (ll. 162–165)

In the fashion of the Lancastrian poet, who cannot help introducing via subordination or negation or passing illustration the very ideas that dare not be acknowledged, Hoccleve here broaches a standard that the Lancastrian kings will not and cannot meet. Hoccleve naturally tries to respond to the very issue he raises, fiddling constantly with the facts of Lancastrian succession. Thus, for example, the *Regement of Princes* attributes Richard's supplantation to the arbitrary operations of fortune's stroke (ll. 22–24), and virtually elides the usurping Henry IV in favor of John of Gaunt, oddly memorialized as a great dresser (ll. 512–520). By such means, Hoccleve joins his fellow genealogists in mocking up a version of just Lancastrian descent – and the right to secure enjoyment and use of the prerogatives and symbols of rule.

So, in a kind of parallel genealogical exercise, does Hoccleve ponder his own relation to his forebears in the order of artistic succession. The standard of true descent turns out to have its counterpart in the realm of letters, and its name is literary tradition. Every Lancastrian poet was some kind of literary genealogist, above all in relation to the example and achievements of 'fadir Chaucer.' In the several discussions of his relation to Chaucer, Hoccleve hastens to disclaim the notion that his father and master might have 'bequeathed' his talent (*Regement*, ll. 1965–1966). But, as in monarchic succession, demise and proper interment necessarily precede the transfer of *dignitas* or royal aura. Even as he describes Chaucer's death, Hoccleve is at pains to suggest that Chaucer's 'resemblance' still lives in him. At this point, Hoccleve causes a portrait of Chaucer to be inserted in his manuscript:

> Althogh his lyfe be queynt, the resemblaunce
> Of him hath in me so fressh lyflynesse,
> That, to putte othir men in remembraunce
> Of his persone, I haue heere his lyknesse
> Do make. . . . (ll. 4992–4996)

Chaucer's portrait concludes Hoccleve's meditation on origins, and introduces another of those digressions, the significance of which has only begun to be felt. This time, Hoccleve concerns himself with the use of images in worship, and inveighs against 'some' who say that no images should be made.[63] For, he argues, by a kind of halo effect or replication, the spiritual aura of the images will propagate inwardly in the thoughts of their beholders:

> . . . when a thing depeynt is,
> Or entailed, if men take of it heede,
> Thoght of the lyknesse, it will in hem brede. (ll. 5003–5005)

Inert images – images that are no more than they seem to be – are unlikely to have such an effect. Dead metal, dead matter, will propagate in no one's heart. But tradition-minded poets, like worshipers of saints and properly anointed kings, can incarnate the ineffable aura of the deceased.

This is as much as to say that tradition is the best guarantee of reference, and best defense against the adulteration of the sign. As R. A. Shoaf demonstrates, the late medieval poet's central fear is that the sign will become irreferential, a semiotic dead letter, when wielded by frauds and counterfeits like Chaucer's Pardoner, whose signs have become wholly inert from the point of view of a sacramental and motile symbol system.[64] Against the threat of the irreferential – the airborne toxic event that would throttle poetry at its source – Hoccleve employs an arsenal of assurances, declaiming against false oaths, flattery, visual deception, and – as we have already seen – counterfeiting itself. But true succession, for poet and for prince, is finally the best guarantee that the sign can be regulated, without negation of its migratory capacity to confer and legitimize new status.

'To live outside the law you must be honest'
(Bob Dylan, 'Absolutely Sweet Marie')

Continually troubling the repose of these facile sign-mongers is, however, an ill-assorted gang of real and imaginary literalists and materialists: counterfeiters like William Carsewell, Lollards like Oldcastle and Sautre who think that what looks like bread must still in some sense be bread, friars like the one from Aylesbury who regard King Henry as the duke of Lancaster still. In their wake and train are alien monks, renegade Welsh, wild Irish, and lapsed priests. These characters inhabit a fascinating border country between the historical and the textual. The irrefutably historical characters like Oldcastle are so written over by imaginative predisposition and so completely violated by Lancastrian designs upon their signification as to seem hardly believable. And the putatively invented characters like Trim and Harlech (named, not impossibly but implausibly, after castles in their native lands) are nevertheless bearers of historical antagonisms that confer a form of reality.

So is the written record of the fifteenth century populated with denizens of this strange border country, including more Lollard counterfeiters than Carsewell alone. Among their ranks is the remarkable Robert Rose, *capellanus* of Herteshorn, Derbyshire, who was charged as a confederate of John Oldcastle and also as a 'launderer of gold and silver and shaver and counterfeiter of the king's coin and as a multi-plier and manufacturer of false money, including groats, pence, and half pence' – in this case, from brass, copper, and lead, rather than silver or gold.[65] Although not an official approver, Rose seems to have concocted a story to assist in his exoneration, according to which, in 1415 or 1416, he encountered and conversed with John Oldcastle at 'Swerstone' bridge and they rode together for three or four leagues and they ate and drank together, he fully knowing the identity of his Lollard companion. Rose's story must have pleased someone, because – despite having been accused of a raft of crimes including not only counterfeiting but also mail fraud, common thievery, highway robbery, rape, theft of kitchen implements, and more – he was found not guilty by jury and delivered from jail.[66]

Less fortunate was another Lollard counterfeiter, John Russell of

London: a member of the Woolpackers Guild, a friend of Lollards like Richard Gurmyn but also an apparent confidence-man who sought inheritance of Gurmyn's goods, a mortal enemy of Mayor Thomas Fauconer who had to be mainprized by his friends for threatening Fauconer's apprentices, a sanctuary-seeker who stuck his friends with the tab, a confessed slanderer, and finally – in the Lollard rising of 1431 – a man convicted of consorting with Lollards *and* publishing their opinions *and* clipping and counterfeiting the money of the king![67] For all his ephemerality, Russell (his treason evidently superseding his Lollardy) met a very material fate: hanged, beheaded, quartered, and his severed head displayed on London Bridge.

These characters' entry into the textual record, or at least the form in which they are permitted to enter it, is detemined by a complex of Lancastrian anxieties and motivations: displaced anxiety about their own legitimacy and vulnerability to charges of counterfeit, and positive motivation to construct a discursive cordon around their own legality and orthodoxy. An ill-assorted gaggle of hopeless connivers and intransigent enemies of self-transformation, these characters seem rarely if ever even permitted to speak in their own voices, let alone to offer anything very satisfying in the way of reasoned or sustained anti-Lancastrian critique. But, occasionally, even in sponsored utterances like Carsewell's confession, a fissured verbal surface yields a possiblity of an anti-Lancastrian interpretation. One must, of course, be aware of the potentially fantastic and self-deluding nature of the quest for the 'unpoliced detail' or the ready-made and transparent found object of unassailable interpretative privilege. Yet, a strained and conflictual extra-textual situation exerts what I have described in the final chapter of this volume as an 'absent pressure,' upon the text itself, under which or in relation to which certain of the text's details acquire an ulterior but socially urgent significance. It is to one such detail in the Carsewell confession that I wish, in conclusion, to turn.

In common conception the counterfeit coin substitutes dross or base metal for the precious metal of which the legitimate coin is composed, thus relying cynically on subjects' trust in the extent to which symbols like the face and name of the king stabilize and guarantee value. But Carsewell and Oldcastle plan on producing coins *already made of silver*. In his confession, Carsewell describes the process as one of melting a bar of genuine (albeit clipped) silver in a fire and casting it into a similitude of the king's money called groats ('in quodam prente ad simulitudinem monete domini regis Anglie de grotes') the die having been artfully made with the letters and signs belonging to a groat ('cum litteris et signis ad grossum pertinentibus'). These letters and signs consisted of the image of the king with his legends and titles on the face, and a cross and the place of minting on the back – all serving purposes of authentication.

In a more traditional economy the silver would have needed no authentication. Our counterfeiters inhabit a more developed culture – more developed, at any rate, in terms of royal aspiration, in which a coin lacks its full measure of authenticity until the Mint has added symbols with the effect of stabilizing its value by incorporating it within the royal aura or *dignitas*. The paradox here is that a 'counterfeit' coin of the sort contemplated by our plotters could possess its full weight of silver but lack value; a clipped or worn coin, supplemented by the king's sacral guarantee, will be redeemed at full value. But the purpose of this royal supplement is not so much to guarantee the coin's weight (although measures to enforce such guarantees were periodically taken), but to effect a symbolic repair of its material deficiencies. In this sense, it is our counterfeiters who are the literalists and traditionalists, recirculating bullion and only redundantly adding the symbolic impedimenta that will permit recognition of their true coin *as* true. Hereby is posed a set of very subtle questions about the meaning of legitimacy and ultimately of kingship.

From the orthodox view the so-called counterfeit coins are of course illegitimate in that they are falsely referent or irreferent to the royal *dignitas* on whose authority they would enter into circulation. But Carsewell's silver coins nevertheless possess at least a fugitive claim to authenticity in their valuable material composition. It is in terms of Carsewell's reliance on the material that his and Oldcastle's objectives may be supposed most deeply to coincide. Whatever other associations might have been elicited by his name, Oldcastle is recognizable in this narrative principally as a Lollard, and the complement to the fervor of Lollard spirituality was a resolute insistence on the persistence, literality, and semiotic reliability of matter.

Stubbornly and resistantly construed, the counterfeit coin signals a previous time when a self-present and unalienated subject might bear precious metal worth its 'actual' value. The coin of the realm, on the other hand, represents a step toward what Žižek (after Rotman) calls 'imaginary money,' or money of which the possessor is an impersonal 'bearer,' relying for the completion of its value upon the supervening presence of the king.[68] Carsewell's arrest occurred at a crucial moment in time, with respect to the monarch's attempt to establish himself as overseer and guarantor of monetary circulation. In earlier medieval centuries, gold (and gold in its 'personality' as silver) had long since established itself as master signifier within the domain of monetary exchange, functioning as the 'general equivalent' which set and regulated economic value.[69] Its role within the system of economic exchange may be seen, in this sense, as coordinate with the function of the monarch as regulator and measure of value within the political system or system of 'social forces.' But the fourteenth and, especially, the early fifteenth centuries in England were the point at which monarchs sought to exert their practical and symbolic authority over monetary circulation, requiring that gold function as monetary general equivalent only under the sign of their approval. To the extent that this step is successful, and the king establishes himself as presiding presence over monetary exchange, the participant in exchange is rendered reliant upon the royal guarantee, and is correspondingly depersonalized. The participant in monetary exchange is, like the reminted coin, at once emptied and reauthenticated by the majesty of the king.[70] Given the regulation and authentication of coinage as one element of royal initiative and assertion in the late Middle Ages, the subject who circumvents or refuses to deal in the king's coin – who returns like these 'counterfeiters of the real' to precious metal itself as the standard of equivalent value – resists the hegemonic project of the king.

Stubbornness, as a form of resistance to Lancastrian designs on the autonomy or self-sufficiency of the subject, characterizes different but interrelated forms of behavior that could put a subject at odds with Lancastrian hegemonic ambitions. The ultimate case in point, to which I can only allude here, is the Lollard heretic Badby, burnt in 1410 for his view that the sacramental host remained material bread. Ostensibly moved by mercy – over-great mercy, in Hoccleve's eyes[71] – Prince Henry offered to make him a royal pensioner for life if he would recant. Yet Badby – possessed, in Walsingham's account,[72] by an evil spirit – stubbornly declined such great honor and was returned to the flames. Badby's refusal appears not only to have been a doctrinal matter, but also a refusal (in this case a literal refusal) to become the prince's 'man,' his creature, living under sufferance.

Carsewell was no Badby, and his confession is to be read as a deliberate self-incrimination rather than an endorsement of resistance. Nevertheless, counterfeiting as he imagines it is a stubborn and retrograde practice, and hence a resistant one. Real counterfeiters – like real thieves, real poachers, real keepers of unlicensed brothels, and the like – were presumably uninterested in seditous acts of symbolic resistance, caught up instead in the far more urgent business of earning a livelihood and getting by. But imaginary counterfeiters were everywhere in this society, and their activity is a site in which resistance can be thought about, both favorably by anti-Lancastrians (with their attraction to any activity evading or escaping the legitimizing claims of the king) and unfavorably by pro-Lancastrians (who uneasily acknowledge the centrality of the metaphor but seek to shift its stigma to anybody's activities but their own). Lending itself best of all to the imagination of resistance is the brand of counterfeiting practiced by Carsewell and his associates, with its reliance upon precious metals as traditional units of value and its refusal to acknowledge the transformative powers of the king. Under the sponsorship of the uneasy Lancastrian imagination, these illicit purveyors of real silver engage in a form of counterfeiting that puts them in the same seditious boat as revolutionary Lollards and arch-traditional Franciscans. All equally attract Lancastrian enmity by treating the world as irreducible matter, as what it seems to be, rather than what it might be made to seem.

6

Joanne of Navarre: That Obscure Object of Desire

This study has already touched on a recurrent problem: historical characters once lived empirical lives separate from surviving records or narrations, but the same texts which promise access to their lives paradoxically screen them from view. No matter how benignly intended, these texts supplant the life, effectively installing themselves in its place. This substitutive power is amply demonstrated in the case of John Oldcastle, whose different narrators freely and variously pronounce upon his presence, his absence, his leadership, his cowardice, his martial prowess, his feminization. Cacophonous as they might be, these varied characterizations have the effect of imposing themselves, occupying the place of the life they would describe. Certainly, with respect to things said of a life, different ethical standards must pertain to one who lives, or once lived, as opposed to a character whose sole existence is textual. But how, or on what basis, is an ethical judgment to be made? How, that is, is the life's supposed 'original' to be found and assessed, when already screened from view by a myriad of bad or even maliciously distorted copies?

A starting-point for the historical life's analysis might rest in subsequent texts' inefficiencies – or, to put it differently, their representational hyper-efficiency, their inevitable production of a narrative and symbolic residue from which alternative motives, traits, and counter-tendencies might be inferred. Teresa De Lauretis speaks relevantly of the 'elsewhere' of discourse, the 'space not visible in the frame but inferable from what the frame makes visible.'[1] This space is not so much beyond or external to the text as within the text, constituted as the text's own tacit admission of inability to control its terms.

The problem for the historian is that, as an epiphenomenon of discourse, still wholly textually produced and enclosed, this residue enjoys no privileged historical status. Nevertheless, the historical life or life external to the text retains the capacity to place the text under an absent 'pressure,' a pressure potentially measurable in certain of that text's enlargements. Texts concerning queens and ladies like Joanne of Navarre, Catherine of France, and Jacqueline of Holland attempt official and stringently limited descriptions, within recognized patterns and representational regimes. Yet, in part because these rambunctious historical actors pressured their biographers with atypical feats and sallies, the same textual records invariably contain internal and concurrent spaces within which alternative possibilities can be discerned.

Here I will consider just one of these women, Joanne of Navarre, and several different elements of her representation: her dower (with special emphasis falling upon the 'material' aspects of her situation); and her portrayal as both mediatrix and witch; her inclusion in an extraordinary narrative of failed recognition.

As 'liquid asset'

Aristocratic marriages of the later Middle Ages might seem unguardedly illustrative of the senses in which women were regarded as property and the marriage relation as a propertied relation. Nakedly foregrounded was the expectation that the woman would bring a substantial dowry or *dot* (in the form of lands, income, or at the very least money and treasure) to the relation. Also understood in later medieval England was the offsetting, but still fully materialistic, expectation that in certain cases a prosperous husband marrying advantageously would return to the wife sums in the form of a dower or *douaire*, available for her household expenses even during the term of his life (above and beyond, that is, the share of his estate which would devolve upon her with his death). The dowry/dower negotiation established an interpretative structure within which the behavior of its participants – or at least their presumed worth to each other – might be weighted and understood.

The experience of Henry IV's second marriage to Joanne (or Jeanne) of Navarre will suggest that a system seemingly intended to reduce women to markers of property and to rationalize the marital relation as a propertied relation might actually serve as an expressive vehicle for the most unpredictable personal and regional interests. The intent of the arranged, aristocratic marriage is obviously to deploy the woman as an asset. But her value as an asset depends in part on her convertibility and transferability; on what Bourdieu calls her value as 'a political instrument, a sort of pledge or liquid asset, capable of earning symbolic profits.'[2] Her ability to function as a pledge or marker is bound up in her ability to cross boundaries and frontiers, to represent differential categories of material and symbolic wealth. Yet this very liquidity renders her difficult of possession – attaches to her a sense of implied profit, but profit that can be difficult or even dangerous to realize. If she indeed remains a property, she represents 'property of a labile and dangerous sort.'[3]

Previously married and possessed of substantial capital in her own right, Joanne might have seemed to promise an economic windfall for this insecure and impecunious dynasty. But the prospective property rights attached to this marriage turn out to be illusory; or, worse still, to have been wired, booby-trapped, and rigged for disaster. If Joanne introduced any 'capital' into her marriage, it needed to be symbolic, because intangibles were the only advantages which Henry was destined to realize as a result of this transaction. In Bourdieu's analysis, symbolic benefits are likely to serve as a screen for more naked economic achievements, with 'the pursuit of maximum material profit . . . masked under the contests of honour and the pursuit of maximum symbolic profit' (p. 56). In the present case, as so often in the mocked-up and topsy-turvy reign of Henry IV, the mask had perforce to become and to *be* the reality, for the presumed or hoped-for material underpinning proved impossible of access.

As daughter of the notorious and well-heeled Charles le Mauvais, king of Navarre, Joanne naturally enough brought a dowry to *a* marriage, a dowry remarkable in its generosity: her father promised the sum of 120,000 gold livres and 6,000 livres annually in rents for her 1386 marriage to the elderly, headstrong, and truculent John IV, duke of Brittany. John, for his part, responded with an equally munificent dower, including the rents of the city of Nantes, and other substantial properties.[4] Charles's death in 1387 meant that substantial portions of the dowry would not be paid,[5] but the dower was unaffected; it was, in fact, renegotiated in 1396, including stipulations that it should comprise one third of his wealth and should be available from the date of the wedding onward, and at her disposal until death, should he predecease her.[6]

After the duke's death in 1399, Joanne served as regent of Brittany until 1401 when her twelve-year-old son John became duke. Negotiations for marriage with Henry IV were begun in March 1402, and completed with considerable rapidity, considering the complexity of the arrangements to be made. The marriage required a papal dispensation for consanguinity; a 3 April 1402 proxy ceremony in England (in the course of which Henry plighted his troth to envoy Antoine Ricze); a further dispensation from the pope to live among schismatics; and a complex and mainly disadvantageous negotiation in which her own nobles, who opposed the marriage, went over her head to the duke of Burgundy, in whose guardianship she was required to leave her male children as a condition of departure.[7] On 20 December 1402 Joanne set out from Nantes, with the marriage finally occurring at Winchester on 8 February 1403 and a ceremony of coronation on 26 February at Westminster. Matters of dowry and dower must have been discussed in the course of the marriage negotiations (the proxy ceremony includes reference to pertinent 'lettres et endentures'), but are absent from the record.

Speculation about Henry IV's interest in marriage to Joanne inevitably included the eventual disposition of this wealthy widow's dower from the duke of Brittany. The Chronicler of Saint-Denys says that initial awareness of the marriage negotiation sparked a rumor to the effect that she had shipped her treasure and jewels abroad.[8] Writing at the end of the seventeenth century, Lobineau lists an interest in the dower prominently among other possible considerations: the likelihood of her continuing influence in duchy affairs, the possibility of an English–Breton alliance against France, access to continental ports, and 'le gros doüaire qu'elle avoit en Bretagne, auquel le feu Duc avoit adjousté trois ou quatre ans avant que de mourir.'[9] If this was indeed Henry's list, he must have been a disappointed man. Joanne left the young duke and her other sons under the hostile guardianship of the duke of Burgundy,[10] the Bretons were in arms against the British within months of the wedding,[11] and Joanne was thwarted in her attempt to raise ready cash by selling the governorship of Nantes to Olivier de Clisson for 12,000 crowns.[12] Although the dower appears to have remained securely in Joanne's possession, its ultimate disposition also eluded whatever hopes Henry might have entertained.

In fact, the ever financially hard-pressed Henry IV was to endure a squadron of monetary disappointments in his alliance with the wealthy countess, at least when the financial aspects of his marriage are compared with generally accepted medieval norms. First, no record exists of any dowry that came to Henry as a result of the marriage. A second area of more promise would seem to be the large dower from her previous marriage which Joanne brought with her to England, and of which medieval precedents would have granted Henry administrative control and enjoyment during his lifetime.[13] Later records confirm Joanne's active interest in the state and amount of her Breton dower, and also suggest that it was paid throughout her lifetime except for certain postponements owing to shifting alliances and states of war.[14] Henry, however, seems to have achieved no control whatever over his wife's inherited revenues and funds. In this sense, would-be *gylour* Henry must be considered *gyled*. For, although Joanne really did have money in her coffer, that coffer might as well have been empty, since Henry was never to enjoy one sou of its contents.

Rather, in another costly decision, he followed a different medieval precedent, acting promptly to assure Joanne of a second dower, from the English Treasury and from lands under his control, together with certain guarantees from the income of the Lancaster estates: on 8 March 1403, a month after the marriage, a sum of 10,000 marks annually was granted to the queen, to be paid from the Exchequer, pending satisfaction of the sum by rents from possessions later to be assigned.[15] This massive sum, amounting to some 10 percent of the annual income of the royal government,[16] was roughly half again as large as the £4,500 granted to English queens in dower over the preceding two centuries. This lavish grant initiated a six-year struggle to assemble lands and rents equal to its proportions – an enterprise aided by convenient confiscations from Scrope, Northumberland, and other convicted traitors, but not to be adequately addressed until 1 July 1409, when annual income from a major settlement of lands nearly (but not completely) yielded the requisite sum.[17] Once again these sums granted to Joanne in dower were not for her enjoyment after Henry's death, but for her expenses during the term of his life; they were, effectively, alienated from his control.

The immense resources available to Joanne from her previous and present marriages, and the autonomy with which she enjoyed them, are emblematized by Henry's 10 December 1404 grant of the new tower at the entrance of the great gate of the great hall within the palace of Westminster across from the royal Treasury, for her use.[18] Nor are we here speaking of a wardrobe or chamber for planning beneficent intercessions; hard business is the order of the day. Specified in the grant is her range of contemplated activities, including councils and business, for handling and auditing her accounts and for (safeguarding) her charters, writings, muniments, and other evidences ('pro consiliis et negociis . . . tractandis ac compotis suis audiendis necnon pro cartis, scriptis, munimentis et aliis euidenciis . . .'). Much could be said and thought about the symbolism of this tower; suffice it to say here that this grant would have been superfluous, had it not been directed to a woman bent on exercising a significant degree of fiscal self-determination.

The amazing thing is not that this 'hopelessly over-generous'[19] dower was interrupted during a three-year period in which Joanne was confined on suspicion of sorcery, but that it was taken so seriously, both before and after her confinement. Henry IV applied himself assiduously to meeting its demands and, drafting his will in 1408, was prepared to meet the sum from Duchy revenues in lieu of other sources.[20] Henry V faithfully met arrears, especially from revenues of alien priories, and, when he took these priories into his hands, from other compensations.[21] Henry V restoring her dower shortly before his death as a matter of 'conscience,' the obligation was honored by parliament in 1423, and the sum was met as fully as the reassignment of certain of its portions would permit.[22] Not just the monarchs, but even parliament, were surprisingly ready to support the dower through most of the thirty-four years it was paid, with parliament even overlooking its unprecedented size in its expressed wish to see the queen 'sufficiantment endowez . . . en manere come autres Roignes ont este endowez davaunt ces heures.'[23]

As an investment, Henry IV's tie with Joanne of Navarre must be rated somewhere between bad and catastrophic, absorbing nearly 10 percent of royal revenues over a period of some thirty hard-pressed years. Yet the populace treated this bad risk with surprising sympathy and forbearance. Even while Joanne was requested by parliament to assume certain of her own expenses from sums made available from her English dower,[24] she was the subject of regular parliamentary commendations to the king.[25] Long after Henry IV's death, she was shown every mark of respect by her stepson Henry V. She is habitually described in the documents of Henry V's reign as 'Regina Angliae' and as 'carissima Mater nostra.'[26] She was assigned the right to live in the royal castles of Berkhamstead and Wallingford while her stepson campaigned in France.[27] Such regard shown for Joanne at a point in her life when she had little to offer in the way of personal power or material resource (since both her dowers would terminate at death) suggests the residual influence commanded by a certain kind of title and affiliation. At these moments, she may be said to have enlisted sympathy above and beyond the promised material benefits of her allegiance.

Of course, those benefits we might loosely designate as 'capital' may be held in many forms, and even a manifestly impractical gesture from the point of view of rent or other material gain may still be self-interested in its motive of acquiring or controlling symbolic resources.[28] From the viewpoint of a usurping king, any sort of marital tie to the ruling houses of Europe evidently made sense as a symbolic contribution to his legitimation, however exorbitant the cost. A precedent (though hardly an encouraging one) was available near at hand in forefather John of Gaunt's marriage to Constanza of Castile, a marriage on which he vainly attempted to capitalize by engaging in proprietary sorties and insisting upon the formal title 'King of Castile' during her lifetime. Henry IV gained all his heirs, as well as a substantial dowry, from his first marriage to Mary de Bohun, yet she ended up obscurely buried in the unfinished church of St Mary in the

Newarke at Leicester, while his consort Joanne shared his royal tomb and joined her effigy to his at Canterbury.[29] As daughter (and co-heiress) of Humphrey X de Bohun, seventh earl of Hereford and his wife Joanne, sister of Richard, earl of Arundel, Mary could hardly have had better domestic credentials. Yet as daughter of the king of Navarre and granddaughter of the king of France, Joanne possessed a continental cachet that was evidently deemed the greater contribution to legitimation.

Shortly after her arrival in England and marriage to the king at Winchester, Joanne's leading role was solemnized in a formal ceremony of coronation, with invitations broadly distributed among the lords, ladies, and knights of the realm. This was, to judge from such indications as its ambitious guestlist,[30] a sumptuous affair, conducted (in the view of one chronicler) with due honor and festivity ('satis honorifica et festiva').[31] An illustration of the event shows Joanne invested with the contradictory symbols of majesty and subjection typical of late medieval queenly coronation: on the one hand enthroned in majesty; on the other, her hair loosely tressed, in the ancillary role of the king's virginal bride.[32] The point of difference from tradition which measures the esteem in which she was held is that, along with the traditional *virga* or rod in her right hand, she extraordinarily holds an orb surmounted with a cross in her left. Before Philippa in 1330, English queens seem to have held only the *virga*. The fourteenth-century recension of the *Liber regalis* grants queens a scepter, but a lesser one, unequal to that of the king: a small gilt one, surmounted by a gilt dove ('paruum septrum deauratum in cuius summitate est columba deaurata').[33] The presence of this orb suggests a breadth of authority which must derive from her own descent from a head of state, her onetime marriage to the dauphin of France, and her ties to the ruling houses of Europe.[34] Of the same import is her depiction in solitary splendor, enthroned under a canopy with the archbishop of Canterbury and the abbot of Westminster supporting a royal diadem on her head, rather than – as was customary in the coronation itself – together with the king but placed at a lower level than him.[35] No formality is spared, with the archbishop of Canterbury and the abbot of Westminster simultaneously placing the crown upon her head. Behind are various emblems of English and continental royalty: at her right the Plantagenet lions and fleurs-de-lys, and at her left possibly a more fanciful evocation of the arms of Brittany.

Evident, when compared with previous coronation practice, is a margin of exceptionality. Certainly, in this case, the exceptionality derives less from Joanne's personal history than from what the Lancastrians wanted or needed from her, what she can be made into. The

4. The coronation of Joanne of Navarre, consort of King Henry IV.

coronation is Joanne's jewelbox, the very special setting in which she is displayed as the precious gem. It both celebrates and consolidates her status as a valued and valuable asset to the English throne. But perhaps – just perhaps – Joanne's own assertiveness and presentational skills may be partially registered in the extravagance of her coronation ceremonial.

The mother and the . . . ?

Despite evidence of respect and special treatment, Joanne nevertheless keeps disappearing into the various material and symbolic valuations placed upon her. With respect, at least, to the written record, she is often absent at a point of crucial determination, when a decision affecting the control or disposition of her resources is being made. Her own ceremony of betrothal – from which she was of course necessarily absent – might nevertheless be considered a figure of other absences to come. At that ceremony, held on 3 April 1402, an august body was assembled at Henry's manor of Eltham, including the king in his own person, the Percies, and other officials of court, household, and Church, together with Joanne's emissary, Squire Antoine Ricze, with whom as stand-in Henry exchanged vows. Proxy betrothals and even proxy weddings were commonplace among the medieval aristocracy, but restriction of the ceremony to a group entirely composed of men is less common; a certain failure, at least of mimesis, may be said to have occurred when Henry IV turned to Ricze and said, 'I Henri of Lencastre . . . You Johanne Duchesse of Bretaigne . . . , in the persone of Antoine Ricze your very procurator in this partie to this matrimoigne take unto my wife and thereto I plight you my troth.'[36]

Her betrothal might be thought to exemplify a persistent aspect of women's treatment, according to which a neglect or effacement of the empirical woman is a precondition of her recasting in a convenient and non-threatening role. The 'persone' of Antoine Ricze uncontroversially 'stands for' or assumes the role of this hectic woman, in a way which elides her complexities and suffices to get the deal done. And so are women generally brought forward in Lancastrian texts in a range of capacities, each of which might be thought a less than adequate representation of the historical woman, but a more than adequate way of shaping her representation to the requirements of the task at hand. This range of capacities includes such superficially different incarnations as mother, mediatrix, sorceress, whore. Yet for all their apparent variety such roles must be seen as alternative forms of effacement, in their complete subservience to processes of male fantasy. If woman is to be discovered in these texts in any capacity separate from what men want her to be, the discovery must perforce be made precisely in the places where she is voided out – either literally absent or (virtually the same thing) concealed behind a male fantasy-screen. The interesting thing about the fantasy-screen is what it conceals. Of greatest analytical interest are those hints that, behind the screen, lies a personality in reserve, a reservoir of unknowable but coherently organized otherness. This other or shadowed place is the lodging of everything else that is known or might be inferred, but cannot be expressed, about Joanne as historical performer. Interestingly, even the most radically opposed presentations of Joanne – as selfless mediatrix in her early years and as conniving sorceress nearer the end of her life – possess a point of similarity: each gestures toward such an unknowable reserve behind the blank façades of her various dictated or permissible enactments.

*

Famed as mediatrix,[37] Joanne achieved her most renowned intervention early in her first marriage, when the choleric count of Brittany staged a spectacular affront to chivalric etiquette by arresting and menacing the ambassadors of the king of France. According to the Chronicle of Saint-Denys, the duchess was alerted to the situation by her brother, who begged her intervention in order to amend this treacherous and barbarous act:

> In the interest of peace and concord, this estimable duchess promised to serve as go-between ['interponere vices suas']. . . . And promptly setting aside her womanly modesty ['muliebri pudore'], although on the brink of giving birth, taking her children in her arms, with only one attendant, wholly unexpected in the gathering night, and neglecting accepted practices ['preter morem solitum'] entered the chamber of the duke. As I learned from reliable report, throwing herself at the feet of the duke upon bended knees, and inciting the duke with grievous sobs ['cum mestis singultibus'] to pity her and her children, she boldly exposes his duplicity, openly declares the names of his co-conspirators, and, the wickedness deepening, earnestly pleads that he reconsider, lest they should alienate through such disobedience our king and the various flowers of the lily, who after his death would be able to protect his offspring.[38]

Here Joanne performs in the most traditional of queenly roles, and she enacts several of the most conventional elements of such performances.[39] As in the paradigmatic precedent of Philippa's plea before Edward III for the burghers of Calais, she appears adventitiously (as a result of her brother's intervention), she intervenes at a time when all hope of conciliation seems to have evaporated, and her fragile femininity and maternal self-abnegation are emphasized (as thrice over in Froissart's depiction of Philippa) by the fact of her pregnancy.[40] Likewise, as in Philippa's intervention, she has the merit of recommending a course of action the duke probably wishes upon sober consideration to adopt, but could not adopt without running the risk of seeming changeable and hence unmanly. Joanne's behavior has the merit of arrogating all the possibilities of disorderliness to itself. Emphasized are her abandonment of female modesty, her relinquishment of traditional ceremony and pomp, her disorderly appearance at the duke's chamber at an unusual time, and the interruption of her speech by choking sobs ['cum mestis singultibus'].[41]

For all the emphasis upon the drastic and anti-conventional nature of Joanne's behavior, she is in some respects doing exactly what a mediatrix is supposed to do: she is creating an intervention from somewhere beyond the norms and conventions of male transactions, creating an occasion for a non-precedential exception to the normal irrevocability of male resolve. At the same time, though, this depiction possesses a hectic quality, a hint of behavior on her part which remains potentially excessive to the requirements of the situation at hand. Her behaviour is portrayed paradoxically. Joanne is, on the one hand, never more female, and never more compliant with her husband's requirements and wishes, than when she casts away *pudor*. Yet, on the other hand, her femininity and her utility are insecurely grounded in a demonstrated potential for spontaneous rejection of the conventions of her station. If she is most capable of fulfilling male needs and desires when she rejects or surpasses them, she must be conceded a dim or fugitive potential for operating somewhere beyond their bounds.

*

Witchcraft rumors pursuant to Joanne's 1419 arrest on charges of treasonous imagining turn out to be rather practical and non-lurid in their inception, but may stand in some secondary relation to her repute as a spirited woman capable of independent calculation and action. The specific charge against Joanne was based upon a 'relation and confession' of a friar, one John Randolph, to the effect that 'Joanne, queen of England has compassed and imagined ['avoit compassez et ymaginez'] the death and destruction of our lord the king, in the most high and horrible manner that could be recounted' ['en le pluis haute et horrible manere, que l'en purroit deviser'].[42] The accusation is framed within the conventional expectation of a treason charge, in which she is said to have planned the death of the king – even though, presumably because of an absence of real evidence, the language characterizing her horrible intentions is both less specific and more lurid than that customary in such cases.

As the simultaneous vagueness and extremity of the language of accusation would suggest, the charges against Joanne had no substance whatever. Their impetus was apparently to gain some kind of control over the immense sums being poured into Joanne's dower; sums that were desperately needed elsewhere.[43] The year in which the charges were filed concluded a period in which Henry had found increasing difficulty in financing his French war (a war which, even in the first flush of enthusiasm, had been financed only by such expedients as sawing up and pawning parts of his royal crown!). Added to these cumulative financial problems was a new strain, connected with negotiations launched in the summer of 1419 over the extent of

Catherine of France's dower. The charges themselves were not only cursory, but devoted the preponderance of their attention to the seizure of Joanne's goods, both dowered and other, by the treasurer of England.[44]

Neither brought to trial nor acquitted, Joanne remained under arrest for nearly three years, her dower at the disposal of the English Treasury. A probable indication of her guiltlessness is the honor with which she was treated, right up to, and after, her incarceration, as well as during the incarceration itself.[45] In contrast with the summary treatment of accused conspirators like Scrope and his Southampton cohorts, Joanne's first months of imprisonment were spent with nineteen grooms and seven pages, a private physician, and (later) a minstrel and private stables. Expenditures throughout on such items as a birdcage for her jay, a fine wine cellar and entertainment expenses for visitors like Duke Humphrey, furred capes and mantles, three dozen pairs of shoes, and spices like green ginger and cinnamon, suggest that she was hardly regarded as a common felon, or as a person under much suspicion of plotting against the king.[46] Even under the comfortable circumstances described, at an average annual expenditure from the Exchequer of just under £1,000, her incarceration still netted a handsome return. The surprise, when the consequences of her accusation are seen in this way, is not that an expedient was found to withhold her dower, but that payments were ever resumed – as they were when Henry, near death, ordered their restoration. Without bothering to assert her guilt of anything, he cited an unwillingness later to bear the charge to his own 'conscience,' and proclaimed his decision not 'to occupie forth lenger the said Douair in this wise.'[47]

The materials seem to lie at hand from which a completely material and functional explanation of Joanne's accusation, derived from financial exigency, might be constructed. But additional, less purely functional, aspects of Joanne's situation may be seen as contributory to the charges against her and the extent to which they were entertained. These aspects all touch in one way or another upon her isolation and estrangement, upon an area of private reserve within which she might, in effect, be conceded an imaginative autonomy; might be 'imagined to imagine' the destruction of the king. Among these aspects is her salient quality – the one which made her most valuable to the king *and* simultaneously rendered her an object of suspicion: her foreignness itself.[48] Certainly, for all the expressions of parliamentary and civic solicitude she received, Joanne was treated throughout her long sojourn with a good deal of grudging suspicion, both as matter out of place in her own right, and as sponsor of a suspect retinue with ties to a country often at war with England. In 1404, the year after her arrival with a scaled-down retinue including only her two daughters at her own social level, she bore some of the brunt of a resolution removing aliens from the royal household; her two daughters were excepted, but only so long as they exhibited anti-schismatic belief.[49] And, in the end, the two daughters themselves were evidently dismissed, along with other Breton retainers.[50] In 1415 Bretons were again an object of suspicion, accused of exporting money and jewels from the realm, and trading in secrets of the realm overheard in the household of the queen.[51] In 1425, even with Joanne back in good grace, a petition complained that 'les estraungers demurrantz . . . ove la Royne Johanne' were betraying the king's counsel to his enemies, and demanded their expulsion.[52] In an age of prevalent xenophobia and insurgent proto-nationalism, Joanne was an outpost of foreignness – and hence of suspicion – in an increasingly English and English-speaking milieu.

Other sorts of preparedness to believe the worst of Joanne resulted in popular amplification of the charges against her. Nothing in the nebulous accusation of treason would seem conducive either to belief or to non-belief. The cautious Walsingham says only that Joanne was accused by certain persons of a certain wrongdoing which would have tended toward injury of the king ('per quosdam infamata de quodam maleficio, quod in laesionem Regis commentata fuisset').[53] Less scrupulous observers, however, elaborated the accusation's hints of independent intrigue, by supposing Joanne guilty of sorcery and necromantic practice. A London chronicler, his mind on treason (having just recounted the treacherous slaying of the duke of Burgundy by the dauphin of France), continues,

> Also this same yere frere Randolf, a mayster of dyvynte, that sumtyme was the quene Johanne confessor, at the excitynge of the forseid quene, by sorcerye and by nygramancie wrought for to astroyd [to (have) destoyed] the kyng: but, as God wolde, his falsnesse at the laste was aspyed; wherefore be comown parlement the quene forfetyd here landes.[54]

Such apparent elaborations of the charge may expand hints already loosed by king and council in the larger environment of the accusation. The original accusation against the queen is included in the order to expropriate her property, dated 27 September 1419. On 25 September 1419 – about the day when action against Joanne must first have been taken – Archbishop Chichele wrote to his bishops, urging a redoubling of prayers for the safety of the king in his dangerous enterprises, 'from all evils, malices, and iniquities intended by his enemies, and from superstitious deeds of necromancers ['superstitiosis necromanticorum

operationibus'], especially such as were recently planned for the overthrow and destruction of his person by many.'[55] In this letter may be
glimpsed the outlines of a campaign of innuendo. Such a campaign
may have been intended to lay the groundwork for an actual prosecution, but was then shelved because its purpose had already been
served by the expropriation of Joanne's goods, and ultimately abandoned because of Henry V's contrition. In keeping with this functional
view is Keith Thomas's analysis of sorcery accusations, in which they
are found to arise with particular frequency in situations like Joanne's:
that is, as a convenient subterfuge and displacement of guilt onto the
victims of a selfish withdrawal of traditional privileges or charities.[56]
Hardly a 'charity' in this case, Joanne's dowry nevertheless stands in
the place of a 'traditional privilege,' having been legally assigned to her
by Henry V's father, the former king, and now standing in jeopardy.
However functional the charge, and its assignment of guilt, it retains a
non-functional and highly emotive dimension, assigning to Joanne an
area of independent, unknowable, and devious practice.

That a person famed for her benign intercessions was thought at a
later point in life to be guilty of sorcery might seem contradictory. But
the 'other' or shadowed implication of each narrative has much in
common with its superficially opposite twin. Even superficially, the
two narratives converge in some respects. Both mediatrices and sorcer-
esses might, for example, be regarded as rule-breakers, operating, if
not outside conventional expectation, at least outside the normal rules
governing social interactions. And each, to the extent that she casts and
pursues a design, is thought to harbor an 'imagining' of how things
might be other than they are. Mediatrices do not seem especially
threatening, in that they normally do things that kings and dukes want
done. But something about the mediatrix links her to her sister, the
sorceress. They are alike in their fervor, their hectic emotionality, their
arbitrary and tumultuous comings and goings and – sometimes –
personal disarray.[57] Whether deservedly or undeservedly, a comment
about Joanne may be taking shape here. The historical Joanne seems to
have possessed an unusual affinity with narratives about disruption
and disarray; or, to put it differently, narratives about Joanne seem
prone to unusual amplification in this regard.

Joanne as problem

Thus far Joanne has been realized and presented within different pre-
existent patterings. What if this representational logic were carried
another step, to an imagining of Joanne as *herself* a manipulator of

roles, a witting and accomplished masquer? The notion of Joanne as masquer has shadowed narratives we have already seen, and explicitly informs one tale told of her. It seems that Joanne, as queen mother of England, was visited by a son from her prior marriage: Arthur, the earl of Richmond and future constable of France, recently captured at Agincourt. The narrative realization of this incident, generally hailed as 'touching' and 'affecting,'[58] bears within itself a hint of the kind of unease a potentially empowered woman can cause, even when seemingly held secure within the bounds of conventionalized and sentimentalized narration. This tale was first recorded as part of a romanticized biography of Arthur, written in the mid-fifteenth century by Guillaume Gruel, who was a member of Arthur's household during his years of mature service as constable of France. According to Gruel, Arthur was dispatched to England with other prisoners of Agincourt, and, soon after his arrival in London,

> the queen, mother of the count of Richmont, asked leave of the king of England to see her son, who was prisoner, and the king agreed. And the guards of the said lord led him to the queen his mother, who, when she learned of his arrival, put one of her ladies (who knew how to speak well) in her place, and thus received him, placing herself in a row of other ladies, with two of them before her. And when the lord of Richmont arrived he supposed that the lady was his mother and saluted her and bowed before her and they spoke together for a time, until he said that he would greet the other ladies with a kiss. When he reached the queen, her heart went out to him ['le coeur luy tendrea'], and she said, 'Bad son, you have not recognized me' ['Mauuais fils, m'auez vous descongneüe']. And both began to cry, because they were so dear to each other. And the queen his mother gave him a thousand nobles, which he divided among his fellow prisoners and his guards, and also gave him shirts and garments, and he did not afterwards dare to speak to her or visit her, as he would have wished.[59]

This tale is told in an account highly sympathetic to Arthur, and its narrator appears to regard it as an affecting scene of maternal–filial affection, first impeded and then allowed. Yet a number of problematic elements perturb its progress.

Although I wish to understand this tale historically, the quest for such understanding must begin with the admission that it may possess no 'kernel' of historical truth. Arthur was indeed captured at Agincourt and was indeed prisoner in England during his mother's reign as queen and they probably did meet; yet they did not necessarily meet nor did the form of any such meeting necessarily inspire the present narration. As with Veyne's Greek myths, rather than seeking a truth *behind* or at the bottom of the lie, we will be better off seeking a truth *in* (that is, *coextensive with*) the lie – in the fantasies it embodies or in the purposes it serves.[60]

This tale's fictitiousness is suggested by its evident status as a framed fantasy: the frame is drawn from romance and the fantasy involves discovery or 'recognition.' Joanne stage-manages, and then awaits, recognition, and the expectation is that Arthur will indeed provide that recognition: of Joanne as woman, as mother, and as true queen. But – surprisingly and fascinatingly – it turns out to be a tale of failed recognition, or even something very like *mis*-recognition – which is, after all, the closest modern English equivalent to the Old French 'descongneüe.' The misrecognition consists of an imaginary displacement of the actual conditions of their relation, and its seriousness is registered in the severity with which each protagonist is treated.

Joanne takes her place in the rank of ladies and awaits discovery, not just as a romance heroine (although this element is not entirely lacking) but also in two additional senses which should clearly distinguish her from the women among whom she stands: as a mother (connected to Arthur by an invisible but sturdy bond of affection) and as a 'true queen' (with some of that 'aura' which permits anointed rulers to expose themselves to hungry lions and other tests, in the confidence that their regal condition will be recognized).[61] But she is to be conspicuously disappointed in all respects. Arthur mistakes a stand-in for his own mother, and then moves on to an indiscriminate mingling among the other ladies (including his true mother) whom he wishes graciously to greet.

Of course, Joanne's reliance upon the maternal bond was never propitious. No evidence of such a bond exists, either in historical records or in this chronicle's quasi-historical rendition. This tale's historical precondition is the prior desertion of the young Arthur by his ambitious mother. Remarrying, and arranging to take the better part of her dower with her, and leaving her children in the guardianship of the duke of Burgundy, Joanne became a 'cruel mother,' in the sense of deserting her children and in the literal sense of taking her dower with her.[62] Joanne's cruelty was mitigated, at least in its economic aspects, by offsetting gifts.[63] The stigmatizing image of the cruel mother may also be partially offset by the counter-image of the victimized mother whose children are stripped away (right down to the last daughter, if the *Annales Henrici Quarti* are correct), and this narrative may tacitly rely upon this counter-image as a basis for its sentimental effects. But the fact remains that, with the exception of a possible visit on the occasion of his investiture as earl of Richmond in 1404,[64] Arthur had not seen his mother for well over a decade, and the case for the constancy of her maternal feelings is not strong.

Additionally remaining in Joanne's arsenal is, however, the expectation of being recognized as 'true queen,' and she exposes her regality – and, even more tellingly, her legitimacy – to review. The whole point of such a scene – repeatedly confirmed by the 'mysterious marks' and other devices of recognition in romance[65] – is that her aura will manifest itself. But what if the aura is not there to be seen? Here we encounter a failure, not just of maternity but of dynastic legitimacy, posed in a stark and embarrassing way. The 'test' which Joanne fails is, moreover, one which most monarchs in most romance-influenced recognition scenes would never have had to risk in the first place. The typical romance recognition scene places the sovereign in the position of needing *to recognize*, rather than to *be recognized*.[66] Typically, the monarch attempts to identify an errant or long-lost child, aided by special garments or other devices of recognition, but is never asked to put his or her recognizability to the test of a child's discernment. Thus, Joanne's position is curtailed by narrative adjustments which erode even her temporary enjoyment of the prerogatives of the stage-manager's role. This tale's denouement then delivers an additional blow to Joanne's own pretensions as architect and scene-shaper of her personal history. Having set out to 'manage' this event, she devolves into a hapless bystander, a 'watcher' of its progress. Having set out to be its judge and subject, she ends up reverting to 'the dreaded category of object.'[67]

Nor does Arthur fare better. Abandoned at an early age by a 'cruel mother' who left seeking a crown and took her dower with her, Arthur is slenderly equipped for recognition.[68] The already vexed situation is additionally complicated by the Oedipal dilemma posed for the reader of this passage, who expects to enjoy a son's recognition of his mother in her maternal capacity, but then finds the son performing as a courtier, seeking a kiss from his unrecognized parent – treating her, that is, like the other ladies of the court and with the same mixture of courteous and, presumably, flirtatious intent. Compounding these other failures is the fact that Arthur, a prisoner out on furlough as a result of Joanne's intervention, not only fails to recognize her as mother or queen, but even as a benefactor and possible instrument in his own freedom.

Affronts are accumulating rapidly here. Affronts to Arthur's perspicacity, to Joanne's maternity and queenship, and finally to the capacity of either for purposeful or effective self-management. In Joanne's case, these affronts might be regarded as the penalty or 'toll' exacted upon assertive women, as a hostile residue resulting from the grudging admission of her capacity to mount and execute her own plans. Nevertheless, these affronts need somehow to be allayed or absorbed, and their palliation is discovered in a proven (and ultimately reassuring) imaginative paradigm. The anticipated recognition of Joanne's queenly aura having failed to occur, she responds with a spontaneous welling up of feelings and an unscripted outburst. Summoned at this critical moment for the narrative's rescue are, in fact, traits which have much in common with those revealed in her mediation episodes, and also, less directly, with those that underpin her treason accusation. At each of these moments she is revealed as possessing, or suspected of possessing, undisclosed emotions and attitudes. Withheld from view, this distinctively feminine reservoir of surplus emotion manifests itself in unpredictable ways, although ways which are, finally, disabling to her ability to carry forward an independent resolve. Her son drawing near to her, her heart softens ('le coeur luy tendrea'), leading to the abandonment of her own stratagem, conveyed in a fervent but tender reproach.

This narration is a prelude to nothing, since Arthur was not to see his mother again. Accomplished and secured with the gifts of money and clothing,[69] their recognition scene strives for a sense of narrative completeness in itself. But, if completeness requires a knitting together of themes and loose ends, then this remains an 'open' structure, raising dilemmas it lacks the power adequately to resolve. The taint of cruel motherhood, Arthur's courtly address to his own mother, the sense of Joanne as something of a plotter and manipulator – all continue as sources of narrative disturbance. Further perturbation surrounds whatever fear prevents Arthur from seeing his mother again. In special disfavor with Henry V, as a result of his allegiance to the cause of France despite his enjoyment of the English earldom of Richmond, he might indeed have been prevented from seeing her in any case. But this is not what the narrative says: it says that he did not *dare* to see her afterwards ('n'osa depuis parler à elle ne la visiter'). His fear and awe might exist in relation to an angry king, or perhaps even (given his original, unknowing but flirtatious approach to his mother) magnified by elements of Oedipal implication.

This narrative plainly fails as a 'sentimental' tale of recognition, and it also fails as an assertion of legitimate queenship. Yet it does, perhaps inadvertently, leave Joanne with something. She rallies from Arthur's oversight, reasserting her control of the situation with gifts of money and clothes, and the narration closes with a hint of her implacability. In other words, this narration leaves its reader with a shadowed suggestion of Joanne as possessed of independent purpose. As Arthur blunders about the room, failing to recognize his mother and benefactor, Joanne's own position, behind two ladies of her court, provides a steady vantage point from which Arthur's failed courtiership *is observed*. The sight-lines of this tale suggest the existence of a woman who means to be a purposeful actor in her own life. Arthur's gaze is unsteady, unfixed, uncertain of its object, and incapable of discernment. Joanne's, albeit veiled, remains in full possession of its field. She is, in this sense, something more than an object of value, to be purchased, owned, and displayed. For this brief moment, in spite of trials to which she has been subjected, Joanne suddenly emerges as the subject of her own counter-narrative, a narrative in which she temporarily becomes the point of focalization and the standpoint from which events are interpreted and understood.[70] A scene-setter and scene-maker, this playful and flirtatious and emotionally hectic woman can hardly be thought an adjunct to male designs, bought or paid for or already interpellated and deployed in the service of 'Power.' She is resistant in the sense in which the counterfeiters of Chapter 5 were resistant, operating somewhere outside the ambit of orthodox power. Like them, and like other figures I have discussed in this book, she is 'stubborn' – obstinate, uninstructed in the necessity of forgoing or subordinating her own wishes. Attempting to sell the city of Nantes; fleeing the Continent with her jewels; ensconced with her accounts and council in her own tower adjacent to Westminster Hall; weathering her sorcery charge in style, with her nineteen grooms and seven pages, ordering a new cage for her jay – the record fitfully but cumulatively accepts evidence of her exceptionality.

Like the displaced and superseded queens of Shakespeare's history plays, Joanne is a personage that nobody appears to have known quite how to accommodate. Lancastrian actions seem always designed to 'contain' her impulses, to return her to a pre-existing frame. The contrite Henry V, restoring her dower and original status after her release from prison, sought to resignify her in what at least now appears as the most banal and condescending possible way, with a grant of attire, providing 'that she have of such Cloth, and of suche colour, as she wol devise hir self, v or vi Gounes, such as she useth to were.'[71] But, despite such efforts to return her to her proper and pre-prepared place within the order of the symbolic, she seems to keep appearing, and problematically so, as the focal point of her own life.

*

Henry V and his brothers are not literally present in this narrative, but their off-frame presence is implied. They are Arthur's captors, and those who permit the brief audience, and who terminate contact between mother and son. In the sense that Henry sets the terms and boundaries of the meeting, and allows its occurrence only under his own sufferance, this may be regarded as a traditionally satisfying narrative from the male (and dynastic) point of view.[72] Yet this narrative also contains a partially suppressed reconsideration of patriarchal expectations and suppositions. A woman who can be described as having engineered an interview with her son, and who stage-manages the encounter, and who is its best-informed participant, certainly defies any simple formulas about women as property. Conceded the power to mount initiatives and reframe situations, she achieves an implied existence beyond any of the more restricted registers in which men might seek to portray her.

Although certainly bilked in their material hopes, Henry IV and his sons may have got what they wanted in the way of symbolic capital from their well-born foreign brides. But a sober assessment of their marriages would suggest that they habitually misread the precedent of their founding father, John of Gaunt. Gaunt's own coup was to parlay his royal parentage into marriage with native heiress Blanche of Lancaster and control of the rich duchy of Lancaster; his subsequent folly was his wasteful and destructive marriage to Constanza of Castile and the fruitless ambitions it fostered (and little honor was accorded to his final marriage, to long-time mistress Katherine Swinford). Henry IV appears, for better or worse, to have followed the first two stages of John's model. Although never again so disastrously as Constanza, the foreign brides of Henry IV (and, at least in the case of Humphrey, duke of Gloucester and possibly that of Henry V) seem to have eluded the expectations accompanying their marriages. A hint of this elusiveness clings to Queen Joanne's written representations. It inheres in these representations, even to the extent of being their discursive production. Granted to Joanne is an area of unknown connivance and reserve, a capacity for intervention in the progress of her own affairs. The existence of such an unknowable area supports the possibility that a historical person might possess disruptive potentialities, might be something more than the sum of the roles to which she or he is assigned.

7

Advising the Lancastrian Prince

Changing styles of admonition

The king is a natural magnet for all sorts of forecasts, desired scenarios, hopeful imaginings. Nor are his advice-givers restricted to those who have entered his service or received his rewards. Traditional notions of 'patronage' must be enlarged to embrace complex filiations of expectation, attachment, and belief between a king and his aspirational advisers. These filiations are often more emotional than pragmatic, and can operate in the absence of contract, contact – or any personal relation at all.

Kings, in other words, often receive unsolicited, or even unwanted, advice. One wonders how a king, besieged by attempted ingratiation, manages to establish anything approximating a personal style or stance toward the receipt of advice. Yet, even within what might appear as an impersonally structured advice-giving regime, a king may register certain points of personal style. Consider, for example, Richard II's and Henry IV's different reactions to the proffered services of the 'Northern Prophet.' Harangued by this self-styled prophet, the intellectually curious Richard invited him to confirm his status by walking on water; similarly approached, Henry ordered, or at least abetted, his would-be adviser's execution.[1] Such regal actions, amplified by other stories about kingly behavior, create a horizon of contemporary expectations. Despite his reputation for tyranny and irascibility, Richard II seems not to have wasted much anger or emotion on people beyond his purview or even his immediate line of vision, unless they happened to engage his personal interest. The odd and solipsistic aura of invincibility within which he moved seems to have allowed Richard to countenance alternative analysis and dissenting speech. Impelled by a broader set of ambitions concerning what might today be called his

'image,' and obsessively interested in how he was perceived by subjects well beyond his entourage or court circle, Henry IV was far more
likely to intervene in the processes by which his conduct was publicly
broadcast and privately imagined. Not only were the boundaries of
permissible speech narrowed in his reign, but those addressing and
characterizing the particulars of his kingship must have realized that
their words would be scrutinized with more than usual care.

Every adviser, whether Ricardian or Lancastrian, decries flattering
intent and espouses plain speaking no matter what the cost. And each
is equally complicitous, in the sense of telling the king things he
already knows and (more important) wants to hear. But, for all its
durability, the role of adviser to princes remains one which can be
differentially inhabited, one which can (for example) be enacted with
varying degrees of assurance and ease. My suggestion here is that
Henry IV's different pattern of interests and preferences, coupled with
the uneasy circumstances of his usurpation, encouraged a noticeably
different and effectively 'Lancastrian' style of advice-giving in his and
his son's reigns. Taking for its examples a celebrated letter by Philip
Repingdon and varied poetical works by Thomas Hoccleve and John
Lydgate, this chapter explores some of the subtle shifts in which an
emergent 'Lancastrian' style might be discerned. A hallmark of that
style turns out to be a quality of unease, a kind of nervous reciprocity
in which the adviser at once experiences a closer identification with his
monarch, and a heightened uncertainty about the spirit in which even
the most complicitous reassurances will be received.

Affording an instructive contrast with Lancastrian advice-giving
practice is a poem I have elsewhere discussed at some length, and will
only mention here: Chaucer's 'Lack of Steadfastness,' a poem advisory
to Richard II, undated, but probably written in 1389–90.[2] In this highly
conventional poem, Chaucer warns of a world grown 'fals and
deceivable' and the spread of a new, self-serving, and collusive ethic:

> ... among us now a man is holde unable,
> But if he can by som collusion
> Don his neighbour wrong or oppressioun ...

In an envoy composed for Richard, Chaucer urges him to 'Shew forth
thy swerd of castigacioun,' and, by honoring law, *trouthe*, and worthi-
ness, to rejoin his people to steadfastness. Although Chaucer adopts a
stern admonitory voice, and does in fact urge his monarch to *do* things,
he probably had little cause to fear Richard's displeasure. After all, the
effect of his advice is to strengthen the king's hand; to urge him to
stiffen up and *be* a king. Moreover, if the poem was indeed written in
1389–90, its stern advice to restore order in the countryside would have

been positively congenial: for this was the period of Richard's own law-and-order campaign, that series of self-representations by which he sought to display himself capable of castigation, to deserve his throne (and to out-deserve his rivals, the Appellants) by curbing local misrule. Sure of his role and buoyed by his consistency with his king's program, Chaucer seems rather at ease with his moralizing voice, and presents his analysis without explanation or apology.

The Lancastrian adviser proves unable to muster such certitude. This incapacity may be glimpsed quite early in Henry IV's reign, in an unexpected place: in the much-praised and apparently courageous admonitory letter addressed to the new king by his supporter and confidant, Philip Repingdon.[3] Repingdon, whose modern repute springs mostly from his early Lollardy and his later activities (including his dealings with Margery Kempe as bishop of Lincoln after 1405), wrote his letter in May 1401, at a time when he was serving as abbot of St Mary de Pré, Leicester, and concurrently, as the king's personal chaplain.[4] It must have reached the king, since it was discovered among the royal papers collected two generations later by Thomas Bekynton.[5] Other versions exist, including one quoted in its entirety by Adam of Usk (as 'apt' for the times), suggesting that Repingdon wrote in part for a larger public.[6] That he did not suffer for his apparent candor is suggested by his subsequent advancement.

As we should expect, this letter presents itself as a self-denying, and possibly even politically risky, espousal of hard truth over slack and advantageous compliance. 'I have chosen,' says Repingdon in paraphrase of Psalm 83:11 '"to be a doorkeeper in the house of the Lord" with the Baptist – rather than with the traitor Judas to mingle with regal delights and to bear the kiss of adulation in my mouth.'[7] His letter goes on to say many hard things to the king about the state of the realm, and it may indeed be accorded the title of a 'manly' performance[8] – but only so long as a 'manly' performance is allowed to embrace the generous quantities of flattery, programmatic conciliation, wary evasion, and self-protective equivocation common to most advice-giving to medieval kings. Stalwart indeed in its tone, this letter constantly modifies and undercuts its own effects with calculated ambiguities and confused implications. Consider its early strictures on the bad condition of law and justice in the second year of Henry's reign:

> For law and justice are exiles from the realm: thefts, homicides, adulteries, fornications, oppressions of the poor, quarrels, and various contumacions abound. And now a tyrannical willfulness replaces law ['nunc pro lege sufficit tyrannica voluntas']. . . . I say,

with the faithful prophet, that 'the Lord God, strong and patient, grows angry day by day,' and 'unless you will have been converted ['nisi conversi fueritis'] He will brandish his sword. He has bent and prepared his bow, and has prepared the vessels of death; he has tempered his arrows with fire,' such that, after the manifest miracles of God and His exceeding and most welcome benefits have in effect or deed been scorned or neglected, He may bring a vengeful fire-storm upon those who are ungrateful, cruel, and contemptuous of Him ['in Ejus ingratos, saevos, et manifestos contemptores'].

Although this passage is arrayed in vigorous utterance, numerous shifts and slippages and evasions operate against its apparent pointed-ness. The reference to 'tyrannical willfulness,' for example, might seem at first to stigmatize Henry IV. But, despite this passage's apparent condemnation, it quickly neutralizes its own effects. This neutraliza-tion is accomplished partially by the shift to biblical quotation, with opprobrium falling, first, on the enemies of the Psalmist, or those of the Hebrew people, who bear the brunt of Psalm 7:12–14. The biblical quotation may then be derivatively applied to a contemporary target, one addressed in the second-person plural of 'nisi conversi fueritis.' The party so addressed might be Henry, respectful object of the second-person plural throughout this passage, but subsequent deter-minants reveal this party, not as Henry, but as a more general and unruly segment of the populace at large. Later in the passage, this populace in need of reform is described as ungrateful, cruel, and con-temptuous: all in the accusative plural – grammatically unnecessary, and in fact impossible if the subject in question were the king.

Having, in a sense, threatened but then rescued Henry,[9] the text then returns him to a zone of possible critique, recalling the hopes attending his arrival in England just two years before:

Although we had hoped that your propitious entry ['vester gratiosus ingressus'] into the realm of England – obviously guided by the hand of God – would have redeemed Israel, and would have reformed those guilty of evils and contempt of God. . . . But now the prudent weep and the peevish laugh; the widows, fatherless, and orphans now wring their hands; tears flow down the cheeks of those who lately, with your entry into the realm of England, were united in their applause, praising God with one voice, with the sons of Israel leading the way for Christ on the day of palms, and exclaiming to the heavens, and of you, their king, anointed like Christ, saying: 'Blessed who comes in the name of God,' our king of England, in hope of a happy reign for this kingdom.

The addressee of this passage – the 'you' of 'vester gratiosus ingressus' – has obviously become Henry again, and he falls within range of the accusation of making widows and orphans wring their hands. Yet, as we now progress to the present time of infelicity, Henry turns out not to be the problem after all; blame is once again shifted, in this case to fall upon bureaucrats, local lords, and, especially, recalcitrant subjects:

> . . . in just punishment and vengeance on the negligences and omissions of the governors of the people ['gubernatorum populi'], God, as a just judge, permits the commons ['plebeios'], like wild beasts, to exert arbitrary and irrational judgment, and unnaturally to assume rule over their superiors, and, without the counter-weight of discretion, to rage bestially against those who are superior, equal, and inferior to them.

Subject to local misrule, the commons rage out of control. And the concern now becomes, not that Henry will fall short of dealing with the situation, but that he will righteously over-react, becoming over-zealous in his godlike wrath:

> And indeed, if I am not mistaken, particularly on account of this popular rebellion ['super rebellione populi'], if it were not unworthy of your royal dignity ['regalis dignitas'], given the affront to your sublimity, I fear lest your military ferocity might be aroused, so that, even in one region of your kingdom, 20,000 of your liegemen might be slain by swords' edges, until the cruelty of the magistrates ['lictorum'] might be sated.

Yet even here Henry is shielded – for the possible over-reaction is attributed not to him, but to his zealous magistrates and royal officials.

As for Henry, the proposed course of action is nearly identical to that proposed for Richard at the end of 'Lack of Steadfastness.' There, it was 'do law . . ./And wed they folk agein to stedfastnesse'; here, it is:

> Nor will the murmur of the populace ['murmur populi'] greatly cease, nor the indignation of our angry God, but it will more and more be roused to fury and, the occasion taken, will rage into vengeance, until the law and justice of your legitimate reign ['legali regni vestri justitia'] being honored, the forementioned injuries, injustices, and popular oppressions will have been removed and extinguished, through right rule of just law ['per rectam regulam regis justitiae'].

Not only is Henry instated where any king would want to be, as the examplar and pivot of law and justice in his realm, but this entire passage has accomplished a good deal of additional ideological labor, in a gracefully incidental and barely visible way. Appearing to dwell upon problems and threats to majesty, Repingdon has actually managed to sound each of the notes most consistently congenial to Lancastrian legitimacy and the Lancastrian claim. Under a general sign of negation (his insistence that a problem exists in the realm), he has managed to rearticulate and reinstall a rhetorical divide in which the king stands on the side of orthodoxy and legitimacy and his adversaries on that of dangerous misrule. For his part, the king is the subject of God's providential interest (entering the country under the hand of God: 'non dubito quin manu Dei factus'); he has been anointed like another Christ ('sicut de altero Christo in regem uncto'); he possesses royal *dignitas* that must not be impaired. For their part, the turbulent people of the land are described in terms reminiscent of those used for the rebels of 1381: they are savage, bestial, prone always to murmur against their superiors.[10] Nor does Repingdon shrink from the central and recurrent Lancastrian accusation against all opposition, that of treasonous rebellion or *rebellio populi*.

For all its pugnacity of tone, Repingdon's letter serves up a feast of overt and covert assurances. For added assurance, its contents had already been orally vetted by the king in advance ('vivae vocis oraculo locutus sum vobis apud vos manens'). From no reasonable standpoint can he be thought to have put himself at risk. Even so, his letter is framed and wreathed in the language of extreme apology and deference. Such deference is common enough in poems and letters advising a prince or other superior. But something in Repingdon's protestations strikes a hectic and excessive note, especially for a churchman, an abbot, and a confessor, arrayed in the full dignity of his office. His imagined posture, for example, is literally abject; he writes as Henry's servant, having cast himself at his sovereign's feet: 'vestris pedibus provolutum.' His letter is written with trembling heart, its author consumed with love-longing: 'scriptum, si vestrae placeat Dominationi, corde tremulo, quia amore langueo.' Not only is his desire to 'please' his sovereign, but he propels himself into what might be considered excessive and unnecessary ingratiation; the letter issues, he tells us, from the hand of 'vestri soliti precatoris' – your customary supplicant. Although his position as the king's friend and spiritual adviser would appear to require less deference than Chaucer's position as one of Richard's minor court officials, Repingdon seems obliged to display this quality in greater measure. His display suggests that the need for a more gingerly positioning by the would-be commentator on royal affairs, even when speaking from the position of *zelator* or arch-loyalist, was already apparent in the first years of Henry IV's kingship.

Repingdon at least indulges in a pretense of admonition. Writing in 1410–11 and dedicating his *Regement of Princes* to the young Prince Henry shortly before his accession to the throne, Thomas Hoccleve altogether abandons the stance of admonitory critic, assuming instead that of wholehearted ally determined in no respect to offend. As he comments late in his poem,

> In al my book ye schul naght see ne fynde,
> That I youre dedes lakke [diminish], or hem despreise.
>   (ll. 4397–4398)[11]

The prince is, to be sure, admonished to end 'maintenance' and local disorder, and to punish misdoers

> . . . by lawful rightwysnesse,
> and suffre naght ich othir thus to oppresse. (ll. 2813–2814)

Yet the terms of the admonition are not just tacitly but specifically congenial to the claims and prerogatives of Lancastrian kingship. The king and prince had already sought by legislation to restrict maintenance to their own use,[12] and the advice to the young Henry to 'wynneth your peples voice' (l. 2885) is a reverent recasting of Henry IV's original claim of free election to the throne.

The extent of Hoccleve's partisanship carries him to a series of ever more ambitious formulations of his Lancastrian loyalty. Chaucer, Repingdon, and the younger Hoccleve of the *Regement* argued that the obligation of the monarch is to heal divisions among his people. By 1413, in a balade evidently written just before the coronation of Henry V, Hoccleve develops a new position: that the king may consider himself entitled to *create* division, if its ultimate effect is to protect the Church and his own estate:

> Strengthe your modir [Church] in chacyng away
> Theerrour which sones of iniquitee
> Han sowe ageyn the feith it is no nay,
> Yee ther-to bownde been of duetee;
> Your office is it now, for your seurtee,
> Souffreth nat Crystes feith to take a fal![13]

'Theerrour' which Henry is to correct is the Lollard heresy, and show trials and public executions during the reign of Henry IV had familiarized Hoccleve's audience with the violence he now tacitly invites; better the persecution of a domestic heresy, he suggests, than any derogation of the Church by 'sones of iniquitee.'

John Lydgate warmly seconds this concept of the Lancastrian poet as
co-conservator of the current dynasty's dignity at any domestic price.
He departs from his sources in *Fall of Princes* to confide his own view of
the responsibilities of poets:

> Ther cheeff labour is vicis to repreve
> With a maner couert symylitude,
> And non estat with their langage greeve
> Bi no rebukyng . . . (III, ll. 3829–3832)

This don't-rock-the-boat attitude may be conditioned by the fact that
Lydgate is getting ready to ask Humphrey for money: for 'fare compe-
tent vnto . . . sustenance' (including a wine allowance). But his intention to deliver no reproof, or to deliver it only incidentally or when it
is temporarily welcome, is consistently borne out in the corpus of
his work. His normal enterprise is to soar over problems in high
generalities, as suggested by these lines addressed to Henry VI upon
his coronation:

> Prynce excellent, be feythful, truwe and stable;
> Dreed God, do lawe, chastyce extorcyoun,
> Be liberal, of courage vnmutable,
> Cherisshe the Chirche with holle affeccyoun,
> Loue thy lyeges of eyther regyoun,
> Preferre the pees, eschuwe werre and debate. . . .

Of course, he is addressing an infant rather than a capable ruler;
nevertheless, given an opportunity to address substantive problems in
the realm, he contents himself with a stale rehash of terms ('do lawe,'
etc.), borrowed directly from Chaucer's 'Lack of Steadfastness' and
recycled for this occasion.

With Hoccleve and, especially, Lydgate, we are to encounter a
program of mollification, complicity, and what might politely be considered strategic unexceptionality. Yet, as a further look at some of
these poets' works will suggest, complicity imposes its own complicated demands. And, in certain exceptional situations (of which usurpation is one example), unexceptionality itself is not always an
achievable end.

Two poets and their prince

Hoccleve's emergence as a poet of large ambition and some visibility
on the national scene may be traced to a cluster of poems on public

themes addressed to Henry of Monmouth, first as Prince of Wales and then as king, especially in the period *c.* 1409–10 to 1415, beginning when Henry first contested his own father's authority and ending several years into his reign.[14] During these half-dozen years Hoccleve seems to have operated within a kind of patronage nexus – a complex of loyalties and attachments which enabled him to perceive himself (and within which he may even have been perceived) as a semi-official commentator, a kind of proto-laureate, anticipating a role which Lydgate was soon and so capaciously to fill. The central work of this period is his *Regement of Princes*, completed in 1410–11 during a period of the prince's ascendancy and unabashedly partisan on his behalf. Moreover, it is a poem wholly consistent with the prince's own program of self-representation as a peerless exemplar of orthodoxy. It embraces an elaborate system of differences which instates both the history-making prince and his poeticizing adviser on the orthodox side of every discursive divide, emphasizing their affinities and even, at times, strategically mingling their identities.

Introducing the *Regement* is a prologue comprising over one-third of its total length, the contents of which are a good deal more personal and topical than is common in such works. Here Hoccleve *in propria persona* meets with 'a poore old hore man' with whom he discusses his personal discontents and the (closely associated) problems of the realm. Turning to his 'matere' of good counsel, Hoccleve is quite explicit about his reliance upon conventionally accepted materials. Cited in his own texts are such broadly circulated guides to statecraft as Giles of Rome's *De regimine principum*, the pseudo-Aristotelian *Secreta secretorum*, and the 'Book of Chess' or *Libellus de ludo scachorum* of Jacobus de Cessolis. Yet the seemingly personal prologue and seemingly impersonal sections of advice are closely united, both by Hoccleve's practice of using his own predicaments to illuminate general issues and by certain recurrent themes related to the new conditions of Lancastrian rule. These include suppressed but ever-present worries about legitimation, concern about the dichotomies of outward show and inner belief, and a propensity for broad strokes of self-definition in which a space is opened and magnified between rulers and their sympathizers on the one hand and internal and external enemies and traitors to the realm on the other.

Issues of legitimacy and title underpin the *Regement*'s continuing concern with matters of genealogy. At the most apparent level, the text embodies an attempt to overcome the trauma of Henry IV's usurpation by eliding his role, and elevating that of various forebears. The first duke of Lancaster (Henry IV's maternal grandfather) is eulogized, as are Edward III (rather fancifully praised for going among his people in simple attire) and John of Gaunt (oddly considered as a discreet dresser, and then even more oddly hailed as an exemplar of merciful conduct). Subordinate to this blizzard of antecedence is Henry IV, mentioned only as 'the kyng which that is now' who is found 'gracious ynow' to Hoccleve, and as one who followed in Gaunt's footsteps. Emphasis falls, instead, on the Prince's unblemished inheritance, which will restore succession and honor to the office ('agayn that the corone/Honoure you shall' – ll. 2157–2158).

Anxiety and reassurance about legitimacy and just descent permeate Hoccleve's poetry in varied forms, of which the most noticeable is his continual deference to his 'maistir . . . and fadir, Chaucer,' himself not only Hoccleve's teacher but part of an imposing lineage stretching back to Aristotle and Virgil. Chaucer appears no fewer than five times in the *Regement*, the last in the celebrated illumination of Harley MS. 4866, cast in an orthodox and virtually hagiographical mode by accompanying anti-Lollard verses defending 'the ymages that in the chirche been.'[15] Hoccleve's repeated invocation of Chaucer has rightly but restrictively been seen as personal aggrandizement; viewed more broadly, Chaucer's unquestioned artistic legitimacy and his adaptability to issues of literary succession offer a convenient and reassuring analogue to the problematic of succession in the political sphere.[16]

Issues of legitimacy and loyalty are also repeatedly joined in disguised or displaced forms. Hoccleve can hardly, after all, make the obvious point: that false display gains particular pertinence when the king as supposed guarantor of legitimacy and meaning sits illicitly on the throne. One restatement of the issue favorable to Lancastrian hopes, or at any rate amenable to Lancastrian solution, equates legitimacy and orthodoxy, and imagines recent dynastic emergence as an asset rather than a liability, so long as it constitutes a needed bulwark against heresy. As I have proposed in Chapter 3, Henry IV and his son were the first English kings to grasp the sense in which orthodoxy and legitimacy might be defined and dramatized via the creation of a decidedly *unorthodox* and *illegitimate* group internal to the realm. Lollardy had been abroad in the reign of Richard II, but without ever quite catching that ruler's erratic attention. The coronation of Henry IV ushered in the first burning for heresy in England, that of priest William Sautre in Smithfield in 1401, and the first authorizing legislation, the statute *De haeretico comburendo*, later that same year,[17] and the prince paraded his own involvement at the burning of layman John Badby in 1410.[18]

The Prince, like his father, viewed the Lollards as an opportunity rather than a threat, and Hoccleve was fully complicit in the interested invocation of anti-Lollard sentiment at crucial junctures in both reigns. In the *Regement* the Prince is praised for his 'tendernesse' for Badby's soul (l. 297), but his attempt to woo and threaten Badby back to orthodoxy also discloses an unprecedented degree of royal interest in the composition of a subject's inner life and belief. Even as Hoccleve praises the Prince's proffered mercy, he adopts the authoritative voice of his old interlocutor to out-prince the Prince on this issue, wishing that not only Badby but that all Lollards were 'I-serued soo' (l. 328). The object-lesson for all loyal Lancastrians is to remain in the 'bridel' of orthodoxy, and the Lancastrian kings saw to it that religious and political orthodoxy were inextricably mixed.

The bridle of orthodoxy is, in fact, persistently recommended in all the political poems Hoccleve wrote during the two-year period following Henry V's coronation in 1413 – dealing with Henry V's accession (1413), the reburial of Richard II (1413), denouncing the Lollard Oldcastle (1415), and addressing Henry and the knights of the Garter (1414–16). To Henry V upon his accession Hoccleve recommends the extirpation of heresy, 'Therrour which sones of iniquitee/Han sowe ageyn the feith,' as the principal emphasis of the new regime. Whereas Chaucer's 'Lack of Steadfastness' had admonished Richard II to 'Suffre nothing that may be reprevable/To *thyn* estat . . . ,' Hoccleve urges Henry V to 'Be holy chirches Champioun eek ay;/Susteene *hir* right; souffre no thyng doon be/In preiudice of hir. . . .' His poem on Henry V's reburial of the bones of Richard II in Westminster Abbey (1413) continues his (and his new king's) elision of Henry IV, by suggesting an emotional and ritual connection between Henry V and his more legitimate predecessor. More importantly, it devotes a single stanza to the reburial itself in a poem which deals principally with Henry V's war against heresy, implicitly suggesting that the reburial functions mainly to close the kind of fissure within which heresy might breed. His diatribe against the Lollard Oldcastle (1415) again joins the subject of the established Church's 'title iust & trewe' handed down by 'our goode fadres olde' to the unattainable Lancastrian daydream of a just succession, handed down in unbroken line from the guarantor-fathers. In this case, the Church's title serves as a haven of the legitimacy Hoccleve will constantly seek but never be able securely to locate in the realm itself. His advice to Oldcastle, as to all heretics, is

> . . . vn-to our cristen kyng
> Thee hie as faste as that thow canst dyuyse
> And humble eeke thee to him for any thyng!

In the meantime, Oldcastle serves his purpose. Joining with a 'hethenly couyne' even as he avoids service in France, he serves the same argumentative convenience as the hapless Southampton conspirators, seized and executed for his role in a partially fabricated plot for treasonous conspiracy on the very eve of the expedition to Harfleur.[19] By the same token, Henry V and the Garter knights (1414–16) are exhorted to attack the common foe – not, as it happens, the French, but 'heresies bittir galle.' Had it not been for Henry's prompt exertions, Hoccleve constantly suggests, the isle would already have fallen to the heathens. As he declares to Henry V and the Garter knights, 'This yle, or [ere] this, had been but hethennesse,/Nad been of your feith the force & vigour!'

This system of differences, in which heresy is set on its feet and sent walking in the land as orthodoxy's foil, is amplified throughout Hoccleve's *Regement* and other works of its decade, with respect to a series of interrelated oppositions, all touching in one way or another on a continuing contrast between superfluity, excess, and false display on the one hand and the solidity and inner integrity of a legitimate claim on the other. Hoccleve's interlocutor in the *Regement* is, for example, highly exercised over the subject of extravagant dress, 'wit pendant sleues downe/On the grounde,' but his anti-fashion agenda does not stop with moralizing concern over vanity and waste:

> 'Nay sothely, sone, it is al a-mys me thinkyth;
> So pore a wight his lord to counterfete
> In his array, in my conceyit it stynkith.
> Certes to blame ben the lordes grete,
> If that I durste seyn, that hir men lete
> Usurpe swiche a lordly apparaille.' (ll. 435–440)

Loose in these lines are several different anxieties, including Lancastrian concern over aristocratic retinues and the potential of liveried retainers to create disturbance in the land.[20] But the principal concern is with outward display, in its potential to falsify or 'counterfete' inner meaning, and such self-illegitimization is linked with the possibility of treasonous usurpation. The Lancastrian counter-example is John of Gaunt, whose 'garnamentes weren noght fel wyde,/And yit thei hym becam wonderly wel' (ll. 519–520). His garments, that is, were in accord with his station, a guarantee of 'trouth' and authenticity in a potentially inauthentic world.

An overdressed man is gendered as 'but a womman' (*Regement*, l. 468), and the possibility of descent into womanly practices is constantly threatened. His poem against Oldcastle, for example, accuses the Lollard knight of deficient manhood, as reflected even in such details as reading practice. Oldcastle joins those thin-witted women who 'Wele argumentes make in holy writ,' analyzing holy texts with questions of, ' "Why stant this word heere?" ' Recommended to him is reading matter appropriate to knights, including *romans d'aventure*, martial romance, and Vegetius on the art of chivalry. It is 1415 and the 'rial viage' to France is underway; Oldcastle is challenged to abandon feminized pursuits and to join the royal and knightly program of victorious conquest.

Also repeatedly stigmatized is flattery, especially as it threatens to dilute the effectiveness of poets and other good counselors of the king. In his early 'Male Regle' he inveighed against Favel (or 'flattery'), whose 'feyned wordes' undermine good governance. In the prologue to the *Regement* he renews the attack, arguing that Favel treasonously blinds lords and the rich to their actual deserts, and suggests (in the voice of his mentor) that he personally would 'bet . . . ben at ierusalem' (l. 1942) than engage in such deceits. In pillorying flattery, Hoccleve gains advantage in his self-portrayal as a plain speaker and truth-teller. But he also taps a broader area of crucial Lancastrian concern by connecting flattery with the ever-present threat of treason and plain dealing with political legitimacy.

In each of these cases, an inauthentic and less wholesome alternative – whether heresy, effeminate fashion, female practices of reading and introspection, or false speech – is considered subversive of Lancastrian practice, which is stabilized around ideas of the orthodox, the identity of inner and outer, the refusal of debilitating speculation and misrepresentation in any of its forms. Here held at bay is the embarrassing fact of the Lancastrians as a usurping dynasty, and the extent to which misrepresentation and false display reach a crisis point during their regime. This is the unacknowledged issue around which Hoccleve's public poems revolve, never explicitly admitting the flawed nature of the Lancastrian title, but never completely free of its demand to be acknowledged.

A surge of present interest in Hoccleve is undoubtedly based less on his topicality than on his creation and deployment of what might be taken for a personal voice. With obvious debts to Chaucer's own skill at self-presentation, and with longer-term reliance on tropes of poetic modesty and first-person confessional practices, Hoccleve achieves a uniquely detailed and persuasive stance as a self-revealing speaker in his 'Male Regle,' in his dialogue with the old man which introduces his *Regement*, and in the 'Complaint' and the 'Dialogue with a Friend' that launch the free-wheeling literary compilation of the 1420s now generally known as Hoccleve's 'Series.' Persuasively arrayed in details about his excessive tavern life and personal misrule (in 'Male Regle'), his economic difficulties and financially disadvantageous marriage (*Regement*), and, especially, a 'wild infirmytie' of several years' duration that checked his professional life and shook his self-confidence ('Complaint' and 'Dialogue'), these revelatory passages have been granted near-autobiographical status – the more so, because of their pertinence to such issues as Hoccleve's apparent cessation of writing between 1414–15 and 1419–20, and because they are supported by some evidence of irregularities in his annuity payments.[21]

In addition to an exciting impression of self-revelation, Hoccleve's insistence on his flawed nature possesses a political dimension. His poem to Henry V and the Garter knights observes that 'an heep of vs arn halt & lame' with respect to matters of faith and (by derivation) loyalty. By the same token, the deficiencies to which he confesses freely may be read as testimonies to his own reliance upon Lancastrian rule, figured by his flaws as a political subject.[22] Even his early 'Male Regle' may be read as a mirror for magistrates in the personal sphere, its constant emphasis on the virtues of submission to the 'mene reule' (l. 352) of good health as an inscription of the flawed subject's responsibilities to a stern but just sovereign. Hoccleve offers himself as 'mirour . . . of riot & excess' (l. 330), whose personal misrule must be checked if it is not to lead to rebellion (l. 65). So, too, does the protagonist of the 'Complaint,' for all his emphasis upon personal psychological catastrophe, hint at a political lesson to be drawn from his 'synfull governaunce' (l. 406). Whatever else we learn about Hoccleve from such apparent disclosures, we most certainly learn of his ultimate deference to his Lancastrian monarchs – extending even to the expression of flaws and deficiencies over which they hold the power and secret of ultimate repair.

*

John Lydgate's own life-chances and literary fortunes received an early impetus from the Prince. His first extended absence from the Abbey of St Edmunds after his ordination in 1389 was a period of several years' study at Oxford in the first decade of the fifteenth century, and while there he seems to have attracted the young Henry's attention; the latter rather exceptionally intervened in 1406–8 with a letter to the abbot and chapter of Bury St Edmunds asking that Lydgate be permitted to continue his studies.[23] The year 1407–8 saw the inception of the Prince's role as an opposition leader, and this author-intellectual's potential political usefulness may have been a factor in Henry's interest. Lydgate had not yet entered the political arena; among surviving works of this period may be numbered Aesopian fables, love visions, and devotional

hymns.[24] But he would soon accept more ambitious and more politically charged endeavors, in which he sought consistently to advance
Henry's prospects, first as Prince and then as King Henry V, as well as
those of his infant son. The first of his mega compositions, the *Troy
Book*, a 30,000-line translation and embellishment of Guido della
Colonna's *Historia*, claims the Prince as its patron, and spans the period
1412–20. His next long work, the *Siege of Thebes*, was composed during
1420–22 and would appear to have been written on speculation –
though its complete identification with Henry V's ambitions in France
is suggested by a series of celebratory allusions to his 1420 Treaty of
Troyes.[25] Then commences that decade of still more heightened activity
called by Pearsall the 'laureate' period,[26] spanning the years 1422–23 to
1433–34, in which Lydgate was associated with the earl of Warwick,
sojourned with the duke of Bedford in France and made himself available for a variety of commissions and state-related tasks, many
designed to bolster the legitimacy of the infant Henry VI. By the end of
this period he had commenced his final great work, the sprawling
36,000-line translation and augmentation of Boccaccio as rendered in
French by Laurent de Premierfait, entitled *Fall of Princes*, under the
patronage of Humphrey, duke of Gloucester. This work, probably
begun in 1431, was facilitated by Lydgate's return to Bury in 1433–34
and not completed until 1438–39. Lydgate received a royal annuity in
1439, was intermittently active in the final decade of his life, and died
at Bury St Edmunds in 1449.

Already at the 1412 start of *Troy Book* Lydgate showed himself adept
in effecting a creative linkage among favored Lancastrian themes of
dynastic succession, legitimacy, and nationalism. He says that then-
Prince Henry had 'comaunded' him to compile the work from Guido,
implying like any good flatterer that his lord does not need the work
for himself (since, acquainted with the story in French and Latin, he is
already fully supplied with all that it might offer) but wants it for his
future subjects:

> . . . By-cause he wolde that to hyge and lowe
> The noble story openly wer knowe
> In oure tonge. (Prologue, ll. 111–113)

Henry's wish is to be obeyed because, 'stok' of his father, to him 'schal
longe by successioun/For to gouerne Brutys Albyoun' (Prologue,
ll. 103–104). Henry's father having gained the throne only by interrupting 'successioun,' and ruling in despite of the superior claims of
the earl of March, Lydgate's dynastic argument would seem less than

ideally secure. But, in another sense, Henry V's direct inheritance from his father will represent a return to the very principle of continuity interrupted by Henry IV.

Lydgate also addresses by other means the Lancastrian affront to orderly succession. In the epilogue and envoy to this work he settles upon a convenient elision of the whole matter, focusing instead upon Henry V's right to rule in France:

> . . . who-so list loken and vnfolde
> The pe-de-Grew of cronycles olde,
> . . . He shal fynde that he is iustly born
> To regne in Fraunce by lyneal discent. (V, ll. 3387–3388, 3390–3391)

The triumphant theme of the 'two crowns' will serve increasingly in Lydgate as a wished-for transcendence of whatever equivocal tarnish remains upon the domestic one. The tracings of the medieval *pie de grue* or 'crane's foot' are not devoted to the embarrassing issue of domestic succession, but are displaced to the less internally divisive subject of the English claim on France. Focusing with ever more intensity on Henry VI's French 'enheritaunce,' Lydgate reaffirms his right in poems like his 'Prayer for King, Queen, and People' (1429), 'Title and Pedigree of Henry VI' (1426) and 'King Henry VI's Triumphal Entry into London' (1432).

The urgent need for a transcendence of bloody local history becomes evident throughout the *Troy Book*, as in its successor work, the *Siege of Thebes* (derived from the French tradition of the *Roman de Edipus*). In each poem, dreams of just succession are continually advanced, as in the *Troy Book*, where Horestes' revenge on his mother (cutting her into small pieces and feeding them to dogs) and Egisthus (severing him 'bon fro bon') leads to the wishful declaration that 'Thus was the toun fro tresoun purged clene' (V, l. 1660). But dreams of dynastic succession are invariably disturbed by the actual motors of history, variously identified as covetousness, suspicion, slander, malice, rancor, treason, female perfidy, flattery, discord, vengeance, newfangledness, and – especially – the doubleness and random malignancy of Fortune. Unavoidably acknowledged in the *Troy Book* and carried to its ultimate development in Lydgate's vastly augmented *Fall of Princes* is the dissolution of providential or teleological history into a chaos of bloody extirpations, usurpations, and dismemberments. History, so seen, is 'tragedie' – not in the classical sense that pits a solitary hero against an inescapable destiny, but in the medieval sense of a finite and abrupt descent from 'ioie' to 'aduersite' (*Fall*, V, ll. 3120–3121).

The Lancastrian artist recasts the problematic of succession at various expressive levels. As with Hoccleve, Lydgate repeatedly lays claim to discipleship and just authorial inheritance, as when he presents the *Siege of Thebes* as his own Canterbury tale, in effect imagining himself as written by Chaucer, or in the *Troy Book*, in which he presents himself in a tradition of truthful historiography that reaches back to presumed eyewitness accounts of Dares and Dictys, or in *Fall of Princes* with a genealogy embracing Boccaccio as *auctour* and compiler. Yet such dutiful imaginings are perturbed by ambition of a different sort. Despite Lydgate's professions of loyalty to Chaucer, he does not fail to take advantage of the older poet's absence from the scene to institute his own, and very different, aesthetic of stylistic decorum and comprehensive treatment. A. C. Spearing has incisively commented on the 'innocent destructiveness' with which Lydgate sets out to survive and supplant this benevolent yet powerful father Chaucer.[27] So, too, is Lydgate's emphasis on good sources in the *Troy Book* undermined by a host of suppressions and substitutions, including the concealment of Benôit de Saint-Maure's enormous influence upon his 'maister' Guido delle Colonne. Guido's own advancement is based on an appropriately Lancastrian (and hence contradictory) assertion: that his is a new kind of authority, self-generated and self-conferred, based on an innovative capacity for stylistic embellishment and narrative amplification. So, too, is Boccaccio in the *Fall of Princes* accorded a degree of respect, even as Lydgate argues that intervening source Laurence de Premierfait is entitled to 'breke and renewe' Boccaccio's vessel in order to amend it for the best (l. 11).[28]

For all his professions of personal subservience to literary authority and continuity, Lydgate seems to acknowledge that succession might involve some displacements along the way. This acknowledgment, in turn, parallels Lydgate's attitude toward dynastic succession and secular rule. Against perfidies of statecraft and the dissipations of history, he sets the ideal of the history-making prince. This self-legitimizing prince is permitted to interrupt and intrude upon established successions, to create new occasions for creative and reparative history-writing, to be the vehicle of his own exceptionality. Reviewing Henry V's achievements as defender of Holychurch and destroyer of Lollards and, especially, as conqueror of France, Lydgate imagines him successful in his exertions, in having created his own permanent and stable 'dwelling-place,' both in heaven and in historical memory:

> I pray to God, so yiue his soule good reste,
> With hooli seyntis in heuene a duellyng-place.
> For heere with vs to litil was the space

That he abood; off whom the remembraunce
Shal neuer deie in Ingland nor in Fraunce. (*Fall*, I, ll. 5981–5985)

Henry's residence with the saints is a matter of prayerful, that is fanciful, transcendence of residual and obstinate difficulties. But, by the
time these verses were written, Lydgate must have known in fact what
he certainly knew in theory: that historical developments elude and
exceed the exertions of even the most temporarily successful princes.

Rather than retiring the mantle of the history-making prince,
Lydgate loaned it to various less propitious candidates. The eligibility
of the duke of Gloucester is, for example, canvassed within the poem
he patronized, as Lydgate launches the *Fall of Princes* with the assertion
that Humphrey (unlike the host of more prepossessing princes who
have already taken the fall) is fortune-proof, 'Settyng a-side alle
chaungis of Fortune' (Prologue, l. 390). So, too, does his 'Title and
Pedigree of Henry VI' attempt to soar over intractable circumstances to
present that unfortunate child as a bearer of larger dynastic destinies.
Indeed, throughout his poetry, Lydgate does what he can to adjust
obstinate circumstances and putative enemies to the requirements of
the Lancastrian solution. In a short piece entitled 'Of the Sodein Fall of
Princes in Oure Dayes,' he supplements the *Fall of Princes* with seven
more modern instances, including that of Richard II who turns out to
have been 'feyne' or 'willing' to resign and die. So, too, did Henry V's
principal French adversary the dauphin conveniently disqualify
himself by the murder of duke of Burgundy Jean sans Peur:

> . . . causing in soth his vnabilite
> For to succede to any dignite,
> Of knyghtly honure to regne in any lond.

Lydgate thus stands continually ready to suspend the depredations of
Fortune and the vanity of princely designs in favor of official optimism
that the Lancastrians will clear their impossible title and find a way to
establish peace through war.

Nevertheless, as Lee Patterson has trenchantly observed, Lydgate's
most ambitious endeavors remain 'ambivalent texts', constantly at
odds with themselves.[29] As he suggests of the *Siege* with its message of
war as a route to peace, none of these texts can avoid incorporating its
opposite: the *Troy Book* with its uneasy acknowledgment of flawed
origins, the 'Pedigree' with its unavoidable inclusion of coincidence
and doubleness, the *Fall* with its reminder that no prince is fortune-
proof. Even as Lydgate's text sets for itself a determined task of Lancas-

trian apology, it cannot prevent the emergence of a more pessimistic counter-awareness in each of its joints and recesses.

Dullness and affect in Lancastrian letters

If the characteristic Ricardian pattern was to chide the monarch even while assenting in the end to things he wants done, the characteristic Lancastrian pattern moves in the opposite direction: an extreme surface deference to the monarch's aims and an attempt to accommodate all aspects of his program eventuates in a text that straddles crisis after crisis of argumentative consistency. Whatever the diplomacy or skill of its author, the Lancastrian text finds itself in such straits because of the deep self-contradiction of its monarchs' political program and the sheer impossibility of its successful textualization. Among other elements of their program, the Lancastrians expected that complicit writers would celebrate the legitimacy of Henry IV's murderous usurpation, the benefits to orthodoxy in burning English subjects as Lollard heretics, and the path to peace through rapine and seizure in France. And herein lies a recipe for inevitable cognitive/aesthetic breakdown.

Even though Hoccleve and Lydgate both *try* to be as complicit as possible in every aspect of the Lancastrian program, their versified arguments for loyalty and continuity repeatedly turn out not quite to fit the purposes they are invoked to serve. The very topics most disturbing to their princes constantly resurface, around and under the sign of their negation. At the end of the *Regement* for example, Hoccleve offers what must seem an unexceptionable plea for peace with France, citing Christ's words to St Bridget to the effect that

> . . . forthi may
> By matrimoigne pees and vnite
> Ben had; cristes plesance is swiche; thus he
> That right heir is, may the reme reioyse,
> Cesynge al strif, debate, or werre, or noyse. (ll. 5393–5397)

Negation of strife, debate, war, and tumult may seem uncontroversial implications, but this 'unity' program is finally a highly partisan Lancastrian performance that embraces every sort of *disunity* and contradiction. Hoccleve's proposal anticipates the solution of the Treaty of Troyes, a treaty whose deep and unresolvable contradictions galvanized, rather than assuaged, the martial anger of the French. In fact, so unstable was the interplay of Burgundian and French factions around the treaty that the Lancastrians themselves could not agree on its coherent prosecution. Nor could the Lancastrians maintain even a coherent family policy; disagreement over the relative merits of assisting the Burgundians and the Armagnacs underlay the quarrel between Henry IV and the Prince in 1412, and in 1424–25 Humphrey, duke of Gloucester enraged the dukes of Bedford and Burgundy by marrying Jaque of Hainault and (in a reprise of his grandfather's Castilian adventures) warring against the Burgundian alliance.[30]

In late 1422 or early 1423, Lydgate wrote celebratory verses on the proposed alliance of Humphrey and Jaque. As widowed heiress of Holland, Hainault, and Zeeland, in flight from an unsuccessful second marriage to Jean of Brabant, Jaque escaped in 1422 to England, where she was received by Humphrey in an atmosphere of royal support and high intrigue. Even though her annulment was incomplete,[31] and even though this marriage threatened the larger contours of English foreign policy by pitting Humphrey against the duke of Burgundy, the remote but seductive prospect of lands on the Continent and a derivative title proved too alluring for Humphrey to resist. This opportunistic and short-lived match thus rested on an entirely acquisitive basis, and Lydgate's rather ingenious celebratory strategy is to praise the marriage exactly for its acquisitive motives. Marriage itself, in a myth of origins influenced by Theseus's peroration in the 'Knight's Tale' reshaped by Lydgate for the occasion of his poem, is introduced by the eternal Lord in furtherance of his first cause, which is elimination of strife by 'allayaunce/Betweene provynces and worthy regyouns.'[32] Many chronicles have told how marriage has functioned in this way, 'Howe maryages haue grounde and cause be/Betwene landes of pees and vnytee' – the most recent example being Catherine of France's function as a 'meene' or conveyance of alliance for Henry V. So, too, Lydgate goes on to suggest (in a stanza riddled with syntactic inconsistencies which I will not pause to analyze here, but which amply suggest the awkwardness of his task), will grace suffice to attain a secondary but related objective:

> To fynde a wey wherby we may atteyne
> That Duchye of Holand by hool affeccoun
> May beo allyed with Brutus Albyoun.

This objective is, of course, to be accomplished by Humphrey's union with 'of Holand the goodely fresshe Duchesse,/Called *Iaques*', the delayed introduction of her name suggesting the lesser importance of the individual than the charged position she occupies as heritor of these lands.

Lydgate's emphasis on dynastic advantage is by no means to be construed as contrary to his celebratory purpose; he writes, as he says, in 'holle entent . . . for tyl do plesaunce' to Jaque, and a recognition of her substantial dower is undoubtedly one aspect of the pleasure to be given. Yet, at the same time, he develops his poems in terms so inherently flawed, contradictory, and unsusceptible of belief as to pose an interpretative problem in their own right. Whether because of the inherent impossibility of his descriptive mandate, or the promptings of his own imp of the perverse, Lydgate constantly veers toward the very things that cannot be said, and the very images that discredit or destabilize his enterprise. Jaque – twice married already, and her current marriage scheme enveloped in international furor as a result of her failure to achieve annulment of her marriage to Jean of Brabant – is extensively praised as the 'fresshe Duchesse,' no less 'truwe and cleene' in love than Lucrece herself. Her flight over the seas to new Troy encourages Lydgate to compare her to fair Helen and Humphrey to comely Paris, without overt acknowledgment of the unfortunate imagistic baggage carried by this duplicitous couple. Humphrey's knightly fame is found worthy of registration in 'the Hous of Ffaame,' without explicit recognition of the scandal such recognition would imply for any careful reader of Chaucer's poem. The marriage of 'Phylogonye and Mercurye' is invoked, with the principal guest turning out in this case to be that noted destabilizer of realms, Fortune herself:

> And thowe, Fortune, bee also of assent
> This neodful thing texecuyt yerne,
> Thorugh youre power whiche that is eterne.

With what might legitimately be taken for an irony as heavy as January's praise of marriage in Chaucer's 'Merchants Tale', Lydgate foresees a trouble-free future for this dynastic union:

> Farewell thanne al trouble and hevynesse,
> Yf so were thees landes were alle oon.

The soon to be revealed reality is that the duke of Burgundy's opposition to Humphrey's meddling would imperil the English–Burgundian axis that formed almost the entire basis for English continuance in France after the death of Henry V.[33] When Bedford finally pulled the plug on the last of the schemes to aid Jaque, it was precisely the inconvenience represented by Humphrey's and Jaque's tie, and the danger to the English interest in France and continued good relations with Burgundy, that decided the day.[34] The marriage was to limp along for some four years, punctuated by absurdities like a contemplated duel between Humphrey and the duke of Burgundy,[35] and was finally terminated four years later, leaving behind Humphrey's next wife (Jaque's lady-in-waiting Eleanor Cobham) as its sordid remainder.[36]

A similar point may briefly be made by a return to a passage with which this chapter began, Lydgate's deliberately banal address to Henry VI upon his coronation:

> Prynce excellent, be feythful, truwe and stable;
> Dreed God, do lawe, chastyce extorcyoun,
> Be liberal, of courage vnmutable,
> Cherisshe the Chirche with holle affeccyoun,
> Loue thy lyeges of eyther regyoun,
> Preferre the pees, eschuwe werre and debate. . . .

Although Lydgate confines himself to an utterly unexceptional series of stances and steps, this serene poetic surface tolerates a number of deeply divisive implications: that the normal Lancastrian way of cherishing the Church is to apprehend and burn heretics, that the claim to the crown of France as well as England ('thy lyeges of eyther regyoun') was customarily adduced to deflect attention from the Lancastrians' uncertain domestic throne, that Henry's claim to the 'two crowns' of England and France was unlikely to be sustained without resort to 'werre and debate.'

The scandal of desertion, the horror of regicide, the injustice of extirpation, the folly of conquest recur constantly in Lancastrian poetry – but mitigated by falsely optimistic solutions, blunted by layers of extraneous commentary, and never in open reference to Lancastrian policy. At best obtuse and at worst dishonest, such evasions (and the indirection and excessive amplification with which they are associated) have encouraged accusations of dullness against Lancastrian poetry. But, beneath the deceptively placid surface of Lancastrian letters roils a veritable ocean of unacknowledged aberration.

A bold and revisionary discussion of the conflict-avoiding surfaces of Lancastrian letters has been inaugurated by David Lawton's essay on 'Dullness and the Fifteenth Century,' in which he argues that a public posture of dullness enabled poets of the period to advance bold propositions and offer unwelcome advice.[37] My own, slightly different, analysis is that Lancastrian poetry indeed assumed a posture of dullness, not only (as Lawton suggests) tactically with respect to the monarch, but also more confusedly with respect to the affective trajectories of its own desire. According to this reading, Hoccleve's and Lydgate's aspiration to full complicity was unwavering, but the impossibility of Lancastrian requirements drove even the most resolutely loyal texts into a morass of embarrassing half-acknowledgments and debilitating self-contradictions. Continually at strife with its own professions, the Lancastrian text is above all a hardworking text, always striving but never succeeding in reconciling its placid surface with its external entanglements and its internal contradictions.

Writing in the most precarious circumstances, on the threshold of the most internecine passage in English history, Hoccleve and Lydgate produced poems which stumble constantly and even obsessively into referential difficulties they cannot afford to acknowledge. Condemned to ceaseless vigilance and interminable labor, their texts evince Herculean exertion in an impossible cause. Unable to close itself to history, Lancastrian poetry reluctantly attempts the task of disavowing what it knows and cannot say about usurpation, tyranny, and terror – and by its very nature this task can never end.

8

Coda: The Amnesiac Text

These studies have revolved around a succession of remarkably amne-siac texts. These are texts which stand dumb in relation to the past, expending much labor and ingenuity in the service of forgetfulness. Such amnesia may be seen as a general condition of textuality itself, with no text found reliable with regard to the whole truth of its origins. Yet the condition of forgetfulness attains unusual dimensions in the Lancastrian period, when the scandalous and disturbing circum-stances of Henry IV's accession gave everybody (except a few diehard Ricardians) so much to forget.

Henry and his sons were committed from the outset to a program of *official* forgetfulness: a forgetfulness embracing their own dynastic ori-gins, their predecessor's fate, the promises and opportunistic alliances which had gained them a throne. I say 'program,' because they did not lack for willing participants. Initial and impressive Lancastrian suc-cesses rested, not only upon the adeptness of their propaganda machine, but also upon the short-term problem experienced by the English populace in 'processing' the displacement and subsequent murder of Richard II. For the English people, including many of Richard's formerly loyal subjects, now found themselves confronted with 'impossible history' – a set of circumstances beyond the capacity of existing explanatory frames or repositories of meaning.[1] Lancastrian self-perpetuation effectively required an exploitation of this initial bewilderment, a prolongation of the somewhat stunned acquiescence with which Henry IV's seizure of the throne was greeted in the beginning.

The early Lancastrian text fulfills its social function by participating in this amnesiac exercise. Would-be Lancastrian ideologues replicated – with varied results – the suppressions, contortions, and reworkings endemic to the Lancastrian propaganda endeavor. But the resulting, aspirationally complicitous, text was never to be free of the absent pressure of banished events, and particularly 'the' event of sovereignty's illicit and violent origin. This pressure may be measured in the extent to which the very texts most bent on eliding or ignoring dynastic origins cannot seem to close themselves or defend themselves from the very things they mean not to say.

My chosen text – Thomas Hoccleve's tale of John of Canace – is not exactly history-denying at first glance. It appears, after all, in a work of 'advice to princes,' Hoccleve's *Regement of Princes*, composed for Henry, Prince of Wales in that charged period in and around 1410–11, when he impatiently awaited the crown.[2] As a representative of the advice-to-princes genre, it invites consideration as an intervention (however deflected or muted) in contemporary discussions of statecraft.[3] During the five or six centuries of this anecdote's popularity it was deployed in all kinds of ways, including, in its personality as a text advisory to princes, its dedication and rededication to many actual and aspirant monarchs, including Prince John of France shortly before his ill-fated kingship began in 1350, and, in Caxton's 1474 first edition, to George, ill-fated duke of Clarence. But, even if the impulse to dedicate is not in itself unique, each dedication attaches itself in a potentially specific way to someone's design. Hoccleve's own text exists in manuscripts with multiple destinations. Obviously addressed to the future Henry V, and including a drawing for presentation to the prince, the splendid British Library MS Arundel 38 also includes evidence of patronage by the Mowbray family (numbering among its recent members the Thomas Mowbray who was executed for his part in the 1405 Scrope conspiracy), and Hoccleve composed dedicatory verses destined for Edward, duke of York or John, duke of Bedford.[4] Clearly, such dedications attach the work in different, potentially specific ways to someone's design.

These points being granted, the 'advice' contained in works like Hoccleve's *Regement* and its antecedents nevertheless remains on an extremely broad plane, constantly shirking and disavowing any potentially embarrassing applications. The *Regement* early on reveals itself as superficially mindful, but in all significant senses forgetful, of its own relation to history. Hoccleve announces at the outset that his state of personal anxiety or 'restless bysynesse' may be connected with the instability of the world he inhabits, citing the recent fall of Richard II as an instance. Yet his allusion remains oddly anaesthetized, assimilating Richard's demise to the tradition of the 'falls of princes,' with Fortune, rather than any earthly hand, delivering the final stroke:

> Me fyl to mynde how that noght long a goo
> Fortunes stroke doun threst estat real

> In to mesche & I tok heede also
> Of many an other lord that hadde a fal. . . .

The attempt to acknowledge a 'fall,' but to render it harmless and agentless, is replicated at many points in this work, in which Hoccleve persistently draws close to the most disturbing and incriminating deeds and deficiencies of Lancastrian kingship, though always with the apparent motive of palliating them and detaching them from telling critique.

Similarly generalized is the tale of John of Canace. Broadly distributed over a half-dozen centuries, it crossed linguistic, generic and political boundaries with an aplomb resistant to topical applications. A further antidote to topicality would seem to rest in the proximity of Hoccleve's own version to its source, the highly influential *Liber de ludo scaccorum*, composed at the end of the thirteenth century by Jacobus de Cessolis.[5] The condition of non-knowledge and amnesia I have claimed for the Lancastrian text is explicitly ascribed to this production. This will, Hoccleve says at the beginning, be the tale of 'oon' John, which 'be fil y not [know not] in what contree.'[6] In its preference for broad moralization over particular application and its evident intent to provide decontextualized wisdom, Hoccleve's tale of John seems a wholly representative Lancastrian text.

How, then, and on what terms, is history to stage a return within a text so determined that contemporary history should not be discovered within its bounds? My own belief is that history was never absent, although its presence is manifested at different levels of acknowledgment.[7] My first stage of consideration will concern some historical things this tale rather overtly 'knows' or 'means to say' about itself: its decided generic self-positioning within an advice-to-princes tradition, for example, and some specific adaptations, deferences, and evasions adopted in relation to its particular political-historical situation. I will subsequently consider this tale's less overt political engagements, discovering a number of respects in which it 'says more than it knows,' or at least more than it 'means to say' about the Lancastrian situation.

Advising the Lancastrian prince

Although this tale possesses no 'ur' or invariable structure independent of its realizations, certain of its elements do tend to persist independently of its particular generic personality. Among these are: a father wastes his substance among his children; now that he is poor, they treat him negligently; he responds by acquiring an empty chest, either empty or filled with sand, stones, or something else heavy, and conspicuously reverences it; the deceived children think the chest contains inheritable treasure and treat him well for the remainder of his life.

In one generic incarnation, this may be considered a 'moral tale,' told within a tradition of mendicant preaching and instruction. Instances include the version of Joannes Herolt in his *Promptuarium exemplorum*, a fifteenth-century Dominican compilation (from thirteenth-century sources)[8] and also the version contained in *De virtutibus et vitiis*, a Franciscan compilation of earlier tales made in Italy in the early fifteenth century.[9] Opprobrium is broadly distributed within these omnipurpose and versatile tellings; the father is blamed for improvident generosity, but the ungrateful children are at least equally criticized; Herolt's version, for example, is placed under the heading of 'Filii et Filiae,' rather than that of the ruler or prince, in his alphabetical scheme.

But, within the alternative genre of collections advisory to princes, emphasis shifts heavily to the father, with his activities presented as a metonym for the prince and his responsibility of good rule. Hoccleve's source, Jacobus de Cessolis's Book of Chess, sets the advice-to-princes mold by centralizing the role of the father/prince, offering an energized father who borrows and temporarily displays real gold in order to stoke his daughters' desires. His guile unexhausted, he additionally deceives them by distributing keys to the chest, redeemable by charitable donations from the daughters' own means before they can discover the chest's contents. True to its generic affiliation, Hoccleve's renarration additionally enhances the fatherly role. Instead of simply allowing inference about the contents of the locked chest filled with stones, or merely dumping borrowed treasure out on a carpet where the ungrateful heirs can see it, this John implicates his children in an inflammatory process of illicit observation. Inviting his daughters and sons-in-law to dinner, he persuades them to spend the night, placing them in a room adjacent to his chamber, through which his chamber can be viewed through a 'parclose' or partition with chinks or 'chynyngs.' The next morning, he stages a dumb show in which he opens his chest, displays its borrowed contents, casts and sorts the coins, assays them for possible counterfeit, and only belatedly bags and coffers them:

> And to the parclos they hem haste and hye,
> To wyte and knowe what hir fader wroughte.
> In at the chynes of the bord they prye,
> And sygh how he a monge the nobles soghte

> If deffectif were any as hem thought;
> And on hys nayle he threw hym ofte & caste,
> And bagged hem and cofred at the laste.

Forbidden knowledge, coupled with a certain requisite distance, turns out to be the perfect condition of desire, which in these bad siblings is whetted almost beyond endurance:

> . . . for hyre hertes depe
> Stak in hys bounden cofre, and al hire hope
> Was good bagges therynne for to grope.

The chest is, of course, now again empty, the gold having been returned to the merchant from whom John borrowed it. But, since these bad daughters' pleasure consists, not in possession of the gold, but in the expectation of their enjoyment, they are easy to fool.

Note that Hoccleve has followed his proximate source in a choice critical for the advice-to-princes genre, by emphasizing that this is a tale about a father's relation to his daughters. Other versions of this tale – and especially those designed for general moral compilations – are likely to portray a father's relation with his male heirs.[10] The choice of daughters – apparently originating in thirteenth-century Italian texts in which, as in *De virtutibus et vitiis*, the high cost of dowries intrudes as a critical consideration[11] – is critical in the consolidation of this tale for purposes of princely advice. For the daughter may be taken as a representation of the prince's subjects (greedy and demanding, but susceptible to discipline) without raising the issue of ultimate rivalry so common (and so inherent) in relations of royal fathers and princely sons.

Hoccleve likewise develops another element of his tale with latent bearing on the issue of princely conduct. One version of the tale substitutes a heavy hammer for the sand or stones which give the chest its weight: the Herolt father fetched a *scrinium* or treasure chest, in which he placed a heavy hammer as if it were money ('in quo posuit malleum gravem quasi esset pecunia')[12] and other versions imagine a *clava* or club in the same role. This hammer or club, in turn, becomes the agent of the tale's disciplinary message, with the father attaching to it a note, to the effect that a parent who wastes his substance among his children deserves to be struck with this instrument. But Hoccleve's chest turns out, uniquely, to contain an explicit emblem of civil authority, 'a passyngly greet sergeantes mace' bearing the inscribed sentiment that 'Who berith charge of other men, & is/Of hem despised, slayn be he with this.' Like its predecessor the club, the mace still menaces the heedless prince. Unlike the club, the mace is an emblem of constituted civil authority, and thus sits two-sidedly in the narration, as an admonition to the prince as well as his subjects. To 'bear charge,' in this case, has an obviously doubled meaning: not just to pay the costs but to bear responsibility, the latter the province of the prince.

Hoccleve seems to be playing a double game here. On the one hand, he adapts his tale more closely than ever before to the situation of rulership and the problem of the ruler who experiences economic destitution or (in a more general symbolic sense) diminution of his legitimacy or 'right to rule.' In this regard, his tale would seem to possess an immense capacity to solace the Lancastrian prince. No sooner, for example, is a loss recognized and recorded (in John's empty chest) than it is narratively remastered (through John's conversion of his destitution to a source of symbolic strength). Sedition and scandal are held at bay by this narrative curvature: not so much repressed as simply not mentioned. Even the bad daughters, while hardly reformed, are made to *seem* good, to behave well, by the force of John's deception. On the other hand, tame as John's narrative might appear to be, Hoccleve seems at pains to muffle its political applicability, effectively to disavow the very implications he seems explicitly to invite. In addition to the other protestations of bafflement and refusals of context in which he cloaks his tale, he goes on to insist that the spendthrift father's predicament is really his *own*; its application, he tells us in one of those disingenuous fifteenth-century moralizations, is to his own wasted substance and to his own hope for repair from the coffers of the prince.

Something in this narrative seems to need extra taming; an extra dash of disavowal. Here arises the question of what a text might 'mean' which it 'means' or intends not to say. What, in an analytical direction contrary to a text's own professed intentions, and in the face of that text's own resolute silences, can still be said of its subversive potential? What considerations might lead us to conclude that John's empty box, and the strategies by which he induces his viewers to imagine it full, comprise a parabolic commentary on the unavoidable insufficiencies of a usurping dynasty?

As anti-Lancastrian narrative

Given its apparent motives of reassurance and recuperation, this anecdote seems an unlikely place for a dynastic 'history in abeyance' to begin its own rematerialization. But history has never been wholly absent from this text; it remains latent and unarticulated within its boundaries, liable to be teased or tricked into visibility by the contemporary discourses by which it is traversed and with which it cannot refuse alignment. Which is to say that this text's mechanisms cannot all be viewed from within, or within the terms in which it presents itself; from the vantage point of several different external discourses, an incriminating and only partially symbolized anti-Lancastrian history may be viewed.[13]

Following are discussions of several moments at which the elements of an alternative history become available to view, or are even summoned, invited to breach and re-enter Hoccleve's carefully drawn and defended narrative circle.

'Emptiness'

One way to render absence visible is to thematize it, to raise to the level of explicit attention the topic of *what is not there*. Consider, in this regard, the attention given to John's empty box as the object-cause of the daughters' desire. As a kind of Lacanian trope before the letter, the revelation that desire is here constituted around an open or empty place might be received in a timeless or transhistorical sense; might seem, that is, to soar over the historically specific. But desire *itself* is never (or at least cannot remain) transhistorical; for the desiring state never exists separately from very particular, inevitably historical, objects of desire. The sublimated objects of our desire are always established (as Lacan observes) 'at a certain historical moment' and the historicity of their insertion and presentation is what opens them to social analysis and historical consequence.[14]

But what, then, is 'historical' and specific to the Lancastrian situation about the choice of an empty box as a figure for the father/prince's legitimation? What possible connection exists between an image of emptiness and the soaring fortunes of a dynasty that a decade earlier had accepted its mandate with near-unanimous acclaim, and whose best years lay a decade ahead with Agincourt and the theoretical repossession of the French throne? The emptiness of which I speak is not just a material emptiness, although the Lancastrians certainly had their revenue problems,[15] or even a ceremonial failure, for the Lancastrians utilized every available element of coronation and related pageantry. But theirs was an also empty sacral center, a center which the wide range of legitimizing ceremonies and testimonies invoked by Henry of Lancaster in compensatory relation to the deposition and eventual murder of Richard II could not fill.

Of course, thrones in the Middle Ages were forcibly vacated all the time, and even the most durable kings fall prey to mortality. But such transitions are, in Bourdieu's apt phrase, normally promptly and suc-cessfully 'euphemized' by well-orchestrated ceremonies of interment and coronation.[16] Moreover, as Kantorowicz demonstrates more subtly than this short summary can convey, the presumption of dynastic continuity succeeded in banishing entirely any scandal or embarrass-ment of an interregnum between the death of a monarch and the accession of his legitimate heir. Although coronation remained a vital and quasi-sacral event in the fourteenth and fifteenth centuries, prac-tice in England and France dictated the heir's accession to full rule on the day of the father's burial, with that accession to be solemnized (rather than inaugurated) by the event of coronation.[17] And, although the concept of the 'Plantagenet' dynasty was effectively a mid-fifteenth-century creation, the fact is that for nearly two and a half centuries England had not lacked an obvious and dynastically sanc-tioned heir to its throne.[18] Now, suddenly, the Lancastrian succession offered a double affront to the concept of orderly succession: given the temporary but awkward persistence of the precursor king, the Lancas-trians needed to declare and demonstrate the very fact that rituals of succession are designed to euphemize: the emptiness of a throne cus-tomarily regarded as uninterruptedly full.

The Lancastrian-sponsored 'Record and Process' of Henry's acces-sion sets the ceremony of Richard's resignation and Henry's acclama-tion on 30 September, in Westminster Hall, before an ostentatiously displayed, gold-draped, and conspicuously empty throne:

> . . . beyng thanne the kyngis See, with clothes off golde and astate ryally apparayllyd, voyde, withoute eny presedent or ocupiour theroff.[19]

In a scene that captured the imagination of the illustrator of Creton's pro-Ricardian *Histoire du Roy d'Angleterre Richard*, the throne is depicted as having been prepared in gracious array ['Le siege royal aprester/ Par tres gracieuse ordonnance'],[20] but as conspicuously empty. The lords spiritual are seated at the right of the throne, the lords temporal at its left. Henry stands, attired in beaver hat, in the honorable second rank of participants, in the place accorded him as duke of Lancaster. He is ready to occupy the throne once his election and coronation are complete. But, for now, he accepts his role as the duke of Lancaster still. The throne is flanked by two figures who may be identified (assuming that the illustrator was working from Creton's text) as Ralph Neville and Henry Percy, already serving in a *de facto* way in the capacities they would soon enjoy, as marshal and constable of the realm ('La estoient par bel aroy/Le conte de northomberlant,/Et

5. Subsequent to Richard II's deposition and prior to Henry IV's accession, the throne is shown empty.

le conte de westmerlant,/Toute iour enestant sans soir').[21] The figure to the right of the throne – probably Neville – raises his hand as if to arrest the moment, when the seat of the realm is found to be vacant. This moment, to which all present stand witness, precedes the institution of Lancastrian kingship: it is the moment of the Lancastrian dynasty's own origin, when all might glimpse the 'open, undecided process that engendered it.'[22] Only a French and anti-Lancastrian text could, in a sense, have been so mischievous as to depict Henry as a solemn witness of his own kingship's inaugural moment, a moment which he would immediately seek by all possible means to disguise and deny.

Henry seems to have occupied this empty throne as quickly as any legitimate successor might have done, and perhaps more so. A scandalized French account has him seated upon the throne even before his coronation ('Adonc le duc ala seoir en la chaiere de justice ains quil fust courone on lieu ou le Roy estoit acoustume de seoir').[23] All accounts agree, in any event, that he moved with the utmost promptitude to fill the vacancy once it had been declared. Thus, Walsingham: 'And immediately ['confestim'], the foregoing deposition having been agreed upon, and England's seat of authority to be vacant ['regnum Angliae . . . vacare'],[24] Henry, duke of Lancaster, rose from his place. . . .' Yet sitting on the throne was not to suffice; Henry's problem was not just that of filling a physical or spatial void, but filling the empty place of legitimacy, its elusive sacral center.[25]

Symbolic self-display

Even the usurper inherits formidable resources of external display. Especially in and around the ceremonies of coronation, these external symbols of legitimacy and plenitude – access to the regalia, anointment and investiture by the archbishop of Canterbury, display of the curtana, the sword of state – seem available for the taking.[26] At this level of external display, kingship can easily be performed, gathered into legitimizing enactments of Lancastrian succession. By such enactments, the king can lay claim to his prepared space within the order of the symbolic. Henry can, duly crowned, take his seat on that empty throne, 'fill' it with his physical presence, and command its symbolism as well.[27]

Yet we are here talking, in effect, about kingship's symbolic 'carapace,' about those external markers which can identify their bearer, or wearer, as a king. They might be likened to the three locks on John of Canace's chest: signs of the worth of its internal contents. But clothes, like the locks on John's empty chest, are treated throughout the *Regement of Princes* as unreliable indicators of inner value. There, virtuous persons are likely to be 'but narwe clothed' (f. 10b), even as 'penylees gromes' and other pretenders to higher estate mop the filth from streets with their trailing sleeves. Unconfined to the poem's actors, this concern finally extends to the text itself – a text for which Hoccleve apologizes (but which he nevertheless also removes from the taint of ingratiation or inauthenticity) by portraying it as rudely arrayed: '[I] thus iangle and clappe/So lewedly in my termes I me wrappe' (f. 19a). In fact, at the end, Hoccleve would rather his own text be completely *unclothed* than more luxuriously but less authentically draped:

> And why approchest thou his excellence
> Vnclothyd sauf thy kyrtyl bar also
> I am ryght seur hys humble pacience
> Ye geueth hardynesse to do so. (f. 98a)

This concern about surplus or unearned array, and preference for simplicity in external attire, is thematized throughout the *Regement*, in a way that cannot be held separate from John's own dissemblings. So deep, in fact, is the affinity of clothing and false array to John's story that one of its earlier renditions literalizes the metaphor, with the father basing his deception not only on an empty chest but on three suits of new clothes made from the most beautiful cloth, the garments and the chest together contributing to the children's deception.[28]

The problem – as affirmed by Hoccleve's decision to portray his poem as clad in humble weeds – is that elaborate legitimizing displays are revealed as potentially misleading, as fostering not rightful recognition but *mis*recognition, of the owner's or bearer's or wearer's entitlements. The usurping claimant encourages an active reworking of his imaginary relation to the subjects, a reworking which abets his misrecognition as entitled ruler. Any references or allusions which invite notice of this necessarily covert process thus pose risky problems for the aspirationally complicitous text.[29] Awareness of legitimizing processes is likely to foster an uneasy suspicion that the emperor's or king's symbolic attire covers nothing at all. The regalia might, in this sense, be seen as analogous to the vase or vacuole by which Lacan figures the Thing or object-cause of desire: all outside, no inside.[30] This anecdote of John's empty box may then, for the period in which it was written, be seen as the product of a double disenchantment. I say 'double disenchantment' because the Lacanian perception of the vacuole, that ultimately empty place that attracts and supports our desires, has (as with all psychoanalytical categories) both its timeless and its time-bound aspects: both its transhistorical and its historically specific elements. The first, or 'timeless,' disenchantment is one in which we can all share: the perception that the supports and incentives of responsible conduct are only symbolic, rather than real. But the second, 'time-bound' or historically specific, disenchantment is medieval, in the sense that this anecdote would have been more problematic for a medieval than a modern audience. For, as Claude Lefort has elegantly argued, the very essence of modern democracy is the assumption that 'power is an *empty place*,' and that an inevitable and unbridgeable gap exists between the symbols of power (which anyone can seize) and the reality of power (which no one can completely seize or continuously enjoy).[31] In the democratic period, every incumbent of high office is, by definition, a temporary occupant; as Žižek succinctly puts it, 'What was at one moment a terrifying defect, a catastrophe for the social edifice – the fact that the throne is empty – [now, in the period of democracy] turns into a crucial prerogative.'[32] But from the medieval perspective the vacant throne was indeed a terrifying defeat, bearing no opportunity or promise – an unmitigated catastrophe. For medieval society still believed in the 'real presence' of the sacral king, in both the theological and Lacanian senses of that phrase. The throne is either occupied by a rightful incumbent (that is, a properly consecrated king) or else it is in the hands of an improperly sanctioned incumbent, a usurper – and the presence of a usurper heralds breakdown and anomie.[33]

Hans Christian Andersen's nineteenth-century tale which shows that 'the Emperor has no clothes' may be understood as a tale of reassurance, a democratic tale, and the wise child who announces the discovery is a democrat rather than an anarchist. For the child's perception is that, even if the symbolic carapace is removed, something remains: the king in his humanness, and thus his flawed potential. The naked king of the nursery tale, his nakedness named, still exists; for all his flaws and gross materiality he still possesses a body which may or may not have certain potentialities for regal reinvention or reinvestment: as a deposed king or a reformed king or a constitutional king or what have you. But the deeper, more specifically pre- and post-modern anxiety would be: what if the symbols are more real than the king who bears them? What if, within the symbolic carapace, resides . . . nothing important, a kingship without a legitimizing center, a desacralized king, and thus no king at all?

Borrowed capital

However furnished with appropriate hardware, a box is only a box, if it is believed or found empty. John takes prompt steps to fill his own 'empty center' by presenting 'borrowed capital' as his own. He asks a merchant friend to *cheuyse* or 'furnish' him with the capital (10,000 pounds) upon which he will base his deception, and he displays and employs it in ways designed to foster the misperception that it is his own. Although borrowed from Jacobus de Cessolis, this detail might well have triggered awareness of the Lancastrians' own constant financial problems and frequent recourse to borrowing, a material possibility explored by Judith Ferster.[34] But, at a more figurative level, John's stratagem alludes to the condition of all royalty, which is to borrow the symbols and terms of its legitimation. Every monarch, for example, effectively 'borrows' the regalia and other trappings of office (coronation garb is checked out only for the day of the ceremony and otherwise remains in the care of the monks of Westminster).[35] But the usurping king presents a special, heightened case of this normal condition, since nothing he employs is his own, since all the terms of his enjoyment are borrowed twice over: from their rightful custodians and from the rightful king.

It happens that Henry IV's own most crucial legitimizing ceremony, of anointment, also required 'borrowed' treasure, in the sense that it employed an exceptional oil, borrowed from his predecessor, Richard II. Accounts of this oil, an oil in a vessel shaped like an eagle presented to St Thomas à Becket by the Blessed Virgin, had been long in circulation before the accession of Henry IV. Edward II, for example, promulgated an account of such an oil, informing Pope John XXII that he had considered coronation with it, but had chosen the customary oil,[36] and only now, as a result of reversals in his reign, was considering a second ceremony of anointment. Originally associated with this oil was the claim that the fifth king from the one then reigning (a slot occupied by Richard II) would, by virtue of this oil, recover the Holy Land from the heathen. Taken up by the Lancastrians, this older legend was first reworked for use by omission of the 'fifth king' in favor of a 'rex futurus' who, anointed with this oil, will recover easily ('sine vi'), not the Holy Land, but the lost lands of Normandy and Aquitaine.[37] Now, stripped of its previous, inopportune association with Richard II and crusades, this legend lay open to new inscription.

We re-encounter it in Walsingham as a fully Lancastrian 'miraculum.' Walsingham gives it a specific Lancastrian genealogy: it is now discovered by Henry, first duke of Lancaster, passed by him to the Black Prince (who, had he lived, would have been worthy recipient and fifth king), then placed in the Tower only to be rediscovered accidentally ('inopinate' – p. 239) by Richard II in 1399 as he was randomly rooting around in relics of his ancestors. But, given Walsingham's Lancastrian rewriting, how is it that Richard is permitted any appearance (even as hapless browser in his own castle) in this new version? The answer is that the authorizing power of the unguent is enhanced by the fact of its spoilage from a previous possessor who did not know how to use it.[38] The point is not that it must be 'your' gold or 'your' oil; rather, that you be the one who knows how to build it into your self-narration, how to *put it to use*. Richard's previous possession of the oil thus, rather than challenging Lancastrian appropriation, has the effect of inserting him in a testamentary chain, reconstituting him as a particularly forceful witness to the necessity of his own supplantation.[39]

By such stratagems, the Lancastrians make a virtue of their 'borrowed' title. In matters of legitimacy, advantage must nevertheless be conceded to those who possess it from the outset, in contrast to those who must effect its capture.

Arbitrating legitimacy

John of Canace displays the source of his recovered legitimacy spectacularly – which is to say, performatively and visually – for the sake of his audience on the other side of the wall. He unbags his gold, 'shoots' it out on a carpet, clanks the coins together, etc. And, once he is certain of being observed, he engages in his most crucial operation. They

> . . . sygh how he a monge the nobles soghte
> If deffectif were any, as hem thought;
> And on hys nayle he threw hym ofte & caste,
> And bagged hem and cofred at the laste.

One element of this scene is its celebration of surplus: both surplus coinage (as a displaced response to the early fifteenth century as a time of severe bullion famine)[40] and surplus legitimacy (in the sense that gold coins metonymically figure the father's legitimacy in relation to his family, his right to summon and bridle their desires). Yet the spectacle of the old man sorting coins becomes, through the children's fantastic addition, something more besides: a scene in which ('as hem thought') the old man practices his arts of discernment or assay upon the coins; separates the good from the bad, the perfect from the defective, the genuine from the counterfeit. This doubled fantasy, then, is exactly what the father would wish it to be: a fantasy of plenitude, but also of plenitude as possessed or wielded by a paternal figure who has the authority to decide on matters of perfection and imperfection, genuineness and counterfeit – who enjoys legitimate possession, and who has the ability to determine or decide upon matters of legitimacy as well.

The ironies are not far to seek here. John, faking an interlude with his borrowed gold, is perceived as an arbiter of the genuine. Henry IV and the prince, arraying themselves in their spurious title, attempt the same. Of course, counterfeiting, defined as treasonous by statutes in 1352 and thereafter, was always a concern of the king, and the Lancastrians had much to say about 'loial moneie' throughout their reign. And properly and shrewdly so, because the king's function as symbolic guarantor of the national currency is one of those arenas in which he exhibits himself as most royal. The king's very character or *carecter*, that set of ineffable qualities by which Richard believed himself so indelibly stamped and which Henry sought so persistently and imaginatively to obtain, is a metaphor derived from minting, coinage, and engraving, and is associated with the king's image as the guarantee of legitimacy in coin.[41] As I argued in Chapter 5, the exposure of counterfeit also becomes a crucial Lancastrian exemplification of the entire range of activities in which the king bolsters his position by displaying himself as arbiter of the authentic, the loyal, the orthodox, over against the false, the treasonous, and the heretical.

So crucial was the Lollard heresy to the establishment of Lancastrian orthodoxy and legitimacy that, had it not existed, they would have had to devise something in its stead. As it is, the language of heresy and its necessary extirpation, and the range of inquisitional procedures by which heresy is identified and punished, come ready-made. A pan-European language of 'assay' and 'proof,' dealing with the procedures by which bogus coin is separated from the genuine article, had been available since the Greeks,[42] and the continental assault against heresy in the thirteenth and early fourteenth centuries had provided the underpinning for a continuing campaign of spiritual discernment and attack on heresy in all its guises. From our period, Jean Gerson is representative, with his injunction that those charged with the defense of orthodoxy should function as numismatists or spiritual money-changers, examining the coin of divine relevation, in order to prove it against demonic substitutions.[43] But it was the Lancastrians who extensively introduced secular authority into the activity of spiritual 'assay.' The 'sect' of Lollards had been identified (and sporadically and incipiently, though mostly non-violently, prosecuted) in the last two decades of the fourteenth century. But Richard II was never dedicated to the identification and separation of Lollards from the body politic. It remained for Henry IV and his son to expose the Lollard as adulterator of the realm's true coin and to separate Lollards, not only from the community of the orthodox but from the purified body of loyal subjects. Conflating heresy and sedition, Henry IV not only gained legislative assent to the proposition that heretics must be burnt, but zealously anticipated his own statute to decree the first civilly sponsored English heretic burning, when William Sautre went to the stake for his views on the eucharist in the second year of Henry's reign.

The most spectacular burning, and the first burning of a layman by lay authority, was that of John Badby in 1410, a recent event which Hoccleve applauds in his *Regement*, cursing the 'stink' of Badby's error (and burning carcass) and wishing that Henry, Prince of Wales, who was present and solicited Badby's last-minute recantation, had been less merciful and that more heretics would be similarly served. The fire had already been lit and Badby cried out (evidently involuntarily, in pain), when the prince ordered the burning wood to be withdrawn, promising the suffering heretic sustenance, pardon, and (according to chronicler Walsingham) a living of three pence a day from the Royal Treasury ('de fisco regio'), in return for his repentance.[44] Badby refused, and the prince ordered him returned to his barrel and the execution to be concluded. McNiven, principal analyst of this scene, thinks the prince was in a hard place here, and that Badby's refusal of what amounted to an invitation to accept the prince's personal allegiance was a blow to his personal prestige.[45] My own analysis is that the prince was in a win-win situation here. Either Badby recants and the prince is seen to be able to convert the dross of heresy into the local coin of orthodoxy, or Badby does not recant and the prince is the ultimate guarantor of the mechanisms which detect and scourge heresy, separating its baser metal from the good coin of the realm. Either way, the prince is at the fulcrum, and whether he remints the bad coin of heresy or casts it out, *his* orthodoxy is affirmed. Like John, and within no less theatrical a frame, he asserts performatively his capacity to test or 'prove' the good and the bad, the fit and the unfit, the counterfeit and the true. And, as with John, the elements of his stage-craft are never wholly absent from view.

Gylour-king

Broadly conceived, Hoccleve's *Regement* and his tale of John constitute a recognition and celebration of the prince's impending kingship and its hoped-for repair of Lancastrian fortunes – both real and symbolic. But, despite the prince's having been confirmed and reconfirmed as heir, this internal succession was itself not to occur without some rather aggravated tensions between father and son – tensions visible in the political crisis of 1412,[46] amplified by later authors like the translator of Titus Livius,[47] and ultimately dramatized by Shakespeare throughout both parts of his *Henry IV*. Hoccleve is somewhat more tacit in his preference for the prince, but his treatment of the matter nevertheless effects what might be considered an act of symbolic parricide. By virtue of this act, Henry IV is virtually expelled from the body of the *Regement*. Scarcely mentioned – less prominent even than his father, John of Gaunt – Henry IV is relegated by Hoccleve to the role of 'vanishing mediator.' This is the figure who, making a transition possible, bears the taint of its own violent or traumatic origins, and must therefore be suppressed in order that the transition may be portrayed as untroubled, legal, just.[48] Further, the king's demotion and the prince's symbolic advancement as the epitome of restoration and hope require implicit acknowledgment of exactly what all Henry IV's elaborate coronation hoopla was designed to elide: namely, a flawed beginning for the dynasty as a whole, a point of traumatic origin which cannot stand direct exposure. Imagistically treated, not just by Hoccleve but by generations of writers, as the prospective problem-solver, Henry V was left with the dilemma that the original problem, once acknowledged, was dynastic in scope, and could not entirely be set aside.

For all the luster of his eventual accomplishments, this matter of a taint, an originary flaw, lingers within Henry V's subsequent representations. John of Canace's story of destitution and mimetic rehabilitation is uncannily predictive of the narrative strategy underlying later accounts of Henry V's career, in the sense that – his father effectively banished from representation – the whole narrative arc from dissipation to restoration will be brought under his son's domain. Despite a complete absence of evidence that the young Henry was in any sense profligate, fifteenth- and sixteenth-century chroniclers, biographers, and dramatists were quick to *assign* to him a series of youthful transgressions, exactly so that his self-abandonment to enjoyment might be seen to yield to a regime of law and restraint.[49] In Titus Livius, in Hall's Chronicle, in the *Famous Victories of Henry V*, we find the profligate Hal among lowlife, practicing robbery and deception, engaging in surprising shifts and transfers and restorations of capital, flaunting weird costumes, playing at kingship with his cronies, engaging in strange theatrics before his father, stealing his very crown.[50]

At one analytical level, these escapades are obviously introduced precisely so that they can be obliterated, if not through inner examination and new resolve then through sacramental action. As I have already argued, the inner deficiencies of the Lancastrian kings were to be understood less as character flaws than as failures of unction, the inefficaciousness of a sacrament wrongly employed; whereas our wild prince's reformation upon his coronation may be seen as an externalization of a successful sacramental ceremony. As a fifteenth–sixteenth century chronicle of British Museum Cotton MS. Claudius A.viii argues, 'in his youthe he had bene wylde recheles and spared nothyngof his lustes ne desires . . . but as sonne as he was crouned enoynted and sacred anone sodenly he was chaunged in to a new man' (f. 17). With the sacramental of coronation as the pivot, Henry's character change becomes an index of the spiritual recovery of his dynasty as a whole – and thus the more sudden and dramatic his change the better.

But, as definitively as his transformation came to be represented, another sense exists in which Henry V could never quite free himself from a certain proclivity for guile, from the implication that he possesses a 'secret.' This secret is in some respects the very secret of rulership and rule – according to which any successful regal impersonation *always* incorporates its own fictionality, with the king enlisting his subjects' imaginations in a cooperative exploration of his own secret, a joint discovery of plenitude within his hidden or veiled recesses.[51] Henry V's secret is inextricable from his wild youth, in the sense that the wildness of his youth constitutes what Louise Fradenburg has described (in the intriguingly parallel case of James IV's wild knight tournament) as a revisitation of 'his own creation as king, through his emergence from the "troubled regions" of his own rebellion, the taint of parricide and regicide.'[52] The wildness, in this case, cannot and does not go away; even the 'reformed' prince, the prince of maturity and self-imposed restraint, cannot immunize himself from this suggestion of his unruly origins. Thus, representations of Henry V's kingship will throw a certain emphasis onto this habit of secrecy, of witting self-deployment. The trick of fabulation by which he ensnares the Southampton conspirators, his disguised passage among his men before Agincourt: such sleights are by no means unique to Henry V, but nevertheless loom large when writers imagine his strategies and technologies of rule. Like his analogue John of Canace, the prince-become-king remains a *gylour* to the end – perhaps even a more consummate *gylour* at the end, although more subtly so, still concerned with the ingenious fabrication of his own impugned legitimacy.

A certain ambivalence or two-sidedness has characterized this narrative throughout: implicitly loyalist in its advice about inveigling subjects into submission, it is recklessly irreverent in identifying the father as *gylour* and the chest's promise as an empty one. It is undeniably shrewd, but also cynical, in its perception that even an empty or vacuous center of authority can constitute subjects as good citizens so long as it engages their desires.

'That absence around which a real complexity is knit'[53]

The historian, fixated upon this text's center like John's bad daughters on their empty box, hopes for a 'nugget' of information, but finds only an enigmatic and transhistorical truism: one which might be encapsulated in the Freudian observation that the profligate father of enjoyment must yield to the Oedipal father of prohibition before social progress can occur.[54] Not that this is a shallow observation; it is profound enough to drive *Totem and Taboo* and other analyses of power and its uses, and the relation of prohibition to enjoyment. But, aside from a broad contextual suggestion that a prince might have something to learn from this paradigm, nothing much is said to speed the historically desirous interpreter on his or her path. It remains nonspecific by inviting application to *each* of the monarchs at hand: to Richard II (himself, ironically, an invader of the public chest);[55] to Henry IV (who sought to represent himself as superior to his contemporary Richard in maturity and self-imposed restraint,[56] but was undermined by his own obscene enjoyment of the crown); to Henry V (who restored the crown's good credit but never shook the implications of guile from his own most favorable representations). Faced with this embarrassment of interpretative possibilities, one must concede the impossibility of stabilizing any one, definite, referent.

Here I would turn to my epigraph, an observation by Pierre Macherey, who finds texts empty at the center, but peripherally fully engaged. He locates the text's unconscious in history, 'the play of history beyond its edges,' and finds the text haunted by history, arguing that this history-at-bay 'is why it is possible to trace the path which leads from the haunted work to that which haunts it' (Macherey, p. 94). The 'path' to external history, as I have tried to define it here, is discursive, via the text's inevitable implication in multiple, historically inflected discourses. Sometimes with and sometimes without invitation, discourses of sacrality, vestment and symbolic array, borrowed capital, probation, legitimacy and orthodoxy, secrecy and guile serve successively to open one or another of this text's unspoken meanings to view. Do these points of contact between a text and its surroundings amount to historical evidence? Not, certainly, evidence of an empirical kind. Nothing is to be learned about concrete actions or intentions, either authorial or Lancastrian. But these discursive linkages or affiliations between a text and the exclusions which 'haunt' it enable us to complete or embody a text's aura of unspoken implication.

These discursive linkages are like 'framing fictions,' like the apertures or *chynyngs* through which John's bad children behold the object of their desires. Peering through these discursive frames, we see things (including things we are not 'supposed' to see). And from these things we constitute a past. The status of that past is more or less reliable, depending on the extent to which we are deluded by our desires. But this reconstituted past need not, like the chest's imagined gold for John's daughters, *only* be a hallucinated product of desire. John's daughters are fixated by desire, gripped only by their hallucination of what lies in the chest's interior, oblivious of its complex staging and its embeddedness in its surroundings. Remembering that the text has an inside and an outside, that its meaning is a joint product of text and con-text, we see more, and learn more, and are rescued from the vain solipsism of our desires.[57]

Certainly, the text possesses no one 'nugget' of historical information. Its historical meaning lies not at its heart but at its edges and unacknowledged affiliations, in the ground it discursively shares with the suppressed history just beyond its own bounds. Because they are inevitably and complexly enmeshed and entrammeled, the texts of Lancastrian succession can never quite complete or finish themselves. They cannot withdraw themselves from a meaning-making process which continually (in spite of contrary resolve) replenishes alternative understanding.

Notes

1 Prophecy and Kingship

1. *Gesta Henrici Quinti*, pp. 54–55. I have here quoted the elegant Taylor–Roskell translation.
2. For this point I am indebted to Taylor and Roskell, ibid., n. 4, p. 55.
3. 'Les Anglois qui estoient dedans, environ quinze cents, rendirent la ville Harfleur au roy de France, s'en allèrent, leurs corps et biens saufs, les ungs en Angleterre, les autres en Normandie, ès places tenantes leur parti' (*Mémories de Jacques du Clercq*, in *Chroniques de Monstrelet*, ed. J. A. Buchon, vol. 12 [Paris, 1826], p. 53). On the French 'recouvrement' of Normandy, and the restoration of claims of those residents who had remained faithful to the Valois cause, see C. T. Allmand, *Lancastrian Normandy, 1415–1450* (Oxford: Clarendon Press, 1983), pp. 284–304.
4. *The Imaginary Institution of Society* (Cambridge: Polity Press, 1987), p. 371.
5. *The Chronicle of Iohn Hardyng*, ed. Henry Ellis (London: Rivington, 1812), p. 354.
6. Ibid., pp. viii–ix.
7. *Continuatio Eulogii*, pp. 169–170.
8. Usk, p. 62. C. Given-Wilson's excellent edition having just appeared, I have substituted his Latin text for the earlier Thompson edition originally used in preparation of this manuscript. Paraphrases of Usk's material are my own. Quoted translations are from Given-Wilson, unless otherwise indicated.
9. Adam's account of these deliberations is corroborated by Hardyng: 'I Iohn Hardynge, the maker of this booke, herde the erle of Northumberlonde . . . saie, how the same kyng Henry, vpon saynt Mathee day afore he wase made kinge September 21, put forth that ilke cronycle claymynge his title to the crown be the seide Edmonde, upon which all the Cronycles of Westminstre and of all other notable monasteries were hade in the counsell at Westmynstre, and examyned amonge the lordes, and proued well be all theire cronycles, that the kinge Edwarde wase the older brother' (p. 353). Despite this rebuff by the *doctores*, Henry IV was not quite ready to let the matter drop. He reintroduced a glancing and slightly sanitized reference to Crouchback in his 'challenge' to the throne 'be right line of the blod comyng fro the good lord kyng Henry thrid.' See Strohm, *Hochon's Arrow* (Princeton: Princeton University

Press, 1992), p. 83.

10. Chronicles naturally lay considerably more open to revisionary tampering than their own authority-claims might imply. That most sober of medieval chroniclers, Walsingham, revised his own writings in expectation of Lancastrian scrutiny, not only adopting a pro-Lancastrian line after 1399, but retrospectively revising his earlier harsh treatment of John of Gaunt in order to align his work with Lancastrian expectations. Beyond the self-censorship employed by chroniclers as a result of changed circumstances and their vulnerable position within the field of textual production, lies the more active endeavor of John of Gaunt, Henry IV, and Henry V to promote the inclusion of chronicle materials favorable to their aspirations. The cardinal illustration of this point is the Lancastrian-sponsored account of Richard II's voluntary abdication, the 'Record and Process' of events that became the formal text of the Rolls of Parliament, and, broadly circulated, was adopted by numerous chronicle accounts.

11. Usk, pp. 64–66. The appeal to chronicles, whether to sustain an argument or to reject it, was an established aspect of this debate. Back when Gaunt first launched his claim, Bolingbroke's fellow claimant Mortimer is said to have asserted that Edward was firstborn and Edmund was a 'vir elegantissimus,' adducing the chronicles in support of his position: 'prout in chronicis patenter continetur' Continuatio Eulogii, pp. 169–170.

12. Strohm, Hochon's Arrow, esp. pp. 75–82.

13. I allude to Certeau's distinction between the secure 'strategies' of those official parties which control space, and the improvisational 'tactics' of those which control no space and must mount their activities within the territory of the other. See Michel de Certeau, The Practice of Everyday Life (Berkeley: University of California Press, 1984), pp. 35–39.

14. Based on the French edition with accompanying English translation by J. Webb, Archaeologia 20 (1824), 374, 169–170, with minor adjustments of the translation. This same prophecy is repeated, also as a prophecy of Merlin, upon the occasion of Henry's triumphal entry into London in the French Chronicque de la Traïson et Mort, ed. Benjamin Williams ' (London, 1846), p. 62.

15. Histoire de France (Paris, 1685), vol. 1, p. 384.

16. A convenient fifteenth-century Englishing of Merlin's prophecy of the last six kings may be found in Brut, ed. W. D. Brie, EETS, OS, no. 131, vol. 1 (London, 1906), pp. 72–76. Other Latin and French versions of the succession of the asinus or assne and the talpa or talpe are printed as appendices to Rupert Taylor, The Political Prophecy in England (New York: Columbia University Press, 1911), pp. 157–164. An English versified rendition appears as an appendix to Poems of Laurence Minot, ed. Joseph Hall, 3rd edn (Oxford: Clarendon Press, 1914), pp. 60–111. The fifteenth-century Englishings edited by Brie and Hall tend to be Yorkist in their selection of detail, especially in their denunciation of the moldwarp, 'ful wrangwis in euerilka wane' (Hall, p. 110). An alternative, Lancastrian tradition, presents Richard as the crowned ass who will trouble the realm ('Asinus coronatus turbabit regnum') and Henry as the fox who will return from exile to

expel the ass ('Reveniet enim vna ex bestiis quam prius absciderat et eum iuxta mare reuertentem opprimet.... Hanc asinus expellet a saltem'); see 'Prophecia Geffridi Eglyne,' BL Cotton MS. Faustina B. ix. ff. 241v–242, and MS. Cotton Vespasian E. vii. f. 88v.

17. Leyden Cod. Lat. Voss. 77, f. 122. Latin text printed in Geoffrey of Monmouth, *Historia Regum Britanniae*, ed. A. Schulz (Halle: Eduard Anton, 1854), as note to Bk. 12, cap. 18: 'aquilae.'

18. Froissart, *Oeuvres*, ed. K. de Lettenhove, vol. 16 (Brussels: Devaux, 1872), p. 235.

19. *Historia Anglicana*, vol. 2, p. 270. The passages in question are drawn, respectively, from Bridlington sec. 3, chap. 9 and sec. 2, chap. 2. See Thomas Wright, ed., *Political Poems and Songs*, Rolls Series, no. 14, vol. 1 (London, 1859).

20. Wright, *Political Poems and Songs*, p. 124.

21. See, for instance, H. L. D. Ward, *Catalogue of Romances in the British Museum*, vol. 1 (London: British Museum, 1883), pp. 203–338.

22. Adam's retrospective use of prophecy is, of course, part of a more general interpretative practice. The free-wheeling possibilities of such practice are suggested by a marginal notation in which one of his early readers glosses Adam's account of Richard's seizure at Flint. Adam says that 'The lord duke came to meet him..., bringing twenty thousand chosen men with him... and advanced toward the king in the castle of Flint' (Usk, p. 59). Adam's reader, acquainted with the Prophecy of the Eagle, adds the following insertion:

> Surrounding it with men-at-arms on one side and archers on the other, thus fulfilling the

prophecy ['illam propheciam implendo'], 'the white and glorious king in the manner of a shield,' etc. (p. 59)

This attempt to decontextualize and harness the thirteenth-century Prophecy of the Eagle for local use leads the commentator somewhat astray. The commentator treats the 'rex albus' as if he were Henry, flanked by his nobles and men-at-arms, already as good as king. But the original prophecy treated the 'albus rex' as victim, checked and defeated by his enemy, the 'pullus aquilae' or eaglet. In point of fact, the marginal commentator's objective was probably well enough performed just in asserting the fulfillment of a prophecy; but, when the prophecy is inspected, it turns out to offer confusion if not embarrassment to the commentator's aims.

23. Although John of Bridlington enjoyed a general reputation as a miracle-worker, he was known more specifically as the author of the prophecies, and the Lancastrians knew how to reward a prophet that had been good to them. Dated 4 October 1400 are letters patent from Henry, in support of an embassy to obtain canonization of John of Bridlington: *Foedera*, vol. 3, pt. 4, p. 191. John's translation occcurred on 5 May 1404, with Archbishop Scrope and other dignitaries attending: 'Anno praesenti, quinto Idus Maii, clarescentibus miraculis circa corpus Sancti Johannis, quondam Prioris Canonicorum de Bridelingtone, de mandato Domini Papae, translatum fuit corpus ejusdem Sancti Johannis, per manus honorabilium virorum, scilicet, Eboracensis Archiepiscopi, et Dunelmensis atque Karleolensis Episcoporum' (*Ypodigma Neustriae*, Rolls Series,

no. 28, pt. 7, (London, 1876), pp. 405–406).

24. I base this observation on the excellent discussion of E. M. Thompson in *Chronicon Adae de Usk*, 2nd edn (London: Frowde, 1904), pp. 172–173.

25. On the dog-days as defined by Bridlington and on Henry's occasional use of the greyhound livery also see ibid., p. 173.

26. Taylor, *The Political Prophecy in England*, prints what he regards as a late thirteenth-century French version, and argues for an older version in Latin: pp. 157–165. The influence of this prophecy requires a shared conviction of its origin prior to the reign of Henry IV, although its broadest currency was undoubtedly in the early fifteenth century.

27. *Brut*, p. 75. For French and Latin versions, see Taylor, *The Political Prophecy in England*, appendix 1, pp. 157–164.

28. See Chapter 4, pp. 106–108.

29. Just consider, in passing, the range of extra-contextual ingenuities by which discrete Old Testament events were reworked from the standpoint of New Testament eventualities, as in the *Pictor in Carmine*, where (for example) Christ Rising from the Sepulcher is found to have been predicted by: Noah waking from vinous sleep, Joseph dreaming that his sheaf was adored by those of his brothers, Joseph freed from prison and becoming lord of Egypt, Samson visiting the cadaver of the dead lion, David fleeing the home of a knight via the window, and Jonah cast up by a whale on the shore of Nineveh (ed. M. R. James, *Archaeologia* 94 [1951], 163).

30. Pp. 231–232.

31. The *Continuatio Eulogii* styles him the 'Northern Prophet' ('Quidam eremita de partibus Borealibus' – pp. 380–381), and again suggests that this is the same prophet who visited Henry, presuming to disclose 'secreta multa' to him (p. 397).

32. The *Continuatio Eulogii* is even more terse: 'Quem rex jussit decollari' (p. 397).

33. *RP*, vol. 3, p. 508. See also *Statutes of the Realm*, ed. Basket (London: Dawsons, 1816), vol. 2, p. 140.

34. *Brut*, ed. W. D. Brie, EETS, OS, no. 131, vol. 1 (London, 1906), p. 75.

35. Printed as appendix to *Poems of Laurence Minot*, pp. 103–111.

36. Usk, p. 151.

37. Slavoj Žižek, *The Sublime Object of Ideology* (London: Verso, 1989), p. 29.

38. Other writings amplify and affirm Glyndwr's provisional belief in prophecy and his possible prophetic mission. On his consultation of a 'maister of Brut,' see BL Cotton MS. Cleo F. iii, f. 116 (printed in *Original Letters*, second series, vol. 1, pp. 3–4).

39. *Incerti Scriptis Chronicon Angliae*, ed. J. A. Giles (London, 1848), p. 40. The authenticity of this document, commonly known as the 'Tripartite Indenture,' has no immediate bearing on my own argument, which is concerned with a certain character of imaginative participation, whether belonging to Glyndwr or merely attributed to him. But, noting its consistency with fourteenth-century and Welsh attitudes toward prophecy and its uses, R. R. Davies does grant it a putative purchase on political possibility, saying that we need not dismiss this Indenture's contents 'as being, at the level of a blueprint, totally beyond the bounds of political possibility' (*The Revolt of Owain Glyn Dŵr* [Oxford: Oxford University Press, 1995], pp. 166–169).

40. *Continuatio Eulogii*, p. 396.

41. P. 365.

42. Percy's rebellion would, ultimately, be captured within the fifteenth-century prophecy of the

Asinus coronatus, a predominantly Yorkist production circulated in support of Edward IV. There (in the version of British Museum Faustina B. ix), a crowned ass (Richard) misrules his land and is supplanted by a fox that he had previously exiled (Bolingbroke or 'taurus in torente'). The ass having been expelled, one will rise against the fox who has been given the name Luna for his brightness. The fox will spill the blood of his domestic adversaries, but scarcely none on foreign shores. Then, 'In eius exaltatione derogabitur leoni propter quod luna patietur eclipsem, quia dua cornua perdet propter iusticiam' ('The lion [Northumberland?] will be diminished in his pride on account of which the moon will suffer eclipse, for it will lose the two horns [sometimes: *dua corona* or dual crowns]). And justly so '– BM MS. Faustina B. ix. ff. 241b–242; compare BM Cotton Vespasian E. vii. f. 88b. In this prophecy, Luna is almost certainly Percy, referring to his emblem of the crescent moon, with the two horns suggesting both the two points of the crescent and the fact that Henry Percy died in the battle and his uncle Thomas was captured in the battle and beheaded in its aftermath. (For a prophecy of similar import, see Usk, p. 83.)

43. Near-contemporaries were familiar with Henry's interest in the reconquest of Jerusalem and with the fact that he died in the 'Jerusalem' chamber at Westminster Abbey (*Continuatio Eulogii*, p. 421), but the quasi-prophetic link between these two details was apparently not made until later in the century (J. H. Wylie, *History of England under Henry IV*, vol. 4 [London: Longmans, 1898], p. 110) – ironically, most likely under the presiding generic influ-

ence of Henry Percy's inadvertent fulfillment of the prophecy that he should die in 'Berwick.'

44. I have attempted to avoid reliance on the word 'popular,' with what I regard as some of its doubtful interpretative implications. Because I think that any idea appearing in a Latin chronicle is already something other than popular, I have difficulty agreeing with the conclusion of Aron Gurevich that popular elements can be discovered within the bounds of learned works (*Medieval Popular Culture: Problems of Belief and Perception* [Cambridge: Cambridge University Press, 1988]). I do, however, believe that the *sharing* of argumentative strategies and perceptual structures among and between social categories is far more widespread than ordinarily allowed, and that the imagined learned/popular divide is constantly traversed by such strategies and structures.

45. Including PRO C54/45 (printed in *English Coronation Records*, ed. L. G. Wickham Legg [Westminster: Constable, 1901], pp. 145–150), and *Historia Anglicana*, vol. 1, pp. 330–339.

46. Legg, *English Coronation Records*, pp. 79–80.

47. Walsingham includes the account of a knight carrying the king to the palace on his shoulders, though without note of the lost slipper: 'portatus est in humeris militum usque ad regale Palatium' (*Historia Anglicana*, vol. 1, p. 337).

48. Hector and Harvey present evidence of monastic concern over the preservation of the regalia, *Westminster Chron.*, p. 417.

49. BL MSS. Cotton Titus C. xv and Royal 13 A. xix, noted by Thompson in his edition of Usk's *Chronicon*, p. 202.

50. Froissart tells the same story, with more gloss, more testimony. In his version, the prescient pooch

deserts Richard in the Conway courtyard, behaving toward Henry as previously toward Richard, including a major caress delivered with his feet on Henry's shoulders. Henry seeking an explanation, Richard himself is caused to say that the dog possesses a 'congnoissance naturelle' of Henry's impending kingship and his own deposition. Securing his claim, Froissart reminds his reader that this event was attested by more than 30,000 men (*Oeuvres*, ed. de Lettenhove, vol. 16, pp. 187–188). As one might suppose, this is a frequently recycled anecdote. Johnes observes that it was applied in another near-contemporary instance, the desertion of Charles of Blois's greyhound shortly before his defeat by John Montfort (*Chronicles* [New York: Leavit and Allen, 1857], p. 617).

51. *CCR*, 1389–92, p. 527.
52. Transcribed and translated from MS. Ambassades, Bibliothèque de Roi no. 8448, ff. 143–144. See Webb, *Archaeologia* 20, p. 179.
53. *Chronicque*, ed. Williams, p. 64.
54. *Oeuvres*, ed. de Lettenhove, vol. 16, p. 200.
55. 'The Accusations against Thomas Austin,' ed. A. J. Prescott, in Strohm, *Hochon's Arrow*, p. 175.
56. *Select Cases*, pp. 123–124.
57. Originally set up to deal with matters of heraldry, this court (as Kay Harris has observed to me in correspondence) 'regularly exceeded its parameters,' becoming a frequent venue for treason cases, and even (as in the trials of the 1405 rebels) spectacularly so. See Alan Harding, *The Law Courts of Medieval England* (London: George Allen, 1973): 'The court was ... an obvious place to bring charges of open rebellion within the realm, and in 1405 the rebels against Henry IV were convicted on the king's

record "according to the laws and usages of arms of the Court of Chivalry in England." The punishments for treason inflicted by the court included degradation from honours – the traitor's loss of his coat of arms and peculiar signs of infamy at his execution' (p. 104). According to G. D. Squibb, the occasional designation of this court as 'military' results from its Latin designation as 'Curia Militaris' – with *militaris* mistakenly taken to refer to *miles* = 'soldier' rather than *miles* = 'knight,' and hence 'Curia Militaris' translated as 'Court Military' rather than (properly) as 'Court of Knighthood' or 'Chivalry.' See *The High Court of Chivalry: A Study of the Civil Law in England* (Oxford: Clarendon Press, 1959), pp. 2–3.
58. As discussed in Chapter 7, pp. 175–178.
59. Isobel D. Thornley, 'Treason by Words in the Fifteenth Century,' *EHR* 32 (1917), 556–561.
60. Samuel Rezneck, who offered the most timely and pointed correction of the claim for novel status for treason by words in the fifteenth century, explained that 'Before 1352 as after, the essence of treason is to be found in the intent to compass the death of the king; everything else, words included, was to be regarded as the outward manifestation and as the proof of that intent.' Rezneck valuably added that the fifteenth-century indictment for treason 'was a narrative tending toward exhaustive comprehensiveness,' and that when spoken words were changed they were part of a 'manifold narrative' designed to establish the compassing and imagining of the king's death. See 'Constructive Treason by Words in the Fifteenth Century,' *American Historical Review* 33 (1927), 544–552. The special status

of treason by words has also been extensively critiqued by J. G. Bellamy, who adds the valuable point that the 1352 statute's requirement of an overt act applies to the special case of aid and comfort to enemies of the realm, and not to the more general case of compassing or imagining the king's death. See *The Law of Treason in the Middle Ages* (Cambridge: Cambridge University Press, 1970), esp. pp. 120–123.

61. *The Book of Memory* (Cambridge: Cambridge University Press, 1990), p. 57.

62. Ann Arbor: University of Michigan Press, 1952.

63. *Piers Plowman as a Fourteenth-Century Apocalypse* (New Brunswick: Rutgers University Press, 1961), p. 171.

64. Conservative strictures on Bloomfield's equation of imagination with prophecy are to be found in Britton J. Harwood, 'Imaginative in *Piers Plowman*,' *Medium Aevum* 44 (1975), 249–263.

65. James Simpson – a participant in the rich dialogue surrounding Langland's *Imaginatif* – is clearly correct in describing this character as a 'natural faculty of the soul'; nevertheless, his role is, as Simpson observes, a potentially ambitious one: 'When he announces himself at the beginning of Passus XII ['I have folwed thee, in feith, thise fyve and fourty wynter, / And manye tymes have meved thee to mynne on thyn ende'], it is clear again that his role is one of moral reflection across time, both towards the past and the future.' See: *Piers Plowman: An Introduction to the B-Text* (London: Longman, 1990), pp. 102–103.

66. *The Literal Meaning of Genesis*, trans. John Hammond Taylor, Ancient Christian Writers (New York: Newman Press, 1982), no. 42, vol. 2, p. 193.

67. *The Riverside Chaucer*, 3rd edn, ed.

Larry D. Benson (Boston: Houghton Mifflin, 1987), vol. VII, ll. 3217, 3322–3324.

68. *Confessio Amantis*, vol. II, ll. 2803–3023, in *The Complete Works of John Gower*, vol. 2, ed. G. C. Macaulay (Oxford: Clarendon Press, 1902).

69. *RP*, vol. 3, pp. 583–584.

70. These contradictions are skillfully surveyed by McNiven, who finds the petition 'uncertain in its purpose, contrived and disjointed in its composition, and calculatedly dishonest in its details' (McNiven, pp. 102–104).

71. As in its anger at certain unnamed persons 'living in diverse privileged places' who seem willing to contemplate such dispossession; Lollards are probably present, not as the statute's actual target, but as a means of implicating these privileged dabblers in dissension and enemies of the realm, and the statute expands the means for their arrest by the secular powers.

72. See Chapter 4, pp. 106–108.

73. Taken together, these considerations cater to the nobility's own sense of opportunistic advantage; this is the bundle of concerns described by K. B. McFarlane in his essay on 'The Wars of the Roses,' when he speaks of the predisposition of the later fifteenth-century nobility to await 'the next *fait accompli*' (*England in the Fifteenth Century*, ed. G. L. Harriss [London: Hambledon Press, 1981], p. 245). See also R. L. Storey's discussion of the advantages naturally accruing to any royal incumbency, *The End of the House of Lancaster* (London: Barrie and Rockliff, 1966), p. 24.

74. Forcefully argued by Nicholas Watson, 'Censorship and Cultural Change in Late-Medieval England: Vernacular Theology, the Oxford Translation Debate, and Arundel's Constitutions of 1409,' *Speculum* 70 (1995), 821–864.

75. On the oppositional imagination see Castoriadis, *The Imaginary Institution of Society*, esp. pp. 340–373.

2 Heretic Burning: The Lollard as Menace and Victim

1. So, of course, were the rebels of 1381 and other social insurgents characteristically arrayed in the imagery of buffoonery and the carnivalesque. I have previously treated this subject, with additional citations, in ' "A Revelle!" Chronicle Evidence and the Rebel Voice,' in *Hochon's Arrow* (Princeton: Princeton University Press, 1992), pp. 33–56, and in ' "Lad with revel to Newegate," Chaucerian Narrative and Historical Meta-Narrative,' in *Art and Context in Late Medieval English Narrative*, ed. Robert R. Edwards (Woodbridge, Suffolk: D.S. Brewer, 1994), pp. 163–176.
2. *Concilia*, p. 258.
3. Consider, for example, the roughly parallel case of Cistercian Henry Crumpe, found guilty in 1392 convocation of being a lapsed heretic, but whose only secular penalty was to be barred by royal edict from teaching at Oxford: *FZ*, pp. 343–359.
4. *Lancastrian Kings and Lollard Knights* (Oxford: Clarendon Press, 1972), p. 226.
5. McNiven, p. 65.
6. R. N. Swanson, *Church and Society in Late Medieval England* (Oxford: Blackwell, 1989), p. 338.
7. Paul De Man, *Allegories of Reading* (New Haven: Yale University Press, 1979), p. 108.
8. Even the coiner of the phrase 'substitutive reversal' is dubious about its interpretative validity, warning that 'it seems unlikely that one more such reversal . . . would suffice to restore things

to their proper order' (ibid., p. 113).
9. Fellow admirers of R. I. Moore, *The Formation of a Persecuting Society* (Oxford: Blackwell, 1987), will recognize a non-specific, but still considerable, debt to his work in my description of this administrative/discursive situation.
10. H. G. Richardson, 'Heresy and the Lay Power under Richard II,' *EHR* 51 (1936), 1–28; McNiven; Margaret Aston, 'Lollardy and Sedition, 1381–1431,' *Past and Present* 17 (1960), 1–44.
11. *FZ*, pp. 311–312.
12. Epistle CXIII (*PL*, vol. 207).
13. See Miri Rubin, *Corpus Christi: The Eucharist in Late Medieval Culture* (Cambridge: Cambridge University Press, 1991), pp. 312–316. Also see Margaret Aston, 'Corpus Christi and Corpus Regni: Heresy and the Peasants' Revolt,' *Past and Present* 143 (1994), 27–31 and Anthony K. Cassell, *Dante's Fearful Art of Justice* (Toronto: University of Toronto Press, 1984), pp. 100–103.
14. *FZ*, p. 277.
15. Text and translation from *Knighton*, pp. 306–307.
16. *CCR*, 1389–92, p. 530.
17. *Concilia*, p. 223.
18. *Knighton*, p. 312. Martin translates this phrase as '[he was] adjudged fuel for the flames,' and considers it a formal sentence: 'This observation, made *c.* 1390, seems not to have been noted in discussions of the death penalty for heresy in England' (p. 313). My own inclination is to treat it as an opinion as to Swinderby's deserts; although, as I am arguing here, the line between speech acts and corporeal acts grows increasingly dim, with hostile speech functioning to erase the barrier between symbolization and concrete action.
19. *Historia Anglicana*, vol. 2, p. 189.
20. Cited in H. G. Richardson and G. O. Sayles, 'Parliamentary

Documents from Formularies,' *Bulletin of the Institute of Historical Research* 11 (1933–34), 147–162.

21. Dymmok, p. 5.
22. Richardson and Sayles, 'Parliamentary Documents from Formularies,' p. 154.
23. Naturally enough, the decision actually to burn heretics always occurs in a climate in which a great deal of thinking, or even fantasizing, about burning is going on. Shortly before the inauguration of large-scale burning in 1413, Arundel's mind was turning to all sorts of thoughts about incineration. In a letter to Pope John XXIII dated by Wilkins in 1412, he presses his scheme of digging up Wyclif's bones, proposing that the pontiff order that they should be thrown in a privy subject to constant use by the faithful or else burned ('. . . ossa ipsius haeresiarchae exhumari, et in sterquilinium a cunctis christicolis profananda, contemptibiliter projeci seu comburi' – *Concilia*, p. 351). The tenor of public feeling in the year of the first large-scale burnings is represented in *The Book of Margery Kempe*, in which, though repeatedly exonerated in official interviews, she reports herself as threatened by the monks of Canterbury (who would appear to indulge in imagining her punishment at their own hands, without waiting for the secular arm): 'Then she went out of the monastery, they following and crying upon her, "Thou xalt be brent, fals lollare. Her is a cartful of thornys redy for the & a tonne to bren the wyth"' (*The Book of Margery Kempe*, ed. S. Meech and H. E. Allen, EETS, OS, vol. 212 [London, 1940], vol. 1, p. 28). So, too, did a woman of Lambeth compass her death, saying '"I wold thu wer in Smythfeld, & I wold beryn a fagot to bren the

wyth"' (p. 36). She was, of course, not burnt, but the idea of burning, and imaginative indulgence in that idea, were very much in the air, in close concert with the turn to multiple burnings in the coming year.

24. *Continuatio Eulogii*, p. 388.
25. Discussion of the convocation, and Sautre's trial, based on *Concilia*, pp. 254–260.
26. Observing that the delegation then went on to request the convocation's support for a generous subsidy, McNiven points out reasonably enough that a bargain appears to have been struck: 'If the Convocation committed itself to a satisfactory grant of clerical taxation, the laity would reciprocate by providing positive support for the drive against the Lollards' (p. 80). One cannot disagree with so reasonable an inference, although the tendency of my analysis is to find that Henry IV and supportive elements in the parliament entertained a good deal more interest of their own in Lollard persecution than McNiven's quid pro quo formulation would imply.
27. *RP*, vol. 3, pp. 466–467.
28. *Statutes of the Realm*, ed. Basket (Dawsons, 1816), vol. 2, p. 126.
29. *Concilia*, p. 260.
30. Ibid. The date of Sautre's deposition and transfer to the secular arm is given as 24 February in the official record of the convocation, whereas the actual date that Saturday was 26 February. This seemingly inconsequential slip may have been deliberate, in order that the royal writ under which Sautre was actually burnt, dated 26 February (although not actually issued until 2 March), may not seem to have been composed in quite so precipitate a fashion. In any event, this royal writ is the one slightly anomalous feature in an otherwise exquisitely synchronized production.

224

Notes to pages 43–48

31. *Historia Anglicana*, vol. 2, p. 247.
See also the instance of one John
Seynonus, who boasted that he
would not abandon his own
(heretical) view of the eucharist,
despite the *decretum* approved
by the convocation and also by
king and parliament, as directed
'contra haereticum in civitate
Londoniensi nuper combustum'
(*Concilia*, p. 249).

32. The writ is issued by authority
of 'H. R. apud Westm' 26
die Febr. Per ipsum regem et
consilium in parliamento.' On
the legal sufficiency of the writ,
and non-necessity of the statute
De haeretico comburendo, see
A. K. McHardy, *'De haeretico
comburendo, 1401,'* in *Lollardy and
the Gentry in the Later Middle Ages*,
ed. Margaret Aston and Collin
Richmond (Stroud: Sutton Publishing, 1997), pp.112–126.

33. *RP*, vol. 3, p. 459.

34. *De Legibus Angliae*, ed. George E.
Woodbine, vol. 3 (New Haven:
Yale University Press, 1918), Tract
ii, chap. 9, no. 2.

35. These texts are all discussed and
documented in G. G. Coulton's
vigorous polemic, 'The Death
Penalty for Heresy,' *Medieval
Studies* 18 (1924), 1–19.

36. Discussed in Henry Charles Lea,
*A History of the Inquisition in the
Middle Ages*, vol. 1 (London, 1888),
pp. 113–114. Lea concludes that
the Cathars died of exposure. He
mentions a possible burning in
thirteenth-century London, but
without documentation.

37. Although some of her followers
may have been burnt. See *A Contemporary Narrative of the Proceedings against Dame Alice Kyteler*, ed.
Thomas Wright, Camden Society,
first series, vol. 24 (London, 1843),
p. 40.

38. Richardson and Sayles, 'Parliamentary Documents from Formularies', pp. 152–154.

39. Elaine Scarry, *The Body in Pain*

(New York: Oxford University
Press, 1985), p. 29.

40. *FZ*, pp. 408–410.

41. Recent scholarship on the theology of the eucharist has increasingly attended not to its rigidity
but to what Gary Macy has called
its traditional 'diversity' – the
wide range of possible orthodox
pronouncements. See his *Theo-
logies of the Eucharist in the
Early Scholastic Period* (Oxford:
Clarendon Press, 1984).

42. See Mansi, *Sacrorum Conciliorum
Nova et Amplissima Collectio*, vol.
22 (Graz: Akademische Druck,
1961), vol. 981. Any attempts
by Innocent to advance a particular view of transubstantiation
occurred in other places, as in
De sacro altaris mysterio, written *c.*
1195 when he was still Cardinal
Lotario dei Segni, in which arguments against Berengar's and
other deviant views were conclusively gathered, and the view of
the sacrament as 'accidentia sine
subjecto' strongly urged (*PL*, vol.
217, cols 862–863).

43. *Summa Theologiae*, part 3a, question 77, article 1 (London: Eyre
and Spottiswoode, 1965), vol. 58,
pp. 128–129.

44. Berengar was extensively an-
swered, by Lanfranc (who argued
that the essence of Christ's
body was present in the host,
though the species of bread remained), by Guitmond of Aversa
(who argued that the substance
of the Lord's body was intact,
concealed under accidents), by
Alger of Liège (who argued
that accidental qualities exist by
themselves), and others throughout the eleventh and twelfth centuries. See Raymond G. Fontaine,
*Subsistent Accident in the Philoso-
phy of Saint Thomas and in His Pre-
decessors* (Washington, DC: The
Catholic University Press, 1950),
esp. pp. 34–41.

45. Thomas's principal influence, at

least upon lay and vernacular discussion, derived from widely dispersed pseudo-Thomistic treatises (*De Sacramento Eucharistiae* and *De Sacramento Altaris – Opera Omnia*, vols 16–17 [Parma, 1864–65]) and from his supposed authorship of the Corpus Christi service.

46. Gordon Leff, *Heresy in the Later Middle Ages*, vol. 2 (Manchester: Manchester University Press, 1967), p. 551.

47. Gary Macy, 'The Dogma of Transubstantiation in the Middle Ages,' *Journal of Ecclesiastical History* 45 (1994), 11–41.

48. *Trialogus*, ed. G. Lechler (Oxford: Clarendon Press, 1869), p. 247.

49. 'The Testimony of William Thorpe 1407,' in *Two Wycliffite Texts*, ed. Anne Hudson, EETS, 301 (London, 1993), p. 55.

50. According to Gary Macy, 'If there was an academic or preacher who others felt needed disciplining, then his theology of the eucharist was a good place to look for heresy' ('The Dogma of Transubstantiation,' p. 40). He goes on to observe that 'The instances of charges against the eucharist which do occur in the Middle Ages usually seem to be part of a larger political or theological agenda' (p. 41). On subsequent protocols for the examination of heretics and Lollards, invariably headed by questions designed to elicit denial of material substance of bread or wine after transubstantiation, see Anne Hudson, 'The Examination of Lollards,' in *Lollards and their Books* (London: Hambledon Press, 1985), pp. 125–140.

51. *Chronicon Angliae*, p. 311.

52. Probably, but not necessarily, in writing.

53. *FZ*, p. 106.

54. See Herbert B. Workman, *John Wyclif*, vol. 2 (Oxford: Clarendon Press, 1926), pp. 140–148.

55. *FZ*, pp. 105–106.

56. 'On the Eucharist,' in *Library of Christian Classics*, vol. 14, ed. Matthew Spinka (Philadelphia: Westminster Press, 1953), p. 61.

57. *FZ*, p. 110.

58. Ibid., p. 115.

59. For example, F. D. Matthew, 'The Date of Wyclif's Attack on Transubstantiation,' *EHR* 5 (1890), 328–330.

60. See Williell R. Thomson, *The Latin Writings of John Wyclif* (Toronto: Pontifical Institute, 1983), p. 6.

61. That is, deployed as a rhetorical trope. *FZ*, p. 110.

62. Ibid., pp. 277–278; from Courtenay's letter to Peter Stokes of Oxford, reporting the results of the synod.

63. *RP*, vol. 3, pp. 124–125.

64. *FZ*, pp. 275–317.

65. McNiven, p. 38.

66. *Knighton*, p. 65. One Cornelius de Clone was, evidently, a royal pensioner, whose annuity was augmented shortly before the alleged miracle. McNiven, p. 38.

67. *RP*, vol. 3, p. 141. The king assented to this counter-petition, but the statute was never rescinded.

68. *Knighton*, pp. 312–314; *FZ*, p. 340. The petitions seem ultimately not to have been successful, but one is struck by the optimism underlying the fact that they were launched at all.

69. Dymmok, p. 89.

70. *FZ*, p. 116.

71. Ibid., p. 353.

72. Ibid., p. 384.

73. *Two Wycliffite Texts*, p. 55. Compare the moment in Oldcastle's trial when (as rendered by Foxe) 'Then asked they him, to stop his mouth therewith, if he believed not in the determination of the church?' See John Foxe, *Acts and Monuments*, ed. G. Townsend and S. Cattley, vol. 3 (London: Seeley and Burnside, 1837), p. 331.

74. The moment of revelation for the dissenting subject seems to

embrace two possibilities (the accused either accepts the authority of the Church or refuses it); in a sense it only embraces one. The first alternative offers a symbolic death, through nullification of belief, projected in the form of a written (and sometimes oral) recantation; the second a real death, by fire, in the public view. In either case, the operation exhibits the same recursiveness that structured Walsingham's anti-Sautre joke. Its intended revelation and dramatization are that, however the accused might fancy an idea of hiding his or her guilt, that guilt is on plain view, it has always been known; the Lollard is designated as the last to know how fully the institutions of orthodox control have preempted initiative and undermined an illusion of autonomy within a larger ideological system.

75. Control of the process by which documents are created and entered as evidence is, of course, crucial to the process of obtaining convictions and making them stick. Early on in the trial, for instance, a written *schedula* is produced, in which Arundel's chancellor has recorded Sautre's current views 'veraciter de verbo ad verbum' (*Concilia*, p. 255), and from which he now reads them, their tenor to be additionally recorded in the conciliar record. Sautre reasonably enough tries to regain a footing within this process of written incrimination, asking for a copy for purposes of response. The trial reconvening, he appears with a *schedula* of his own, from which he delivers his answers. The oral interrogation, however, quickly leaves his rejoinders behind, while he continues to be responsible for the original, written charges.

76. *FZ*, p. 348.

77. This phrase is borrowed from Michel de Certeau, *The Writing of History* (New York: Columbia University Press, 1988), p. 157. Its context is Certeau's remark on ways in which seventeenth-century political institutions have learned to use religious institutions: 'The weakened Christian "system" is transformed into a sacred theater of the system which will take its place.' Lancastrian uses of religious institutions and structures in their consolidation of political power suggest that Certeau's insight is equally applicable to situations preceding his own early modern examples.

78. Despite the presumed congeniality of either outcome, the trial record sometimes suggests a preference for one alternative or the other. The trial of Richard Wyche, *c*. 1403, contains evidence that compromises were sought at each juncture, whereby ecclesiastical authority would be recognized even as the plaintiff went free (*EHR* 5 [1890], 530–544). The trial of Sautre tends rather obviously toward another result, in which the plaintiff's compromise formulations about the coextensiveness of Christ's body and the consecrated bread were rejected out of hand on the way to his conviction.

79. Emphasis mine. *RP*, vol. 3, p. 459.

80. A subject in literature or in life who offers himself or herself as an example, might, as Larry Scanlon puts it in the case of Chaucer's Parson, 'become exemplary precisely by transforming his or her actions into a moral narrative' (*Narrative, Authority, and Power: the Medieval Exemplum and the Chaucerian Tradition* [Cambridge: Cambridge University Press, 1994], p. 34). Or a subject like Sautre might *be* transformed, willy-nilly, into a moral narrative.

81. *RP*, vol. 3, p. 473.

82. *Statutes of the Realm*, vol. 2, p. 128.

83. *Continuatio Eulogii*, p. 388.

84. As McNiven has observed, pp. 90–91.
85. *Concilia*, p. 260.
86. See, for example, the case of Johannes Beket, who in 2 Henry IV appeared 'spontaneously' before Arundel, tearfully confessing prior Lollard belief and seeking appropriate punishment – *Concilia*, pp. 247–248.
87. *Concilia*, p. 249.
88. 'The Testimony of William Thorpe,' in *Two Wycliffite Texts*, p. 36.
89. Scarry, *The Body in Pain*, pp. 38–45.
90. *Two Wycliffite Texts*, p. 36.
91. Although the *Concilia* backdates the occasion by two days, perhaps reluctant to reveal the fact that Henry's letter was already written.
92. Any review of motives for postponement must include McNiven's altogether reasonable suggestion pp. 89–92 that the delay was intended to break Purvey, whose case came to trial immediately after Sautre's, and was then postponed until several days after his death.
93. An instance of the careful consideration given to the symbolic dimensions of an execution was to occur with the burning of Jan Hus in 1415: 'He was made to stand upon a couple of faggots and tightly bound to a thick post with ropes, around the ankles, below the knee, above the knee, at the groin, the waist, and under the arms. A chain was also secured around the neck. Then it was observed that he faced the east, which was not fitting for a heretic, and he was shifted to the west' (Lea, *A History of the Inquisition* vol. 1, pp. 552–553).
94. As recounted in most of the chronicles. See also the official city account, in *Letter-Book H*, f. cxxxiii.

95. Strohm, *Hochon's Arrow*, pp. 182–184.
96. 'The Smithfield Tournament of 1390,' *Journal of Medieval and Renaissance Studies* 20 (1990), 6.
97. See, for example, the cases of Jan Hus (Lea, *A History of the Inquisition*, vol. 1, pp. 552–553), Oldcastle hanged 'by a stronge Cheyne' (*Great Chronicle of London*, ed. A. H. Thomas and I. D. Thornley [London, 1938], p. 96), and Savonarola (L. Landucci, *A Florentine Diary*, trans. A. Jervis [London: Dent, 1927], p. 143).
98. *Historia Anglicana*, vol. 2, p. 282.
99. *The Historical Collections of a Citizen of London*, ed. James Gairdner, Camden Society, NS, vol. xvii (London, 1876), p. 105.
100. *Concilia*, p. 328.
101. The thoroughness of Sautre's burning, so that only ashes remained, may be understood as precautionary in nature, in order to prevent subsequent veneration of his remains. Subsequent accounts of better-known heresiarchs foreground the importance of complete bodily destruction, and the rationale of the practice. Prominent Bohemian heretic Jan Hus's body was broken into pieces and re-burnt to prevent this eventuality. (Lea, *A History of the Inquisition*, vol. 1, pp. 552–553). An apparent eyewitness account of the burning of Savonarola and his companions adds that,

> In a few hours they were burnt, their arms and legs gradually dropping off; part of their bodies remaining hanging to the chains, a quantity of stones were thrown to make them fall, as there was a fear of the people getting hold of them; and then the hangman and those whose business it was hacked down the post and burnt it to the ground, bringing a lot of brushwood, and stirring the fire up

over the dead bodies, so that the very last piece was consumed. Then they fetched carts, and accompanied by the mace-bearers, carried the last bit of dust to the Arno, by the Ponte Vecchio, in order that no remains should be found.

And such precautions were indeed necessary; some of Savonarola's followers evidently did gather ashes from the flowing river and, several days later, women were found kneeling at his burning-place (Landucci, *Florentine Diary*, p. 143). For a parallel English case, consider the cult of Richard Wyche, burnt in 1440. The city of London *Journals* contain evidence of the bearing away of relics from his burning-place, and of attempts by his followers to worship there; see Caroline Barron, rev., 'The Later Lollards', *Journal of the Society of Archaeologists* 3 (1965–69), 258–259.

102. The choice of an everyday object to exemplify his separation has its own kind of horror, again as captured by Elaine Scarry's discussion of everyday apparatus – lightbulbs, bathtubs – in twentieth-century torture.

103. On the use of protocols to elicit heretical views, see Anne Hudson, 'The Examination of Lollards,' in *Lollards and their Books*, pp. 125–140.

104. Pope Martin V, writing in the aftermath of the Council of Constance to endorse the all-out effort against Wyclif's followers, is at pains to be certain that no one will escape with pretended ignorance or other frivolity: 'Verum ne in prejudicium et scandalum praefatae fidei orthodoxae religionis Christianae, praetextu ignorantiae quemquam in hoc circumveniri, aut versutos homines sub frivolae excusationis velamine in hac materia palliare

contingat' (Mansi, *Sacrorum Conciliorum . . . Collectio*, vol. 27, col. 1207).

105. An alternative argument for Sautre's centrality, in this case based upon more extensive evidence of important Lollard connections, has recently been offered by A. K. McHardy, in '*De Heretico Comburendo, 1401,*' esp. pp. 119–123.

106. *FZ*, p. 408.

107. Cp. *Concilia*, p. 257 with *FZ*, pp. 408–410.

108. PRO E37/28. The document exists now in a category known as Court of the Marshalsea and Court of the Verge, and informally known as pleas of the hall. I have been alerted to its existence by Dr Simon Walker, and assisted in its location and categorization by A. N. Lawes of the Public Record Office.

109. That this was the verdict in Sautre's case – and that the Sautre in question is our man – is confirmed by the enrollment of his royal pardon, dated 6 February 1400, for diverse treasons and felonies. In its entirety, the document confirms that William was not only indicted but found guilty, and that the royal pardon saved him from a judgment of death:

> . . . William Sautre, chaplain ['capellanus'] recently adjudged for diverse treasons and felonies ['nuper iudicatus fuisset de diuersis prodicionibus et feloniis'] which he was considered to have committed against our peace, because of which he was convicted and judged to death ['convictus fuit et ad mortem adiudicatus']. We from our special grace pardon the same William from these treasons and felonies and also withdraw him from execution of the judgment rendered against him.

See PRO C66/358, mem. 16.

Incomplete summary in *CPR*, 1399–1401, p. 190.

Adam of Usk says that 'plures alii' were arrested as co-conspirators of the earls, and he names several (including Richard imitator Maudelen) who were hanged and beheaded for their knowledge of the crime (p. 42). The Patent Rolls for February also contain a number of other pardons, many clearly related to the same event, of which the most conspicuous is given to Hugh Blount, esquire, brother of Thomas Blount, one of the convicted conspirators.

110. A passive sympathy for the rebellion of the earls is often attributed to Despenser, whose brother, Thomas le Despenser, was an active participant who died in the aftermath.

111. On alleged London meetings, see the indictment against Merks, in *Select Cases*, pp. 102–103. On the involvement of Colchester, see E. F. Jacob, *The Fifteenth Century* (Oxford: Clarendon Press, 1961), p. 25.

112. Various linkages between Lollardy and treasonous endeavor are explored in Chapter 4, p. 120ff. The classic study of this imagined (and perhaps occasionally real) interpenetration remains Aston, 'Lollardy and Sedition,' 1–44.

113. *Concilia*, pp. 254–255.

114. Mansi, *Sacrorum Conciliorum . . . Collectio*, vol. 27 (Venice, 1784), cols 632–634.

115. As Gordon Leff and others have observed, emphasis on the eucharist remained an 'egregious theological anomaly' in the Lollards' primarily moral and social agenda. Leff, *Heresy in the Later Middle Ages*, vol. 2 (Manchester: Manchester University Press, 1967), p. 579.

116. Thus Sautre can find in the cross of Christ, and in the host as well, an occasion for vicarious or symbolical adoration, 'adoratione vicaria' (*Concilia*, p. 255). The consecrated bread can remain bread, but can also now be symbolically or by common consent the body of Christ, just as a person consecrated to the priesthood or in marriage remains the same person, but advanced to a new symbolic status.

117. As Žižek observes of this privileged signifier and sublime object of desire, 'the element which only holds the place of a certain lack, which is in its bodily presence nothing but an embodiment of a certain lack, is perceived as a point of supreme plenitude' (*The Sublime Object of Ideology* [London: Verso, 1989], p. 99).

3 Plots

1. *Historia Anglicana*, vol. 2, p. 248.

2. On Walsingham's increasingly Lancastrian outlook after 1397 see Antonia Gransden, *Historical Writing in England*, vol. 2 (London: Routledge and Kegan Paul, 1982), pp. 140–144.

3. The same anecdote appears in various chronicles. See, for instance, its appearance in the related, but non-identical, text of *Annales Henrici*, pp. 337–338.

4. As described, for example, in *Chronicque de la Traïson et Mort* (London, 1846), pp. 85–92.

5. *Annales Henrici Quarti*, p. 323.

6. According to Gregory's *Chronicle of London, Historical Collections of a Citizen of London*, ed. J. Gairdner, Camden Society, NS, vol. 17 (London, 1876), p. 108 – a highly unreliable source. But some corroboration might be found in the Exchequer Issue Rolls for February 1414, pertaining to events of the previous month; payment is authorized for manacles 'for certain traitors recently captured at Eltham and elsewhere, and

imprisoned' (PRO E403/614/mem.12).

7. The most ingenious of these supposed plots (though eschewing the Christmas season) involved a group of 1401 conspirators who intended to 'arrange by necromancy and spell to make an ointment with which to anoint the saddle of . . . the king secretly and cunningly so that no one would know about it, and before he had ridden ten miles he would be quite swelled up and die suddenly, sitting up in the saddle' (*Select Cases*, p. 113).

8. 'Petite Économie libidinale d'un dispositif narratif: La Régie Renault raconte le meurtre de Pierre Overney,' in *Des Dispositifs pulsionnels* (Paris, 1973), p. 205.

9. See Nicholas Watson, 'Censorship and Cultural Change in Late-Medieval England,' *Speculum* 70 (1995), 821–864.

10. This act of reinvention was equally a product of programmatic rereading on the one hand and rigorous textual analysis on the other. In *A brefe Chronicle concerning . . . sir Johan Oldcastel* (London, 1548), John Bale stunningly argued for the bogus nature of the supposed Oldcastle event, claiming no armed rebels had actually gathered that day: that the king in fact 'found no such company' in the field and that ensuing prosecutions were actually the king's reprisal against those whom he supposed to have assisted John Oldcastle's escape from the Tower earlier that autumn. As John Foxe was to tell it in the second and subsequent editions of his *Acts and Monuments*, Bale's argument in turn had such an impact on the Tudor chronicler Edward Halle that it caused the latter to rip out his pages on the rebellion and to adopt a less partial account: 'It so befell that as Hall was entring into the story of Syr John Oldcastle . . . the booke of John Bale . . . was the same time newly come ouer, which booke was priuely conueied by one of his seruaunts into the study of Hall. . . . At the sight wherof, when he saw the ground and resons in that booke contained, . . . he taking his pen, rased and cancilled all that he had written before. . . . And thus your autor Hall, hauing recited the varietie of menes opinions, determineth himselfe no certaine thing therof . . .' (*Acts*, 4th edn, London, 1583, pp. 578–579). And, Foxe triumphantly exclaims, he possesses Halle's own marked copy! Whatever his motivation, Halle most certainly did initiate a substantial retreat from the fifteenth-century contention, observing tepidly that 'Some saie that the occasion of their death was the conueighance of the Lorde Cobham out of prisone. Other write that it was bothe for treason and heresy as the record declareth. Certain affirme that it was for feined causes surmised by the spiritualite more of despleasour then truth' (*The Union of the Two Noble and Illustre Families* [1548], pp. 48–49).

Finally, and most influentially, Foxe himself set forth a closely argued 21-folio-page critique of the fifteenth-century 'record,' concluding that no body of Lollards was in the field in martial array, and those who were there came more for a simple prayer meeting than by seditious design: 'might they not,' he urged, 'come to those thickets neare to the felde of Seint Giles, hauing Beuerly theyr Preacher with them . . . to pray & to preach in that woody place, as wel as to fight?' (*Acts*, 4th edn, p. 569).

If conscientious and skeptical textual analysis is to be considered an essential historiographical skill, then I would assert that John

Foxe's archival interest and close analytical attention make him incomparably the more formidable historian than the Victorians who succeeded him. Foxe has his prejudices, to be sure, as represented by anti-papist tirade and rant, but he stations them where they belong: on the visible surface of his text. Although he lacked access to materials such as the original Oldcastle indictment or the 1414 county commissions, Foxe's analysis of the Oldcastle indictment (in the form as he discovered it in the Rolls of Parliament – available for consultation in *RP*, vol. 4, pp. 107–108) and the text of the anti-Lollard legislation passed at Leicester in March 1414 (available for consultation in *RP*, vol. 4, pp. 24–25) reveal a remarkable capacity both closely to read a text and to 'read through' to its forced junctures, its inconsistencies, its other fissures. 'How vnlikely and vntidely,' he observes of the Oldcastle indictment, 'the poynts of this tale are tide and hang together' – p. 569). Foxe's own research notes and transcriptions of historical records are available for consultation as British Library MS. Harley 420, ff. 67a–73a.

11. Writing in the *DNB*, vol. 42 (London, 1895), pp. 86–93.

12. *The Reign of Henry the Fifth*, vol. 1 (Cambridge: Cambridge University Press, 1914), pp. 261–280.

13. 'Sir John Oldcastle,' part II, *EHR* 20 (1905), 637–658.

14. These historians dismiss Foxe and the other Oldcastle apologists as blinded by sectarian impulse, and advocate a corrective return to the fifteenth-century written record. Grounded on an appeal to objectivity and scientific history over sectarian claims, these historians' authority claims were predicated on the reintroduction of previously lost or neglected documents and sources – most particularly the 10 January indictment and associated texts, together with the writings of early fifteenth-century chroniclers like Walsingham. Egregious and unbelievable claims made within these documents – such as those concerning the number of persons supposedly involved – were addressed via selective emendation. These historians do, as promised, use their documents 'with great reserve' (Waugh, 'Sir John Oldcastle', p. 649), but the reserve in question is limited to such particularities and matters of detail. This strategy of a return to 'documents' amounts to a preference for any written source's structuration of an event, with certain local emendations introduced *mutatis mutandis*, over any interrogation of that source's truth claims from a ground outside its own framework of assumptions. Thus, in the course of his rehabilitative renarration, Waugh observes that 'in the foregoing description the accounts of contemporary chronicles and official records are assumed to be substantially correct' (ibid., p. 645). The basis of this endorsement is explanatory convenience; as Waugh observes, his reason for accepting 'the accounts of the London chroniclers' is that 'they . . . furnish a coherent story which adequately explains the subsequent development of events' (ibid., p. 641).

15. Waugh and subsequent commentators adopt an extreme and seemingly endless series of awkward postures in order to discover and maintain consistency in the Lancastrian account. Consider, for example, this egregious series of conjectures on the motives and strategies of the presumed rebellion: 'It follows that the leaders of the rising were prepared to

sanction a considerable amount of violence. Perhaps, indeed, after Henry's removal from Eltham, Oldcastle intended to use his main force as a mere screen for an attempt on Westminster.... Malcontents of the lower classes, among whom the ideas of 1381 may still have lingered, were doubtless only too ready to join a movement directed against a part of the existing order of things. But it is improbable that this section of Oldcastle's followers would have been content with making a mere demonstration outside the walls of London, where there was no chance of murdering a few of the wealthy or gathering any plunder. It is conceivable, too, that many of the real Lollards were anxious to play havoc with some of the available churches and monastic houses. The official description of the objects of the rising to some extent bears out these conjectures. It is just what was likely to be deduced from the incoherent statements of ignorant rustics' (Waugh, 'Sir John Oldcastle', pp. 650–651). 'Follows that ... perhaps ... doubtless ... it is improbable that ... conceivable ... to some extent... conjectures ... likely.' Not only do the fudge-words of this passage betray its utterly fanciful nature, but its concluding sentence certainly dispatches any presumption on the part of Waugh or those who have followed his analysis that they are operating outside ideology, or free of predispositions.

16. In her splendid and otherwise groundbreaking essay on 'Lollardy and Sedition, 1381–1431,' Margaret Aston embraces and works from Waugh's conclusions, citing the acceptability of his description of the 'rebellion' as her reason for not pursuing the subject in more detail (in *Lollards and Reformers* [London: Hambledon Press, 1984], p. 25, n.

95). Anne Hudson is more circumspect in *The Premature Reformation*, pointing out the advantages of a presumptive connection between Lollardy and rebellion to the anti-Lollard cause, and observing that 'the absence of a modern monograph on the rebellion is one of the stranger lacunae in late medieval historical writing' (Oxford: Clarendon Press, 1988), pp. 117–119. Materials bearing on such a reconsideration have been partially developed, though not pursued to conclusion, in C. Kightly, 'The Early Lollards: A Survey of Popular Lollard Activity in England, 1382–1428,' York University Ph.D. thesis, 1975. Most revisionary in its possible implications is Edward Powell's assessment of the legal records of 1414 in his *Kingship, Law, and Society*, pp. 141–167; Powell notes the sparse turnout at St Giles's Fields, the hyperbole of Lancastrian claims, and effective Lancastrian control of each stage of the event – though his inquiry's emphasis upon legal records leaves the Lancastrian-influenced narrative framing of the event effectively intact.

17. On this stratagem, also central to Lacanian and other analyses of the claims of the future upon the past, see Luce Irigaray, *Speculum of the Other Woman* trans. Gillian C. Gill (Ithaca, NY: Cornell University Press, 1985), pp. 244–246.

18. Issues of the Exchequer: PRO E403/614/mem. 9.

19. Patent Rolls: PRO C66/393/mem. 22 (*CPR*, 1413–16, p. 157). Similar payments were made to Thomas Burton in February, for activities related to the month of January (E403/614/mem. 16).

20. PRO C54/263/mem. 6d [*CCR*, 1413–16, p. 114].

21. PRO E403/614/mem. 12.

22. *RP*, vol. 3, pp. 583–584.

23. *Statutes of the Realm*, ed. Basket (London: Dawsons, 1816), vol. 2,

pp. 181–184 (coupled with an even more ambitious proscription of *all* illegal assemblies, pp. 184–187).

24. PRO C66/393, mem. 30d. I describe this commission as 'broadly worded' in part because of its inclusion of 'castigari & puniri' as its charge; Andrew Prescott has observed in his discussions of the commissions of 1381 that this deliberately broad phrase is there invoked to permit a range of arrests and sanctions. See 'The Judicial Records of the Rising of 1381,' Ph.D. thesis, University of London, 1984, p. 57.

25. This item and the following are part of the record of King's Bench, PRO KB 27/611/ (rex) mem. 7. It is conveniently transcribed and translated in *Select Cases*, pp. 217–220.

26. This item, from Issues of the Exchequer, for Michaelmas 1 Henry V (PRO E403/614/mem. 12), is not conclusively dated; however, since the King's Bench (*Coram Rege*) records suggest that the commissioners' business began and ended on the morning of 10 January, the assignment of this date seems warranted.

27. Latham, *Revised Medieval Latin Word-List* (British Academy, 1965), connects this term with the Christian tradition of 'a celebratory breakfast that breaks a period of fasting or abstinence.' The notion of celebration on the morning of so supposedly harrowing an event would, again, suggest its planned nature.

28. PRO KB 9/204, 205.

29. *CCR*, 1413–19, pp. 106–107; printed in *Foedera*, vol. 4, pt. 2, p. 61.

30. *CLBI*, p. 166.

31. Their activities, and those of other itinerant preachers and provocateurs, are conveniently documented in Charles Kightly, 'The Early Lollards'. Evidence of their activities is supplemented by additional evidence of laymen willing to offer temporary shelter (PRO KB9/204/1/ff. 59–60, 65–67); of pamphleteers like Thomas Ile (or Scot) (ibid. f. 141); of laymen ready to act as go-betweens and to arrange meeting-places (ibid. f. 58). The extent and formality of their activities are, however, very much open to question, as is the subject-matter of their communications.

32. These written records, narratively contextualized by the chronicles, the *Gesta Henrici Quinti*, and other prose and verse accounts, form the evidentiary background of Waugh's treatment of the rising, and also the more exacting but essentially parallel and corroborative chapters written by Charles Kightly on the same subject in his rigorously detailed study, 'The Early Lollards.'

33. PRO KB 9/204/13.

34. The commissions thus functioned, as Edward Powell has observed, as intelligence sources for the King's Bench, rather than as independent authorities: 'The commissioners were empowered only to receive indictments and order arrests, whereas justices of oyer and terminer could also try and convict offenders. The findings of these inquiries were returned to chancery and forwarded to the court of king's bench for determination' ('The Restoration of Law and Order,' in *Henry V: The Practice of Kingship* [Oxford: Oxford University Press, 1985], pp. 66–67). This circumscription may thus been seen more as centralizing, rather than as restricting, the authority of the commissions.

35. In only one case – the vivid account of the assignation at the Wrestler on the Hoop – is the nature of the armament specified: 'cum palettis, doublettes de defenso, et aliis...' (PRO KB9/204/58).

36. On the conventionality of the language of these returns, and their frequent repetitiveness, Powell observes that, 'Juries before the local commissions also seem to have relied upon information obtained by the government. ... The returns are formulaic and repetitive.... The commissioners in each county were probably sent a brief account of the revolt which they read to the jurors, together with a list of suspects from that county' (*Kingship, Law, and Society*, p. 154).

37. As when, for example, the language of the 23 January and 28 March pardons repeats substantial sections of the original 10 January commission (the 23 January pardon appears as C66/393/mem. 16, and in *CPR*, 1413–16, p. 162; see the 28 March pardon as printed in *Foedera*, vol. 4, pt. 2, pp. 72–73). The former text insists that the rebels were 'modo guerrino arraiat'; the latter repeats the charge that the Lollards conspired 'in Mortem nostram.'

38. See PRO KB9/204/mems 118–126. In a typical case, the preamble of the indictment states the general charge, which is to inquire into the deeds of those Lollards 'qui mortem ... domini Regis ... falso et proditorie ymaginauerunt, etc.' and then applies it to one Johanne Cok, already under arrest, who, 'modo guerrino araiatus ... falso et proditorie morte ... domini Regis imaginando, etc.' (taken at Thaxstede, mem. 116). Other documents use the same technique, but in a more subtle form, in which the language of the original commission is simply digested and played back, as when various persons, 'false et proditorie imaginando mortem domini Regis insurrexerunt, etc.' (mem. 99).

39. *Kingship, Law, and Society*, p. 155.

40. This latter category of accusation affords a fascinating glimpse of what Lollards either thought or were supposed to think in the second decade of the fifteenth century. The majority are simply said to harbor Lollard *opiniones* (nos 4, 15, 58, 60, 63, 65–67, 104, 132, 134, 137). But others are said, slightly more concretely, to own Lollard books (2–4, 11), to have designs against the cross at St Paul's (no. 5), to despise pilgrimages (nos 104, 130, 134, 137, 139), to believe in confession to God alone (no. 130), to doubt the importance of churchyard burial (nos 130, 139), to refuse adoration to images (no. 139). More troubles awaited persons from Braybrook, Leicestershire, who doubted the power of the pope. One was accused of being a prominent speaker against the pope and his powers, another of believing that there hasn't been a (real) pope since Clement ('quod nullus fuit papa a tempore sancti clementi pape vsque in hunc diem' – no. 141). Another not only complained about the pope, but had hard words for Archbishop Arundel as well, branding him secretly among the disciples of Antichrist and murderers of men ('discipulorum antechristi et murdratorum hominum' – no. 141).

41. PRO KB 27/611/(rex) mem. 7; here in consultation with *Select Cases*, p. 218.

42. St Giles outside Temple Bar (to distinguish it from St Giles Cripplegate, also outside the city walls and also, at that time, surrounded by fields) lay near the intersection of High Holborn and what was to become Oxford Street, though before New Oxford Street joined the two thoroughfares, near the base of present-day Tottenham Court Road. A village did exist along High Street and Broad Street St Giles, and it was

indeed surrounded by fields, and would indeed have provided a convenient meeting-place for persons arriving from Oxford, Bristol, and other locations in the north and west. However, seemingly gratuitously, a number of other early commentators substitute an alternative location, a half-mile to the south and east and a good deal closer to Temple Bar. This location is Fickett's field, west of Chanceler – now Chancery – Lane and near the site of St Clement's well, near the southern end of the present Lincoln's Inn Fields. Some early commentators, like Walsingham, stood firm with St Giles as the site of the rising ('in campum qui dicebatur "Sancti Egidii," prope Londonias' – *Ypodigma Neustriae*, Rolls Series, no. 28, pt. 7, p. 447). Others silently altered the record. Adam of Usk, nearly as early a reference as Walsingham, places the event at Fickett's field ('ad congregandum Fykettsfelde noctanter . . . ordinat campum' – Usk, p. 141). The relatively authoritative Thomas of Elmham wavers between the two locations (making St Giles into a prophesied site of the encounter in his *Liber Metricus*, in *Memorials of Henry V*, Rolls Series, no. 11, pp. 98–99) and opting in his *Vita et Gesta Henrici Quinti* for 'Fykettesfelde, non procul a Westmonasterio' (ed. Thomas Hearne [Oxford, 1727], p. 30). This confusion might be traced through many texts, most of which struggle in one way or another with its contradictions. For example, this attempt at rationalization from later in the century: 'The king . . . was warned of their fals purpos and ordenaunce, and took the feld that is callid Fiketts feld. . . . And many of thaym were take, and drawe and hanged and brent on the galowes in saint Giles feld' (*An

English Chronicle of the Reign of Richard II, Henry IV, Henry V, and Henry VI*, ed. J. S. Davies [Camden Society, series 1, vol. 64 (London, 1855)], p. 39). In the meantime we are left with a purported event, which even the most credulous commentators have some difficulty situating in a single, identifiable place.

43. Consider in this regard the retrospective analysis of a Benedictine preacher: 'The strength of this [Lollard] camp terrified many boldhearted men. . . . Unless the soldier of God, our liege lord that now is, had attacked and besieged it manfully, in human estimate it was most unlikely to have been conquered.' (Translation and Latin text in Patrick J. Horner, 'The King Taught Us the Lesson: Benedictine Support for Henry V's Suppression of the Lollards,' *Mediaeval Studies* 52 [1990], 213.) Here, the contradiction is partially managed by an emphasis on Henry's timing. Things *would* have been out of hand, had he not arrived at the precise moment when conquest was possible.

44. A standard claim against conspirators, since the stratagem was attempted by the rebellious earls in 1400.

45. The offer of this reward was repeated in 1417, the year of Oldcastle's ultimate capture, in Wales. Close Rolls for 4 March 1421 record the satisfaction of Oldcastle's takers with their settlement (*CCR*, 1419–22, p. 196). This version is based on *Ypodigma Neustriae*, Rolls Series no. 28, pt. 7, pp. 446–448; it is effectively identical to the version in *Historia Anglicana*, vol. 2, pp. 297–299.

46. *CCR*, 1413–19, pp. 106–107, etc.

47. Subsequent, circumstantial evidence places Oldcastle in the vicinity of London; on 4 October 1416 Lollard William Parchemener of Smithfield was

accused of having harbored Oldcastle between his escape from the Tower until 10 January, when he and Oldcastle were said to have joined the assembly in St Giles's Fields. See *Letter-Book I*, f. xliii; Riley, *Memorials of London Life*, p. 641.

48. *Foedera*, vol. 4, pt. 2, p. 61.

49. *RP*, vol. 4, pp. 107–108.

50. An honorable exception to the general credulousness with which this document has been accepted is: Luke Owen Pike, *A History of Crime in England*, vol. 1 (London: Smith, Elder, 1893), pp. 488–493.

51. To this excerpt may be compared the fuller original of the commission as contained in the king's letter patent (as published in PRO C66/393/mem. 30d *CPR*, 1413–16, p. 175). Unrepeated in the present indictment, but contained in the commission, is the phrase which constitutes it as an inquiry of unusual breadth: the Lollards are to be castigated and punished according to their demerits in this matter ('iuxta eorum demerita in hac parte castigari et puniri'). Without this phrase, and insisting on the intent to handle the case 'secundum legem et consuetudinem regni,' the judicial indictment has gained a more serene surface, concealing its own genesis in a grant of exceptional investigative and prosecutorial powers.

52. The content of the erasure can probably not be recovered. Andrew Prescott has examined it under ultraviolet light, and concludes that, although some traces of the original script remain, the erasure was sufficiently complete to render it illegible.

53. Even aside from the evidence of the erasure, hand, and ink, the status of this passage as insertion may be deduced on internal grounds; the 'dominus' of the insertion is a bad juncture, imply-ing but lacking space for 'Cobham.' Separating the words 'chiualer' and 'dominus' is the abbreviation ÷, yielding the possible sense, 'knight, that is, lord' – yet even this friendly and somewhat strained interpretation fails to establish a coherent juncture. Moreover, and more importantly, the remainder of the first-state text proceeds as if Oldcastle had not been named at all; his first mention is as an absent object of the rebels' designs, their choice as possible regent of the realm.

54. A formidable scholar of these documents, Maureen Jurkowski, has observed to me that this erasure and insertion were not necessarily a matter of conscious duplicity; that the original indictment might have been purpose-written for the arrest of felons already in custody – Acton and Blake – and that no indictment was needed for Oldcastle since he was still at large. By this reasoning, his name might have been properly and unashamedly added to this document of record at the time of his capture. Nevertheless, the effect of the document is not limited to persons already under arrest. To be sure, Blake and Acton were almost certainly in custody when the jurors presented; but the legal fiction of the indictment is that they were not yet necessarily taken (it notes conventionally that the sheriff should not fail in arresting them: 'non omitteret quin caperet eos').

55. *RP*, vol. 4, pp. 107–108 adds that the records particularly sought were those of Oldcastle's outlawry: 'les record & processe de l'utlagarie.'

56. As pointed out by Paul Brand, after the 1997 Matthews Lectures at Birkbeck College, in which some of these materials on John Oldcastle were included.

57. Pike, *History of Crime*, pp. 346–351.

58. The fairly slender thread connecting the fifteenth-century Oldcastle to his Shakespearean counterpart would seem to be a suggestion, developed by late-century chroniclers, that he and Henry had been close companions, and that he was repudiated when Henry assumed the throne. See, for example, Titus Livius, on 'Johannes Oldecastell (qui ante coronationem regis ab ipso propter has opiniones dimissus fuerat, & ab ejus famulatu penitus abjectus)' – in *Vita Henrici Quinti*, ed. Thomas Hearne (Oxford, 1716), p. 6.

59. As discussed in the cases of John Carsewell and Robert Rose, in Chapter 5.

60. Lacan, *Seminars*, pp. 270–283.

61. As discussed in Chapter 4, pp. 119–124.

62. See Jacques Derrida, *Specters of Marx* (New York and London: Routledge, 1994), esp. p. 161.

63. H. Ellis, *Original Letters*, second series (London, 1827), vol. 1, p. 59.

64. *Gesta*, pp. 2–11.

65. See, in this regard, Wylie, *Reign of Henry the Fifth*, vol. 1, p. 265, or Gairdner, who attempts to integrate this exorbitant detail into a rational explanatory scheme by suggesting that Henry 'was assisted by some flashes of lightning to discover the enemy' (*Lollardy and the Reformation in England*, vol. 1 [London: Macmillan, 1908], p. 81). In citing Gairdner's suggestion, I do not intend a gratuitous gibe at a distinguished historian's work. I wish, rather, to make two points: first about credulousness in the use of sources; second, about the misguided temptation to correct certain details in an account. I would compare Gairdner's interpretative effort to other, simpler instances like the scaling down of the 20,000 participants to 100 or 60, when the entire account itself is rather clearly concocted. In this case, it is the larger providential motive that would seem to govern the creation of details like the heavenly apparition, and it is to the larger motive, rather than to the correction of individual details, that interpretative attention should be directed. On the fallacy of seeking the true 'kernel' lodged at the heart of the exaggeration or myth, see Paul Veyne, *Did the Greeks Believe in their Myths? An Essay on the Constitutive Imagination* (Chicago: University of Chicago Press, 1988), pp. 1, 51.

66. *Gesta*, pp. 98–99.

67. Edward Powell finds that, of the total number of known indictments, only 58 of 242 were treated both as Lollards and as rebels (*Kingship, Law, and Society*, pp. 154–155).

68. PRO C54/263/9d (*CCR*, 1413–16, pp. 109–110). An analogous concern surfaces in the minutes of Henry IV's privy council when, in the period following the rebellion of the earls in January 1400, the council expressed its concern about the danger of unsupervised actions and reprisals, including improvisations 'sanz aucun processe de la loy' (*Privy Council*, p. 107).

69. PPO C66/393/mem.16; *CPR*, 1413–16, p. 162.

70. *Foedera*, vol. 4, pt. 2, pp. 72–73.

71. PRO Pardon Roll C67, nos 37, 49 (see J. A. F. Thomson, *The Later Lollards, 1414–1520* [Oxford: Oxford University Press, 1965], p. 12).

72. *Foedera*, vol. 4, pt. 2, pp. 72–73.

73. 'Misereri eligimus' – PRO C54/263/9d.

74. A subject not pursued here, but ably pursued elsewhere, is Henry V's monastic foundations at Syon and Sheen. Variously interpreted as celebratory gestures marking the Lollard defeat and as penitential gestures atoning for

the murder of Richard II, these benefactions were central to the Lancastrian fusion of the secular and religious spheres. For general introduction and bibliography see Jeremy Catto, 'Religious Change under Henry V,' in *Henry V: The Practice of Kingship*, ed. G. L. Harriss (1985; repr. Alan Sutton: Stroud, 1993), esp. pp. 109–111. Recent doctoral work by Rebecca Krug (now at Harvard University) and Nancy Warren (Indiana University) promises extensive new insight into these foundations and their context in political action.

75. Documents of the case, including the three confessions and pleas for mercy from the three conspirators, as well as indictments and other court records, have all been edited, and have been authoritatively analyzed with respect both to their contents and backgrounds, by T. B. Pugh. In distinction from Pugh's, my interest in the case is particular to this study, and concerns its standing and uses within the larger project of Lancastrian consolidation. For Pugh's analysis, and appendices including the conspirators' letters and the record of the treason trials in modern English, see *Henry V and the Southampton Plot of 1415* (Alan Sutton: Wolfboro Falls, New Hampshire, 1988). The originals are contained in British Museum MS. Cotton Vespasian, C.xiv, f. 39. Transcriptions of the letters are published as James Gairdner, *Report of the Deputy Keeper of the Public Records*, vol. 43, no. 5, pp. 579–594. The two separate letters of the earl of Cambridge are available in H. N. Nicolas, *History of the Battle of Agincourt* (1832; repr. London: Muller, 1970), pp. 19–20, and in *Original Letters*, pp. 45–49. Court records may be found in *RP*, vol. 4, pp. 64–67.

76. As argued by Gairdner, *Report*, p. 580.

77. Appendix to Nicolas, *Agincourt*, pp. 19–20.

78. For his successful 1414 petition see *RP*, vol. 4, p. 37; Gairdner, *Report*, prints the other documents bearing on restoration of Percy's lands, including a 27 July annuity to the duke of Bedford in compensation for lands to be returned to Henry Percy (*Report*, p. 581; see also *CPR*, 1413–16, p. 321.

79. *RP*, vol. 4, p. 212. For payment of a first installment of 2,000 pounds, see *CCR*, 1413–19, p. 240.

80. On garrisons, see Nicolas, *Agincourt*, p. 15.

81. See ibid., p. 17.

82. This sense of inevitable failure is inscribed in every detail of the conspiracy. Gray reads a letter from the earl of Cambridge (delivered by one Skranby) and then casts it in a *goung* or latrine. Gray and March's man Lucy agree that the earl of March (upon whom their prospects must rise and fall) is a timid and unambitious *hogge*. The idea of displaying a second-hand crown of Spain, on pawn from the Lancastrians, figures their inevitable infiltration at every point in this sorry adventure.

83. Compare Edmund Mortimer's 1402 letter to his tenants, announcing his decision to join with Glyndwr, with the object that 'si le Roy Richard soit en vie de luy restorer a sa coronne, et sinoun qe mon honore Neuewe [the earl of March] q'est droit heir al dit coronne serroit Roy d'Engleterre.' *Original Letters*, pp. 24–25.

84. J. H. Wylie, *History of England under Henry IV*, vol. 2 (London: Longmans, 1884), pp. 40–43.

85. Waurin: 'sans queres grans languages et sans jehynne les seigneurs dessusdis confesserent' (Rolls Series, no. 39, vol. 5, London, 1891, p. 179).

86. The participants themselves seem at something of a loss with respect to more particular descriptions of

motive. Gray specifies 'powert' or poverty and 'cofetice' or covetousness as his fatal spurs, and Pugh (*Henry V*, pp. 103–104) has demonstrated his chronic insolvency. Cambridge would seem to have some reason for contentment with King Henry, having been named earl as recently as May, 1414, though – as Pugh also establishes (ibid., pp. 97–99) – his was the only unlanded peerage in the realm. His situation as the earl of March's brother-in-law (coupled with his intention of declaring Henry V to be a usurper) might suggest sincere conviction about the validity of March's claims, although he finally trails off into lame protestations of 'stirring' and 'egging' by other folk. Scrope observes that the conspirators approached him on the supposition that because of the death of his uncle, Archbishop Scrope, he might favor the earl of March, but he seems rather unheated on the matter. The closest thing to an assignable motive in his case might be a misgiving about Henry's forthcoming invasion of France; Gray observes that he found it 'best to breke this viage if hit meghte be done' – though this is one of the moments at which Gray might be motivated by a desire to bring down his better-positioned co-conspirators.

87. Edward Halle, *The Union of the Two Noble Families of Lancaster and York* (1550; repr. London: Scholar Press, 1970), ff. xii–xiii.

88. *RP*, vol. 4, p. 62.

89. *Gesta*, p. 18.

90. *Historia Anglicana*, vol. 2, pp. 305–306.

91. Ibid., p. 306.

92. EETS, OS, vol. 124, no. 12 (London, 1904).

93. *RP*, vol. 4, p. 66. 'Lingua' is here employed in the sense of 'tongue' or 'language' and in the emergent sense of 'nationality' as well.

94. BL Harley MS. 565, f. 104.

95. *An English Chronicle of the Reigns of Richard II, Henry IV, Henry V, and Henry VI*, ed. J. S. Davies, Camden Society, series 1, vol. 64 (London, 1856), p. 40.

96. *Chronicle of England*, ed. F. C. Hingeston, Rolls Series, vol. 1 (London, 1858), p. 309.

97. Jean de Waurin, *Recueil des Croniques et Anchiennes Istories de la Grant Bretaigne*, ed. William Hardy, Rolls Series, no. 39. vol. 5, pp. 177–179; *Collection of the Chronicles and Ancient Histories of Great Britain*, ed. William Hardy, Rolls Series, no. 40, vol. 5, pp. 182–183.

98. Robert Redmann, *Vita Henrici Quinti, Memorials of Henry V*, ed. C. A. Cole, Rolls Series, no. 11 (London, 1858), p. 39.

99. *Chronique de Jean le Févre, seigneur de Saint-Remy*, ed. F. Morand (Paris: Société de l' Histoire de France, 1876), vol. 1, pp. 222–224.

100. And hence – as Annabel Patterson has observed of late medieval and early modern fabulation – inherently about power. *Fables of Power: Aesopian Writing and Political History* (Durham, NC: Duke University Press, 1991), esp. pp. 15–16. Although here, unlike Patterson's example, the fable is enlisted in support of, rather than in opposition to, established power relations.

101. Here quoting the translation of William Hardy, Rolls Series, no. 40, pt. 5 (London), pp. 182–183.

102. *Motif-Index*, vol. 5, p. 263. The *Index* lists numerous occurrences, including Halm, *Aesop*, nos 18, 326.

103. *Caxton's Aesop*, ed. R. T. Lenaghan (Cambridge, MA: Harvard University Press, 1967), bk. 5, table 9, p. 149.

104. Ibid., p. 172.

105. Accounts of how Henry came by his information vary. The most common explanation involves a spontaneous confession by the anxious earl of March – as when

the *Gesta* credits God with working 'through the Lord Mortimer, the earl of March, whose innocence they had assaulted as part of this murderous design' (p. 19). This supposition is borne out by Henry's prompt pardon exonerating March of any part in the scheme (Pugh, *Henry V*, p. 82). Other explanations involve a blaze of public opinion ('it was there publisshid and openli knowe' – Davies Chronicle, p. 40) and the discreet operations of informers ('regi nuntiatum est . . .' – Redmann, *Vita Henrici Quinti*, p. 38).

106. For records of Lancastrian counter-espionage, see Corporation of London, Plea and Memoranda Rolls, A25, mem. 8 and A27, mem. 16b.

107. Alan Sinfield and Allon White note a similar phenomenon in Holinshed and Shakespeare, in which the conspirators are motivated only by greed and incomprehensible evil, and in which 'such arbitrary and general "human" failings obscure the kind of instability in the ruling fraction to which the concurrent career of Essex bore witness.' See *Faultlines: Cultural Materialism and the Politics of Dissident Reading* (Oxford: Clarendon Press, 1992), p. 121.

108. *RP*, vol. 5, p. 377.

109. Ibid., pp. 463–464.

110. Ibid., p. 465.

111. Ibid., p. 375.

112. *Union of the Two Noble Families*, f. xiii.

4 Reburying Richard: Ceremony and Symbolic Relegitimation

1. Usk, p. 84.

2. 'forasmoche as some peple seyde that Sr. Henry Percy was alyve, he was taken up ayen out of his grave, and bounded upright betwen to mille stones, that alle men myghte se that he was ded' (*Chronicle of London* [London: Longman et al., 1827], p. 88). Percy's head was evidently also displayed upon London Bridge: 'And thanne sir Thomas Percy was Juged to the deeth. And he was drawe and hanged and his heed smyten of atte Showesbury. And his heed sente to London and there sette upon the Brigge' (*Great Chronicle of London*, ed. A. H. Thomas and I. D. Thornley [London: George Jones, 1938], p. 85).

3. J. Nichols, *A Collection of all the Wills . . . of the Kings and Queens of England*, 1780; repr. New York: Kraus, 1969, p. 203. The establishment of the shrine of Edward the Confessor at Westminster Abbey, followed by the creation of substantial monuments to Henry III and Edward III – not to mention the presence of Richard II's own tomb there – had established the Abbey as the precedential royal resting place, by the time that Henry IV made his decision to lie elsewhere. See *The History of the King's Works*, vol. 1, ed. R. Allen Brown *et al.* (London: Stationery Office, 1963), pp. 477–490. On the translation of Edward the Confessor, I am grateful to John C. Parsons for allowing me to consult his 'Rethinking English Coronations, 1216–1308,' unpublished manuscript. Parsons has observed to me in correspondence that the burial of the Black Prince at Canterbury, as well as other considerations such as the tradition of the Virgin's gift to Becket of the holy oil with which Henry IV had been anointed king, would have militated in favor of the latter site. Taking note of the impropriety of a Westminster burial for Henry, but also asserting the positive symbolism of Canterbury as the

site at which the holy oil was dis-covered, is Christopher Wilson, 'The Tomb of Henry IV and the Holy Oil of St Thomas of Can-terbury,' in *Medieval Architecture and its Intellectual Context*, ed. Eric Fernie and Paul Crossley (London: Hambledon Press, 1990), pp. 182–190.

4. Henry was ultimately to be associ-ated with another burial, almost as illustrious and equally fraught with symbolic importance. During his French campaign of 1420, upon capture of Montereau and the burial place of murdered Duke Jean sans Peur of Burgundy, Henry supervised his exhumation and burial with increased honor in the Charterhouse at Dijon. See Monstrelet, *Chronique*, 6 vols (Paris: Société de l'Histoire de France, 1857–62), vol. 3, p. 404.

5. Nichols, *Wills*, p. 194.

6. Froissart, *Oeuvres*, ed. De Lettenhove, vol. 16 (Brussels, 1872), p. 408. Such an occurrence could hardly have been possible, given the size and composition of the entourage accompanying his corpse (J. H. Wylie, *History of England under Henry the Fourth*, vol. 4 [London: Longmans, 1898], p. 113). But the idea was undeni-ably attractive to his French detractors, who challenged his legitimacy to the end.

7. *Archaeologia* 28 (1840), 87–95.

8. The pertinence of Freud's reflec-tions on the uncanny ('das Unheimliche') cannot be ignored, since they are taken for granted (although not explicitly explored) within the body of this chapter. Their applicability resides not just in the surface sense noted by Freud – that of a difficulty in dis-tinguishing between animate and inanimate, living and dead – but more ambitiously in his sugges-tion that the experience of the uncanny consists in the recur-rence of something repressed. The

repression in question results from a general societal experience of subterfuge and denial, rather than a singular experience of the individual psyche, although Lancastrian machination would have created the preconditions for recognition of Richard's 'un-canny' return among many of his former subjects. See Freud, 'The "Uncanny,"' *Standard Edition*, ed. J. Strachey (London: Hogarth Press, 1953–74), vol. 17, pp. 218–232.

9. Lacan, *Seminar*, pp. 243–287.

10. *Looking Awry* (Cambridge, MA: MIT Press, 1991), p. 22.

11. Kantorowicz, pp. 12–13, 59, etc. On the importance of the effigy, see pp. 419–437. On grounds not clear to me, Kantorowicz selects Edward II as his initial example, rather than, for instance, the earlier bronze effigy of Henry III by William Torel. Kantorowicz's political biography has recently come under scrutiny and the applicability of his theories under attack; for the former see the bizarre screed of Norman Cantor, 'The Nazi Twins,' in *Inventing the Middle Ages* (Cambridge: Lutterworth Press, 1991), pp. 79–117; for the latter see the much more reasoned discussion of David Norbrook, 'The Emperor's New Body?', *Textual Practice* 10 (1996), 329–357. Arguing that Kantorowicz's reading of Shakespeare's *Richard II* was 'rooted in a long tradition of counter-revolutionary discourse,' Norbrook suggests that 'Critics who have drawn heavily on Kantorowicz have therefore unwittingly inherited a set of assumptions which they might be reluctant to endorse explicitly.' Indeed, many elements of our language and gestural and signi-fying structures come trailing significations we might not be hasty to endorse. But Norbrook

seems to me over-hasty in his assumption about the obtuseness of those who have found Kantorowicz's formulation usefully descriptive of a medieval structuration. My own experience of *Richard II* discovers Richard at the mercy of his own illusions of transcendence, with the doctrine of the two bodies proving useful exactly in allowing a more precise description of the nature of that confused character's self-deception; whatever sentimental investments may lurk in the recesses of Kantorowicz's formulation, I must doubt Norbrook's suggestion that its broad adoption by subsequent medievalists is predicated on this element of ulterior and unspoken allure. A more useful critique of Kantorowicz is that of Claude Lefort, in *Democracy and Political Theory*, trans. David Macey (Cambridge: Polity Press, 1988). Lefort argues for the artificiality of Kantorowicz's separation of the theological and the political, the king's sublime and human bodies, finding his actual zone of inquiry to be 'the already politicized theological and the already theologized political' (p. 250). His suggestion that the king's sacrality rebounds upon and mystifies his human body bears an important explanatory relation to my inquiry, where the locus of the king's human remains continues as a subject of urgent importance, with continued bearing upon matters of succession. The proper interment of the body is required to put the spirit to rest, but the material body of the king acquires its own uncanny importance too; on the varying supplementary importance of the king's corporeal body see Elizabeth A. R. Brown, 'Burying and Unburying the Kings of France,' in *Persons in Groups*, ed. Richard C. Trexler (Binghamton,

New York: MRTS, 1985), pp. 241–266.

12. A royal tomb, bearing the arms of Richard II flanked by patron saints Edward the Confessor and Edmund Martyr and also the arms of Anne of Bohemia's father and the sons of Edward III, has been located at the Parish Church of All Saints, King's Langley. This tomb may, H. C. Baker speculates, have been begun for Richard prior to the commissioning of the Westminster tomb in 1394 and then turned to the use of Isabel of Castile. A barely possible alternative is that this was Richard's tomb at the Church of the Friars Preachers at Langley, subsequently turned to other use. It is by no means an ignoble tomb, though of lesser dignity than the memorial for Richard and Anne commissioned for Westminster. See Baker, 'The Royal Tomb at King's Langley,' *Transactions of the Monumental Brass Society* 2 (1969–74), 279–283.

13. Material and symbolic initiatives cannot finally be distinguished at any level of analysis. Consider, for example, the Welsh volunteers who were said by the *Eulogium* continuator to have joined Henry Percy at the battle of Shrewsbury, three years after Richard's well-documented death, wearing Ricardian badges of the white hart. No analysis can disaggregate the practical self-interest and obstinate belief and wild surmise which brought them to this bloody battle in such redundant array. See *Continuatio Eulogii*, p. 396. The issue of Richard's improper burial was most obviously engaged at the symbolic level, through pageantry and written commentary and judicial process, but it was simultaneously a material matter, involving expenditure and bodily punishment and military muster.

14. Thus Derrida, in his discussion of

Hamlet's father, suggests that the ghost and its beholder are conspirators in a complex feat of conjuration, the ghost posing its demand and the beholder embracing the ghost in reciprocal desire. Jacques Derrida, *Specters of Marx* (New York and London: Routledge, 1994), pp. 24, 28–29.

15. In this respect see Ian Duncan, 'The Upright Corpse: Hogg, National Literature and the Uncanny,' *Studies in Hogg and his World* 5 (1994): 'Spectral persistence ... unsettles that linear, developmental unfolding which constitutes the progressive chronology of modern history' (p. 35).

16. Even the staunchly pro-Lancastrian Adam of Usk says that Henry's lieutenant Swinford starved Richard to death at Pontefract (Usk, p. 90). See E. M. Thompson's very full note on this matter, *Chronicon Adae de Usk*, 2nd edn (London: Frowde, 1904), pp. 199–200. The belief that Henry IV's murder of Richard had effectively negated his right to the throne surfaces, among other places, in the words of the intransigent Leicester friar who boldly told Henry that 'If he is dead, he is dead by your hand. And if he is dead through you, you have lost your title, and every right to the throne' ('Si mortuus est, per vos mortuus est. Et si per vos mortuus est, perdidistis titulum, et omne jus quod habere potestis ad regnum' – *Continuatio Eulogii*, p. 392).

17. British Library Cotton MS. Cleopatra F. iii, f. 9b (now 14b). This transcription may be compared with the much freer rendering of N. H. Nicolas, *Privy Council*, pp. 107, 111–112.

18. According to Walsingham (*Historia Anglicana*, vol. 2, p. 245). The traditional date of 14 February for St Valentine's Day coincides well, but perhaps a bit belatedly, with the first entry in the Issues of the Exchequer pertaining to the death of Richard: in 17 February 1400 Thomas Tuttebury, a clerk associated with the Royal Wardrobe, was granted 100 marks for expenses incurred for the transportation of Richard's body from Pontefract to London (Issues of the Exchequer: PRO E403/564).

19. According to Thomas Walsingham, '... [corpus] monstratum est post Officium Mortuorum, et in crastino post Missam peractam. Cumque in ecclesia Sancti Pauli Londoniis celebratae fuissent exequiae, Rege praesente et Londoniarum civibus.' See *Historia Anglicana*, vol. 2, p. 246. See also F. Devon, *Issues of the Exchequer* (London, 1837), p. 275.

20. So generously was Richard displayed that Lancastrian commentators and ideologues would continue to express dismay that his death could be a subject of any doubt. A 1413 jury of the King's Bench would, for example, recall that, in spite of rumors to the contrary, Richard had been long dead and was seen dead by thousands of thousands of citizens of London and elsewhere in the realm ('et sic mortuus visus fuit per millia millium infra ciuitatem London' et alibi infra regnum Anglie' – *Select Cases*, p. 212).

21. On Richard's will, including detailed provisions and commissions for Anne's and his burial, see Nichols, *Wills*, pp. 191–196. On the tomb itself, designed by Yevele and Lote with effigies by coppersmiths Broker and Prest, see Brown, *History of the King's Works*, vol. 1, pp. 487–488.

22. *RP*, vol. 3, pp. 415–427.

23. *Historia Anglicana*, vol. 2, p. 246.

24. One set of annual expenses for such observances, for 1406–7, still exists as Westminster Archives

MS. 23986b. It records such items as 'p[ro] pulsacione campanarum' and 'pro illuminatione cereorum circa tumbam' and 'distribut[io] pauperibus.' Foundational grants by Richard survive as MSS. 5257A and 5258A. For a puzzling item of 8 November 1413 in which Henry V orders payment to the prior and convent of Christ Church, Canterbury, for observances at Richard's tomb in Westminster, apparently by order of his father, recently entombed there ('de ordinacione domini Regis iam raro tumulatur') see PRO E403/614, and Devon, *Issues of the Exchequer*, p. 325.

25. Certainly, Henry had made every effort to effect the symbolic capture of Richard's kingly essence, including elaborate ceremonies of deposition and election, bogus narratives of Richard's voluntary resignation ('with glad countenance') and initiative in placing his signet on Henry's finger, and a coronation ritual considerably expanded to emphasize Henry's own anointment and sacred unction. (For a discussion of these matters see my 'Saving the Appearances,' in *Hochon's Arrow* [Princeton: Princeton University Press, 1992], pp. 75–94.) But Richard may have understood better than Henry the senses in which the transcendent properties of kingship might elude forcible appropriation. Richard seems to have suggested at one point that Henry assume guidance of the realm but that Richard retain the distinctive, sacral qualities conferred upon him by divine unction ('noluit nec intendebat renunciare carecteribus anime sue impressis a sacra unccione' – BL Stowe MS 66, cited in *Hochon's Arrow*, p. 81). In addition to considerations of self-interest, Richard would seem to have understood that the kingly aura is

not so easily transferable, but is more securely inherited by orderly succession at the time of the rightful king's death.

26. *Archaeologia* 20 (1837), 213. For his death in 1400 see *Historia Anglicana*, vol. 2, p. 245.

27. The dimensions of the rumor have recently and very capably been surveyed by Peter McNiven, 'Rebellion, Sedition, and the Legend of Richard II's Survival in the Reigns of Henry IV and Henry V,' *Bulletin of the John Rylands Library* 76 (1994), 93–117. McNiven suggests that the phenomenon served as a kind of half-way house for protest movements of all kinds, 'a rallying cry in successive and otherwise uncoordinated gestures of protest, directed against a particular king or against authority in general, but not necessarily carrying sufficient conviction, in the absence of a viable alternative, to pose serious threats to the occupant of the throne' (p. 117). McNiven here catches very nicely what I will describe as the 'hypothetical' status of remarks on Richard's availability and status, but with somewhat more emphasis upon the rational or calculable dimensions of the belief in a living Richard. The same material has also concurrently been assessed by Philip Morgan, 'Henry IV and the Shadow of Richard II,' in *Crown, Government and People in the Fifteenth Century*, ed. Rowena E. Archer (New York: St Martin's Press, 1995), pp. 1–31. Working separately from McNiven, but in close agreement with his conclusions, Morgan argues for a tradition of 'loyalist rebellion,' making pragmatic use of a living Richard as a 'legitimizing framework . . . for redress of grievance . . . or for a programme of religious or political change' (p. 11), a framework which did not necessarily

28. *Foedera*, vol. 4, pt. 1, p. 27.

29. Ibid., p. 29.

30. 27 June 1402 payment for the messengers and their expenses is recorded in the Issue Rolls (Devon, *Issues of the Exchequer*, p. 286).

31. This observation is made upon the death of the pro-Ricardian Serle, and expresses the premature hope that such rumors are now at an end. *Annales Henrici*, p. 391.

32. De Lettenhove cites expenditures from the *Rotuli computorum Scotiae* for the support of 'Richardum regem Angliae' for 1408, 1414, 1415, and 1417, and a notation of his death in 1419. This was undoubtedly the 'Thomas Ward of Trumpington,' who played the part of Richard in Scotland for twelve years, and probably longer, until his death in 1419 (Froissart, *Oeuvres*, vol. 17, pp. 407–408).

33. *Historia Anglicana*, vol. 2, pp. 262–263; see also *Select Cases*, pp. 151–155.

34. Usk, p. 94.

35. Rumor theorist Edgar Morin suggests that the most powerful support for a rumor rests with face-to-face testimony of trusted persons: 'The rumor's remarkable powers of self-perpetuation derive from the fact that what people trusted was not so much the information *per se*, but rather *the person* who passed it on, because he was known (a good friend or acquaintance on whose 'word of honour' one automatically relied)' (*Rumour in Orleans* [London: Anthony Blond, 1971], p. 227). The proliferation of such personal testimonies baffled contemporary commentators; the author of a canceled passage in the St Albans Chronicle reports with apparent surprise that the promulgators of such tidings deceived many persons, who listened patiently to them and received them into their homes ('pacienter audierant vel receperant in domos suas'). See *St Albans Chronicle, 1406–1420*, ed. V. H. Galbraith (Oxford: Clarendon Press, 1937), p. 135.

36. *Select Cases*, pp. 126–127.

37. Bernard's trust had its limits. Richard having failed to appear, and these confederates arrested for treason, Bernard turned approver, defeated Balsshalf in combat, and received a royal pardon. *Foedera*, vol. 4, pt. 1, p. 30. Sayles cites other, similar confessions in the same roll, *Select Cases*, p. 127.

38. Derrida, *Specters of Marx*, pp. 24, 28–29.

39. '... venerunt omnes in Litchfeld' insignati signis Regis Ricardi, videlicet, cervis. Et fecit ibi Henricus proclamari, dicens quod ipse fuit unus de illis qui maxime agebat ad expulsionem Regis Ricardi et introductionem Henrici, credens se bene fecisse. Et quia nunc cognovit quod pejus regit Henricus quam Ricardus ideo intendit corrigere errorem suum' (*Continuatio Eulogii*, p. 396).

40. *City, Marriage, Tournament: Arts of Rule in Late Medieval Scotland* (Madison: University of Wisconsin Press, 1991), pp. 70–71.

41. *Archaeologia* 28 (1840), 87–95.

42. In a certain sense we may say that Creton's letter, although composed two years after Richard's death, indeed arrived at its destination. For, as Žižek says of the message in a bottle thrown into the water without an addressee, 'its true addressee is namely not the empirical other which may receive it or not, but ... the symbolic order itself, which receives it *the moment the letter is put into circulation*' (Slavoj Žižek, *Enjoy Your Symptom!* [New York and London: Routledge, 1992], p. 10).

43. *Continuatio Eulogii*, p. 389.
44. Ibid., p. 391. This is likewise the position of his fellow, also condemned to death, who, asked what he would do with Henry if Henry were in his power, replied 'I would make you the Duke of Lancaster' ('Et Rex: "Quid faceres mecum si super me haberes victoriam?" Cui frater: "Facerem vos ducem Lancastriae"' – p. 390). The point of each would appear to be that Henry, despite his pretensions, has no just claim to kingly *dignitas*, but remains the duke that he was; that if he lives Richard yet possesses the *dignitas*, and that if he does not live his *dignitas* remains at large, unsecured by Henry and still as much Richard's as anyone's.
45. *Original Letters*, pp. 24–25.
46. Ibid., p. 45 (corrected).
47. *Historia Anglicana*, vol. 2, p. 264.
48. The effect of their behavior is, in Lacanian terms, the concealment of an 'impossible kernel' or an insupportable social 'antagonism' – in this case, presumably, the secularity and appropriability of kingship, the unthinkable extent to which kingship is coextensive with the enjoyment and exercise of secular power (Slavoj Žižek, *The Sublime Object of Ideology* [London: Verso, 1989] pp. 28–47).
49. 'In communi audientia omnium dominorum et communitatis Rex comitem Marchiae heredem fore proximum ad coronam Angliae post ipsum publice fecerat proclamari' (*Continuatio Eulogii*, p. 361).
50. *Select Cases*, pp. 123–124.
51. *Original Letters*, p. 25.
52. Summarized by T. B. Pugh, *Henry V and the Southampton Plot of 1415* (The Southampton Record Series, 1988), p. 78.
53. *Original Letters*, p. 45.
54. *CPR*, 1401–5, p. 108; on arrangements after 1405 see *CPR*, 1405–8, p. 276.

55. *CPR*, 1405–8, p. 408.
56. *CPR*, 1408–13, p. 149.
57. Beginning with the first year of his reign, Henry V maintained regular payments to Queen Joanne, for those marriage rights that Henry had previously 'bargained' from her when he was Prince of Wales: in part payment of the larger sum 'dicte Regine debitur de certis secretis convencionibus inter ipsam Reginam & dominum nostrum Regem nunc confectis & tangentibus in speciali maritagio comiti March de dicta Regina empto & barganizato per dictum dominum Regem nunc dum erat Princeps Wall' (PRO E403/614). See also Devon, *Issues of the Exchequer*, pp. 324–325, 329.
58. *CPR*, 1413–16, p. 45; *CCR*, 1413–19, p. 20.
59. *RP*, vol. 4, p. 212. For a first installment of 2,000 pounds, see *CCR*, 1413–19, p. 240.
60. *CPR*, 1313–1416, p. 349.
61. *Henry V and the Southampton Plot*, p. 82.
62. Appendix I to the 43rd Report of the Deputy Keeper of the Records, *British Sessional Papers, House of Commons* 36 (1882), 584.
63. Commenting on Serle's confession and very public death, the *Eulogium* continuator rather sourly comments that the rumors of Richard's survival did not end: '...tamen adhuc non quievit rumor ille de vita ejus' (p. 403). Among the continuing rumors, see Walsingham's account of a 1407 campaign well furnished in written materials: 'Eo tempore fixae sunt scedulae multis in locis Londoniis, quibus continebatur quod Rex Ricardus viveret...' (*Historia Anglicana*, vol. 2, p. 276).
64. *Select Cases*, p. 213.
65. *Historia Anglicana*, vol. 2, p. 297.
66. British Library Cotton MS. Claudius A. viii, f. 7.
67. *Chronicle of London* suggests that

the formal decision was made by king and council on 4 December (p. 96), although certain expenditures precede that date.

68. All expenditures from PRO Issue Rolls, E403/614.

69. PRO E403/564 (20 March 1400).

70. Nichols, *Wills*, p. 193.

71. PRO E403/614; Devon, *Issues of the Exchequer*, p. 327.

72. *A Chronicle of the Reigns of Richard II, Henry IV, Henry V, and Henry VI*, Camden Society, vol. 64 (London, 1855), p. 39.

73. British Library Cotton MS. Claudius A. viii, f. 17.

74. Fredric Jameson, 'Marx's Purloined Letter,' *New Left Review* 209 (1995), 103.

75. Basing his hopes on fictitious accounts of Richard's voluntary resignation and on his own elaborate coronation rituals, Henry sought to strip Richard not only of the natural but also of the sacral elements of kingship – though with only partial success. Consider, for example, the 1402 retort of the Leicester friar to Henry's claims of election, note 16 above.

76. 'The Ceremonial of Royal Succession in Capetian France: The Double Funeral of Louis X,' *Traditio* 34 (1978), 227–271. A second funeral is, of course, less ceremonially ambitious than a second burial. The model for the latter is the translation of the remains of a saint or a king, as in the relocations of Edward the Confessor in Westminster or King Arthur in Glastonbury; see, in these cases, Parsons, 'Rethinking English Coronations.'

77. *Vita et Gesta Henrici Quinti*, ed. Thomas Hearne (Oxford, 1727), p. 5. See also Froissart, *Oeuvres*, vol. 20, p. 87, and Titus Livius, as translated in *The First English Life of King Henry the Fifth*, ed. C. L. Kingsford (Oxford: Clarendon Press, 1911), p. 8.

78. Henry V may indeed have had little love for his late father; though partially obscured, the Rolls of Parliament and other sources disclose publicly contentious relations between Henry and his father during the last years of the latter's life. See Peter McNiven, 'Prince Henry and the English Political Crisis of 1412,' *History* 65 (1980), 1–16. McNiven suggests that Henry might have had some basis for believing that his father intended to 'disturb the line of succession' by naming his second son Thomas as his heir (p. 13). See also Christopher Allmand, *Henry V* (Berkeley: University of California Press, 1992), pp. 50–58. The bottom line would seem to be that his carnal tie (whatever its quality) was an embarrassment to the firmer succession claims the new king had become interested in mounting, at the level of symbolic attachment.

79. My thanks to Linda Charnes for challenging me to consider the operations of transference in this situation; initially reluctant to generalize an aspect of the therapist–client relation to this historical situation, I have become increasingly convinced that the process of transference (and, especially, its potential rejection or refusal by Lollards and other stubborn subjects) is indeed relevant here. The crucial aspect, for me, is the element of misrecognition upon which transference depends; a refusal to transfer allegiance to a usurping king is, in effect, a refusal to misrecognize the legitimacy of the usurper's claims.

80. Readers of Lacan and Žižek will recognize the sources of my terminology here, especially in the latter's essay on 'Why Are There Always Two Fathers?' (in *Enjoy Your Symptom!*, esp. pp. 158–160). He observes that the excessively

present father – in this case, Henry IV, who made himself present for his son in more ways than his son would have chosen – 'cannot be reduced to the bearer of a symbolic function' (p. 158), a role for which Richard II was better suited both by secure entombment and impeccable and guiltless title to the throne. Entombed Richard is, in Žžek's terms, a 'father living up to his symbolic function,' and thus rendering possible 'a viable, temperate relation with a woman' (p. 160). To the years after Richard's reinterment may be assigned Henry V's successes in France, recognition as fully legitimate king of England and France, and dynastically advantageous marriage.

81. Here see McNiven, 'Rebellion,' and Morgan, 'Henry IV and the Shadow of Richard II' for more complete documentation.

82. *Letter-Book I*, fl. clxxxi, recto (*CLBI*, p. 164).

83. *Journal*, Proceedings of the Court of Common Council, 1 (1416) Corporation of London, 83b.

84. *Select Cases*, pp. 248–253.

85. The authoritative survey of this linkage is by Margaret Aston, in 'Lollardy and Sedition,' *Past and Present* 17 (1960), 1–44.

86. Also encouraging to this convergence was the external climate of opinion, in which Innocent III and other pan-European figures were responsible for the emergent doctrine that the heretic is the ultimate traitor. For this linkage in Innocent, see *PL*, vol. 214, p. 539.

87. *RP*, vol. 3, pp. 583–584.

88. *Select Cases*, pp. 237–239.

89. Talbot's cryptic line of defense appears to have excited the concern of king and council. Issue Rolls of 5 Henry V suggest that the king sent William Scalby, a clerk of the King's Bench, to York to spy out matters connected with

the Talbot case ('pro commodo Regis explorandis'), and that Thomas Horneby, 'explorator regis,' was appointed to handle travel arrangements and all expenses for the jury coming from York for the trial (PRO Issue Rolls, E403/630, 21 April 1417). Certainly, the justices were more than compliant; they consulted Henry V in person to learn his wishes, and his wish is evidently reflected in the final verdict, which was that Henry Talbot should be drawn, hanged, cut down while alive, beheaded, his body divided into four additional quarters, and the pieces sent for display to whatever parts of England should please the king and his council. Talbot's putative Lollardy receives confirmation from his mention among those prominent members of the sect refused pardon at the St Giles rising, in a proclamation of 28 March 1414 (*Foedera*, vol. 4, pt. 2, pp. 72–73).

90. PRO KB 27/624/rex mem. 9a. Lucas was found not guilty and released, but the link between pro-Ricardian activities and Oldcastle – and the link between heresy and sedition in Oldcastle's own activities – may be considered significant.

91. *Historia Anglicana*, vol. 2, p. 328. See also Elmham, *Liber Metricus de Henrico Quinti*, in *Memorials of Henry V*, ed. C. A. Cole, Rolls Series, no. 11 (London 1858), p. 158:

Regem Ricardum fore
    viventem simulavit,
Ut sua fictitia fortior inde foret.

92. The mid-fifteenth-century Phillips manuscript introduces the poem as 'faite tost apres que les osses du Roy Richard feuerent apportez a Westmouster,' and the contents of the poem would seem to confirm this claim. See *Hoccleve's Works:*

I, *The Minor Poems*, ed. F. J. Furnivall, EETS, ES 61 (London, 1892), pp.47–48.

93. Hoccleve similarly elides Henry IV in the *Regement of Princes*, creating an ideal progression from Edward III to John of Gaunt to the future Henry V, with only incidental mention of Henry IV and one veiled and neutral allusion to Richard II (ed. F. J. Furnivall, EETS, ES, no. 61, pt. 3 [London, 1897]).

94. Elmham, *Liber Metricus*, p. 158.

95. In accordance with a tradition already established in the case of William Sautre, Oldcastle is said to have babbled incoherently from the gallows about such matters as his projected resurrection on the third day. I would suggest that his reference to Richard participates in the same tradition, in which condemned heretics and others are allowed to incriminate themselves by the self-evident idiocy of their views. On Sautre, see Usk, p. 122; on Oldcastle, see *Historia Anglicana*, vol. 2, pp. 328.

96. *Gesta*, p. 9.

97. A point made incisively (though via different argumentative routes) by McNiven, 'Rebellion,' p. 17 and Morgan, 'Henry IV and the Shadow of Richard II,' pp. 25–26.

98. British Library MS. Royal 15 E. vi, f. 3. See the acute discussion of Lee Patterson, 'Making Identities: Henry V and Lydgate,' in *New Historical Literary Study*, ed. Jeffrey N. Cox and Larry J. Reynolds (Princeton: Princeton University Press, 1993), pp. 69–107. Relevant observations are also to be found in J. W. McKenna, 'Henry VI of England and the Dual Monarchy: Aspects of Royal Political Propaganda,' *Journal of the Warburg and Courtauld Institutes* 28 (1965), 145–162.

99. Jameson comments in 'Marx's Purloined Letter' that 'To forget the dead altogether is impious in ways that prepare their own retribution' (p. 103).

100. *RP*, vol. 5, pp. 463–464.

5 Counterfeiters, Lollards, and Lancastrian Unease

1. Printed in *Select Cases*, pp. 244–246.

2. On approvership, what was expected of an approver, and the doubtful prospects it afforded, see Frederick C. Hamil, 'The King's Approvers: A Chapter in the History of English Criminal Law,' *Speculum* 11 (1936), 238–258.

3. Barbara Harvey explains that the 'misericord' functioned in the late-medieval English monastery as a dining room for irregular meals (and especially meals involving consumption of meat) as opposed to the refectory in which regular (and more ordinary) meals were consumed. See *Living and Dying in England, 1100–1540: The Monastic Experience* (Oxford: Clarendon Press, 1993), p. 40.

4. See J. A. F. Thomson's discussion (*The Later Lollards, 1414–1520* [Oxford: Oxford University Press, 1965], pp. 13–14), in which he notes that Carsewell was found guilty of a false appeal against the prior, that the cellarer incurred a charge of outlawry, and that Carsewell 'who was clearly making desperate attempts to save his skin, also laid an appeal against the sub-seneschal of the prior of Leominster, for not acting on information he had given him about Oldcastle'.

5. *CPR*, 1416–22, p. 83. This proclamation was made in English; see *A Book of London English, 1384–1425*, ed. R. W. Chambers and M. Daunt (Oxford: Clarendon Press, 1931), p. 287.

6. F. Devon, *Issues of the Exchequer* (London, 1837), p. 353. Carsewell told his story in April 1417 at the zenith of revived interest in Oldcastle. In the last days of November, Oldcastle was finally captured in the marches of Wales, whence he was speedily brought by a 'posse' of men for sentencing in London and put to death in the month of December (*CPR*, 1416–22, p. 145).

7. I am speaking here of a doubled sense in which Ireland and Wales were understood as sources of treasonous trouble: English attempts at invasion and domination had, of course, the effect of constructing these territories as sites of resolute opposition (just as, more figuratively, orthodox definition of Lollardy as a dangerous heresy had the effect of constructing an armed Lollard opposition), even as, once subject to rebellious construction, these territories and people naturally enough became unruly in their own defense. Thus, the unsubdued portions of Ireland and Wales, and the ranks of persecuted Lollards, remained the crucial imaginative *and* tangible sites in which rebellious activity might be formed and from which it might be launched.

8. *RP*, vol. 3, p. 567.

9. Capgrave, *Chronicle of England*, ed. F. C. Hingeston, Rolls Series, no. 1 (London, 1858), p. 259.

10. *Historia Anglicana*, vol. 2, p. 250.

11. Ibid., pp. 250–251.

12. Capgrave, *Chronicle* p. 258; *RP*, vol. 4, pp. 16, 190.

13. Dr Brendan Smith of Bristol University has helpfully observed to me that Castle Trim retained a Mortimer, and hence Yorkist and insurrectionary, implication before, during, and after the years 1417–19.

14. Harlech may have possessed added symbolic prestige as the site of a Welsh parliament convoked by Glyndwr in 1405. At any rate, so reported the king's steward John Stanley in an intelligence report sent from Cheshire in that year. See R. R. Davies, *The Revolt of Owain Glyn Dŵr* (Oxford: Oxford University Press, 1995), pp. 163–164.

15. The accusation is summarized in *RP*, vol. 4, p. 65.

16. R. R. Davies points out that, although Glyndwr had died in 1415, his son was offered a pardon by the English in 1417 and did not accept it (bringing a formal end to hostilities) until 1421. See *The Age of Conquest* (Oxford: Oxford University Press Paperbacks, 1987), p. 457.

17. These observations on Cluniac Wenlock are indebted to David Knowles, *The Religious Orders in England*, vol. 2 (Cambridge: Cambridge University Press, 1955), pp. 157–164.

18. *RP*, vol. 4, p. 22.

19. Knowles, *Religious Orders*, p. 160.

20. Ibid., p. 161.

21. *Statutes of the Realm* (London, 1763), vol. 1, p. 320. On the prominence of counterfeiting in medieval definitions of treason see J. G. Bellamy, *The Law of Treason in England in the Later Middle Ages* (Cambridge: Cambridge University Press, 1970), pp. 8, 15, *et passim*. The linking of coin and seal as objects of counterfeit is, of course, indicative; both are seen as extensions of the king's authority. Bearing his physical image and secured by his position and majesty, the coin and seal of the realm are themselves expected to be *loial* in the sense of 'true,' and to secure and command loyalty and fidelity among the king's subjects. The effect of the parliamentary actions and statutes relating to the debasement and fabrication of coin is to secure a particular status for the counterfeit as *disloyal*, as

opposed to legitimacy as defined and embodied by the king.

22. Richard G. Doty, *The Macmillan Encyclopedic Dictionary of Numismatics* (New York and London: Macmillan, 1982), pp. 154–155.

23. Both doctrines are very much in evidence in the treatment of John Badby in 1410. See McNiven, pp. 79–92.

24. *Foedera*, vol. 4, pt. 2, p. 61. The perceived fusion of treason and heresy in Oldcastle's activities is illustrated by his carefully orchestrated execution, as described by Walsingham and numerous other sources: he was sentenced to be drawn and hanged from a gallows (the punishment for treason), and to be burnt even as he hung there (the punishment for heresy).

25. *RP*, vol. 4, p. 15.

26. *Torture and Truth* (London: Routledge, 1991).

27. Jean Gerson, in *Oeuvres Complètes*, vol. 3 (Paris: Deselée, 1962), p. 38. I am grateful to Dyan Elliott for directing my attention to this treatise.

28. *Gesta*, p. 3.

29. 'To Sir John Oldcastle,' in *Works*, vol. 1: *The Minor Poems*, ed. F. J. Furnivall, EETS, ES, 71 (London, 1892), ll. 10, 17, 32.

30. Cotton MS. Claudius A. ii, associated with Myrc's Festial. Published in *Instructions for Parish Priests*, ed. Edward Peacock, EETS, OS no. 31, London, 1902, p. 65. I am grateful to Andrew Cole, currently completing his doctoral work in English at Duke University, for suggesting this passage to me after I presented a preliminary version of this chapter in October 1996. Also derived from our conversation is my later reference to the sermon of Ms. Royal 18 B, in note 42.

31. As suggested by the native term of 'Whitsunday' based on the white garments worn by those baptized during the vigil.

32. Frederick Brittain, *Latin Verse* (Harmondsworth: Penguin, 1962), pp. 146–147.

33. See Etienne Gilson, 'La Grâce et le Saint Graal,' in *Les Idées et les lettres* (Paris: Vrin, 1932), pp. 59–91.

34. The symbolic density of the host is explored and richly documented by Miri Rubin, *Corpus Christi: The Eucharist in Late Medieval Culture* (Cambridge: Cambridge University Press, 1990).

35. *Money, Language, and Thought* (1982; Baltimore: Johns Hopkins University Press, 1993), pp. 24–46.

36. Ibid., esp. pp. 41–44.

37. See R. H. Britnell, *The Commercialisation of English Society 1000–1500* (Cambridge: Cambridge University Press, 1993), pp. 179–185. On the general subject of shortage and coin-clipping in the first decades of the fifteenth century, see T. F. Reddaway, 'The King's Mint and Exchange in London 1343–1543,' *EHR* 82 (1967), esp. 13–14. Carsewell's invention occurs in the midst of what Edward Powell has described as 'an epidemic of counterfeiting coin which swept the country from 1415 onwards' ('The Restoration of Law and Order,' in *Henry V: The Practice of Kingship* [Oxford: Oxford University Press, 1985], p. 73).

38. *Cursor Mundi*, ed. R. Morris, EETS, OS, vols 62, 66 (London, 1876–1877), pp. 1092, 1101–1103, 1121.

39. *Concilia*, p. 260.

40. The most exhaustive contemporary statement of the orthodox position is contained in Dymmok, pt. 4, esp. p. 96. So widespread was the Aristotelian vocabulary of subject and accident that even a relatively popular chronicle account, like the *Eulogium* continuation, which does not even repeat Sawtry's name, knows his offense: 'In this parliament the archbishop of Canterbury degraded a certain heretic, [for]

denying the possibility of accident without a subject in the sacrament of the altar [and for saying that] bread remains bread; he was [later] burned at Smithfield.' See *Continuatio Eulogii*, p. 388.

41. On these points see *Historia Anglicana*, vol. 2, pp. 295, 326.

42. *Middle English Sermons*, ed. Woodburn O. Ross, EETS, OS, no. 209 (London, 1940) p. 127. This sermon is from MS. Royal 18 B, xxiii.

43. *Given Time: Counterfeit Money* (Chicago: University of Chicago Press, 1992), p. 1n.

44. *Continuatio Eulogii*, pp. 369–370.

45. See Strohm, *Hochon's Arrow* (Princeton: Princeton University Press, 1992), pp. 84–85.

46. Dymmok, pt. 6, pp. 129–131.

47. *Concilia*, pp. 255–256.

48. In her forthcoming book, *Imaginary Publics: Extraclergial Writers and Vernacular Audience in Late-Medieval England*, Fiona Somerset notes the stylized nature of this dialogue, nevertheless finding it valuable as an indication of a possible perspective on Henry's claim: 'The reporting of the disputes as dialogues is of course a stylistic device for presenting opposed views: but they are valuable precisely as a digest of those opposed views from a fraternal perspective.'

49. *Historia Anglicana*, vol. 2, p. 390.

50. British Library Cotton MS. Cleopatra F. iii, f. 112 (now: 145).

51. *Historia Anglicana*, vol. 2, p. 328.

52. I borrow this phrase from Franco Moretti, *Signs Taken for Wonders* (London: Verso, 1983), p. 33.

53. See Alan S. Ambrisco and Paul Strohm, 'Succession and Sovereignty in Lydgate's Prologue to the *Troy Book*,' *Chaucer Review* 30 (1995), 40–57.

54. *Hoccleve's Works: – I The Minor Poems*, ed. F. J. Furnivall, EETS, ES, no. 61 (London, 1892), 'Complaint,' ll. 211–212.

55. John Burrow, the most acute of Hoccleve's explicators over the years, says of the 'Dialogue' that 'The main blemish – and it is a serious one – is the passage in which the poet harangues his friend on the evils of tampering with coin of the realm.' See 'Hoccleve's *Series*,' in *Fifteenth-Century Studies*, ed. Robert Yeager (Hamden, CT: Archon Books, 1984), p. 263.

56. An emphasis elegantly illustrated in Antony J. Hasler, 'Hoccleve's Unregimented Body,' *Paragraph* 13 (1990), 164–183.

57. *RP*, vol. 4, pp. 154–155.

58. See Strohm, *Hochon's Arrow*, pp. 57–74, 179–185.

59. *Statutes of the Realm*, ed. Basket (London: Dawsons, 1816), p. 126.

60. *Foedera*, vol. 4, pt. 2, p. 44.

61. *The Regement of Princes*, ed. F. J. Furnivall, EETS, Extra Series, no. 72, [no. 61, pt. 3] 72 (London, 1897), l. 301.

62. Ibid., ll. 281–329.

63. See the insightful discussion of Chaucer's image in Derek Pearsall, 'Hoccleve's *Regement of Princes*: the Poetics of Royal Self-Representation', *Speculum* 69 (1994), 386–410.

64. Shoaf observes that the mutability of the sign is the concern of poets as well as forgers, and that 'with the mutability of the sign we enter the arena of the poet's agon' – since 'the poet, as wielder of signs, must always struggle with their indeterminacy' – *Dante, Chaucer and the Currency of the Word* (Norman, OK: Pilgrim Books, 1983), p. 32; see also pp. 211–227.

65. According to PRO, Gaol Delivery Rolls, Just 3/195/50, 'Robertus Rose . . . capellanus de Herteshorn in com' Derb' captus pro eo quod ipse est communis allocutor cum domino Johanne Oldcastell' . . . et unus abettatorum, fautorum, auxiliatorum et consiliatorum suorum et fatebatur . . . se . . .

fuisse cum praedicto domino Johanne Oldecastell' apud Swerstone Brygge et quod ipse cum eodem domino Johanne equitavit per spacem trium leucarum vel iiii et cum illo bibit et comedit sciens ipsum felonem et proditorem regis.' Accused of everything under the sun, he was most relevantly taken into captivity for a wide range of counterfeiting activities: 'Et eciam captus pro eo quod ipse est communis lotor [launderer] auri et argenti ac tonsor [shaver] et contrafactor cunagii domini regis multiplicator et factor false monete videlicit grossorum, denariorum, et obolorum de falso metallo eneo, cuprino, et stanneo simul mixto.' Rose's Oldcastle story is included among the varied counts on which he is charged, but may reasonably be inferred to have been an item of useful or welcome information, which he volunteered subsequent to his arrest, rather than one of the causes of his arrest. In this sense, he would seem to occupy a position similar to that of Carsewell, although without the status of formal approvership.

66. For his delivery (and a rehearsal of the charges against him, now canceled) see PRO Just. 3/56/14/1/14.

67. On 7 September 1415, Richard Gurmyn, baker and accused Lollard, was convicted of diverse errors and heresies and burnt in Smithfield that same day (British Library Cotton MS. Cleopatra E ii, vol. 2, p. 335b). His sometime associate John Russell was indicted in July 1416, accused of repeatedly slandering Thomas Fauconer (mercer, alderman, and recent mayor), to the effect that Gurmyn had actually possessed letters patent of pardon from the king, but that Fauconer as mayor and escheator in the city of London, caused him to be burnt anyway, along with his letters patent, in contempt of the king – *Letter-Book I*, f. cxcv (see *CLBI*, p. 180); Riley, *Memorials of London Life* [London, 1868], p. 630). As it happens, Russell's accusation of Fauconer was motivated with more particularity, and prosecuted with more vigor, than this account fully reveals. Documents of the King's Bench record an accusation by Russell, together with John Eston, joiner, and Richard Anable, 'peauterer,' to the effect that before his death Gurmyn had written, signed, and sealed a document giving his goods and chattels to the three, but that after Gurmyn's death Fauconer, acting as escheator, had wrongfully seized the goods (PRO KB 27/620, mem. 7 [a and b + added leaf). Other records reveal the intensity of the quarrel. On 1 January 1416, Russell (together with Eston and Anable) complained that Fauconer had caused windows of their shops to be closed in reprisal for their actions (PRO Corporation of London Plea and Memoranda Rolls A45, mem. 2), and Fauconer brought separate suit against Russell for threatening his apprentices and servant (including apparent turncoat Eston) in the summer of 1416 (ibid., mem. 4). Mainperned or ransomed by his friends, Russell then fled the city in the autumn of 1416 (A46, mem. 1) and ultimately sought sanctuary in Westminster throughout the winter of 1416–17, leaving his unfortunate friends to bear the expense (*LBI*, f. 196v). The short-term consequence was Russell's personal and written apology to the mayor and aldermen in April 1417, in which he acknowledged that he had 'spak and noysed en diuerses places of London diuerses wordes and matiers sclaunderous of Thomas Fauconer, . . . late meire'

(*LBI*, f. 196v; Riley, *Memorials*, pp. 633–634).

The link between Russell as a possible falsifier of documents and as possible Lollard is solidified in the final indictment lodged against John Russell, woolman, in King's Bench in 1431, in which he is formally accused of consorting with Lollards and conspiring with them to overthrow the kingdom and the Church, *and* of publishing and promulgating Lollard opinions, *and* of clipping and counterfeiting the money of the king ('de falsis et mixtis metallis ad similitudinem bone monete domini Regis contrefecit et fabricavit' – PRO KB27/681/(rex) mem. 8). The jury made certain distinctions, finding him guilty of counterfeiting at Finsbury but not guilty of other counterfeiting charges. Any guilt at all was, of course, sufficient for condemnation, and Russell was sentenced (in this case as traitor rather than heretic) to be hanged, beheaded, quartered, and to have his severed head displayed on London Bridge. (For another account of Russell see Margaret Aston, *Lollards and Reformers* [London: Hambledon Press, 1984], pp. 32–36.)

68. Slavoj Žižek, *Tarrying with the Negative* (Durham, NC: Duke University Press, 1993), esp. pp. 22–29.

69. I am here borrowing the terminology of Jean-Joseph Goux, *Symbolic Economies after Marx and Freud* (Ithaca, NY: Cornell University Press, 1990), esp. pp. 47–63.

70. This is a point of transition to the Lacanian 'barred subject,' the subject no longer present to itself but possessed only of a 'posited' identity. This is the compromised subject of Žižek's 'nonequivalent exchange,' who gets nothing (symbolic guarantees) in return

for everything (a conviction of self-present volition) – *Tarrying with the Negative*, pp. 22–29.

71. *Regement*, ll. 281–329.

72. *Historia Anglicana*, vol. 2, p. 282.

6 Joanne of Navarre: That Obscure Object of Desire

1. Teresa De Lauretis, *Technologies of Gender* (Bloomington: Indiana University Press, 1987), pp. 25–26. I want to thank E. Jane Burns for a lively discussion of De Lauretis, as well as the more general range of theoretical issues surrounding this chapter. I make no claim that my current argument is necessarily to her liking, but I can certainly say that she has greatly affected its form.

2. Bourdieu, *Outline*, p. 54.

3. Eve K. Sedgwick, *Between Men* (New York: Columbia University Press, 1985), p. 50.

4. Pierre-Hyacinthe Morice, *Histoire ecclésiastique et civile de Bretagne*, vol. 1 (Paris, 1750), p. 395.

5. Although a negotiation of 1405, in which Joanne sought arrears on her dower from Duke John, might suggest that half the promised sum, together with the rents, was paid. This is the amount which she seeks to have added to the lands and rents already given her in dower by Duke John in negotiations of 1386 and 1396. See Gui Lobineau, *Histoire de Bretagne*, vols 1 and 2 (Paris, 1707), vol. 1, p. 507.

6. Ibid., vol. 2, cols 661–662.

7. On these matters see the excerpts from the *Chronicon Briocense*, ibid. cols 874–879.

8. *Chronique du Religieux de Saint-Denys*, ed. M. L. Bellaguet (Paris, 1841), vol. 3, p. 40.

9. *Histoire*, vol. 1, cols 500–501.

10. *Chronique . . . de Saint-Denys*, p. 40.
11. Lobineau, *Histoire*, vol. 1, p. 503.
12. Morice, *Histoire . . . de Bretagne*, vol. 1, col. 395. Joanne's inability to conclude this transaction confirms Christiane Klapisch-Zuber's observation that a dower (or, in this case, an Italian wedding portion) might include income *from* land, but rarely or never actual ownership or proprietorship *of* land. See *Women, Family, and Ritual in Renaissance Italy* (Chicago: University of Chicago Press, 1985), p. 221.
13. Frederick Pollock and Frederick William Maitland, *The History of the English Law*, 2nd edn, vol. 2 (Cambridge: Cambridge University Press, 1952), pp. 407–408, 427. On dower in the fourteenth and fifteenth centuries, see Judith M. Bennett, *Women in the Medieval English Countryside* (New York: Oxford University Press, 1987), pp. 110–114 and Diane Owen Hughes, 'From Brideprice to Dowry,' *Journal of Family History* 3 (1978), 282.
14. Lobineau, *Histoire*, vol. 1, pp. 507, 512, 581, and esp. 575.
15. *CPR*, 1401–5, p. 213.
16. A. R. Myers, 'The Captivity of a Royal Witch: The Household Accounts of Queen Joan of Navarre, 1419–21,' *Journal of the John Rylands Library* 24 (1940), 277.
17. *CPR*, 1408–13, pp. 85–87. See also the parliamentary confirmation, *RP*, vol. 3, p. 632. The fiscal stresses involved in assembling this dower are described by Anne Crawford, 'The King's Burden? – the Consequences of Royal Marriage in Fifteenth-Century England,' in *Patronage, the Crown and the Provinces in Later Medieval England*, ed. Ralph A. Griffiths (Gloucester: Alan Sutton, 1981), esp. pp. 41–44.
18. Patent Rolls, PRO C66/372/no.21; see *CPR*, 1401–5, p. 473. Although not built for Joanne, this tower

had only recently been completed (*c.* 1401), and she was the first queen to be granted so prime a property for this purpose. On details of construction and use see R. Allen Brown et al., *The History of the King's Works*, vol. 1 (London, 1963), p. 533.
19. Crawford, 'The King's Burden?', p. 45.
20. J. Nicholas, *A Collection of Wills . . . of the Kings and Queens of England* (London, 1780), p. 204.
21. *CPR*, 1413–16, pp. 164–167, 341.
22. The term is taken from an English writ dated 13 July 1422, included with the parliamentary action on restoration of the dower, October 1423; see *RP*, vol. 4, pp. 247–248.
23. *RP*, vol. 3, p. 577. The rapidity with which a royal marriage, first considered as a potential revenue source, might end up in major financial hemorrage may be illustrated with equal vividness from cases like that of Henry V's Queen Catherine – where the dreams of possession were even more grand and the consequences even more disappointing. The English first requested a dowry of one million crowns, and the French countered with an offer of 800,000, from which 600,000 should be deducted as arrears of payment for deposed Queen Isabel and 400,000 for her unreturned jewels. In the end, the English once again agreed that no dowry would be expected, and that a 10,000 mark dower would be paid. See J. H. Wylie, *The Reign of Henry V*, vol. 3 (Cambridge: Cambridge University Press, 1929), pp. 157, 166, 268. Yet, as Wylie observes, the chronicler Titus Livius could still suggest that the wedding was conducted in haste so that Henry could gain possession of Catherine's dowry! An even more egregious instance is afforded by Humphrey, duke of Gloucester's calculated marriage

to the experienced and well-endowed Countess Jaque or Jacqueline of Holland, Hainault, and Zeeland. As heiress of those lands, Jaque the bride might have seemed to offer title to a great deal of property indeed – but Humphrey was to find her property more elusive than he had supposed. Contemporary theories of marriage and property seem to offer a basis for Humphrey's claim, if not to be duke of Holland in his own right, at least to rule over her lands and possessions. Arguing his case to John, duke of Bedford and Philip, duke of Burgundy, he pointed out that by virtue of the conclusion of his marriage to Jaque, he had acceded to rule, not only of her person, but of her lands as well ('vigore hujusmodi matrimonii sic consummati, non solum regimen dicte domine, sed etiam omnium terrarum ejusdem, pertinuit et pertinet ad predictum dominum ducem Clocestriae' – *Cartulaire des Comtes de Hainaut*, ed. L. Devillers, vol. 4 (Brussels, 1889), p. 386). Yet, arriving in the country two years after his marriage as head of an invading force, he seems to have had difficulty gaining address as anything other than 'monsgr de Gloucestre'; the warmest titles that seem freely to have been granted him were 'mambourcq et advoet' (or, in effect, 'guardian and advocate' – *Cartulaire*, vol. 4, p. 423) and his most prepossessing (but brief) accomplishment was to rule, not as prince or governor or count, but 'ou non [au nom] de très puissant princesse Jaque de Baivière, comtesse et hiertière' – (ibid., p. 425).

24. *RP*, vol. 3, p. 588.
25. Ibid., pp. 634, 658.
26. See *Foedera*, vol. 4, pt. 2, p. 135 and pt. 3, p. 58.
27. *CPR*, 1413–16, p. 342.
28. Bourdieu, *Outline*, p. 195.

29. Brown et al., *History of the King's Works*, vol. 1, p. 488. It remained for Henry V, acting soon after his coronation, to commission an effigy for his mother's grave. F. Devon, *Issues of the Exchequer* (London, 1837), p. 321.
30. Devon, *Issues of the Exchequer*, p. 296.
31. *Annales Henrici Quarti*, p. 350.
32. A good reproduction may be viewed in *Pageant of the Birth, Life and Death of Richard Beauchamp Early of Warwick K.G., 1389–1439*, ed. Viscount Dillon and W. H. St John Hope (London, 1914). On the ramifications of these symbolic inflections, see John Carmi Parsons, 'Ritual and Symbol in the Medieval English Queenship to 1500,' in *Women and Sovereignty*, ed. Louise O. Fradenburg (Edinburgh: Edinburgh University Press, 1992), pp. 61–66.
33. L. G. W. Legg, *English Coronation Records* (Westminster: A. Constable, 1901), p. 100.
34. At the far end of Joanne's life, her funereal alabaster makes the same point by providing her with two scepters – the only medieval queen to be so provided: 'At first sceptres were lacking. . . . In contrast, the effigies of Eleanor of Castile and Philippa of Hainaut held one sceptre each, Joan Navarre two; Elizabeth of York . . . sheds the ensigns of royalty and clasps her hands in prayer' (John C. Parsons, '"Never was a body buried in England with such solemnity and honor": The Burials and Posthumous Commemorations of English Queens to 1500,' unpublished conference paper.) On this carving, and the possibility that Joanne may have had a hand in planning it, see Brown et al., *History of the King's Works*, vol. 1, p. 488.
35. Parsons, '"Never was a body buried . . . with such solemnity and honor"', p. 64.

36. Lobineau, *Histoire*, vol. 2, cols 874–877.

37. As a young duchess, she mediated between her choleric husband and his arch-enemy de Clisson (see ibid., vol. 2, p. 862), and in 1399, ruling as duchess in her own right, she again achieved an accord with de Clisson (ibid., vol. 1, p. 499). As queen of England, she quickly established a high profile for merciful interventions – some interested (a restoration of captured ships from Navarre at 'special request of the king's consort the queen' – *CPR*, 1401–5, p. 199) and others of a more routine and less interested character (ibid., pp. 207, 209, 229, and, in the more visible case of Maud de Vere's treasonous machinations, p. 480). On the standardized character of such interventions, and the sense in which they accommodate themselves to (rather than disrupt) male governance, see Paul Strohm, 'Queens as Intercessors,' in *Hochon's Arrow* (Princeton: Princeton University Press, 1992), pp. 95–119.

38. *Chronique . . . de Saint-Denys*, vol. 1, p. 726.

39. See Strohm, 'Queens as Intercessors,' pp. 99–105. Two especially valuable recent studies of queenly intercession are Lois L. Huneycutt, 'Intercession and the High-Medieval Queen: the Esther Topos,' and John C. Parsons, 'The Queen's Intercession in Thirteenth-Century England,' both in *Power of the Weak*, ed. Jennifer Carpenter and Sally-Beth MacLean (Urbana: University of Illinois Press, 1995), pp. 126–146, 147–177.

40. See John C. Parsons, 'The Pregnant Queen as Counsellor and the Medieval Construction of Mothering,' in *Medieval Mothering*, ed. J. C. Parsons and B. Wheeler (New York: Garland, 1996), pp. 39–61.

41. Certainly, this scene's elements of disarray impressed themselves most heavily on its subsequent commentators. Bernard d'Agentré has her casting herself ('se ietta') before the duke (*L'Histoire de Bretaigne*, 3rd edn [Paris, 1618], p. 666); F. E. de Mézeray thinks that she entered the duke's chamber 'demy deshabillée' (*Abregé chronologique de l'histoire de France*, vol. 2 [Amsterdam, 1673], p. 142); Lobineau combines these elements and embroiders the account to emphasize the innocence (rather than the dynastic prospects) of her children: 'elle courut tout en desordre, ses enfans entre les bras, se jetter aux pieds de son mari, qu'elle conjura par ses larmes et par l'innocente jeunesse de ces Princes' (*Histoire*, vol. 1, p. 475).

42. *RP*, vol. 4, p. 118.

43. As argued by A. R. Myers, 'The Captivity of a Royal Witch: The Household Accounts of Queen Joan of Navarre, 1419–21,' *Journal of the John Rylands Library* 24 (1940), 263–284.

44. *RP*, vol. 4, pp. 118–119.

45. In the years prior to the charges, Joanne seems to have been held in the highest regard by the king, for whom (as queen mother) she performed valued functions. When Henry first set sail for France, his leave-taking with Joanne was, along with an offering at St Paul's and an obeisance to St George, among his last ceremonial observances (*A Chronicle of London*, ed. N. H. Nicolas [London: Longmans, 1827], p. 219) and he arranged for her to dwell in Windsor and other castles while he was gone (*CPR*, 1413–16, p. 342).

46. On which see Myers, 'Captivity.'

47. *RP*, vol. 4, p. 248.

48. Pertinent in this regard is Jo Ann McNamara and Suzanne Wemple's shrewd observation about the growing suspicion surrounding foreign queens and

their retinues in fourteenth- and fifteenth-century England: 'Queens normally were foreigners and often were cut off from their friends and retainers, who were suspected of pursuing inimical interests. During the Hundred Years' War, the "foreign woman" frequently became the focus of popular discontent, a scapegoat for the follies of her husband as often as the victim of her own thwarted ambition' ('Sanctity and Power: Medieval Women,' in *Becoming Visible: Women in European History*, ed. Renate Bridenthal and Claudia Koonz [Boston: Houghton Mifflin, 1977], p. 113).

49. *RP*, vol. 3, p. 527. See also *Annales Henrici Quarti*, p. 379.

50. In 1406, according to *Annales Henrici Quarti*, p. 419.

51. *RP*, vol. 4, p. 306; cites petition of vol. 3, p. 527.

52. *RP*, vol. 4, p. 306.

53. *Historia Anglicana*, vol. 2, p. 331.

54. *A Chronicle of London*, ed. Nicolas, pp. 107–108.

55. *Concilia*, p. 393.

56. I am, of course, suggesting an analogy only, since Thomas deals with a later period, and with instances occurring in small communities, rather than kingdom-wide. See *Religion and the Decline of Magic* (New York: Scribner's, 1970), pp. 448–449, 552–568.

57. Dyan Elliott explores the interrelated roles of female saint, heretic, and witch in 'The Physiology of Rapture and Female Spirituality,' in *Medieval Theology and the Natural Body*, ed. Alastair Minnis and Peter Biller and Alastair Minnis (Woodbridge, Suffolk: Boydell and Brewer, 1997), pp. 141–173.

58. By Harris Nicholas, *History of the Battle of Agincourt*, 2nd edn (London: Johnson & Co., 1832), p. 157; Agnes Strickland, *Lives of the Queens of England*, vol. 1 (New York: James Miller, 1843), p. 475.

59. *Histoire d'Artus III, Duc de Bretaigne*, ed. Théodore Godefroy (Paris, 1622), pp. 11–12.

60. Paul Veyne, *Did the Greeks Believe in their Myths? An Essay on the Constitutive Imagination* (Chicago: University of Chicago Press, 1988), p. 60.

61. Marc Bloch, *The Royal Touch* (London: Routledge, 1973), pp. 1–2.

62. The term and its particular application are borrowed from Christine Klapisch-Zuber, 'The "Cruel Mother": Maternity, Widowhood, and Dowry in Florence in the Fourteenth and Fifteenth Centuries,' in *Women, Family, and Ritual*, pp. 117–131. Klapisch-Zuber discusses the sense in which the term embraces behavior which is 'affectively' cruel, but, even more importantly, is also 'financially' cruel. Her examples deal mainly with cases in which the sums at issue are recovered from the wife's original dowry, but sums retained from the wife's dower would appear equally to be implied.

63. E.g., Lobineau, *Histoire*, vol. 2, cols 921–924.

64. Morice, *Histoire . . . de Bretagne*, vol. 1, p. 434.

65. Bloch, *The Royal Touch*, pp. 141–148.

66. Based on her dissertation research in the Department of English at the University of North Carolina, Suzanne Craymer has given me examples of several recognition scenes in Middle English romance – including scenes of Ponthus and the Fair Sidone (in which King Ponthus recognizes his mother), Sir Eglamour of Artois (Degrebell is recognized by his noble mother), Sir Isumbras (recognized by his wife, now a queen), and Sir Degare (recognized by his noble mother) – in all of which, as she observes in correspondence, 'the person in power recognizes the long lost love or family

member.' An analogue to the present story may, however, be found in another moment of quasi-historical romance, told by Peter Damian of the young Hugh of Tuscany. Hugh's father who had never seen him doubted his paternity, and a test of recognition ensued wherein 'The father sat with the crowd without any special seat to distinguish him from the rest and, bypassing everyone else, the boy promptly went up to him, and took hold of him as if attracted by one whom he knew very well' (*Peter Damian, Letters 61–90*, trans. Owen Blum, Fathers of the Church, Medieval Continuation, vol. 3 [Washington, DC: Catholic University Press, 1992], p. 84). Here the father's 'aura,' both as marquis and as parent, is sustained.

67. I here borrow the felicitous phrasing of E. Jane Burns, *Bodytalk* (Philadelphia: University of Pennsylvania Press, 1993), p. 59.

68. His general muddle, both about Joanne as a woman among women and about Joanne as his biological parent, amply corroborates Lacan's suggestion that the male always and inevitably misrecognizes the female object of his desire. *Seminar*, pp. 139–154.

69. Compare that moment at which the contrite Henry V, restoring Joanne's dower and original status, resignifies her new position with a grant of attire: 'that she have of such Cloth, and of suche colour, as she wol devise hir self, v or vi Gounes,' (*RP*, vol. 4, p. 248).

70. Implied here is the existence of what Carolynn Van Dyke has very subtly described in narratological terms as 'a second center of intention, a second focalization' (in her review of A.C. Spearing, *The Medieval Poet as Voyeur*, in *Chaucer Yearbook* 3 (1996) p. 224). Also very pertinent to my analysis

here is her identification of 'the force of . . . unresolved counter tales in which women are protagonists,' 'The Clerk's and Franklin's Subjected Subjects,' *Studies in the Age of Chaucer*, 17 (1995), 68. As Page Dubois says of Helen of Troy in one of Sappho's poems, she becomes 'an "actant" in her own life, a *subject* of eros, exemplary not only for her beauty but also for her desiring' (*Sappho is Burning* [Chicago, University of Chicago Press, 1996], p. 121).

71. *RP*, vol. 4, p. 248.

72. Additional mollification and assuagement of Lancastrian interests were subsequently to occur, as Joanne attempted to mobilize a Breton response to ransom demands. *Chronique d'Arthur de Richemont*, ed. Achille le Vavasseur, Société de l'Histoire de France, no. 249 (Paris, 1890), p. 21, n. 1.

7 Advising the Lancastrian Prince

1. As discussed in Chapter 1. See *Annales Ricardi*, pp. 231–232; *Continuatio Eulogii*, p. 397.

2. See Strohm, *Hochon's Arrow* (Princeton: Princeton University Press, 1992), pp. 57–74.

3. My discussion of Repingdon's letter runs parallel in certain respects to that of Frank Grady in 'The Lancastrian Gower and the Limits of Exemplarity,' *Speculum* 70 (1995), esp. 552–555, including his perception, for which he shares credit with Derek Pearsall, that for all its tone of admonition Repingdon's poem abets the construction of Henry as a monarch 'receptive to sage counsel' (p. 554). My estimate of the letter's complicity does, however, exceed Grady's, and differs from his analysis with respect to its

particular mechanisms. On Repingdon's reputation for fearlessness, see James H. Wylie, *History of England Under Henry IV*, vol. 1, p. 201. Noting this reputation, Wylie goes on to observe, however, that this seemingly contentious letter 'was a harmless remonstrance, addressed to an amiable and friendly patron. . . . It produced no practical effect whatever' (p. 201).

4. For an excellent condensed biography, documenting his personal friendship with Henry IV, see E. M. Thompson, ed., *Usk's Chronicon Adae de Usk*, 2nd edn (London: Frowde, 1904), p. 231, n. 3.

5. Printed in *Official Correspondence of Thomas Bekynton*, ed. George Williams, Rolls Series, no. 56, pt. 1 (London, 1872), pp. 151–154. I employ this version as my base text.

6. I have consulted Usk's version, edited both by Given-Wilson and by E. M. Thompson in his edition of the *Chronicon*, pp. 65–69. Yet another version is to be found in British Museum Stowe MS. 67.

7. I thank Richard Pfaff for his assistance in identifying the source of Repingdon's quotation.

8. As characterized by George Williams, in his preface to Bekynton's correspondence, vol. 1, p. lxii.

9. This same operation is repeated at many levels in the course of the letter. The most prominent, example is Repingdon's mention of Richard II – an example of which the possible threat is then neutralized. 'Within the last two years,' he says, 'we have seen King Richard examplified, as in a wondrous mirror.' But his exemplification is general in nature: he is summoned to represent not kingship gone wrong, or royal tyranny, but the bad ending of *all* despisers of the law ('contemptores').

10. See Strohm, ' "A Revelle!": Chronicle Evidence and the Rebel Voice,' in *Hochon's Arrow*, pp. 33–56.

11. *The Regement of Princes*, ed. F. J. Furnivall, EETS, ES, no. 72 [no. 61, pt. 3] (London, 1897).

12. *RP*, vol. 4, p. 428.

13. Hoccleve's *Works*, EETS, ES, no. 61, p. 40.

14. K. B. McFarlane, *Lancastrian Kings and Lollard Knights* (Oxford: Clarendon Press, 1972), observes that 'by 1407 Prince Henry had become the centre and nominal head of a strong and largely baronial opposition,' and that 'for nearly two years, from January 1410 to November 1411 a Council consisting of the prince and his friends administered the country in the king's name' (pp. 102–113). See also Peter McNiven, 'Prince Henry and the English Political Crisis of 1412,' *History* 65 (1980), 1–16. Hoccleve's shorter poems, including all works other than *Regement* cited in this chapter are found in *Hoccleve's Works: I The Minor Poems*, ed. F. J. Furnivall, EETS, ES, no. 61 (London, 1892).

15. On the relationship between Hoccleve's celebration of Chaucer's image and the Lancastrian anti-Lollard program, see Derek Pearsall, 'Hoccleve's *Regement of Princes*: The Poetics of Royal Self-Representation,' *Speculum* 69 (1994), esp. 403–404.

16. The more so because of the emerging link between the mobilization of vernacular literacy and the enjoyment of political power. See Larry Scanlon, *Narrative, Authority, and Power* (Cambridge: Cambridge University Press, 1994), pp. 299–322.

17. *RP*, vol. 3, pp. 466–467.

18. See McNiven, see abbreviations pp. 199–219.

19. As discussed in Chapter 3.

20. Henry IV took the occasion of his first parliament to introduce a major statute on livery and reten-

tion. For relevant texts, see *Statutes of the Realm,* ed. Basket (London: Dawsons, 1816), vol. 1, for 1400, 1402.

21. For useful discussion of annuity payments, see John Burrow, *Thomas Hoccleve,* Authors of the Middle Ages, no. 4 (Aldershot, Hants: Variorum, 1994), p. 22 and notes. On the biographical dimension of Hoccleve's poems, see Burrow, 'Autobiographical Poetry in the Middle Ages: The Case of Thomas Hoccleve,' *Proceedings of the British Academy* 68 (1982), 389–412.

22. See Antony J. Hasler, 'Hoccleve's Unregimented Body,' *Paragraph* 13 (1990), 164–183, to which my comments here are indebted.

23. Derek Pearsall, *John Lydgate* (London: Routledge and Kegan Paul, 1970), pp. 29–30.

24. See *Minor Poems,* part 1, EETS, ES no. 107 and part 2, EETS, OS no. 192. Other works to be discussed in this section include *Troy Book,* EETS, ES nos 97, 103, 106, 126; *Siege of Thebes,* EETS, ES nos 108, 125; and *Fall of Princes,* EETS, ES nos 121–124.

25. For example, ll. 4690–4703 (to which may be compared the language of the treaty itself), and also the *Troy Book,* V, 3410–3412, where the treaty is explicity celebrated.

26. *John Lydgate,* pp. 29–30.

27. Spearing, *Medieval to Renaissance in English Poetry* (Cambridge: Cambridge University Press, 1985), p. 109. Derek Pearsall, in 'Lydgate as Innovator,' *Modern Language Review* 53 (1992), comments on Lydgate's apparent intention of surpassing Chaucer in each of the genres in which he wrote (p. 7).

28. On the general subject of Lydgate and literary/political succession, see Alan S. Ambrisco and Paul Strohm, 'Succession and Sovereignty in Lydgate's Prologue to the *Troy Book,*' *Chaucer Review* 30 (1995–96), 40–57.

29. 'Making Identities in Fifteenth-Century England: Henry V and John Lydgate,' in *New Historical Literary Study,* ed. Jeffrey N. Cox and Larry J. Reynolds (Princeton: Princeton University Press, 1993), p. 95.

30. Meanwhile, Hoccleve's own optimistic argument is predicated on a whole series of unspoken but vulnerable assumptions: that female France will be subordinate to male England, that the child of an English- and Burgundian-sponsored marriage will be acknowledged 'right heir' by France, that 'noyse' in any of its forms (including its most common form of strife between and among different social orders within political units) can be stifled by an enforced dynastic alliance.

31. British Library Cotton MS Vitellius E. vi, fl. 152.

32. 'On Gloucester's Approaching Marriage,' in *Minor Poems* part 2.

33. A year later Henry Beaufort would write to the council of the protectorate warning them of the dangers of Humphrey's designs, describing Burgundy as 'radix et origo' of English successes in France. J. Stevenson, ed., *Letters and Papers Illustrative of the Wars of the English in France,* vol. 2, pt. 2 (London, 1864), pp. 386–387.

34. *Cartulaire des Comtes de Hainaut,* ed. L. Devilliers vol. 4, (Brussels, 1889), pp. 624–625. These considerations might not have been fully evident to the English in 1422, but the postponement of Humphrey's and Jaque's marriage until after the death of Henry V suggests that they were visible at an early date to the perspicacious observer.

35. *Chroniques de Monstrelet,* ed. J. A. Buchon, vol. 5 (Paris, 1826), pp. 98, 104, 133.

36. *Privy Council,* vol. 3, pp. 290–291. *Cartulaire,* p. 623.

37. *ELH* 54 (1987), 761–799.

8 Coda: The Amnesiac Text

1. I borrow this phrase, and several succeeding observations about trauma, from Cathy Carruth, *Trauma: Explorations in Memory* (Baltimore: Johns Hopkins University Press, 1995), pp. 5–6.

2. On the dating of the poem, see John Burrow, *Thomas Hoccleve*, Authors of the Middle Ages, no. 4 (Variorum, 1994), pp. 17–18. On the prince's political expectations during these years see Peter McNiven, 'Prince Henry and the English Political Crisis of 1412,' *History* 65 (1980), 1–16.

3. Two recent studies delineate the contours of this tradition as it affects medieval English literature, each with some specific reference to Hoccleve. See Larry Scanlon, *Narrative, Authority, and Power: The Medieval Exemplum and the Chaucerian Tradition* (Cambridge: Cambridge University Press, 1994) and Judith Ferster, *Fictions of Advice: The Literature and Politics of Counsel in Late Medieval England* (Pennsylvania: University of Pennsylvania Press, 1996). Each is a vigorously argued and informative study, although the former may be regarded as somewhat more coincidental with mine in its analysis of authorial complicity in the creation of royal authority, the latter as more inclined to argue for the corrective, and occasionally oppositional, role of the moralist-poet.

4. Quotations in this chapter are taken from British Library MS Arundel 38. The presentation portrait to the prince has led to the conclusion that this was the manuscript destined for him, but Kate Harris has pointed out the Mowbray connection. See 'The Patron of British Library MS Arundel 38,' *Notes and Queries* n.s.,

31 (1984), 462–463. On other dedications, see M. C. Seymour, 'The Manuscripts of Hoccleve's *Regiment of Princes*,' *Edinburgh Bibliographical Society Transactions* 4 (1974), 255–297.

5. The standard edition of Jacobus is that of Ernst Köpke, *Mitteilungen aus den Handschriften der Ritter-Akademie zu Brandenburg A. H.*, II, Iacobus de Cessolis (Brandenburg, n.d.). Jacobus's work is one of the first translated and printed by Caxton, in 1474, for which see William Axon, ed., *Caxton's Game and Playe of the Chesse* (London, 1883), pp. 148–151. For Hoccleve's indebtedness to Jacobus, and for additional bibliographical information, see Friedrich Aster, *Das Verhältnis des Altenglischen Gedichtes 'De Regimine Principum' von Thomas Hoccleve zu seinen Quellen* (Leipzig: Oskar Peters, 1888), pp. 47–50.

6. Whether Canace (or Cavaza or Ganazath in other versions) refers to Canatha in Palestine or to somewhere else probably matters little; Hoccleve's initial disclaimer announces a more prevalent refusal of context and disavowal of its own implications.

7. On the sense in which a text possesses an 'unconscious,' comprised by those things which it denies or means not to say, see Paul Strohm, 'Chaucer's Lollard Joke: History and the Textual Unconscious,' *Studies in the Age of Chaucer* 17 (1995), 23–42.

8. British Museum MS. Royal 7.D.i, ff. 84b–85a. Published as J. Herolt, *Discipulus redivivus . . . cum Prompuaris exemplorum*, vol. 2 (Stroetter, 1728), p. 621.

9. British Library Additional MS. 27336, fl. 17.

10. In the case of Royal 7.D.i the father's unwise distributions – in this case to sons rather than daughters – occur after their mar-

riages (as an acknowledgment of their new and more adult status) rather than, as with daughters, in order that the marriage might occur. From the viewpoint of princely responsibility, these distributions would seem even less provident, and less wise, than observation of established dowry practices. An ungrateful son is also featured in Bromyard's rendition, printed in Thomas Wright, ed., *Early English Poetry, Ballads, and Popular Literature* (London: Percy Society, 1843), vol. 8, pp. 28–29.

11. There the father divests himself of his goods so that his daughters can marry well, trusting that they will repay him later in life.

12. *Promptuarium exemplorum*, vol. 2, p. 621.

13. Viewed by whom? Presumably not by the prince, its dedicatee, or others committed to the Lancastrian cause. But certainly its ironies could not have escaped diehard Ricardians, or later-century Yorkists, or the modern analyst seeking an understanding of that unstable and reversible state of cynical acquiescence in a belief which makes usurpation possible and allows a patina of respectability to usurping regimes.

14. Lacan, *Seminar*, p. 112. Copjec reiterates this view, drawing from it a somewhat sparer conclusion than I aim to pursue: the desire (and object-cause of desire) 'that causes the subject has historical specificity (it is the product of a specific discursive order), but no historical content. The subject is the product of history without being the fulfillment of a historical demand' (*Read My Desire: Lacan against the Historicists* [Cambridge, MA: MIT Press 1994], p. 56). My demurral is simply that the partial objects of desire presented to us within the symbolic are not only

pre-existing desire's temporary focus, but play their own role in the incitement and deployment of desire. Whatever inchoate desires precede the subject's historical insertion cannot finally be discussed or measured independently of the historical objects in relation to which they are summoned and to which they attach themselves.

15. A subject explored in the context of Hoccleve's tale by Judith Ferster, *Fictions of Advice*, pp. 143–145.

16. *Outline*, p. 191. Kantorowicz's magnificent formulation recognizes that, in addition to the king's sublime body or sacral 'character,' he possesses a mortal body which poses a constant challenge to sacral perfection. Incumbents, for example, sicken and fall into delirium, or (in modern instances) vomit on prime ministers' laps or call their mistresses on cellular phones. Nevertheless, lapses are normally minimized, and transitions euphemized, by an array of rites and ceremonies. Even in the extreme case of bodily death, rites of interment and coronation allow the maintenance of an unfissured façade, of self-evident surfaces. But usurpation at least temporarily severs the monarchy from its panoply of rituals and symbolic supports. For, in the case of usurpation, the space reserved for the monarch within the order of the symbolic is briefly, and traumatically, either *over*occupied – finds itself with two or more aspirant incumbents or, worse yet, voided, seen to have no occupant at all.

17. Kantorowicz, esp. pp. 328–336.

18. Although the 'Plantagenet dynasty' was actually a retrospective construction, dating from Richard, duke of York's attempt to bolster his claims in the mid-fifteenth century, the fact remains

that England had been successively ruled by descendants of Geoffrey, count of Anjou and the Empress Maud, for two and a half centuries, prior to the displacement of Richard II. Even Edward II, overthrown and murdered, left a single, obvious, legal heir behind: his young son, the future Edward III. The continuing vitality of this presupposition of regular succession is demonstrated in the fact that infant Richard, as son of older brother Edward the Black Prince, was chosen over Edward's younger brother John of Gaunt, the most powerful man in the kingdom at that time. Richard had, on earlier occasions, been threatened with deposition, but such initiatives had always foundered upon a certain deference to, and perhaps even awe at, the claims of an anointed king.

19. Julius B. ii, in *Chronicles of London*, ed. C. L. Kingsford (Oxford: Clarendon Press, 1905), p. 23.

20 Ed. and trans. J. Webb, *Archaeologia* 20 (1824), 1–402.

21. Neville and Percy had represented the lords temporal in the delegation which received Richard's resignation at the Tower on 29 September. The next day, Neville was made Marshal of England for life. Percy joined Neville to convey Henry's message to the convocation of clergy on 7 October, and was made constable of the realm on 8 October, coronation day.

22. Slavoj Žižek, *Tarrying with the Negative* (Durham, NC: Duke University Press, 1993), p. 228.

23. *Chronicque de la Träison et Mort*, ed. B. Williams (London: English Historical Society, 1846), p. 69. And Henry did evidently meet with a parliamentary assembly (though not a formally convened parliament) on 6 October, two days before his coronation (*Annales Henrici Quarti*, p. 288).

24. *Historia Anglicana*, vol. 2, p. 239.

25. This deficiency must be understood in relation to late medieval belief and practice. Unction is the sacramental (or quasi-sacramental) moment, a moment technically excluded from sacramental status at the level of dictate and high theology in the twelfth and thirteenth centuries, but nevertheless unevenly and popularly regarded as sacramental in nature throughout the fourteenth century. See, especially, Marc Bloch, *The Royal Touch*, trans. J. E. Anderson (London: Routledge, 1973), p. 113. Bloch's opening chapters have, of course, served as my introduction to the subject of sacramentality and kingship. See also G. L. Hahn, *Die Lehre von den Sakramenten in ihrer geschichtlichen Entwicklung . . . bis zum Concil von Trient* (Breslau, 1864), p. 104. Ricardian apologist Roger Dymmok, writing against Lollards in the 1390s, likens coronation to other sacraments (such as marriage or ordination) in that it effects an inward transformation without external or apparent alteration. See Dymmok, p. 130. (The rationale by which unction was regarded as sacramental is not far to seek; as a spiritually and episcopally sponsored ritual, unction causes an invisible transformation, central to which is the addition of a character the king did not previously possess. 'The sacrament of unction therefore augments the dignity of kingship' ('Adicit igitur regiae dignitati unctionis sacramentum'), Grosseteste explained in response to an inquiry of Henry III [*Epistolae*, ed. H. R. Luard, Rolls Series, vol. 25 [London, 1861], p. 350].)

Richard II evidently believed himself, as a result of unction, to possess a character that he was unable to resign; he is represented as offering to resign the administrative functions of the kingship to Henry but reserving the spiritual character conferred by sacred unction ('noluit nec intendebat renunciare carecteribus anime sue impressis a sacra unccione' [G. O. Sayles, Stowe MS. 66, in 'The Deposition of Richard II: Three Lancastrian Narratives,' *Bull. Inst. Hist. Research* 54 (1981), 266. See also *Annales Henrici Quarti*, p. 286]). Suggested in Richard's reported remark is a belief that certain aspects of legitimacy, as conferred by sacred unction, are irreversible. Shakespeare, of course, has it exactly. 'Not all the water in the rough rude sea/Can wash the balm off from an anointed king' (*Richard II*, III, ii, pp. 55). You possess royal 'character' or you do not, and (in the Yorkist view) the illegitimate king crucially lacks this attribute of inner transformation.

26. On the proposed Lancastrian order of the coronation procession, see Rymer, *Foedera*, vol. 3, pt. 2, pp. 163–164. On innovations in the coronation ceremony, see Strohm, 'Saving the Appearances,' in *Hochon's Arrow* (Princeton: Princeton University Press, 1992), pp. 84–85.

27. Here my analysis parallels that of Larry Scanlon, who regards John's sleight as illustrative of the 'ideological' and 'constructed' nature of medieval kingly authority. *Narrative, Authority, and Power*, pp. 320–321.

28. British Library Additional MS 27336, fl. 17.

29. The king does not, of course, have to create the frames within which he is observed. The place of the king is already fantastically framed within the realm of the symbolic; it is, in a sense, pre-existent and held open for him. The king's regality is, as Jacobus says in the introducton to his Book of Chess, a co-possession of his people, and their eyes must be drawn to him ('ad regem enim oculi omnium attendere debent' – p. 3). He is always being *shown* to the people within the frame of one ceremony or another, and his task is simply to gain recognition as the rightful occupant of that frame. This recognition is always, of course, a *mis*recognition, given the inevitable physical and intellectual inadequacies of any incumbent, and in the case of the usurper this is doubly so.

30. Lacan, *Seminar*, p. 150. The Thing, according to Lacan, marks the place from which the real has been expelled (p. 121).

31. Claude Lefort, *Democracy and Political Theory* (Cambridge: Polity Press, 1988), pp. 17, 225–228.

32. *For They Know Not What They Do: Enjoyment as a Political Factor* (London: Verso, 1991), p. 267, n. 52.

33. As proposed by the old woman who told John Sperhauke that since the accession of Henry IV the weather had gone bad (*Select Cases*, p. 123).

34. 'Having given away too many resources, both John and the government must borrow money to keep up the appearance of wealth,' *Fictions of Advice*, p. 145.

35. As observed by L. G. W. Legg, the only parts of the regalia ever to leave the Abbey are the scepters and orbs, and they are returned to the chapter of Westminster immediately after the coronation banquet. *English Coronation Records* (Westminster: Constable, 1901), pp. lxii–lxiii.

36. Ibid., p. 71.

37. Ibid., p. 169. Legg translated the phrase 'recuperabit sine vi' as 'shall recover by force,' on the apparent assumption that Henry IV wanted to represent himself as a conquering king. In fact, the Lancastrians proposed to effect this recuperation as an easy and beneficent side-effect of their ascent to the throne. Before and

during Richard's negotiation of the peace treaty of 1396, the English feared the alienation of Aquitaine through its reversion to the Duchy of Lancaster; with the crowning of Henry IV, Aquitaine would once again become crown land.

38. We are told that Richard, learning of the oil's properties, had sought to be recrowned and reanointed with it, but was refused. He then (pathetically) carried the ampule around with him, along with other items of regalia, until handing it over to the archbishop of Canterbury, observing (in words assigned him by the Lancastrians) that it was not the divine will that he should be so anointed but that this noble sacrament was intended for another.

The manipulation of Richard as unsuccessful claimant is carried one step farther in *Continuatio Eulogii*, which first relates his discovery (in the 'stripped,' Lancastrian version), then passes on to other subjects, then returns to it in recounting Henry's coronation with the previously mentioned oil ('cum oleo aquilae innotatae' – pp. 380, 384). The oil here functions as a prophetic object, carried around unwittingly by Richard II until its meaning is retrospectively conferred. Opening a temporal and narrative division between the oil's discovery and its use, this account preserves the innocence of its own corroborative scheme.

39. Of course, a less fervent Lancastrian than Walsingham had in his later years become might harbor a doubt. A marginal commentator to the Arundel manuscript of Walsingham's *Historia Anglicana* adds, 'unguentum fictitium.' And, the unguent being found false, the critical inner transformation cannot occur. In that case, the king is left only with his corporeality, his 'natural body,' and even that body is denied that measure of

'charm,' of amorous identification which is inevitably exchanged between the sacral and physical bodies of the king. On this point, an interesting supplement or corrective to Kantorowicz's theory of the two bodies, see Lefort, *Democracy and Political Theory*, pp. 242–244. Consider, in this respect, the comments of early (though later disenchanted) Lancastrian loyalist Adam of Usk, who details Henry IV's moral agonies and putrefaction at death, and connects them with his improper coronation: 'This festering was foreshadowed at his coronation, for as a result of his anointing then, his head was so infected with lice that his hair fell out, and for several months he had to keep his head uncovered' (Usk, pp. 242–243).

40. On the bullion famine see R. H. Britnell, *The Commercialisation of English Society 1000–1500* (Cambridge: Cambridge University Press, 1993), pp. 179–185.

41. As observed by Professor David Armitage, who read and incisively commented upon an early draft of this chapter.

42. Page DuBois, *Torture and Truth* (London: Routledge, 1991).

43. See Chapter 5, p. 134.

44. *Historia Anglicana*, vol. 2, p. 282.

45. McNiven, pp. 216–219.

46. McNiven, 'Prince Henry and the English Political Crisis of 1412.'

47. See *The First English Life of King Henry the Fifth*, ed. C. L. Kingsford (Oxford: Clarendon Press, 1911), esp. pp. 11–16.

48. Žižek, *Tarrying with the Negative*, pp. 226–232. Henry IV is, as I have said, omitted in favor of his son the Prince as dedicatee. The focus shifts, instead, to the prospects for the prince's speedy accession:

Beseche I hym that sitte on hye
  in trone,
That, when that charge
  receyued han ye,

> Swych gouernance men may
>   feele and se
> In yow, as may be vn-to his
>   plesance,
> Profet to vs, and your good
>   loos avance.

That very governance, and self-imposed restraint, expected of Henry IV is now assigned to his son, whose own 'gouernance' will produce 'profet' – either material profit for the realm as a whole or symbolic profit founded on his own good repute.

49. The historical record (of Hal's distinguished military and administrative service in Wales, and on the royal council, and his own regal ambitions) sugggests that he was *always* a person of self-imposed restraint. The legend of his wasted youth may be seen as an invention, designed to install the entire passage from profligate enjoyment to sober self-regulation within a single life.

    An early, and comparatively modest, imposition of this pattern occurs in the near-contemporary account of the *Historia Anglicana*. Noting that Henry V's April coronation was visited by snow, Walsingham ventures a symbolic interpretation, in which winter is to be followed by spring. He then adds that, as soon as the new king was invested with the regalia, he immediately changed into another man ('in virum alterum'), a man of honesty, modesty, and *gravitas*, seeking that no virtue should be omitted which he desired to exercise (vol. 2, p. 290). Subsequent accounts, in which the prince disports himself in robbery and other law-breaking with fictitious low companions, were elaborated in the sixteenth century, as was Thomas Elyot's wholesale fabrication of another imagined confrontation between the Prince and the Law, in this case his quarrel with the chief justice of the realm and subsequent imprisonment. This anecdote was promptly embraced by chroniclers Hall and Holinshed, biographer Redmayne, and the dramatist of *The Famous Victories of Henry V* – not to mention Shakespeare's own willing use of it. (These sixteenth-century elaborations are conveniently summarized in Charles L. Kingsford, *Henry V* [New York, 1901], pp. 87–93.) In point of fact, as demonstrated in the nineteenth century by Solly-Flood, in the early years of this century by Kingsford, and more recently by Christopher Allmand (*Henry V* [Berkeley: University of California Press, 1992], pp. 16–58), Henry as prince had spent his time in the most blameless ways. He acquitted himself assiduously in military campaigns in Wales (1403–7), as a member of the king's council (1407–9), as virtual regent and artful fabricator of a pro-Burgundian strategy (1410–11), and as somewhat impatient and self-publicizing but altogether serious heir-in-waiting (1411–12). Yet we find as respected a historian as K. B. McFarlane ludicrously reiterating, 'That with some wild friends he had lain in wait and robbed his own receivers, that he attracted to himself low and riotous company ... and that William Gascoigne, the Chief Justice, had then so far offended him as to be dismissed at the beginning of his reign, can now hardly be doubted' (*Lancastrian Kings and Lollard Knights* [Oxford: Clarendon Press, 1972], p. 123).

50. The most innovative and complete text in regard to this reading of the Prince's character is composed by the English translator of Titus Livius, early in the sixteenth century, edited and published by Kingsford, *The First English Life of King Henry the Fifth*, esp. pp. 11–12, 17.

51. Louise Fradenburg has observed

in correspondence that 'I think sovereignty always has to "include" its own ficticity, for it to *be* sovereignty.' On the sovereign's 'hidden interiority' see Fradenburg, *City, Marriage, Tournament* (Madison: University of Wisconsin Press, 1991), p. 89.

52. Fradenburg, *City, Marriage, Tournament*, p. 240. Noting that 'the reform of promiscuity and aggressivity thus promises the resolution of maturational crisis,' she observes that 'Shakespeare's Hal charts something of the same course' (p. 241).

53. Pierre Macherey, *A Theory of Literary Production*, trans. Geoffrey Wall (London: Routledge, 1978), p. 101.

54. Our anecdote actually conflates two paternal identities: the wastrel John who scattered his resources and the guileful John who recouped his losses and regained control. These two parental functions generally correspond to the two fatherly roles defined by Freud in one of his own historical exercises, *Totem and Taboo*. His paternal function is divided between a father who defies, and one who accepts, his symbolic function. These roles are offered to us as a progression: from the primal or obscene father, who defies his symbolic function and who commands excess or profligate enjoyment, to his assassin and successor, the father of the law, who interdicts enjoyment (thus paradoxically guaranteeing its perpetuation). On the murder of the primal father and the deferred forms of Oedipal obedience observed by his successor-sons, see Freud, *Totem and Taboo* (New York: Anchor Books 1950), pp. 140–146. With respect to the Oedipal or 'ideal' father, Copjec observes that his prohibitions actually foster a form of limited enjoyment in their own right: 'his *interdictions* give the subject a whiff of hope; it is they that suggest the possibility of transgression. In forbidding excess enjoyment, they appear to be its only obstacle; the subject/prisoner is thus free to dream of their removal and of the bounty of pleasure that will then be his.' See *Read My Desire: Lacan against the Historicists*, p. 156.

55. At his deposition, he was accused of breaking into chests belonging to Arundel left in his safe keeping at the time of the latter's exile. See BL MS. Julius B. ii, as printed in *Chronicles of London*, ed. C. L. Kingsford (Oxford: Clarendon Press, 1905), p. 40.

56. On representation of Henry as a man, see Daniel Rubey, 'The Five Wounds of Melibee's Daughter,' paper delivered at the International Medieval Congress, Kalamazoo, Michigan, May 1996.

57. I here allude to Derrida's conception of 'iterability,' according to which a text's repetition in new contexts, and in relation to new programs or possibilities of understanding, transgresses all attempts to fix meaning within a particular and limited program of truth. Iterability returns us to 'an incessant movement of recontextualization,' in relation to a limitless history-beyond-the-text. (Derrida, 'Afterword' to *Limited Inc* [Evanston: Northwestern University Press, 1988], p. 136.) However complicit his intentions, Hoccleve thus proves unable to give us a tale which suspends reference or stops meaning things; it cannot help but disclose multiple meanings, within that larger (historical) context over which its author can no longer enjoy control.

Index

'Chronicles' and 'prophecies' appear under collective headings. Literary works are indexed under names of their authors. References to Henry IV and Henry V are selective rather than exhaustive. Names of modern scholars appearing in footnotes are indexed only in cases of unusual importance, or when the footnote includes additional comment or discussion.